Keep this book. You will need it and use it throughout your career.

About the American Hotel & Lodging Association (AH&LA)

Founded in 1910, AH&LA is the trade association representing the lodging industry in the United States. AH&LA is a federation of state lodging associations throughout the United States with 11,000 lodging properties worldwide as members. The association offers its members assistance with governmental affairs representation, communications, marketing, hospitality operations, training and education, technology issues, and more. For information, call 202-289-3100.

LODGING, the management magazine of AH&LA, is a "living textbook" for hospitality students that provides timely features, industry news, and vital lodging information. For information on subscriptions and student rates, call 202-289-3113.

About the Educational Institute of AH&LA (EI)

An affiliate of AH&LA, the Educational Institute is the world's largest source of quality training and educational materials for the lodging industry. EI develops textbooks and courses that are used in more than 1,200 colleges and universities worldwide, and also offers courses to individuals through its Distance Learning program. Hotels worldwide rely on EI for training resources that focus on every aspect of lodging operations. Industry-tested videos, CD-ROMs, seminars, and skills guides prepare employees at every skill level. EI also offers professional certification for the industry's top performers. For information about EI's products and services, call 800-349-0299 or 407-999-8100.

About the American Hotel & Lodging Foundation (AH&LF)

An affiliate of AH&LA, the American Hotel & Lodging Foundation provides financial support that enhances the stability, prosperity, and growth of the lodging industry through educational and research programs. AH&LF has awarded hundreds of thousands of dollars in scholarship funds for students pursuing higher education in hospitality management. AH&LF has also funded research projects on topics important to the industry, including occupational safety and health, turnover and diversity, and best practices in the U.S. lodging industry. For information, call 202-289-3100.

PLANNING and CONTROL for FOOD and BEVERAGE OPERATIONS

Fifth Edition

Educational Institute Books

UNIFORM SYSTEM OF ACCOUNTS FOR THE LODGING INDUSTRY
Ninth Revised Edition

RESORT DEVELOPMENT AND MANAGEMENT
Second Edition
Chuck Y. Gee

PLANNING AND CONTROL FOR FOOD AND BEVERAGE OPERATIONS
Fifth Edition
Jack D. Ninemeier

TRAINING FOR THE HOSPITALITY INDUSTRY
Second Edition
Lewis C. Forrest, Jr.

UNDERSTANDING HOSPITALITY LAW
Fourth Edition
Jack P. Jefferies/Banks Brown

SUPERVISION IN THE HOSPITALITY INDUSTRY
Third Edition
Raphael R. Kavanaugh/Jack D. Ninemeier

ENERGY AND WATER RESOURCE MANAGEMENT
Second Edition
Robert E. Aulbach

MANAGEMENT OF FOOD AND BEVERAGE OPERATIONS
Third Edition
Jack D. Ninemeier

MANAGING FRONT OFFICE OPERATIONS
Sixth Edition
Michael L. Kasavana/Richard M. Brooks

STRATEGIC HOTEL/MOTEL MARKETING
Revised Edition
Christopher W. L. Hart/David A. Troy

MANAGING SERVICE IN FOOD AND BEVERAGE OPERATIONS
Second Edition
Ronald F. Cichy/Paul E. Wise

THE LODGING AND FOOD SERVICE INDUSTRY
Fourth Edition
Gerald W. Lattin

SECURITY AND LOSS PREVENTION MANAGEMENT
Second Edition
Raymond C. Ellis, Jr./David M. Stipanuk

HOSPITALITY INDUSTRY MANAGERIAL ACCOUNTING
Fourth Edition
Raymond S. Schmidgall

PURCHASING FOR HOSPITALITY OPERATIONS
William B. Virts

THE ART AND SCIENCE OF HOSPITALITY MANAGEMENT
Jerome J. Vallen/James R. Abbey

MANAGING COMPUTERS IN THE HOSPITALITY INDUSTRY
Third Edition
Michael L. Kasavana/John J. Cahill

MANAGING HOSPITALITY ENGINEERING SYSTEMS
Michael H. Redlin/David M. Stipanuk

UNDERSTANDING HOSPITALITY ACCOUNTING I
Fourth Edition
Raymond Cote

ACCOUNTING FOR HOSPITALITY MANAGERS
Fourth Edition
Raymond Cote

CONVENTION MANAGEMENT AND SERVICE
Fifth Edition
Milton T. Astroff/James R. Abbey

HOSPITALITY SALES AND ADVERTISING
Third Edition
James R. Abbey

MANAGING HOUSEKEEPING OPERATIONS
Second Edition
Margaret M. Kappa/Aleta Nitschke/Patricia B. Schappert

CONVENTION SALES: A BOOK OF READINGS
Margaret Shaw

DIMENSIONS OF TOURISM
Joseph D. Fridgen

HOSPITALITY TODAY: AN INTRODUCTION
Fourth Edition
Rocco M. Angelo/Andrew N. Vladimir

MANAGING BAR AND BEVERAGE OPERATIONS
Lendal H. Kotschevar/Mary L. Tanke

ETHICS IN HOSPITALITY MANAGEMENT: A BOOK OF READINGS
Edited by Stephen S. J. Hall

HOSPITALITY FACILITIES MANAGEMENT AND DESIGN
David M. Stipanuk/Harold Roffmann

MANAGING HOSPITALITY HUMAN RESOURCES
Third Edition
Robert H. Woods

FINANCIAL MANAGEMENT FOR THE HOSPITALITY INDUSTRY
William P. Andrew/Raymond S. Schmidgall

HOSPITALITY INDUSTRY FINANCIAL ACCOUNTING
Second Edition
Raymond S. Schmidgall/James W. Damitio

INTERNATIONAL HOTELS: DEVELOPMENT AND MANAGEMENT
Chuck Y. Gee

QUALITY SANITATION MANAGEMENT
Ronald F. Cichy

HOTEL INVESTMENTS: ISSUES & PERSPECTIVES
Second Edition
Edited by Lori E. Raleigh and Rachel J. Roginsky

QUALITY LEADERSHIP AND MANAGEMENT IN THE HOSPITALITY INDUSTRY
Robert H. Woods/Judy Z. King

MARKETING IN THE HOSPITALITY INDUSTRY
Third Edition
Ronald A. Nykiel

CONTEMPORARY HOSPITALITY MARKETING
William Lazer/Roger Layton

UNIFORM SYSTEM OF ACCOUNTS FOR THE HEALTH, RACQUET AND SPORTSCLUB INDUSTRY

CONTEMPORARY CLUB MANAGEMENT
Edited by Joe Perdue for the Club Managers Association of America

RESORT CONDOMINIUM AND VACATION OWNERSHIP MANAGEMENT: A HOSPITALITY PERSPECTIVE
Robert A. Gentry/Pedro Mandoki/Jack Rush

ACCOUNTING FOR CLUB OPERATIONS
Raymond S. Schmidgall/James W. Damitio

PLANNING and CONTROL for FOOD and BEVERAGE OPERATIONS

Fifth Edition

Jack D. Ninemeier, Ph.D., CHA

EDUCATIONAL INSTITUTE
American Hotel & Lodging Association

Disclaimer

This publication is designed to provide accurate and authoritative information in regard to the subject matter covered. It is sold with the understanding that the publisher is not engaged in rendering legal, accounting, or other professional service. If legal advice or other expert assistance is required, the services of a competent professional person should be sought.

    —From the Declaration of Principles jointly adopted by the American Bar Association and a Committee of Publishers and Associations

The author, Jack D. Ninemeier, is solely responsible for the contents of this publication. All views expressed herein are solely those of the author and do not necessarily reflect the views of the Educational Institute of the American Hotel & Lodging Association (the Institute) or the American Hotel & Lodging Association (AH&LA).

Nothing contained in this publication shall constitute a standard, an endorsement, or a recommendation of the Institute or AH&LA. The Institute and AH&LA disclaim any liability with respect to the use of any information, procedure, or product, or reliance thereon by any member of the hospitality industry.

Contents

Preface

THE FIFTH EDITION of *Planning and Control for Food and Beverage Operations* continues its emphasis on practical activities that managers in all sizes of foodservice operations can use to plan and control their operations. Managers are busy people who must make the most cost–effective use of their time as they control resources, which are always in limited supply. The primary topics of this book—food and beverages, labor, and revenue—are carefully analyzed; the very best strategies for their management are included in this "primer" for the control of commercial and noncommercial foodservice operations.

This book is meant to be read *and* used. For example, students in formal educational programs and trainees in hospitality operations may read the book from cover to cover as part of formal or informal professional development and career training activities. Others, such as managers, can turn to the book for "How–to–do–it" help with problem–solving tasks on the job.

The primary objective of the book has not changed from the earlier editions: to help practicing hospitality managers and students understand the complexities of controlling the primary resources—products (food and beverages), labor, and revenue—in food and beverage operations. With today's emphasis on cost reduction, quality and service optimization, and guests' ever–increasing desire for value in the hospitality dollars they spend, the foundation of information that this book brings to the reader has become increasingly important.

The author would like to acknowledge the significant contribution to the first edition of this book by members of the American Hotel & Lodging Association's Food and Beverage Committee. They, along with several others, provided valuable help with the second edition as well. The third edition was strengthened by significant input from two professionals with the Educational Institute: George Glazer (Senior Vice President, Publications) and Dan Davis (Editor). The fourth edition also benefited from the thoughtful input of the editor (Richard Keener). Frank Holcomb of ACD Computers, Inc., also provided important help with the fourth edition by developing and assembling many of the sample screens used as exhibits illustrating computer applications throughout the book. The information provided by contributors to earlier editions still provides a solid foundation of information upon which the content was revised to keep up with the ever-changing world of food and beverage operations.

Food service continues to be a vast, important, and growing segment of the hospitality industry worldwide. Students and practicing managers who learn the fundamentals of food and beverage planning and control will likely increase their career opportunities. It is sincerely hoped that this book will play a small but important role in their personal and professional success.

Students in literally hundreds of hospitality education programs worldwide are using this and other Educational Institute texts. These students, who will be tomorrow's industry leaders, are the ones to whom this text is dedicated.

Jack D. Ninemeier, Ph.D., CHA
Professor
The School of Hospitality Business
Michigan State University

Part I

Introduction to Food and Beverage Control

Chapter 1 Outline

Travel and Tourism: The Umbrella Industry
    The Hospitality Segment
An Overview of the Organization of a Hotel
    The Food and Beverage Department
Commercial and Institutional Food Services
    Everything Begins with the Menu
    The Operating Control Cycle
    Management System
    The Management Process
    Integrating the Process
    Important Differences
A Common Problem: The Labor Shortage

Competencies

1. Identify differences and similarities between commercial and noncommercial food service operations. (pp. 3–5, 20–24)

2. Describe the basic responsibilities of line and staff managers in a full-service hotel. (pp. 5–9)

3. Identify characteristics that distinguish hotel food and beverage operations from free-standing restaurants. (pp. 9–11)

4. Distinguish revenue centers from support centers in hospitality organizations. (pp. 11–12)

5. Describe the management tasks involved in planning , organizing, coordinating, staffing, directing, controlling, and evaluating. (pp. 13–22)

1

The Challenge of Food and Beverage Operations

MANAGING A FOOD AND BEVERAGE operation, whether small or large, is challenging for many reasons. For one, food and beverage service involves both manufacturing and service-related operations that demand that the manager have not only technical knowledge and skills but also business knowledge and people skills. The manager must know how a product is manufactured, how it is marketed to the consumer, and numerous other operational aspects. Above all, the manager must be able to relate well to people and to work effectively with them.

Since food and beverage operations are part of the hospitality industry—just as the hospitality industry itself is part of the travel and tourism industry—it will be helpful to view the interrelationships that exist among these related enterprises.[1]

Travel and Tourism: The Umbrella Industry

Exhibit 1 shows travel and tourism as an umbrella industry covering five segments—lodging operations, food and beverage operations, transportation services, retail stores, and destination activities—all of which provide products and services for the traveler. Most of these businesses also provide products and services to residents of their communities. In fact, whether a business considers itself part of the travel and tourism industry likely depends on how much of its revenue is derived from travelers, compared with how much is derived from local residents. When reviewing Exhibit 1 note that food and beverage service is an important part of each segment of the travel and tourism industry. Many lodging operations and all food and beverage outlets offer these products and services. Ships, airplanes and trains (in transportation services), food outlets in shopping malls and markets (retail stores) and food service offered as part of recreation, entertainment, meetings, and sporting events, etc., (in destination activities) are examples.

The Hospitality Segment

The hospitality industry comprises lodging operations—hotels, motels, resorts, casinos, and other facilities offering sleeping accommodations—and food and beverage operations. Again, both the traveling public and local residents are served by these segments—particularly by food and beverage operations. Consider, for example, the use of lodging properties by local businesses and organizations for meetings or special occasion dining events. Some lodging properties actively market their room accommodations to local residents. Weekend "escape" packages,

Exhibit 1   Overview of the Travel and Tourism Industry

Lodging Operations	Food and Beverage Operations	Transportation Services	Retail Stores	Destination Activities
Hotels	Restaurants	Ships	Gift Shops	Recreation
Motels	Lodging Properties	Airplanes	Souvenir Shops	Business
Resorts	Retail Stores	Autos	Arts/Crafts Shops	Entertainment
Time-Share Hotels	Vending	Buses	Shopping Malls	Meetings
Condominiums	Catering	Trains	Markets	Study Trips
Conference Centers	Snack Bars	Bikes	Miscellaneous Stores	Sporting Events
Camps	Cruise Ships	Limousines		Ethnic Festivals
Parks	Bars/Taverns			Cultural Events
Extended Stay	Banquets			Seasonal Festivals
Bed and Breakfast	Contract Food Services			Gaming
Casinos				
Convention Hotels				
Cruise Ships				

which may include some meals and the use of the property's recreational facilities in addition to the guestroom, are one example.

Just as the traveling public and local resident markets overlap, so do industry segments. Consider, for example, that many lodging properties have one or more food and beverage outlets, and they may have retail shops and offer various activities as well. Similarly, food and beverage service extends to the transportation, retail, and recreation segments of the industry. Food and beverage operations are indeed crucial to the world of hospitality, travel, and tourism.

There are two basic categories of food and beverage operations. Those in lodging properties, clubs, restaurants, and other for-profit enterprises are considered **commercial food service operations** (see Exhibit 2); those in institutions such as schools, nursing homes, hospitals, and military services are considered noncommercial or **institutional food service operations** (see Exhibit 3). Increasingly, however, the distinctions between these two categories are blurred. For example, a for-profit contract management company may operate a food service program in a nonprofit facility such as a school or hospital. While the facility would not seek to

Exhibit 2   A Commercial Food Service Operation

Founded in 1976, Bennigan's operates restaurants in the United States and in seven other countries and territories. Bennigan's is part of Metromedia Restaurant Group® (MRG®), one of the largest multi-concept, table-service restaurant groups in the world. This site can be found at http://www.bennigans.com.

generate a profit from food sales, it would want the contract management company to minimize the expenses of the food service program. Similarities and differences between these categories will be discussed after we examine more closely the relationship between a lodging property and its food and beverage operation. First, let's look briefly at how a hotel is organized. (Except where otherwise noted, the term "hotel" will be used to represent any type of commercial lodging property.)

An Overview of the Organization of a Hotel

A hotel's organizational plan divides the total management responsibility among divisions or departments, with specific duties required in specific positions. This organizational structure varies from property to property, even when size, levels of service, and other factors seem similar. While each property is different, certain divisions and/or departments, functions, and responsibilities are relatively common.

Exhibit 3   An Institutional Food Service Operation

"Serving more than **15 million people** at over **500,000 locations worldwide**" EVERY DAY   **ARAMARK**

ARAMARK Serves State and National Parks and Other Tourist Attractions

Catering Services
Whatever the event, ARAMARK provides every catering need from delectable entrees, outstanding service and comfortable accommodations.

Restaurant Services
Open for breakfast, lunch and dinner, ARAMARK's restaurants tempt guests with regional specialties and traditional favorites in the midst of picture-perfect views.

Snack Bars & Food Concessions
ARAMARK snack bars and food concessions offer burgers, sandwiches, pizza and beverages to help "re-fuel" tourists during their long days of site seeing.

Uniforms & Career Apparel
Every employee apparel need can be met by ARAMARK's Apparel One program.

Facilities
Whether it's groundskeeping, housekeeping, meeting planning or maintenance operations, ARAMARK manages every aspect of a facility.

Exhibit 3   *(continued)*

Lodging Services

ARAMARK manages lodges, cabins and modern suites whether in the center of the activity or "off the beaten path" with dining rooms, snack shops, gift boutiques and lounges.

Tour Operations & Interpretive Services

ARAMARK tours provide expert guides to help guests fully explore the sites in the area.

Recreational Activities

ARAMARK manages activities such as houseboat rentals, personal watercraft, speedboats and rafting trips as well as hiking, nature walks, horseback riding and wildlife viewing for the whole family to enjoy.

Retail Merchandising

ARAMARK maximizes your product sales and visitor satisfaction with a variety of permanent and portable retail shops.

Marketing Support Services & Reservations

ARAMARK provides staff that can produce brochures and other marketing materials, as well as a team to support a toll free telephone number to answer questions and make reservations.

The **ARAMARK Food and Support Services Group** manages a growing number of integrated services—including food, refreshment, facility and other support services—for a wide range of clients. ARAMARK serves customers such as corporations, healthcare systems, school districts, college campuses, conference and convention centers, national parks, sports and entertainment venues, and correctional institutions in 15 countries. This site can be found at http://www.aramark.com.

Exhibit 4   Typical Management Levels in a Large Hotel

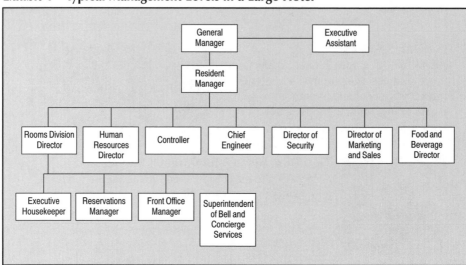

Exhibit 4, for example, shows typical management levels in a large hotel. A representative list of divisions and departments and their responsibilities follows, with the title of the individual in charge indicated in parentheses:

* Rooms Division (Rooms Division Director)—a line department that usually consists of several departments responsible for reservations, front office, bell and concierge services, telephone (PBX) services, laundry, and housekeeping. A **line manager** has decision-making authority within the organization.

* Human Resources (Human Resources Director)—a staff department that assists other departments in recruiting and selecting employees and in a wide variety of other activities involved in the management of employees. The primary role of a **staff manager** is to help managers of line departments make decisions by providing them with information and expert analysis.

* Accounting (Controller)—a staff department responsible for accounting tasks for the entire operation. This department is often responsible for purchasing, receiving, storing, and issuing food and beverage products. A food and beverage controller in a large property performs many of the property's control activities. Sometimes, in multi–unit hotel companies, the hotel's controller reports to a regional manager or other official outside the property rather than to the hotel's general manager. This is seen to provide increased control over the financial aspects of the operation.

* Engineering and Maintenance (Chief Engineer)—a line department responsible for physical plant and equipment maintenance and repair as well as energy conservation practices.

* Security (Director of Security)—a line department responsible for protecting the guests, employees, property, and equipment of the hotel.

- Marketing and Sales (Director of Marketing and Sales)—a line department responsible for attracting guests to the property, making group bookings, and handling convention services. This department is often involved with advertising and public relations.

- Food and Beverage Department (Food and Beverage Director)—a line department responsible for all food and beverage services provided by the property. The operations of the food and beverage department are addressed more specifically in the following section.

The Food and Beverage Department

Separate and distinct from other hotel departments, the food and beverage department typically encompasses such diverse services and operations as:

- Coffee shops

- Dining rooms

- Room service

- Lounges, bars, and other alcoholic beverage services

- Banquet services

- Other (vending machines, employee cafeterias, takeout and specialty shops, within-guestroom snack/beverage centers, etc.)

The food and beverage department is an integral part of the operation of a lodging property. The average **full-service hotel** (a hotel offering a variety of facilities and amenties, including food and beverage services) generates almost 29 percent of its total revenue from the sale of food and beverage products.[2] In some large convention hotels, food and beverage sales may account for 50 percent or more of a property's total revenue. Obviously, the food and beverage department is not "a necessary evil." The hotel's economic success or failure is directly tied to the ability of the food and beverage department staff to effectively plan and control its operations and to provide food service which will attract hotel guests.

It is important to note that the food and beverage department generally cannot survive by providing services to hotel guests only. In many properties, a significant percentage of food and beverage revenue is generated from the local area. Many hotel managers can use basic marketing techniques to attract community residents to the food and beverage operations. The following sections examine some of the major responsibilities associated with managing food and beverage operations within a hotel.

Production Facilities. Managing food production is a major responsibility in every food and beverage department. Older lodging properties were often built with separate food production facilities for each food service outlet. Increased costs of space, equipment, and operations, however, have reduced the usefulness of this design concept. Many newer facilities feature centralized commissary-style-kitchens that make many of the products used in service outlets throughout the

---

The Meaning of Industry Terms

In the hospitality industry, terms with different meanings are sometimes used interchangeably (and, therefore, incorrectly). Consider the following:

- *Revenue* and *Sales*. Revenue refers to money generated when a certain number of items are sold. For example, *revenue* of $25 is generated from the *sales* of five chicken sandwiches costing $5 each.

- *Catering* and *Banquets*. *Catering* refers to selling public functions involving food and beverage services. *Banquets* refers to the setup, production, service, and clean-up of food and beverages in public function space. Frequently, catering is a function of the marketing and sales department, while banqueting is a function of the food and beverage department.

---

property. For example, a central kitchen may produce bakery products, sauces, and products requiring specialized equipment or extensive labor, while finishing kitchens in the food service outlets prepare items requiring less equipment and labor. As a result of this newer design concept, food and beverage managers must be increasingly concerned with transport and delivery systems and with the sanitation, food quality, and production problems involved in large-volume preparation processes.

Operations Challenges. In their efforts to be profitable, food and beverage operations in lodging facilities often have to overcome several challenges that free-standing restaurants do not face. Consider the following:

- Free-standing restaurants are built in locations where food and beverage service is judged to be profitable; hotels are located in areas where the rental of guestrooms is judged to be profitable.

- Food service in hotels must operate at times convenient to hotel guests. For example, an airport hotel's restaurant may need to stay open to accommodate passengers from a late-night flight. By contrast, a restaurant's operating hours are scheduled to best accommodate food service guests.

- Food service in hotels must be provided to guests even on low-occupancy days. A restaurant manager may elect to close (for example, on all Mondays during the summer).

- Hotels often feel obligated to offer room service, even though this service frequently operates at a loss. In addition, room service must generally be available at all hours of the day or night in first-class properties.

- Hotel food service operations frequently offer dining benefits for all employees—not just those in the food and beverage department. While some direct costs may be allocated to departments based upon their employees' use of the dining privileges, other indirect costs are often "buried" in the food and beverage department.

- A hotel often has multiple food outlets. While some operating costs are reduced as central commissary kitchens are used, a free-standing restaurant does not incur the same costs for the transportation of food within the property.

- Free-standing restaurants usually are highly visible to potential guests, whereas restaurants in hotels are often more difficult to see and to get to—even if a direct off-the-street entrance is provided.

- The owner and the manager of a free-standing restaurant are very involved in its operation. In a hotel, by contrast, restaurant managers must often have decisions approved by the hotel manager, who has concerns extending beyond those of the food and beverage department.

Revenue and Support Centers. A food and beverage department contributes departmental income (revenue minus direct expenses) that contributes to the hotel's overhead (fixed costs) and profit requirements. Departmental income is based on the revenue and related expenses of each separate food and beverage outlet in the property. To effectively plan for and control the operation of each outlet, food and beverage managers must know the specific revenues and expenses applicable to each outlet. The concept of dividing departments into revenue and support centers helps managers organize their planning and effectively operate each service outlet. For example, a hotel's banquet operation may generate revenue in excess of costs, and the room service operation may suffer a loss. However, since they create revenue, both the banquet operation and room service are revenue centers within the hotel's food and beverage department. The facilities and activities of the hotel's operation that support revenue centers and supply them with what they need to generate revenue are often referred to as support centers. Examples include purchasing and laundry operations.

Many properties develop accounting and control plans that separate revenue and expense by revenue center—individual restaurant or banquet and room service, for example. In a commissary operation, such as a bakeshop or sauce/soup preparation station, revenue centers may "buy" necessary products from the production unit. The production unit, then, can be referred to as a support center. As a second example, some hotels consider the beverage storeroom to be a support center. The storeroom buys necessary products from suppliers and "sells" them to the beverage outlets, passing along labor and related costs incurred in operating the beverage storeroom.

As this need to identify and separate revenue and expenses by specific revenue and support center within the lodging property increases, food and beverage operations, at least in large facilities, actually become "mini-multi-unit" operations. All the management principles and procedures involved in planning, coordinating, marketing, recordkeeping, and related functions of chain operations apply, on a smaller scale, to the hotel's food and beverage department.

This discussion of a typical large food and beverage department has emphasized the diversity of services for which it is responsible and the complexity of its operations. The organization necessary to provide such services is also complex.

Overall Responsibility. Overall responsibility for the food and beverage department in a typical hotel lies with the food and beverage department head, whose title may be food and beverage director or something similar. The director is responsible to the hotel's general manager or assistant general manager and may receive help from those in other managerial positions within the department. For example, an assistant food and beverage director may be responsible for overseeing the activities of managers in each specific revenue center. Likewise, an executive chef, responsible for all food production in all outlets within the property, may report directly to the food and beverage director. In a large facility, there may be a beverage director who is responsible for all beverage operations and who reports to the director or assistant director of the food and beverage department. A food and beverage controller reporting to the accounting/controller's department may also be employed. This staff member serves in an advisory capacity to the food and beverage director and is responsible for many of the accounting/recordkeeping aspects of the food and beverage operation. Finally, a wide array of employee positions can be found within the specific revenue and support centers of the food and beverage department.

Management System Design. The diverse services and complex organization of a food and beverage department require an effective management system designed according to a carefully developed plan. The management system designed for food and beverage operations must be comprehensive, encompassing all necessary management activities and all aspects of available or potential resources—people, money, products (food and beverage), time, procedures, energy, facilities, and equipment.

Commercial and Institutional Food Services

The above discussion about hotel food and beverage operations addressed the complexity created by the diverse range of services these operations generally provide and their need for specially designed management systems. This point should not hide a more important fact: at their most basic level, quantity food production and management systems—whether developed for commercial or institutional operations—are more similar than different. This common ground determines the basic requirements of a food and beverage management system. Therefore, while our focus is on food and beverage operations in commercial (for-profit) properties, most of what we discuss will apply to other food service operations as well.

First of all, food service is a people business—as is the hospitality industry in general. People are the common factor in all segments of the industry and at all levels of operation. The persons being served, whether they are called guests in a hotel or patients in a hospital, are at the center of all concerns, procedures, and considerations. The guest's perspective must be factored into every process of analyzing and solving problems. For example, responding to a problem of high costs by reducing quality will likely cause guest dissatisfaction and larger problems in the long run. The staff members must work together to deliver services and achieve the goals of the operation—regardless of whether the operation is commercial or institutional.

Everything Begins with the Menu

All food and beverage management systems begin with the menu. The operation's menu determines what production, service, and managerial responsibilities must be met. Many food and beverage operations have a variety of menus for different meal periods and seasons of the year. The menu itself is the result of marketing efforts designed to identify the wants and needs of guests. These guests may vary from hotel or restaurant customers, to hospital patients, nursing home residents, or school students. In each case, the effort is to develop strategies to satisfy the guest's needs, while at the same time achieving the operation's own goals.

Developing the menu is only the first, and most basic, step in planning food and beverage operations. Once the menu is developed, plans and procedures for determining necessary products, equipment (purchase and maintenance), facility design and layout, and production systems must be developed and implemented. The goal is to implement an efficient operating control cycle for all revenue and support centers within the entire operation.

The Operating Control Cycle

An **operating control cycle** divides food and beverage operations into a series of activities involved in providing food and beverage products to guests. Systems must be designed to manage the flow of food and beverage products through each of the following stages of the cycle:

- Menu planning
- Purchasing
- Receiving
- Storing
- Issuing
- Production (includes preparing, cooking, and holding)
- Serving (from production to service personnel)
- Service (from service personnel to the guest)

Management System

All food and beverage operations must develop and implement management programs and establish procedures for managing all available resources. To do this, an effective recordkeeping and accounting system is necessary. This system must be able to provide meaningful, accurate information on a timely basis so that appropriate operating and control decisions can be made and evaluated.

The basic system for management of a food and beverage operation is outlined in Exhibit 5. As the exhibit shows, the **components of management**—planning, organizing, coordinating, staffing, directing, controlling, and evaluating—are the umbrella under which the entire program operates. This is true for any business enterprise. Under the umbrella, external marketing plans and

Exhibit 5   Overview of Management System for Food and Beverage Operations

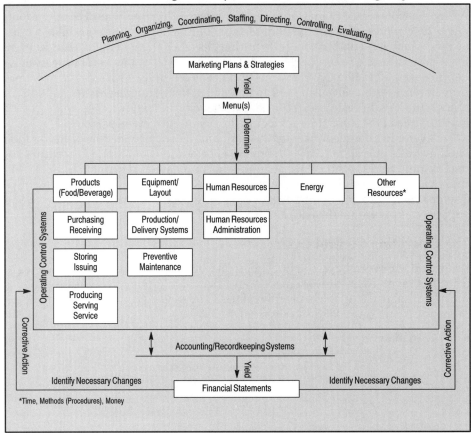

strategies lead to the basic menu decisions. The menu determines what resources are needed and, therefore, what specific operating control systems are necessary. Finally, the accounting/recordkeeping system takes information from the various components in the operating control system and develops statements about the operation's current financial status. The financial statements become the "barometer" of how well the operation is meeting its economic—whether profit or cost containment—objectives. When problems are identified, corrective action—one step in the control system—becomes necessary to ensure effective management of all resources.

The Management Process

The management process can be separated into seven basic components: planning, organizing, coordinating, staffing, directing, controlling, and evaluating (see Exhibit 6). These management components are fundamental activities or tasks that apply to all managers, regardless of the type of food service operation.

Exhibit 6 The Management Process

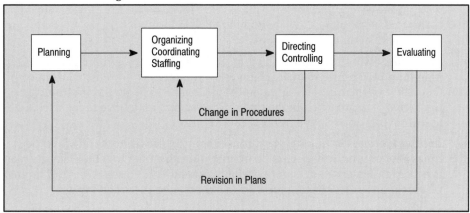

Planning. **Planning** is the management task of creating goals and objectives, and programs of action to reach those goals and objectives. Goals and objectives indicate what you want to do; action plans tell how you propose to do it. Planning should be done before other management tasks are undertaken.

Every manager, regardless of position or type of food service organization, must plan. At the highest management levels, long-range planning is undertaken by executives to develop long-term goals and strategies helpful in attaining those goals. At intermediate management levels, operational plans are developed by managers to attain short-term goals. At lower management levels, supervisory planning involves the day-to-day process of running the operation.

Let's look at how this might work at a large restaurant company with many units. At top management levels, the board of directors, the board chair, and the chief executive officer may establish long-term goals that may not be attained within two, three, five, or even ten years. An example of such goals might be: "To be the number one restaurant chain in gross revenues in the Midwest region within ten years." Intermediate levels of management—unit managers and department heads—focus on meeting current budget objectives and on short-term economic planning. At lower levels of management, supervisors cost next month's banquet, plan next week's labor schedule, or set goals that can be met within a short time period.

Whether the organization is a multi-unit chain or a single property, planning must start at the top. Only when top management establishes a definite course of action can managers at all organizational levels develop plans that fit into the organization's long-range plans.

Other factors in effective planning include:

- *Information.* You must have access to complete information to plan effectively.

- *Communication.* Managers at all levels should communicate with each other when developing plans. For example, when a food and beverage director develops an operating budget, it is wise to get input from the chef and the beverage manager. Whenever possible, managers should also communicate with employees when making plans that affect them. Employees are more likely to follow plans they have helped develop. Such plans become "our plans," not "management's plans."

- *Flexibility.* Plans should be flexible. Some food service managers develop plans and then refuse to make changes even though conditions warrant them. One obvious example is the operating budget. What if sales volume is less than what was projected in the budget? Managers may have to make changes to lower costs and/or generate increased business.

- *Implementation.* Obviously, plans must be implemented to be effective. Sometimes a lot of time and discussion go into putting a plan together, but the plan is never implemented or is only partially carried out. This is a waste of limited resources and is frustrating for staff members who provided input.

Managers should not plan only when they get around to it. Time should be set aside regularly for managers at each organizational level to establish objectives, create plans to attain them, and make revisions as necessary. If planning time is not set aside, the organization may drift into one crisis after another and managers may become "fire fighters," running from one unexpected situation to the next to combat problems that could have been avoided through effective planning.

Organizing. The management activity of **organizing** answers the question, "How can we best assemble and use our limited human resources to attain organizational objectives?" Organizing involves establishing the flow of authority (power) and communication among people.

In any organization, care should be taken to make sure each employee has only one supervisor. If an employee has two bosses, problems can occur if conflicting orders are given.

The number of employees each supervisor should manage must be carefully determined. The right number of employees for each supervisor depends on many variables, including: the supervisor's experience, the complexity of the work, the amount of supervision employees require, the frequency with which problems are liable to occur, and the amount of help the supervisor can expect from higher-level managers, and other variables. What is important is that supervisors not be given more people than they can handle.

The authority to make decisions about using resources should be available at all levels. It is inefficient for a supervisor to have the responsibility to do something, but not have the authority necessary to get it done. Supervisors should not need to seek higher management approval for tasks that must be routinely done as part of the job. Increasingly, employees are **empowered** to make decisions as well; for example, a food server might be given the discretion to replace an incorrectly prepared meal rather than be required to check with a manager first.

Because an organization's structure evolves throughout the life of the business, many food service operations have organization charts that do not reflect current operating procedures. For example, an organization chart can indicate that the cook's supervisor is the chef when in fact the food and beverage director has assumed the responsibility for directing the cook. An organization chart should be updated regularly so that it gives a current, accurate picture of how the operation's human resources are organized.

Coordinating. Coordinating is the management task of assigning work and organizing people and resources to achieve the operation's objectives.

Coordinating depends on communication. There must be effective channels of communication to transmit messages up, down, and across the organizational structure. It is also necessary for peers (those at the same organizational level) to communicate with each other. Achieving the organization's goals can happen only if there is open communication among department heads and other department managers.

Delegation is an important aspect of coordinating. Delegation means that authority can be passed down the organization. Ultimate responsibility or accountability, however, cannot be delegated. For example, the food and beverage department head is responsible to the hotel's general manager for all aspects of the food and beverage department's operating budget. He or she may delegate the authority to make some decisions about food and beverages to the head chef and the beverage manager, but the department head will still be responsible to the general manager for meeting budget goals.

Staffing. Staffing involves recruiting and hiring applicants. The goal of staffing is to bring the best-qualified employees into the food service operation. At large properties, you may be asked to select from applicants screened by the human resources department; at smaller properties, the general manager may give you the total responsibility for finding, screening, and hiring applicants.

Application forms, selection tests, reference checks, and other screening devices should all be a part of the recruitment and selection process. Often, however, very little screening is done. When someone quits, the next person who walks through the door is hired.

It's important to match the applicant to the vacant job rather than hiring someone and then asking what he or she can do. To do this, jobs must be defined in terms of the tasks to be performed. Job descriptions list required job tasks for each job and make it easier to match applicants to jobs.

A second staffing tool, job specifications, lists the personal qualities necessary to perform jobs effectively. We all bring different amounts of knowledge, experience, and common sense to a job. A job specification indicates the personal attributes judged necessary for successful job performance.

Consider all possible sources of job applicants. Human resources departments in large properties may recruit from within the organization. You can also ask currently employed staff members for suggestions, work with employment service agencies, and advertise.

Some managers think that the more applicants who apply, the more work it will take to sort them out, so they try to limit the number of applicants. From the perspective of the total organization, this is a poor strategy. The chance of finding the right person for the job increases if a large number of people are encouraged to apply.

Part of staffing is making sure new hires get off to a good start. An employee's early experiences on the job strongly affect his or her relationship with the organization. A well-planned employee orientation program is necessary to properly introduce new employees to supervisors, co-workers, and the organization in general.

Directing. Directing is a big part of most managers' jobs. Management is often defined as getting work done through other people. In the labor-intensive food service industry this is certainly true. Employees are absolutely critical to the success of every food service operation. All human beings are complex and at times difficult to understand. However, understanding the wants, needs, and expectations of your employees helps you direct them more effectively.

Directing includes supervising, scheduling, and disciplining employees. Supervising comprises all the ways you relate to your employees when work is being done. When supervising employees, you should know how to motivate, gain cooperation, give orders, and bring out the best in people. Ways to mesh organizational goals with the goals of employees become important. Employees can be motivated when their personal needs are addressed on the job. Whenever possible, employees should have input to decisions that affect them.

Scheduling employees effectively is very important. You must know exactly how much labor is needed, then be able to work within those parameters and treat all employees fairly.

Disciplining employees is a task many managers dread. However, it can be a positive experience if you keep in mind that discipline is not a form of punishment. Rather, discipline is a way to address and correct improper behavior and help employees become productive members of the organization. Discipline can consist of informal coaching and counseling sessions as well as more serious meetings between the manager, employee, and perhaps a higher-level manager or (in large organizations) someone from the human resources department. Written warnings and suspensions may be used in some situations. Following a formal, written disciplinary action program is the best way to protect yourself and your organization against charges of favoritism, discrimination, and unfair practices.

Directing people is complex and sometimes difficult. In many directing situations, it is useful to think about how you would like to be treated. Chances are, your employees share many of the same concerns you have.

Controlling. There is no assurance that goals will be attained just because effective plans have been developed, resources organized, staff selected, and directions carried out. For this reason, you must attend to the **controlling** function of management, which includes developing and implementing control systems.

Many food and beverage products pass through a food service operation. Therefore, control procedures for purchasing, receiving, storing, issuing, preparing, and serving products are necessary.

But control includes much more than just the physical tasks of locking storeroom doors, checking standard recipes, or weighing incoming products on a scale. The process of control actually begins with establishing a budget. A budget indicates expected revenue and cost levels. You may look at your recent financial statements—especially income statements—or use statistics developed in-house as a base to project anticipated revenue and expense levels. Once the budget is established, you must measure the extent to which budget goals are met. If the variance between expected results and actual results is excessive, corrective action must be taken and the results evaluated to assess whether the corrective action was effective.

You should develop control systems that will alert you to problems on a timely basis. Obviously, it is not ideal to learn many weeks after it started that a control problem exists. Food service managers often develop daily or weekly control procedures to supplement monthly budget information provided by their accountants or bookkeepers.

Be aware that controls must be worth more than their cost. For example, to use a system that costs $50 weekly to save $35 weekly is not a good idea. On the other hand, spending $500 for a piece of equipment that will save $50 a week is reasonable because the payback period is only ten weeks.

Evaluating. **Evaluating** is the management task of: (1) reviewing the operation's progress toward achieving overall organizational goals, (2) measuring employee performance, and (3) assessing the effectiveness of training programs. The constant question for managers must be, "How well are we doing?"

You must continually evaluate whether organizational goals are being attained because complacency can spell trouble for the future of the operation. If you are on target, you can move on to accomplish new goals. If goals are not being met, the evaluation process served its purpose: it identified a problem. Awareness of a problem is the first step toward solving it.

Managers must also evaluate themselves and their own performance. Some managers believe they always do a good job, so self-evaluation is unnecessary. Others believe they are doing the best possible job and cannot do any better—again, evaluation is judged unnecessary. Both of these approaches are unproductive. Taking an honest look at their own performance from time to time can help managers improve their professional and interpersonal skills.

Evaluating is too important to be done "whenever there is time." Managers should regularly make time for this step in the management process.

Integrating the Process

In the previous section we discussed each activity in the management process separately. In the real world, management activities are not so neatly categorized. Managers at all organizational levels perform many management activities each day, sometimes simultaneously. For example, during a typical day a food service manager might:

- Help develop next year's operating budget (planning, controlling)

- Deal with problems caused by improper delegation (coordinating)

- Work with a colleague in another department to plan an upcoming special event (planning, coordinating)

- Revise job descriptions and job specifications (organizing, staffing)

- Carry out routine supervisory activities (directing)

- Revise standard food and labor costs (controlling)

- Conduct employee performance reviews (evaluating)

As managers gain and learn from experience, they get better at performing all the various management activities and tasks that arise every day.

Important Differences

A major difference between commercial and institutional food services lies in the "language" used to describe management and the results of operations. For example, the language of commercial food service operations refers to "management" and "profits"; the language of institutional food service operations refers to "administration" and "operating surplus."

Also, among the various kinds of food and beverage operations there are important differences in the methods used to collect revenue for services the properties provide. For example, the typical hotel and restaurant generally collects revenue in the form of cash, check, or charge card. Also, they typically collect this revenue when the service is provided. There may also be some house accounts that are billed separately for charges incurred during a monthly or other billing period. The "payment upon receipt of services" policy and timely billing methods make revenue collection relatively simple and straightforward.

Many hotel guests are permitted to charge food and beverage services to their accounts. Guest charges complicate the revenue collection system the hotel needs to manage its operations. The hotel must use an **accounts receivable system** to handle revenue that is due but not yet collected. Gathering and channeling all the information involved in this revenue collection system can be a tedious and error-prone process, but computerized equipment—both at the point of sale and at the front office where guest folios are automatically updated—has greatly simplified the revenue collection process. Nevertheless, there is still an obvious need for an expanded revenue control and collection system for the management of hotel food and beverage operations.

Revenue from banquet sales, a large aspect of food and beverage operations in many hotels, frequently involves a combination of billing methods. To account for "up-front" (advance) payments and to assess the amounts still due, there must be a system to accurately determine the quantity of products sold for which revenue must be collected.

Commercial operators may appreciate the special problems of institutional administrators in allocating and assessing operating and related costs of food services so that charges can be calculated. First, food and beverage service is only one part of the "bill" to patients, residents, students, or others being served. Also, the process of allocating expenses to each cost center, such as dietary services, is frequently much more detailed and complicated in large hospitals and institutions than that used by many hotel properties (See Exhibit 7). Finally, institutional operations may collect cash; they may allow the use of credit cards (in which guests pay when billed); and they may allow the use of debit cards (in which guests pay a lump

Exhibit 7   Food and Facilities Management Services

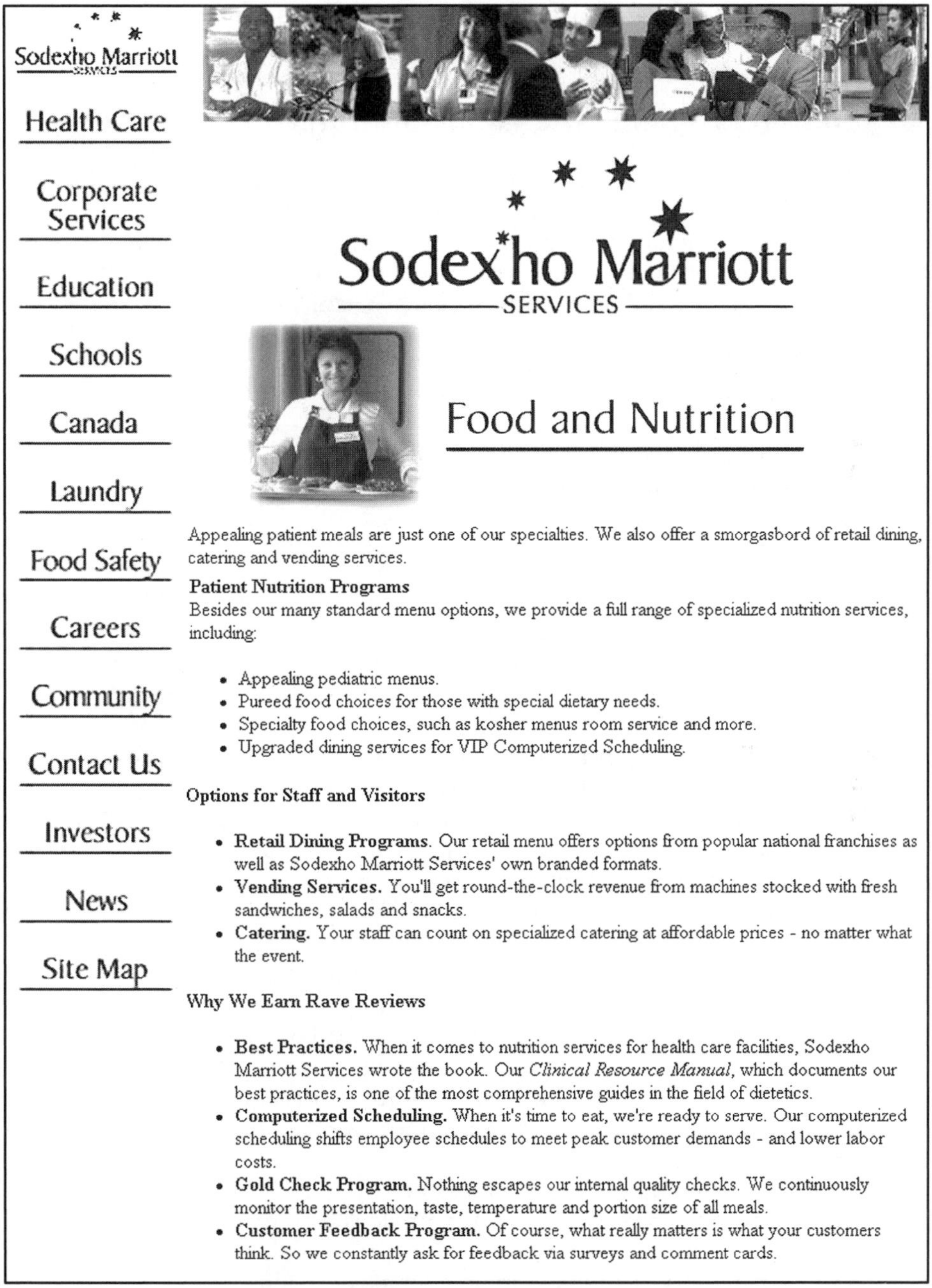

Sodexho Marriott

- Health Care
- Corporate Services
- Education
- Schools
- Canada
- Laundry
- Food Safety
- Careers
- Community
- Contact Us
- Investors
- News
- Site Map

Sodexho Marriott
SERVICES

Food and Nutrition

Appealing patient meals are just one of our specialties. We also offer a smorgasbord of retail dining, catering and vending services.

Patient Nutrition Programs

Besides our many standard menu options, we provide a full range of specialized nutrition services, including:

- Appealing pediatric menus.
- Pureed food choices for those with special dietary needs.
- Specialty food choices, such as kosher menus room service and more.
- Upgraded dining services for VIP Computerized Scheduling.

Options for Staff and Visitors

- **Retail Dining Programs.** Our retail menu offers options from popular national franchises as well as Sodexho Marriott Services' own branded formats.
- **Vending Services.** You'll get round-the-clock revenue from machines stocked with fresh sandwiches, salads and snacks.
- **Catering.** Your staff can count on specialized catering at affordable prices - no matter what the event.

Why We Earn Rave Reviews

- **Best Practices.** When it comes to nutrition services for health care facilities, Sodexho Marriott Services wrote the book. Our *Clinical Resource Manual,* which documents our best practices, is one of the most comprehensive guides in the field of dietetics.
- **Computerized Scheduling.** When it's time to eat, we're ready to serve. Our computerized scheduling shifts employee schedules to meet peak customer demands - and lower labor costs.
- **Gold Check Program.** Nothing escapes our internal quality checks. We continuously monitor the presentation, taste, temperature and portion size of all meals.
- **Customer Feedback Program.** Of course, what really matters is what your customers think. So we constantly ask for feedback via surveys and comment cards.

Sodexho Marriott offers a full range of outsourcing solutions to the corporate, healthcare, and education markets, including food services, housekeeping, groundskeeping, plant operations and maintenance, and integrated facilities management. This site can be found at http://www.sodexhomarriott.com.

sum in advance and then draw on this amount as charges are made) (see Exhibit 8). As another example, private clubs typically permit charges only with members paying amounts owed on a monthly, quarterly or other basis.

A Common Problem: The Labor Shortage

One of the most serious problems confronting the food and beverage industry is the growing labor shortage. The need for qualified and trained professionals in food and beverage operations is great. Large, rapidly expanding companies cannot find, either within or outside their organizations, enough competent staff. Basic strategies managers can adopt to address this problem are:

- Increase productivity

- Reduce turnover

- Offer competitive salaries and fringe benefits

- Revise recruiting and hiring procedures to accommodate non-traditional workers

Managers can also use training, cross-training, self-improvement, and other personal and professional development programs to build leadership talent and improve employees' work skills.[3] The Educational Institute of the American Hotel & Lodging Association, for example, offers courses, seminars, and certification programs, and sponsors professional development chapters for current and prospective hospitality managers and employees.

Another effective strategy for managing the labor shortage involves developing standardized procedures for routine, and even occasionally encountered, situations. This approach tries to resolve all problems in the operation by applying proven procedures and standard policies, rather than by calling upon the creative problem-solving methods of ongoing managerial control and monitoring. The hope is that, after training in these procedures, more people will be qualified to work within a highly structured food and beverage operation and that most operational problems will be solved in advance by applying standard operating procedures. For example, in today's multi-unit fast-food and family restaurants, on-site managers have few opportunities to make decisions about menus, pricing, layout and design, purchase specifications, development of employee training programs, or wage and salary schedules. In each instance, standardized operating procedures and the decisions of district or regional level management personnel take the place of on-site management discretion.

This standardization strategy is of less use in most hotel food and beverage operations. Although almost every hotel chain does have standard operating procedure manuals, they usually provide only the most basic structure and allow a great deal of flexibility for on-site management decisions. These manuals frequently indicate that several different procedures can be used to solve various problems. Finally, standard operating procedures in most hotel food and beverage operations are often designed more to provide consistency from the guest's

Exhibit 8   Campus Restaurants and Food Courts

Restaurants and Food Courts

We provide many choices for dining across campus for students, faculty, staff and visitors. Two locations on campus have food courts; Crossroads Food Court located in the International Building is located in the middle of MSU off Shaw Lane. One Union Square is located inside the MSU Union Building at the north end of campus on West Circle Drive. Michigan State University also has several restaurants for everyone to enjoy. For formal fare, Kellogg's State Room has an enjoyable atmosphere and a delicious selection of entrees. For a great pasta bar, try the River Cafe for lunch, and if you find yourself in the east end of campus, stop in at Owen Cafe located in Owen Graduate Hall.

Layfayette Square	Union Station Cafe
Owen Cafe	Crossroads Food Court
River Cafe	One Union Square Food Court
The State Room	

Lafayette Square is a restaurant of fine dining located in the main building of Brody Complex. It is open to the students and the public on Friday and Saturday evenings only. Residence halls students on board plans are offered reduced rates.

Spartan Cash is accepted here.

The River Cafe is located in the lower level of the Kellogg Hotel and Conference Center on Harrison Road, across from Brody Complex. It features sandwiches, soups and a great pasta bar, stir-fried on the spot. Open for lunch only.

The Department of University Housing at Michigan State University operates the largest residence hall system in the country. Some meal plans allow students to use an electronic card to gain access to food courts, express carry-out cafés, and campus restaurants like Lafayette Square.

perspective and to allow cost comparisons between properties than to ease the tasks of managers and reduce the need for on-site problem solving.

The labor shortage problem emphasizes the fact that competent managers are a critical factor determining the ultimate success—or failure—of all food and beverage operations. Food and beverage managers must know a great deal about many functions to offer the guidance needed at every stage of the operation. A strong educational background provides a base for analyzing and thinking about the dynamics of a large food and beverage operation, and experience must provide an understanding of exactly how the information is applied to effectively solve real and practical problems. Furthermore, management staff must have and maintain a strong positive attitude to succeed. The phrase "the business gets into your blood" reflects the sustaining interest and enthusiasm necessary to work as a food and beverage manager. The high-energy manager will be "turned on" by the challenges of management problems and will have the ability to direct this energy toward effective solutions.

The job of a food and beverage manager is never the same; each day is different. The work can present constant mental and physical challenges. The manager must develop long-range plans while resolving daily crises across the entire spectrum of the department.

Food and beverage managers must thoroughly understand the basic principles integral to each component of the management system for food and beverage operations illustrated in Exhibits 5 and 6. This information provides a foundation upon which control aspects of the operation can be developed.

Endnotes

1. Those interested in a detailed explanation of the role of food service operations in relation to travel and tourism should read Joseph Fridgen's *Dimensions of Tourism* (Lansing, Mich.: Educational Institute of the American Hotel & Lodging Association, 1991).

2. *Trends in the Hotel Industry—USA Edition 1997* (San Francisco: PKF Consulting, 1997), p. 70.

3. The reader interested in strategies managers can adopt to address the labor shortage problem should read Robert H. Woods's *Managing Hospitality Human Resources*, 3d ed. (Lansing, Mich.: Educational Institute of the American Hotel & Lodging Association, 2001).

Key Terms

accounts receivable system—A system to handle revenue that is due but not yet collected.

commercial food service operations—Food service operations found in lodging properties, clubs, restaurants, and other businesses that exist to make a profit from the sale of food and beverage products.

components of management—Activities for managing available resources; activities include planning, organizing, coordinating, staffing, directing, controlling, and evaluating.

controlling—The management task of measuring actual results with expected results, as in measuring actual sales against expected or budgeted sales. Controlling also refers to safeguarding the operation's property and income.

coordinating—The management task of assigning work and organizing people and resources to achieve the operation's objectives.

directing—The management task of supervising, scheduling, and disciplining employees. Supervising includes such things as training and motivating employees.

empowerment—The redistribution of power within an organization that enables managers, supervisors, and employees to perform their jobs more efficiently and effectively. The overall goal is to enhance service to guests and increase profits for the organization by releasing decision-making responsibility, authority, and accountability to every level within the organization.

evaluating—The management task of: (1) reviewing the operation's progress toward overall organizational goals, (2) measuring employee performance, and (3) assessing the effectiveness of training programs.

full-service hotel—A hotel offering food and beverage services.

institutional food service operations—Organizations such as schools, nursing homes, hospitals, and military services that are nonprofit and exist primarily for reasons other than to provide food or lodging services to guests.

line manager—A position within the "chain of command" that is directly responsible for all decisions involved in using the hospitality operation's resources to generate revenue and attain other goals of a department or organization.

operating control cycle—A system that divides food and beverage operations into a series of activities involved in providing food and beverage products to guests.

organizing—The management activity that attempts to best assemble and use limited human resources to attain organizational objectives. It involves establishing the flow of authority and communication among people.

planning—The management task of creating goals, objectives, and programs of action to reach those goals and objectives. It should be done before undertaking other management tasks.

revenue center—A revenue-producing department within a hospitality operation.

staffing—The management activity of recruiting and hiring applicants.

staff manager—A position in a hospitality operation that is responsible for providing expert advice and information to assist management in making decisions; staff specialists collect information and provide advice, but do not make decisions for line managers.

support center—A department within a hospitality operation that is not directly involved in generating revenue but that incurs costs as it provides support services to revenue-generating departments.

Review Questions

1. Why is it important for hotel food and beverage operations to market services to residents in the community as well as to hotel guests?

2. What aspects must be considered when designing a food and beverage management system?

3. What is the difference between a revenue center and a support center?

4. Why must food and beverage managers know the specific revenues and expenses related to each food and beverage outlet in the department?

5. What is the first step in planning food and beverage operations?

6. What are some examples of standard operating procedures that may be important in the management of resources available to the food and beverage manager?

7. What are some factors that complicate revenue collection systems in commercial and institutional food service operations?

8. What are some of the basic skills and traits a food and beverage director must have to be successful?

9. Why is an effective recordkeeping and accounting system necessary in a food and beverage operation?

10. What strategies can managers adopt to address the industry's labor shortage problem?

Internet Sites

For more information, visit the following Internet sites. Remember that Internet addresses can change without notice. If the site is no longer there, you can use a search engine to look for additional sites.

Associations

American Culinary Federation (ACF)
http://www.acfchefs.org

American Hotel & Lodging Association (AH&LA)
http://www.ahlaonline.org

American School Food Service Association (ASFSA)
http://www.asfsa.org

Club Managers Association of America
http://www.cmaa.org

The Educational Foundation of NRA
http://www.edfound.org

The Educational Institute of AH&LA
http://www.ei-ahla.org

Hospitality Financial and Technology
Professionals
http://www.hftp.org

Hotel and Catering Institutional
Management Association
http://www.hcima.org.uk

Institute of Food Technologies
http://www.ift.org

International Council of Hotel
Restaurant and Institutional Education
http://www.chrie.org

International Hotel & Restaurant
Association
http://www.ih-ra.com

National Association of College and
University Food Services
http://www.nacufs.org

National Restaurant Association (NRA)
http://www.restaurant.org

Hotels

Bass Hotels
http://www.basshotels.com

Four Seasons Hotels
http://www.fshr.com

Hilton Hotels
http://www.hilton.com

Hyatt Hotels
http://www.hyatt.com

Marriott International
http://www.marriott.com

Ritz Carlton Hotels
http://www.ritzcarlton.com

Sheraton Hotels
http://www.sheraton.com

Starwood Hotels and Resorts
http://www.starwood.com

Westin Hotels
http://www.westin.com

Restaurants

Burger King Restaurants
http://www.burgerking.com

Canlis Restaurant
http://www.canlis.com

Hard Rock Cafe
http://www.hardrock.com

Houston's Restaurants
http://www.houstons.com

McDonalds
http://www.mcdonalds.com

Olive Garden
http://www.olivegarden.com

Outback Steak House
http://www.outback.com

Rainforest Café
http://www.rainforest.com

Spaghetti Warehouse
http://www.meatballs.com

Steak and Shake
http://www.steaknshake.com

Taco Bell
http://www.tacobell.com

TGI Fridays
http://www.tgifridays.com

Top of the Cove
http://topofthecove.com

Management Companies

ARAMARK
http://www.aramark.com

HDS Services
http://www.hdsservices.com

Bon Appetit Management Company
http://www.bamco.com

Sodexho Marriott
http://www.sodexhomarriott.com

Compass Group
http://www.compass–na.com

White Lodging
http://www.whitelodging.com

Publications—Online and Printed

Chef Educator Today
http://www.chefedtoday.com

Journal of Nutrition
Journal of the American Society of
Nutritional Sciences
http://nutrition.org

Club Management Magazine
http://www.club–mgmt.com

Lodging Food and Beverage
http://www.lodgingnews.com/
lodgingfnb/

Electronic Gourmet Guide
http://www.foodwine.com

Lodging Hospitality Online
http://www.lhonline.com

Food and Hospitality Magazine
http://www.foodserviceworld.com

Lodging News
Journal of the American Hotel &
Lodging Association
http://www.ei–ahla.org/webs/
lodging/index.html

Food Management
http://www.foodservicesearch.com

Food Network: CyberKitchen
http://www.foodtv.com

Lodging Online
http://www.ei–ahla.org/webs/
lodging/index.html

Food Processing
http://www.foodprocessing.com

Hospitality and industry news
www.hospitalitynet.nl

Nation's Restaurant News
http://www.nrn.com

Internet Food Channel
http://www.foodchannel.com

On the Rail—News for Food
Professionals
http://www.ontherail.com

*International Hotel and Restaurant
Association*
www.hotelsmag.com

Prepared Foods
Product development, ingredients,
 suppliers
http://www.preparedfoods.com

*International Journal of Hospitality
Management*
http://www.mcb.co.uk/ijchm.htm

Restaurants and Institutions
http://www.rimag.com

*Restaurant Business, Food Service,
and ID magazines*
http://www.foodservicetoday.com

Restaurant Hospitality
www.foodservicesearch.com

Restaurants USA
Publication of National Restaurant
Association
http://www.restaurant.org/rusa

World Hospitality
http://www.worldhospitality.com

Chapter 2 Outline

Management Resources and Objectives
The Manager in the Management
  Process
The Control Process
  Establish Standards
  Measure Actual Operating Results
  Compare Actual Results with
    Standards
  Take Corrective Action
  Evaluate Corrective Action
Considerations in Designing Control
  Systems
Responsibilities for Control

Competencies

1. Identify the resources managers use to attain organizational objectives. (p. 31)

2. Identify the tools managers use to plan organizational objectives. (pp. 31–33)

3. Explain how control procedures help managers assess operational results. (p. 32)

4. Describe the basic steps in the control process. (pp. 32–45)

5. Identify issues that managers consider when designing control systems. (pp. 45–48)

2

The Control Function

CONTROL IS ONE of the most important functions of the very broad and complex system of activities loosely referred to as "management." Within the hospitality industry there are many definitions of management, reflecting the vast number of concepts included within the term. For our purposes, a workable and practical definition of management is: Management is using what you've got, to do what you want to do. A manager uses available resources to attain the organization's objectives.

Management Resources and Objectives

Resources are the assets of an operation. Food and beverage managers are responsible for eight basic types of resources:

1. People
2. Money
3. Products (food and beverages)
4. Time
5. Procedures
6. Energy
7. Facilities
8. Equipment

All resources are in limited supply. No manager has all the people, money, products, and other resources that he or she would like to work with. Therefore, part of the manager's job is to decide how best to use the limited resources available to attain the organization's objectives.

Objectives state what the management of the operation wishes to accomplish. They indicate why the business exists and what it is trying to do. The objectives of a food and beverage operation often center on such things as:

- **Profit** and/or **cost** levels
- Maintaining or increasing financial strength during changing social and economic conditions
- Guest (marketing) concerns
- Management and employee interests

- Professional obligations

- Societal concerns

Without objectives to lend direction and focus to all activities, managers can easily become sidetracked, and become involved in tasks that are unimportant or unrelated to meeting the organization's goals.

As we shall soon see, management's first activity must be to plan organizational objectives. Management must establish broad courses of action designed to move the operation from where it is to where management wants it to go. Exhibit 1 shows the process by which the initial vision is organized into specific, interdependant steps for achieving the property's goals.

The Manager in the Management Process

A manager is a staff member who: (1) decides the best way to use organizational resources to attain objectives, and (2) participates in the management tasks of planning, organizing, coordinating, staffing, supervising, controlling, and evaluating.

Since most managers supervise employees, they are also responsible for the performance of those staff members. To a large extent, managers are only as successful as their employees. Said another way, managers—not employees—are responsible for many of the problems which food and beverage operations encounter. Being held accountable for their own work as well as the work of others is common to those in management positions.

An effective manager not only knows the basic management principles but is able to put them into practice. While knowledge alone cannot replace experience and common sense, it is a vital ingredient in creative decision making. The remainder of this chapter focuses on basic concepts of control.

The Control Process

A simple definition of control emphasizes its relationship with planning: **Control** is a series of coordinated activities that helps managers assess the extent to which *actual* results of operations match the *planned* results.

An effective control system is important because managers must know how the operation is doing—whether, and to what extent, it is meeting its goals. Control procedures can help managers:

- Determine whether delegated tasks are being carried out correctly.

- Assess the effect of changes required by the economy, market, and/or reactions to competition.

- Identify problems early so they can be resolved before they create bigger problems.

- Determine where problems are occurring.

- Identify mistakes and lead to actions to correct these mistakes.

Exhibit 1   The Sequence of Planning

Planning is a process that involves the development of six management tools. Some managers incorrectly believe that these tools can be developed without regard to each other. However, effective planning requires that these tools be developed in the following order:

Vision

↓

Mission

↓

Long-Range Plan

↓

Business Plan

↓

Marketing Plan

↓

Operating Budget

A vision is a broad and abstract view of what the property should be like. (For example, a property's vision may be "to become the very best hotel in the community for the convention and business traveler.") The vision shapes the mission, which is a more specific statement about what the property will do and how it will do it. (For example, concepts in a mission might include "being the first choice of convention travelers by offering the finest food and beverage services.")

The long-range plan indicates what the property desires to accomplish in a specified time period (often five years) in relation to the mission. (Continuing our example, the property's goal may be to have 75 percent of the city's convention business within five years.) The business plan indicates specifically what will be done within the next year and may include revenue goals. (The property in this example may want to achieve 40 percent of the city's convention business within the next year.) After the business plan is developed, the property determines a marketing plan, which indicates specific procedures that will be used to accomplish the business plan. A wide range of strategies and action plans with associated schedules are included in a marketing plan.

Finally, an operating budget is established. An operating budget details revenue to be generated from the successful marketing plan, costs associated with the products and services, and the property's financial goals.

Exhibit 2   Basic Steps in the Control Process

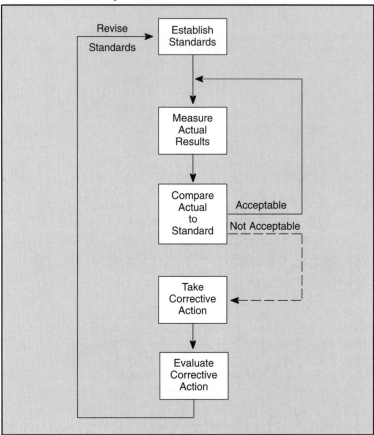

The control process follows a series of basic steps as illustrated in Exhibit 2. The process begins with the establishment of standards. Next, accurate information about the actual results achieved by the operation must be gathered. The food and beverage manager can then compare actual results to standards. If actual results do not conform to the standards, **corrective action** must be taken. The action taken will probably be a change in operating procedures. Finally, results of the correctiveaction must be evaluated. This process may lead to a revision of the standards. By repeating the cycle, the effects of implementing corrective action can be evaluated. Throughout the process, remember that while all resources must be controlled, the primary areas—food, beverage, labor (also called **prime costs**), and revenue—have highest priority.

Establish Standards

The first step in the control process is the establishment of standards. From a broad management view there are several types of standards:

- Quality standards—Quality is the consistent delivery of products and services according to expected benchmarks which help define when and how quality is attained. For example, the quality of dining service might be judged by the extent to which basic standard operating procedures are followed. A review of comment cards from guests and from mystery shoppers might be used to assess whether and to what extent quality service is consistently attained.

- Quantity standards—The volume of output can reflect a benchmark of expected productivity. For example, the number of guests served per labor hour or number of minutes per guest meal are examples of quantity standards.

- Control standards—In the context of control, **standards** are the planned or expected results of the operation and are expressed as a level of performance.

It is important to recognize that standards are not limited to expected levels of performance for individual employees. Depending on the resource to be controlled, standards might involve anything from revenue goals to sales and production targets and employee attendance and safety records. Consequently, the unit of measurement in which the standard is expressed changes from one situation to another. Most operations establish standards for each of the key services or products that they provide.

In general, establishing financial standards involves determining the expected amounts of revenue and the allowable costs of the resources used to generate that revenue. In commercial food and beverage operations, control procedures for the prime costs (food, beverage, and labor) are based on determining allowable amounts for the expenses to be incurred in generating the planned revenue. Standards often express the costs of resources in terms of a percentage of the revenue they generate. For example, if the standard (expected) food cost is set at 31 percent, this means, of all food revenue generated, 31 percent will be required to buy the food necessary to generate that revenue. (Food cost percentage is determined by dividing total food cost by total food revenue.) Exhibit 3 shows how a manager applies costing principles to determine the correct menu price.

In institutional food service operations, expenses are often stated as a percentage of the total expense. For example, a 35 percent food cost means that, of the total expense incurred by the food service operation, 35 percent is required to purchase food products.

Sources of Control Information. One reason that it is so difficult to establish effective standards against which to measure actual performance is that it is hard to find reliable information to use as the basis for setting the standards. There are several readily available sources of information, but each has its own disadvantages in serving as a basis for standards. Sources of information include:

- Averages developed by the industry nationally, statewide, and/or even locally.

- Property financial statements from past fiscal periods that reveal allowable expense and revenue information based on financial results for those previous periods.

Exhibit 3   Establishing Control Standards

Home	Glossary of Terms	Label Ingredients	Nutrition Report	Links

Chef Central Topics

Health & Safety • Food & Beverage • Human Resources • Administration • Quality Assurance •
Weights & Measurements • Tips NEW • Discussion NEW • Search the WEB.

Welcome to Chef Central

Chefcentral is your free hospitality resource provided by a fellow chef and restaurant manager, I hope you enjoy what you learn here and if you have any suggestions to improve the site, please do not hesitate to email me.

Cheers! Stephen.

🌑 Food & Beverage Topics

Costing • Inventory Control • Purchasing & Receiving

Costing

Costing is the most important part of running an efficient, cost effective operation; it's important to have food and beverage costs in line with menu–selling prices. The following formulas will help ensure this objective is achieved.

Add all food and beverage costs for the menu product; do not include non–food and beverage costs like napkins. Remember to include items used to prepare the product like salt, pepper, ketchup, and sugar used at the table; i.e., the oil in the fryer used for frying food. To do this, add all fried items sold in a period, add the cost of the oil used in the same period and divide by the number of items sold; this will give you a dollar amount to add to the cost of each item, probably two to three cents per item.

When all the costs have been totaled, divide the amount by the food and beverage cost percent you wish to achieve; this will give you the menu–selling price; i.e., a chicken finger dinner costs $2.45; divide by 32 percent, this will give you a $7.66 selling price for a food cost of 32 percent.

To ensure you are achieving the food and beverage cost percent at which you set the menu–selling prices, you must observe the following procedure and formula. Track all purchases in a period, track sales for the same period, track inventory for the same period. Add opening inventory for the period (last period's closing inventory), add all purchases of the same period and subtract the closing inventory; i.e., add opening inventory of $6,568.00 and purchases of $5,200.00; this equals $11,768.00; now subtract closing inventory of $5980.00, the costs are $5,788.00 for the period.

Divide cost by sales to find out what the cost percent is; i.e., cost for the period is $5,788.00; divide by sales for the same period of $17,980.00; this equals the cost of 32.19 percent. If by chance the costs are off, either too high or too low, check all the numbers. Start with the inventory; this is an area where lots of mistakes may occur due to human error. If all checks out, then check the opening inventory for accuracy, then check out the purchases. This is another area where mistakes may occur. Remember to include all credits for this period even if you do not receive them for a week or so.

The restaurant manager must regularly track costs, sales, and inventory to ensure that the property is operating at a profit. If food and beverage costs go up, the manager may need to increase the menu price. Adapted from Chef Stephen Johnson at Chef Central. This site can be found at http://www.ncf.carleton.ca.

- Property operating budgets specifying anticipated levels of revenue and expense for a current fiscal period.

- In-house measurements that consider potential costs matched with anticipated revenue.

The two best sources of information are operating budgets and in-house measurements. Basing standards on information obtained from these sources will provide numbers that are most directly relevant to the specific food and beverage operation. Using industry averages presumes, probably incorrectly, that one food and beverage operation is enough like another so that the numbers will mutually apply. In fact, average costs (in dollars and/or as a percentage of revenue) vary significantly between segments of the food service industry and even dramatically within the same segment and the same geographic area. For example, properties that use a significant amount of convenience foods (those that have some or all of the labor built into them which otherwise would need to be provided on site) tend to have higher food costs and lower labor costs. By contrast, properties that make a large amount of food "from scratch" will likely have lower food costs and higher labor costs. Using a property's past financial statements provides information that is relevant to the particular food and beverage operation, but it assumes the company is satisfied with past operations, and that they were managed effectively. If this is not the case, past financial statements are much less useful as a source for measurement information.

Effective Standards. To be effective, standards must accurately reflect results desired by the manager, based on the expectations of the target markets. Standards must also be high enough to offer a challenge and encourage excellence but not so high as to be unattainable and to result in frustration. Effective standards must also:

- Be specific and measurable. For example, "Food revenue will be $225,000, food costs will not exceed $75,000 for the first three months of operation, and the quality of food service will not drop below the following minimum requirements" is a much better statement of standards than "Food costs will be kept as low as possible while ensuring maximum food revenue and without sacrificing quality."

- Once attained, be adjusted slightly to encourage further creativity and challenge. For example, if a desired food cost of 31 percent of revenue is attained, a future food cost goal might be reduced to 30 percent with no reduction in quality. (Or, in times of rising food costs, the 31 percent cost goal might be continued.)

- Include feedback as part of the control system. Affected employees must know how they are doing. In addition, they will likely have practical suggestions about how control procedures can be made more effective.

Measure Actual Operating Results

After standards are established, management must develop procedures for collecting and assessing actual operating information. For example, if the standard food cost is set at 31 percent, how close to this goal is the actual food cost? At this point, some basic principles for assessing information about actual operating performance will be helpful.

Information about Actual Operating Performance Must Be Simple and Easy to Collect. Most managers are very busy and consider time-consuming activities to be impractical. Therefore, a system must be cost-effective; the information collected must be worth more than the cost to collect it. Very accurate data requiring a great deal of time to generate is not practical. The perceived practicality of a system correlates directly with the extent to which it is used.

Actual Information Must Be Collected in a Manner Consistent with the Procedures and Formats Used to Establish Performance Standards. For example, to include values of food and beverage transfers and/or salaried labor in standard costs and to exclude them in the calculation of actual costs does not permit meaningful comparisons. Actual information should be expressed in the same format as standard information. One would not, for example, determine standard costs as a percentage of revenue and actual costs as dollars per day or per meal.

Actual Information Generated for Control Purposes Should Be Compatible with the Formats Used in Accounting Systems. Since the source documents for control and accounting purposes are often the same, the problems of keeping two sets of figures can be avoided if control information is compatible with the accounting system. Exhibit 4 shows how computer software systems can help food and beverage managers collect and analyze control data.

Information Must Be Collected Consistently for Each Fiscal Period. This ensures that trending, indexing, and other measures can be used to identify problems. If this is not done, the meaning of comparisons between fiscal periods is difficult to interpret.

Checks on the Controls Should Be Part of the Control System Itself. Normally, those responsible for attaining a standard should not collect actual information. While collusion is still possible, one person working alone cannot "beat" the control system.

Compare Actual Results with Standards

After collecting actual operating information, the next step in the control process is to compare these actual operating results with the standards that have been established. This comparison measures how well actual performance meets standards expressing planned or desired results. In this way, food and beverage managers can determine the extent to which operational goals are being met. It is important that comparisons are made:

- Frequently, so that observed problems can be corrected as early as possible.
- Routinely; not just when problems are suspected.
- During different time frames, so, for example, standard and actual costs can be compared both daily and monthly.
- As soon as possible after actual costs are known.

Exhibit 3   Collecting and Assessing Operating Information

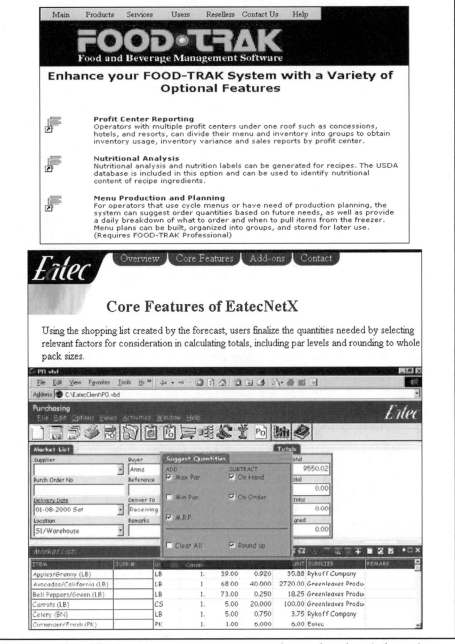

These examples of food and beverage management software show how information can be collected consistently and accurately. Many management software programs are designed so control information flows directly into the property's accounting system. These sites can be found at http://www.foodtrak.com and at http://www.eatec.com.

Comparisons should be analyzed by top management personnel in addition to other managers responsible for attaining cost goals.

Take Corrective Action

The comparison of actual results to standard (expected) results sometimes reveals a significant variance that requires corrective action. (A small variation may be permitted; for example, if standard food costs are set at 31 percent of food revenue, corrective action might not be required unless actual food costs exceed 32 percent of food revenue.) Food and beverage managers often consider corrective action equivalent to the entire control process. But it is important to recognize that control is more than just taking corrective action. If the variance between standard and actual costs is excessive, reasons for the higher cost must be discovered before corrective action can be determined. In some cases, the cause of the variance is obvious and can quickly be brought under control. For example, higher-than-expected food costs may mean that changes in inventory management, product purchasing, portion control, and/or other aspects of the operation are needed. (See Exhibit 5.)

However, some variances are not easily explained, and these call for special analysis. For example, while a greater-than-standard labor cost may be indicated in the comparison step, some basic causes such as decreasing productivity or fraud in reporting labor hours are often not readily detected. These situations can only be discovered by a thorough review of operating practices and procedures.

Once the cause of an unacceptable variance between standard and actual results is determined, corrective action must be taken. That action may lead to a change in operating procedures.

Evaluate Corrective Action

After corrective action has been taken, it is important to evaluate the effects of the changes. Careful evaluation is necessary to determine whether the corrective action has, in fact, resolved the problem(s) that caused an unacceptable variance between the standard and actual costs. Furthermore, it is necessary to determine whether any changes in operating procedures as a result of corrective action have themselves caused unforeseen problems in other areas.

Evaluation ensures that corrective procedures are acceptable, reveals whether additional decisions are needed, or indicates that more problems need to be resolved. Several principles guide the evaluation process:

1. The answer to the question, "How will we know whether the corrective action is successful?" helps define what the situation should be like after successful corrective action has been taken. (See Exhibit 6.)

2. Timing of the evaluation is important. Begin the evaluation as soon as practical after corrective actions are implemented. Often staff must first become familiar with changes, or new procedures must be revised slightly. This may delay the impact of the corrective actions on the original problem. An

Exhibit 5   Analyzing and Preventing Waste in a Prison Food Service

State of Delaware
Office of Auditor of Accounts
R. Thomas Wagner, Jr.

About R. Thomas Wagner, Jr.	What's New	About the Office ...	Audit Reports	Contact Us
Report Fraud 1/(800)55Fraud	State Financial Information	Press Releases	Internal Controls	Links

401 Federal Street - Suite One - Townsend Building - Dover, DE 19901   PHONE: (302) 739-4241   FACSIMILE: (302) 739-2723
OFFICE HOURS: 8:00 a.m. - 4:30 p.m. (EST) - Monday through Friday

EXECUTIVE SUMMARY
FOOD SERVICE OPERATIONS

Projection of Annual Waste

We reviewed the food service operations at the Department of Correction (DOC) to evaluate the controls in place to prevent the waste of food relative to inmate meals. Our tests disclosed that food items of approximately $1.1 million per year were wasted. The waste was identified in the following areas:

1. Overpreparation of Food
2. Ingredients Used
3. Overserving of Food
4. Overordering of Food
5. Paper/Plastic Product Usage

Overpreparation of Food

The audit disclosed one contributor of waste was that each facility is instructed to prepare meals for the total inmate population for every meal. The number of meals the facilities serve, which is a key factor in computing accurate costs per meal, was not kept by any facility. Based upon site visits to seven kitchens and observations of different meals being served (breakfasts, lunches, and dinners), we noted some significant variations in the percentage of inmates who attended meals. Percentage of attendance at meals ranged from 46 percent to 63 percent.

This report addresses the problem of overpreparation and recommends that production control records be maintained so that production might be more closely related to consumption.

Ingredients Used

The audit disclosed a major weakness in that many facilities utilized food items far in excess of what was called for on the portion cards. It appeared that a lack of internal controls existed whereby correctional officer/cooks and cook managers did not adhere to the portion cards as a tool for measure. Additionally, no one in management provided a proper monitoring of food orders of each facility that would have also detected this problem.

Overserving of Food

Quantity and/or serving size portions were not adhered to at the majority of facilities visited. Extremely large initial servings were observed by the audit team that far exceeded the DOC approved menu. Second servings were given at the facilities mainly due to overpreparation for the entire inmate population and vast quantities of uneaten food was returned on trays to be thrown away.

(continued)

Exhibit 5 *(continued)*

Overordering of Food

Once again, kitchen personnel did not adhere to the portion cards provided by the Food Services Director. Several instances were noted whereby one of the most expensive menu items (roast beef) was ordered in quantities that exceeded the required amount shown on the portion cards. A lack of internal control existed whereby no one in management reviewed facility orders periodically and compared them to quantities needed to prepare the menu item.

Paper/Plastic Usage

A close examination was given to the increased usage of paper/plastic products by the facilities. Historical records and costs were gathered on each facility, and based upon our analysis, paper/plastic usage has dramatically increased over the years.

Food Service Alternative

The DOC has an opportunity to save the taxpayers of the State $1.1 MILLION ANNUALLY by modifying their Department policies, strengthening internal controls, and operating the food service operations in a responsible and prudent manner. Management at every level should make a concerted effort to reduce the costs of meals. For each $.01 saved per inmate meal, approximately $45,000 of public resources can be saved. It is anticipated that DOC would need to initiate a cost reduction of approximately $.24 per meal to achieve the savings cited in this report.

Furthermore, should acceptable results not be achieved, the Commissioner should solicit Requests for Proposals for contract feeding at each facility.

FOOD SERVICE ALTERNATIVE

We evaluated the merits of privatizing the food service operation. To that end, we visited a correction facility where a contract vendor was responsible for providing meals. We found that the vendor was able to feed over 500 inmates a well-balanced meal without affecting the internal security. The company purchases all food products and ensures delivery without requiring warehousing facilities. The vendor provided a 3,200 calorie menu prepared by their dietitian. Through adequate training, appropriate menu portions were served.

The food service company was able to project needs and reduce the amount of food prepared by maintaining a "production control log" which indicates the amount of food necessary to feed the inmates. As a result, the company drastically reduced overpreparation and waste of food items. A benefit to the facility which was not anticipated, was the reduction of trash disposal costs of approximately $12,000 annually.

We found that facility personnel were relieved of the administrative functions of ordering, receiving, storing, inventorying, and delivering food items. Therefore, the correctional officers were able to devote more of their time supervising inmates who prepared and served the food. This permitted correctional officers additional time to perform other security-related duties.

Through nationwide volume purchasing, the company was able to purchase food items at a much lower cost than the facility previously expended.

Other savings realized by this facility were the salary and other benefit costs of one employee whose position was eliminated. In areas of warehousing/delivery, salaries, volume purchases, and trash removal, the facility reduced its expenditures under the alternative food service operation by over $437,000 in one year.

A detailed study showed the State of Delaware Department of Correction that food was being overordered and overserved. After analyzing the data, the department concluded it would be more economical to contract the prison food service to a private company. This site can be found at http://www.state.de.us/auditor/foods.htm.

Exhibit 6   How Will We Know Whether the Corrective Action is Successful?

American Society for Healthcare
Food Service Administrators

About ASHFSA

Members Only

Membership

Products & Services

Events

Chapters

Jobs

Links

ASHFSA Home

What Does A 10 Patient Tray Look Like? How To enhance Your Cafeteria?
by
Don Miller, R.D., C.E.C. - Success Coach
Nancy Yezzi, R.D., L.D. - Success Coach

Patient Tray - **PORK ENTREE, ETC**
Hospital Year 2000
Score = 1
(Click for a larger view)

Critique of Tray

This critique is based on the fact that this is a hospital tray in a setting where most of the customers are seniors who frequently complain that they get too much food. The recommendations are based on my experience, and "trial and error" while working in hundreds of different hospitals over a 30 year period. If you find yourself thinking that you just can't make

- Overall the tray is messy and disorganized due to a lack of specific standards for the location of all the products on it. It looks like everything was just thrown on the tray.
- It is better to have the silverware, napkin and diet kit on the right since most folks are right handed.
- A roll on a small bread and butter plate with a doily is more elegant than the prewrapped bread concept.
- In a salad, iceberg lettuce alone is anemic looking. The mix should have 25 or 30% dark green lettuce such as Romaine or green leaf. It also needs a very small amount of shredded carrots and purple cabbage. And, there is too much lettuce in the bowl. Most hospital patients prefer small servings.
- Angel food cake or pound cake by itself on a paper plate is just about as low as you can go on the "class", and "quality" scale. Since people eat with their eyes first, these bland, boring desserts either have to be enhanced or eliminated. In general, use paper only when your dish machine is broken down, your food service team didn't show up for work, your facility is near bankruptcy, or you're in the middle of some sort of major crisis. Paper may work on insulated trays because it's nearly impossible to make insulated trays look great. The paper doesn't stand out as much with insulated trays.
- All condiments need to be in a 3 to 4 oz. clear, disposable plastic, low profile cup, or in the re-usable plastic fluted cup. The practice of simply tossing the condiments on the tray is "tacky" and sends the wrong message. You can afford the plastic cup because you'll save $20,000 to $50,000 per year (due to forced portion control) if you use a very small "monkey"/fruit dishes for all of your side dishes such as canned fruit.
- Look at the hot plate. They have served 100% too many wax beans. This is not uncommon. What's more, wax beans (because they are anemic looking) should be avoided on patient menus. Using wax beans is like shooting yourself in the foot.
- Notice that there's no gravy. This is not as uncommon as you think. We believe a gravy, glaze or sauce is necessary on almost all meats to make them more palatable. Not instant gravy either, but gravy made from natural defatted drippings, quality meat base, and a thickener of your choice. The mashed potatoes should be indented and have gravy on them. The meat should be located at 6 o'clock not 3 o'clock.

(continued)

Exhibit 6   *(continued)*

- This hot plate needs a garnish. Also, an ideally written menu would offer scalloped apples (Stouffers for example) with the pork as an extra touch of excellence. It's like cranberry sauce and turkey- they go together naturally. Perhaps the hot plate wouldn't need a garnish if a beautiful, upscale vegetable blend was offered. We recommend lots of the new attractive vegetable blends on patient menus.
- We have more constructive comments but space is limited, so now look at the next photo of a more attractive patient tray that we would score at the 10 level.

 Nice Looking patient tray - SALISBURY STEAK (after D/10 "makeover")
Year 2001
Score = 10
(Click for a larger view)

The Key Positive Points

- Everything is divided up so that the tray looks organized, balanced, attractive and inviting.
- All the side dishes are very small. This is good. There's no room for 6" bread and butter plates on this small tray.
- The condiments are all placed in a clear container. Now the customer can find them.
- The dessert is simple and garnished.
- The fresh fruit has a green leaf liner. It's "showbiz".
- The coffee mug is in the perfect location
- The roll has a doily under it. Good, but if you can find a 4", or very small bread and butter plate, it would look even better. But the plate has to be small. Minimize or delete pies on small trays because they require a bread and butter plate which normally takes a lot of tray space.
- The soup is in the correct location. You'll be surprised to know that this is a 4 oz. insulated bowl as opposed to the larger version. Do we get away with the smaller portion? Yes! It isn't even noticed in average hospitals who serve primarily seniors. Seniors don't want a lot of food. In fact, they complain that we give them too much food.
- The flatware is on the right. Good!
- Bottom line - this tray scores a 10 on a scale of 1 to 10. Way to go Donna Young, R.D. and team at Mercy Medical Center, Sioux City Iowa.

The mission of the American Society for Healthcare Food Service Administrators is to enhance and advance the practice of healthcare food service management in a broad range of healthcare settings. This critique of hospital food trays includes a step-by-step plan for corrective action. To view additional critiques and food service references, see http://www.ashfsa.org.

evaluation performed too soon may not accurately measure the results of the actions which were taken for problem resolution.

3. The evaluation should be objective and rational. Has the problem been resolved, and is it more likely that organizational goals will be attained? While these may seem obvious questions to consider, evaluations often focus incorrectly upon such concerns as: "What is the easiest? Which way makes my

department look the best? Which way will meet with the least resistance from employees? Which method will my boss like the best? Which is the cheapest and fastest?"

4. If the evaluation identifies other problems or indicates that corrective action has not been successful, reconsider the corrective action. The cycle of control procedures may need to be repeated. New corrective action(s) may be required, or standards may need to be revised. However, great care should be taken before management decides to revise the standard. It is all too easy to rationalize the inability to achieve a standard by saying that the standard is too high. Consequently, revisions of standards should only be considered after a complete examination of operating procedures.

Considerations in Designing Control Systems

In this discussion of the steps in the control process for a food and beverage operation, it is obvious that management's role in control is critical. To ensure that management's time spent in the control function is productive, there are several factors that should be considered in the design of a control system.

Accuracy. While the control system must provide a reasonably accurate assessment of the extent to which goals are being attained, accuracy must be balanced against the time spent developing control systems. For example, it would be impractical for most small and medium-sized operations to determine and monitor the expected cost per meal for meats and poultry. It is extremely important to recall that all procedures must be cost-effective in terms of the labor involved; it must be worth the time necessary to carry out the control procedure.

Timeliness. To be useful, control systems must provide evidence of performance as soon as possible after business activities occur. Many food and beverage operations design control procedures to provide information on a daily basis about actual food and/or beverage costs. Other systems use "to-date" data that accumulates information as a fiscal period progresses. Most food and beverage operations provide reports, such as a monthly financial statement giving actual operatingresults, at the conclusion of a fiscal period. Many properties now use computer-based systems to provide complete daily financial reports.

Objectivity. To be objective, measurements of the level of performance must accurately reflect the desired results that control procedures are designed to monitor. For example, if profit is incorrectly defined as a desired percentage of revenue rather than as a required return on investment, control procedures may indicate satisfactory performance during a time of declining revenue when bottom-line profits are actually lower. Objectivity requires designing the best control system, not necessarily the one that is the easiest to implement. Objectivity is more likely to be achieved when control systems are designed by a team of managers with help from all affected staff; systems designed by a single manager or a few staff members are more likely to be shortsighted.

Consistency. When actual results are measured, management must assess the operation's level of performance in a manner consistent with the definition of the standard. A number of elements may or may not be included when determining a particular standard. When a control system is designed, it is important to decide whether those elements will be included or excluded in the definition of that standard. For example, a manager may decide to include (or exclude) food in work station storage areas when calculating the value of food inventory.

Priority. The control system must give priority to those factors that are most relevant to attaining the operation's goals. For example, control systems for food costs or revenue should be developed before those for supplies expense.

Cost. A well-designed control system is cost-effective. This can be measured by comparing the cost of implementing the control system with the cost reductions achieved by using the system. A system costing $5,000 annually that reduces costs by $2,000 annually probably indicates management did not wisely design its control procedures.

Realism. A realistic control system is first of all a practical system. This involves all the considerations that we have been discussing, such as cost-effectiveness and accuracy. Another realistic consideration has to do with the chain of command. A junior staff member cannot be responsible for controlling operations managed by a senior department head. Also, control systems need a reward/motivation system that acknowledges high levels of performance when identified.

Appropriateness. The control system must fit into the work flow. If following control procedures decreases productivity, reduces guest acceptance, or in other ways hinders the operation, then that system is inappropriate and new control procedures must be designed.

Flexibility. The food and beverage business is always changing and organizational goals are continually evolving. For instance, new ways of doing things will affect what and how control procedures are used. The control system must be flexible enough to adapt to these changes.

Specificity. The main purpose of a control system is to help identify what corrective action is necessary to bring actual results closer to standards set by management. Well-designed control systems provide specific information. For example, there is a big difference between a labor control system that merely indicates "labor costs are too high" and one that says "in the lunch shift, dishwashing labor is 15 percent over budget."

Acceptability. Staff members must understand and accept the control system. They must be trained and updated in the use of control procedures. Where possible, all affected staff members should participate in designing the system. This greatly facilitates acceptance and use of the system. In any event, all procedures should be fully explained and justified in writing. This not only helps the staff understand and appreciate the rationale behind the procedures, but it also is useful when the control procedures are evaluated. It is important for staff members to view the procedures as beneficial to both themselves and the food and beverage operation.

Responsibilities for Control

The food and beverage manager who has ultimate responsibility for the department or operation should provide a great deal of input in the design of data collection systems and in the interpretation of actual operating results. The manager should make control decisions based on information supplied by other managers, departments, and food and beverage personnel.

In many food and beverage operations, the accounting department is responsible for determining how costs should be assessed. This involves determining what elements should be included in calculating costs. For example, someone must determine whether food and beverage transfers and/or salaried labor are to be included in the calculation of costs. In most operations, the accounting department determines the recordkeeping forms used to assemble financial information for income statements, balance sheets, and other financial reports.

In addition, after actual income and cost levels are assessed and reported on income statements, the controller may provide observations about the "meaning of the numbers." For example, if actual food costs are higher than those estimated in the operating budget, the controller will point this out and may make suggestions about why cost variances are excessive and, even, what strategies might be helpful in reducing the problem.

The food and beverage manager should consider the information from the controller to be advice—not a dictate about what must be done. Rather, the food and beverage manager, experienced in all areas of food and beverage management, should consider input from other sources (such as his or her own staff and, of course, higher management levels), and additional facts, to make a decision about whether and what corrective action is necessary. An example may help illustrate this. Based upon the small amount of revenue generated after 9:00 P.M. in a hotel restaurant, the controller may determine that the operation should close at this time: costs to remain open exceed revenue that is generated. However, the food and beverage manager, who is a key member of the property's management team, may recognize the restaurant's need to stay open to serve guests arriving from late airline flights into the community. In fact, these guests may choose the hotel because of available dining service; revenue from room rentals must be considered when making the decision. The food and beverage manager with knowledge of the "big picture" (what's best for the entire property) would likely choose to keep the restaurant operation open—even if the restaurant-related costs for doing so exceed the revenue the restaurant generates.

Large hospitality operations frequently have a **food and beverage controller** employed by the accounting department. The responsibilities of this person may include developing food and beverage standard costs, assisting in budget development, analyzing income statements, directly supervising receiving and/or storeroom personnel, and participating in end-of-period inventory valuations. The food and beverage controller may also be responsible for supervising cashiers in restaurants and lounges. This person often becomes the accounting representative with whom the food and beverage manager has the most contact. However, the role of the food and beverage controller should still be one of providing assistance andadvice—not making operational decisions for the food and beverage department.

It is often noted that the management of a food and beverage operation is complex. This is true. A great deal of teamwork involving personnel in a number of different departments is required. The food and beverage manager should be the leader of the hospitality team that helps meet financial and other organizational goals for the food and beverage operation.

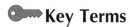

Key Terms

control—A series of coordinated activities that helps managers ensure that the actual results of operations closely match the planned results.

controlling—The management function of developing standards and collecting information to compare actual performance with expectations so that corrective action(s) can be taken if necessary.

convenience foods—Products which have some or all of the labor built into them which, otherwise, would need to be added on-site.

corrective action—The selection, design, and implementation of new or revised procedures or policies to reduce the level of variance between standards and actual operating results.

cost—An expense; a reduction of an asset, generally for the purpose of increasing revenues.

food and beverage controller—The staff member in the accounting department who develops food and beverage standard costs, assists in budget development, analyzes income statements, directly supervises receiving and/or storeroom personnel, and participates in end-of-period inventory valuations.

objectives—Statements that indicate why a business exists and what it is trying to do.

profit—The difference between revenue and expense when there is more revenue than expense.

prime costs—Those costs—product (food and beverage) and labor—which comprise the most significant costs in a food and beverage operation.

standards—Planned or expected results of the operation expressed as a level of performance.

Review Questions

1. What resources are necessary to successfully operate a food and beverage operation?

2. Why is it important to have objectives?

3. Define control. Why is it important? What does control mean to many food and beverage managers? What control elements are missing in the traditional definition?

4. How can an effective control system reduce daily operating problems?

5. What are the four sources of standard control information? Which are the easiest to use? The best to use?

6. Why would a variance be permitted between standard plans and actual operating results?

7. What factors should be considered when implementing a control system?

8. What are some of the duties typically assigned to a food and beverage controller?

9 Why must managers be careful when deciding to revise a standard?

 **Internet Sites** ——————————————————————————————————

For more information, visit the following Internet sites. Remember that Internet addresses can change without notice. If the site is no longer there, you can use a search engine to look for additional sites.

Associations

American Culinary Federation (ACF)
http://www.acfchefs.org

American Hotel & Lodging Association (AH&LA)
http://www.ahlaonline.org

American School Food Service Association (ASFSA)
http://www.asfsa.org

Club Managers Association of America (CMAA)
http://www.cmaa.org

The Educational Foundation of NRA
http://www.edfound.org

The Educational Institute of AH&LA
http://www.ei-ahla.org

Hospitality Financial and Technology Professionals
http://www.hftp.org

Institute of Food Technologies
http://www.ift.org

International Hotel and Restaurant Association
http://www.ih-ra.com

National Association of College and University Food Services
http://www.nacufs.org

National Restaurant Association (NRA)
http://www.restaurant.org

Food and Beverage Resources

Club Management Online
http://www.club-mgmt.com/dining/index.html

Microbrewery and brewpub guide
http://www.realbeer.com

Prepared Foods. Product development, ingredients, suppliers
http://www.preparedfoods.com

Management Companies

ARAMARK
http://www.aramark.com

Bon Appétit Management Company
http://www.bamco.com

Compass Group
http://www.compass-na.com

Sodexho Marriott
http://www.sodexhomarriott.com

Publications—Online and Printed

Club Management Magazine
http://www.club-mgmt.com

Electronic Gourmet Guide
http://www.foodwine.com

Food and Hospitality Magazine
http://www.foodserviceworld.com

Food Management
http://www.foodservicesearch.com

Food Network: CyberKitchen
http://www.foodtv.com

Food Processing: The Magazine of
Strategy, Technology and Trends
http://www.foodprocessing.com

Food Service
http://www.foodservicetoday.com

ID
http://www.foodservicetoday.com

Internet Food Channel
http://www.foodchannel.com

International Hotel and Restaurant
Association journal
www.hotelsmag.com

International Journal of Hospitality
Management
http://www.mcb.co.uk/ijchm.htm

Lodging Food and Beverage
http://www.lodgingnews.com/
lodgingfnb/

Lodging Hospitality Online
http://www.lhonline.com

Lodging News, journal of the American
Hotel & Lodging Association
http://www.ei-ahla.org/webs/
lodging/index.html

Nation's Restaurant News
http://www.nrn.com

On the Rail—News for Food
Professionals
http://www.ontherail.com

Restaurant Business, Food Service, and
ID magazines
http://www.foodservicetoday.com

Restaurant Hospitality
www.foodservicesearch.com

Restaurants and Institutions
http://www.rimag.com

Restaurants USA, publication of
National Restaurant Association
http://www.restaurant.org/rusa

World Hospitality, management
magazine for hotel executives
http://www.worldhospitality.com

Part II

Planning for Food and Beverage Control

Chapter 3 Outline

Competencies

1. Explain how managers use standard purchase specifications as cost control tools. (pp. 53–54)

2. Explain how managers use standard recipes and portion control techniques as cost control tools. (pp. 54–59)

3. Determine standard yields for food products. (pp. 59–60)

4. Calculate the cost per servable pound of a food product. (pp. 60–62)

5. Use an adjustment factor to increase or decrease the yield from a standard recipe. (pp. 62–63)

6. Calculate standard portion costs and standard dinner costs for food items on the basis of standard recipes and standard portion sizes. (pp. 63–70)

7. Identify the functions of files typically maintained by recipe management software applications. (pp. 71–75)

8. Explain how managers use standard food and beverage costs and ideal food and beverage costs to evaluate actual results of operations. (pp. 75–83)

3

Determining Food and Beverage Standards

Dᴇᴠᴇʟᴏᴘɪɴɢ sᴛᴀɴᴅᴀʀᴅs (levels of expected performance) is part of the process of controlling food and beverage costs. Standards specific to the property's current plans will better indicate problems (variances from planned costs) than will standards adopted from industry averages or standards developed from the property's past operating statistics.

The usefulness of control information can be increased by establishing standards for each revenue center within the food and beverage operation. For example, instead of computing a standard food cost covering all outlets, a property might establish separate standard cost levels for its coffee shop, dining room, room service, and banquet operations. An advantage of this alternative is that each outlet can be evaluated separately based on its own set of anticipated costs.

However, food and beverage managers realize that as a standard becomes more specific, more time is required to develop and monitor it. The longer the time needed to collect information on which to base the standard, or later to measure actual results, the less practical managers may judge the task; and as a result, the less likely they may be to undertake the control activity. In addition, the more complex the development of standard costs becomes, the more likely the task will be met with resistance by those who must collect the information.

Therefore, an ideal control system must strike a balance between the time and effort spent developing the control system and the usefulness of the results the system provides. Simplified, time- and cost-effective systems for determining food and beverage standards are offered in this chapter. The principles for establishing standards are the same regardless of whether the property is commercial or institutional, large or small, fast food or gourmet, hotel or restaurant. Managers in any kind of operation who want to develop in-house food and beverage standards can use the procedures discussed in this chapter.

Systems for developing food and beverage standards must begin with the menu. The menu should be designed to implement the property's marketing plan as it relates to the food and beverage operation. Because it establishes which food and beverage items will be served, the menu is the most basic and important control tool. Once a menu is created, five standard cost tools can be developed:

- Standard purchase specifications
- Standard recipes
- Standard yields

- Standard portion sizes
- Standard portion costs

Standard Purchase Specifications

A **purchase specification** is a concise description of the quality, size, weight, count, and other factors needed to describe a desired item. The specified factors should be described in sufficient detail to properly guide the company's suppliers and receiving personnel in the delivery and receipt of the desired products.

Management should establish standard purchase specifications based on menu requirements and the operation's merchandising and pricing policies. Once developed, standard purchase specifications should be given to those responsible for purchasing, the property's suppliers, and receiving personnel. In this way, all of the parties involved in ordering, supplying, and receiving will have the necessary written guides to permit the operation to consistently obtain the quality and kind of food and beverage items desired.

In addition to providing a knowledge of what is required by the operation, standard purchase specifications offer several other advantages:

- Fewer products may be required. Analyzing the menu may suggest ways to duplicate product use (use an ingredient for several menu items) so that fewer ingredients have to be purchased.
- Reduced purchase costs are possible if proper quality items are purchased. Developing purchase specifications based on the needs of the menu means that the property will not have to pay a higher price for a product of greater quality than necessary.
- If purchase specifications are properly established, more than one supplier will likely be able to quote prices and compete for the operation's business.

The development of specifications involves time and effort. Time is needed to create the specifications and then to monitor the need for changes as the operation's business evolves. Furthermore, their use will create increased duties for the receiving staff. Finally, since specifications establish the minimum quality expected, over time they may become the maximum quality that will be purchased.

However, considering the many advantages to the use of purchase specifications relative to the few disadvantages, it should be clear they are a critical standard cost control tool. It is only through carefully developed and rigidly enforced specifications that the operation can help assure that the "right" quality product is consistently available for production and service. Remember, however; use of standard purchase specifications will not, alone, guarantee that products of the correct quality will be received unless effective receiving control procedures are in use.

Standard Recipes

A **standard recipe** is a formula for producing a food or beverage item. It provides a summary of ingredients, the required quantity of each, specific preparation

Exhibit 1 Sample Standard Food Recipe

Fish Fillet Amandine

IX. MAIN DISHES—FISH 2
Baking Temperature: 450°F
Baking Time: 14–15 min

Yield: _____

Size: _____

Yield: 60

Size: 6 oz

Amount	Ingredients	Amount	Procedure
_____	Fish fillets, fresh or frozen 6 oz portion	22¹/₂ lb	1. Defrost fillets if frozen fish is used. 2. Arrange defrosted or fresh fillets in single layers on greased sheet pans.

_____	Almonds, toasted, chopped or slivered	1 lb	3. To toast almonds:
			  a. Spread on sheet pans.
			  b. Place in 350°F oven until lightly toasted.
			    Approximate time: 15 min.

_____	Margarine or butter, softened	2 lb 8 oz	4. Add almonds, lemon juice, lemon peel, salt, and pepper to softened margarine or butter.
_____ _____ _____	Lemon juice Lemon peel, grated Salt	¹/₂ cup 2³/₄ oz 4 tbsp	5. Mix thoroughly. 6. Spread margarine mixture on fillets as uniformly as possible. *Amount per fillet:* #60 scoop
_____	Pepper, white Weight: margarine-almond mixture	1 tbsp 4 lb	7. Bake at 450°F for approx. 15 min or until fish flakes when tested with fork. 8. Sprinkle lightly with chopped parsley or sprigs of parsley when served.

Source: Adapted from G. Boyd, M. McKinley, and J. Dana, *Standardized Quantity Recipe File for Quality and Cost Control* (Ames, Iowa: Iowa State University Press, 1971).

procedures, portion size and portioning equipment, garnish, and any other information necessary to prepare the item. The advantages of standard recipes are equally relevant in both food and beverage preparation. The primary advantage of following a standard recipe is that, regardless of prepares the item, *when* it is prepared, or to *whom* it is served, the product will always look, cost, and taste the same. The consistency in operations provided by the standard recipe is at the heart of all control, and many marketing, systems.

Exhibit 1 presents a sample standard food recipe. Note that this recipe yields 60 portions, each with a standard portion size of 6 ounces. The "Amount" column on the left margin can be used to adjust the yield to a larger or smaller quantity. To aid in portioning, the recipe's "Procedure" column specifies that a #60 scoop (which equals 60 level scoops, or servings, per quart) should be used. Note also that the recipe clearly indicates baking time, temperature, and the exact procedures for preparing the menu item.

There are several other reasons to use standard recipes in addition to the advantages of consistency in appearance, cost, and taste:

- When managers know that the standard recipe will yield a specific number of standard-size portions, it is less likely that too many or too few items will be prepared.

- Since standard recipes indicate needed equipment and required production times, managers can more effectively schedule food production employees and necessary equipment.

- Less supervision is required since standard recipes tell the employees the-quantity and preparation method for each item. Guesswork is eliminated; employees need only follow recipe procedures. Of course, managers should routinely evaluate the quality of items produced and ensure that standard recipes are followed correctly.

- If the chef is ill or the bartender doesn't show up, a product can be produced if a standard recipe is available. Granted, inexperienced employees will be slow and may make mistakes. However, if the recipe is in the head of an absent employee instead of on a standard recipe card or available for printout, management will be in an even more awkward position.

Many persons think about the importance of standard recipes for food production; as suggested above, however, they're also critical to control the consistency (quality and cost) of beverages. Today in the U.S. it is critical that standard recipes specifying ingredient and portion sizes of alcoholic beverages be available in consistent use. Liquor liability concerns often arise when standard recipes are not available and/or when standard portion controls are not in use. It is always necessary to be able to verify the actual quantity of alcohol (not just number of drinks!) that has been consumed by a guest.

Using a standard recipe does not require that the recipe be physically in the work area during production times. After a cook prepares a menu item several times, or a bartender mixes a drink several times, he or she will remember ingredients, quantities, and procedures. It would obviously be impractical if, before preparing a drink, a busy bartender had to refer to a standard recipe. *A standard recipe must always be followed and must always be available, but it does not always need to be read.*

Developing Standard Recipes

Developing standard recipes does not require throwing out existing recipes and starting over. Rather, it often requires standardizing existing recipes according to a series of steps.

Select a time period for standard recipe development. For example, you may choose to standardize three recipes at each weekly cooks' meeting, or spend one hour each week with the head bartender to develop standard beverage recipes. At these meetings, ask the cook or head bartender to talk through the preparation of the item. What are the ingredients and how much of each ingredient is needed? What are the exact procedures? What are cooking/baking temperatures and times? What portion-control tools are, or can be, used? On what plate or in what glassware is the item served? What garnish is used? Double-check the recipe by closely observing the cook or bartender as the item is actually prepared. See Exhibit 2 for an example of a standardized recipe that clearly describes each procedure.

Record the recipes in a standard format that will be helpful to those preparing the items. For example:

- Decide on the desirable yield. If 25 portions of a food item are normally prepared for slow periods and 60 portions are needed for busy times, recipes should be designed to yield these servings.

- List all ingredients in the order they are used.

- Decide whether to use weights or measures or both. Weighing is always more precise than measuring, and it is just as practical to weigh liquids, flour, etc., as it is to measure them. Avoid confusion by using consistent abbreviations throughout all the standard recipes you are developing.

- Whenever possible, express all quantities in amounts that are practical for those preparing the item. For example, convert all measures into the largest possible units. Change $^4/8$ cup to $^1/2$ cup, four cups to one quart, or three teaspoons to one tablespoon. At this point you need to be sure that the proper equipment is available. It does little good to specify a three-ounce quantity when an accurate measuring scale is not available. Also, when applicable, recipes should be developed that call for standard-size pans and other equipment.

- Record procedures in detailed, concise, and exact terms. Avoid ambiguous statements. For example, what does "one cup whipping cream" mean? Does it mean one cup of cream that has been whipped or does it mean one cup of cream that must be whipped? When mixing is called for, tell how to mix (by hand or by machine) and provide the exact time and speed if a machine is used. State the size and type of equipment and small wares such as pans or bowls needed and always list exact temperatures, cooking times, and other necessary controls.

- Carefully consider potential sanitation problems which can arise in each step of recipe production; note these and incorporate food handling precautions directly into the recipe. For example, if the operation uses a hollandaise sauce (this sauce is potentially hazardous and is highly susceptible to contamination by microorganisms), a last step in the recipe for hollandaise sauce might state: "Hollandaise sauce is a potentially dangerous food which can become contaminated by microorganisms; always prepare in small batches and do not hold on the serving line for more than one hour."

- Provide directions for portioning. Indicate the type and size of the serving dish. Also, indicate portioning equipment, such as ladle or scoop, and specify the expected number and size of portions. Be sure all required portioning equipment is available for use. If garnishes or sauces are needed, these should be listed.

After the standard recipes have been recorded, share them with other production staff. Solicit their ideas about accuracy and possible refinements. Finally, test

Exhibit 2 A Standard Recipe Uses Detailed, Concise, and Exact Terms

GreatChefs®

MONDAY THROUGH
THURSDAY AT 4 AND
4:30 P.M. ET/PT

MAIN
CHEF PROFILES
RECIPES
COOKING BASICS
WE'VE GOT NEWS!
FAQs
CONTACT US
TALK ABOUT IT
DISCOVERY DAYTIME
DISCOVERY CHANNEL

Find out what the Great Chefs
are preparing, and get their
recipes here!

Get to know the Great Chefs!
Read their profiles.

Register through "My Discovery"
to receive the Great Chefs
monthly newsletter.

Recipes

Lemon Ice Box Pie
Restaurant: Leonard's Barbecue
Memphis, Tenn.

Makes one 9-inch pie

Crust
1¼ cups graham cracker crumbs
1/4 cup sugar
1/3 cup butter, melted

Filling
3 egg yolks
one 14-ounce can sweetened condensed milk
1/2 cup lemon juice

1 cup heavy (whipping) cream, beaten to soft peaks

To make the crust: In a 9-inch pie pan, toss the graham cracker crumbs with
the sugar and melted butter. Press the mixture onto the bottom and sides of
the pan, then refrigerate 30 minutes before filling.

To make the filling: Beat the egg yolks about 10 minutes, until they turn
pale yellow and are thick enough to form a ribbon. Do not underbeat. Add the
condensed milk and beat at slow speed just until smooth. Incorporate the
lemon juice at low speed. The mixture will thicken almost immediately. Beat
briefly, then pour the filling into the chilled crust. Refrigerate the pie overnight.

To serve: Cut into individual slices. Top slices with whipped cream.

The Discovery Channel Great Chefs website offers hundreds of recipes developed by
chefs around the world. http://dsc.discovery.com

the recipes to be certain that they yield products of the desired quantity and quality. After successful testing, the recipe may be considered standardized.

Despite the advantages of using standard recipes, there may be some difficulties encountered in implementing them. Cooks or bartenders, for example, may feel that they can no longer be creative in the kitchen or behind the bar. They may resent the need to put things down on paper. Other difficulties may be related to concerns about time. It takes time to standardize existing recipes, and it takes time to train production employees to precisely follow them.

These concerns, however, are minor when compared to the points already noted in favor of using standard recipes. In addition, managers can minimize difficulties with implementing standard recipes by explaining to employees why standard recipes are necessary and by involving them in developing and implementing the recipes.

Standard Yields

The term **yield** means the net weight or volume of a food item after it has been processed and made ready for sale to the guest. The difference between the raw or "as purchased" (AP) weight and the prepared or "edible portion" (EP) weight is termed a **production loss**.

In general, there are three steps in the production process. The first step is preparation, which includes such activities as meat trimming and vegetable cleaning. The second step is cooking. Holding, the third step, includes the portioning of those products that have not been preportioned. A "loss" can occur in any of these steps.

A **standard yield** results when an item is produced according to established standard production procedures outlined in the standard recipe. They serve as a base against which to compare actual yields. For example, if the standard purchase specifications are adhered to and a meat item is properly trimmed, cooked, and portioned, the actual yield should closely approximate the standard yield.

Determining Standard Yield

Standard yields are determined by conducting a yield test. Ideally, everything that does not have a 100 percent yield should be tested. (Examples of items with 100 percent yield [100 percent edible portion] are some portion-controlled products such as meats and those convenience foods that only need to be plated.) However, from a practical standpoint, yield tests are typically performed only on high-cost items or on lower-cost products used in large quantities.

The yield from a product depends upon several factors, including the grade, original weight, and preparation and cooking methods. Therefore, it is helpful for a food and beverage purchaser to compare the yields for similar products from different suppliers. It may be possible to substitute a raw product with a lower cost per unit that provides a yield similar to that of a higher cost product, without compromising the operation's quality standards.

An example of the results of a yield test (sometimes called a butcher test when done for meat) is shown in Exhibit 3. In this example, eight oven-prepared beef

Exhibit 3   Summary of Yield Test Results

#109

Item: *Oven Prepared Beef Rib*   Grade: *USDA Choice*
Pieces: *8*   Total Weight: *162 lb*   Average Weight: *20 lb, 4 oz*
Average Item Cost: *$120.49 at $5.95/lb*
Supplier: *Various*

Summary of Yield Test Results

Cooking and Portioning Details	Weight	% of Original Weight	Cost Per Servable Lb	Cost Factor
Edible Portion (EP) Weight	11 lb 3 oz	55.25%	$10.77	1.81
Loss due to fat trim & bones	5 lb 3 oz	25.62		
Loss due to cooking	3 lb 14 oz	19.13		
As Purchased (AP) Weight	20 lb 4 oz	100.00%		

Other Data:
   Cooked at 300°F for 4 hrs, 45 min

ribs, averaging 20 pounds, 4 ounces each, were cooked, trimmed, and the bones removed according to a property's standard recipe and standard preparation and cooking procedures. (Note that eight ribs were used in this example to provide a more accurate base for the yield calculations.) By weighing the meat at each step, the loss due to cooking and trimming can be assessed.

Since the AP weight is already known, the meat must next be weighed when it is removed from the oven after cooking. By subtracting the cooked weight from the original weight, you can determine the loss in cooking—in this example, an average of 3 pounds, 14 ounces per beef rib. Next the fat cap and bones must be removed, and the remaining meat weighed. This is the edible portion or servable weight—in this example, an average of 11 pounds, 3 ounces per beef rib. Subtracting the edible portion (servable) weight from the cooked weight indicates that the loss in carving and bones averaged 5 pounds, 3 ounces.

Cost per Servable Pound

Once the edible portion (servable) weight is determined, a **cost per servable pound** can be determined. To find the cost per servable pound, first establish the yield percentage. The **yield percentage** (sometimes called **yield factor**) is the ratio of servable weight to original weight and is calculated by dividing the servable weight by the original weight (normally both weights are expressed in ounces; there are 16 ounces in one pound), and multiplying by 100 to change the decimal to a percentage. For example:

$$\frac{\text{Servable Weight}}{\text{Original Weight}} \times 100 = \text{Ratio of Servable Weight to Original Weight}$$

$$\frac{11 \text{ lb} \times 16 \text{ oz per lb} + 3 \text{ oz}}{20 \text{ lb} \times 16 \text{ oz per lb} + 4 \text{ oz}} = \frac{179 \text{ oz}}{324 \text{ oz}} \times 100 = 55.25\% \text{ (rounded)}$$

This means that 55.25 percent of the purchase weight of the beef ribs can be served to guests.

The cost per servable pound is found by dividing the AP price by the yield percentage. For example:

$$\frac{\text{AP Price}}{\text{Yield Percentage}} = \text{Cost per Servable Pound}$$

$$\frac{\$5.95}{.5525} = \$10.77 \text{ (rounded)}$$

The cost per servable pound is the information needed to calculate standard portion costs, discussed later in this chapter.

One can make a similar calculation to determine the total AP quantity needed once the yield percentage is known. Assume that 50 8-ounce edible portions of beef ribs in the above example are required for a banquet and that there is a 55.25 percent yield. What quantity of beef ribs will be needed to yield the 25 pounds (50 portions at 8 ounces per portion) that are requested?

$$\frac{\text{Quantity Needed} \times \text{Edible Portion}}{\text{Yield Percentage}} = \text{Quantity to Purchase/Prepare}$$

$$\frac{400 \text{ oz } (50 \text{ portions} \times 8 \text{ oz/portion})}{.5525} = \frac{724 \text{ oz (rounded)}}{16 \text{ oz per pound}} = 45.25 \text{ pounds}$$

The cook will have to prepare approximately 45.25 pounds (724 ounces divided by 16 ounces per pound) to yield the 25 pounds that are needed.

The Cost Factor

The **cost factor** is a constant value that may be used to convert new AP prices into a revised cost per servable pound, assuming that the standard purchase specifications, standard recipe, and standard yield remain the same. The cost factor is obtained by dividing the cost per servable pound, calculated as part of the yield test, by the original AP cost per pound. For example:

$$\frac{\text{Cost per Servable Pound}}{\text{AP Price}} = \text{Cost Factor}$$

$$\frac{\$10.77}{\$5.95} = 1.81$$

Anytime the AP cost changes from the amount used to calculate the original cost per servable pound in the yield test, a new cost per servable pound can be rapidly computed. This is accomplished by multiplying the cost factor by the new AP price. For example, if the AP price for the beef rib increased to \$6.29/lb, the new cost per servable pound would be:

New AP Price	×	Cost Factor	=	New Cost per Servable Pound
$6.29	×	1.81	=	$11.38

One final note: it is critical that all established standards remain the same. The proper use of the cost factor is dependent upon the operation following the same standard purchase specifications and preparation and cooking methods as those used in the yield test.

Adjusting Standard Recipe Yields

The yield from a standard recipe can be easily increased or decreased by using an **adjustment factor**. An adjustment factor is found by dividing the desired yield by the original yield. For example, if a recipe yields 100 portions, and you want 225 portions of the same size, the adjustment factor would be:

$$\frac{\text{Desired Yield}}{\text{Original Yield}} = \text{Adjustment Factor}$$

$$\frac{225 \text{ portions}}{100 \text{ portions}} = 2.25$$

Each recipe ingredient is then multiplied by the adjustment factor to determine the amount needed for the desired yield. For example, if the original recipe required 8 ounces of sugar, the adjusted quantity would be:

Original Amount	×	Adjustment Factor	=	New Amount
8 oz	×	2.25	=	18 oz (1 lb, 2 oz)

A similar procedure can be used to determine the new amount required if the portion size is altered. For example, if a recipe yields 40 servings (12 ounces each), and you want 40 servings (8 ounces each), the adjustment factor would be:

$$\frac{\text{Desired Amount}}{\text{Original Amount}} = \text{Adjustment Factor}$$

$$\frac{8 \text{ oz}}{12 \text{ oz}} = .67 \text{ (rounded)}$$

Each recipe ingredient must then be multiplied by this factor to determine the amount of the ingredient required for the recipe. For example, if a recipe required 30 pounds of ground beef to yield 40 servings (12 ounces each) to prepare 40 servings (8 ounces each), you would need approximately 20 pounds of ground beef.

Original Amount	×	Adjustment Factor	=	New Amount
30 lb	×	.67	=	20.1 lb

A recipe can also be adjusted if both the number of portions *and* the portion size change. First, determine the total volume of the original and desired amounts, then calculate the adjustment factor. For example, if a recipe yields 50 servings

(4 ounces each) and the desired yield is 75 servings (6 ounces each), the adjustment factor would be:

$$\frac{\text{Total Volume of Desired Yield}}{\text{Total Volume of Original Yield}} = \text{Adjustment Factor}$$

Total Volume of Desired Yield $= 75$ portions $\times$ 6 oz/portion $= 450$ oz
Total Volume of Original Yield $= 50$ portions $\times$ 4 oz/portion $= 200$ oz

$$\frac{450 \text{ oz}}{200 \text{ oz}} = 2.25$$

Using an adjustment factor can provide very accurate ingredient quantities when the total volume of a recipe's yield does not change significantly. However, the use of an adjustment factor for a recipe in which the yield changes substantially must be done carefully. For example, it is unlikely that a recipe yielding 10 portions of a specific size can merely be multiplied by an adjustment factor of 100 to yield 1,000 portions of the same size. In such situations, it is best to start with the indicated adjustment factor and then carefully modify it until the recipe yields the desired volume. Likewise, one must be careful when calculating revised quantities for spices and herbs. It is often best to add these ingredients on a "to-taste" basis until you are certain about the exact quantity needed.

Standard Portion Sizes

Each food and beverage standard recipe indicates a **standard portion size**. This is the fourth standard cost tool for ensuring consistency in operations. Because a given menu item or drink will be the same size each time it is portioned, no guest will get a larger or smaller portion or a stronger or weaker drink. The benefit is twofold: portion costs for the same food and beverage items will be consistent, and the guest will always receive the same value for the dollars he or she spends.

Value is the relationship between price and quality. Basing the selling price of the food or beverage item, at least in part, upon its cost will help to establish a fair selling price, or value, from the guest's perspective. Assume that an operation does not provide a standard portion size. On one occasion, a guest may receive a very large portion—a great value. Returning at a later time, the same guest may receive a smaller portion at the same selling price—a lesser value and a disappointment for the guest. Consistency, then, in terms of value perceived by guests, is a primary advantage of standard portion sizes.

Portion control tools must be available and used every time a recipe or beverage is prepared. Portion control tools include such items as weighing and measuring equipment, ladles and scoops to portion food, jiggers and shot glasses for beverages, or automated beverage-dispensing equipment.

Employees must know about portion sizes in order to follow them. Required portion sizes from each standard recipe should be posted in production areas for cooks and bartenders to refer to. A sample standard portion size sheet for food and a standard drink size list are shown in Exhibits 4 and 5, respectively. In addition to these lists, some operations use pictures of each item. When these are posted in

Exhibit 4   Sample Standard Portion Size Sheet

Items	Portion Size	Product Form	Other Data	Work Station Responsible
APPETIZERS				
Shrimp Cocktail	5 ea.	AP	21–25 Count	Cold
Fruit Cup	5 oz	EP	See Recipe No. P12	Cold
Marinated Herring	2¹/₂ oz	AP		Cold
Half Grapefruit	¹/₂ ea.	AP	27 Count	Cold
Soup, Cup	6 oz	EP	6³/₄ oz Cup	Hot
ENTREES				
Sirloin Steak	14 oz	AP	AP—Bone-in	Hot
Prime Rib of Beef	9 oz	EP		Hot
Lobster	1¹/₂ lb	AP		Hot
Ragout of Lamb	4 oz	EP		Hot
Chicken	¹/₂ ea.	AP	2 lb Average	Hot
VEGETABLES & SALADS				
Whipped Potatoes	3 oz	EP		Hot
Baked Potato	1 ea.	AP	90 Count	Hot
Asparagus Spears	3 ea.	AP	Jumbo Spears	Hot
Half Tomato	¹/₂ ea.	AP	4 × 5's	Hot
Garden Salad	2¹/₂ oz	EP		Cold
Hearts of Lettuce	¹/₄ head	EP	5's	Cold

AP—As Purchased; EP—Edible Portion

serving line stations, employees can see how the item should look or how it is placed on the plate.

Standard Portion Costs

After standard recipes and standard portion sizes have been developed, a standard portion cost—the fifth standard cost tool—can be calculated. A **standard portion cost** is, simply, the cost of preparing and serving one portion of food or one drink item according to the standard recipe. The process of establishing this cost is called **pre-costing**.

A standard portion cost is determined by dividing the recipe's total ingredient costs by the number of portions the standard recipe yields. For example, if the cost to prepare a recipe is $75.00 and it yields 50 portions, then the standard portion cost for one item is $1.50 ($75.00 ÷ 50 portions).

The prices for ingredients listed in standard recipes can be obtained from current invoices. Today, many operations use computerized precosting systems to

Exhibit 5 Sample Standard Drink Size List

Beverage	Drink Size In Ounces	Glass Used
Whiskies (Bourbons & Ryes)	$1^1/_4$ oz	Highball (8 oz)
Canadians	$1^1/_4$ oz	Highball (8 oz)
Irish	$1^1/_4$ oz	Highball (8 oz)
Scotch	$1^1/_4$ oz	Highball (8 oz)
Rum	$1^1/_4$ oz	Highball (8 oz)
Brandies	$1^1/_4$ oz	Line Brandy (2 oz)
Cordials	$^7/_8$ oz	Cordial (1 oz)
Wines (by the glass)		
Appetizers	$1^3/_4$ oz	Sherry (2 oz)
Desserts	$2^1/_4$ oz	Port ($2^1/_2$ oz)
Cocktails	See Standard Recipe Manual	

Exhibit 6 Sample Standard Portion Cost Worksheet: Menu Item

A. **Name of Menu Item** *Fish Fillet Amandine*

B. **Portion Size** *6 oz Fish/#60 Scoop Sauce*

C. **Number of Portions** *60*

Ingredient	Amount	Cost/Unit	Total Cost
1	2	3	4
Fish Fillets	*22 lb 8 oz*	*$4.85/lb*	*$109.13*
Almonds	*1 lb*	*4.26/lb*	*4.26*
Butter/Margarine	*2 lb 8 oz*	*1.35/lb*	*3.38*
Lemon Juice	*$1/_2$ cup*	*1.90/16 oz*	*.48*
		(2 cups)	
Lemon Peel	*3 lemons*	*.75/each*	*2.25*
Salt	*TT*	*–*	*–*
Pepper	*TT*	*–*	*–*
		Total	*$119.50*

$119.50 Total Cost (col. 4)	÷	*60* Number Portions (C)	=	*$1.99* Standard Portion Cost

keep the per-portion cost of standard recipes current. For example, if the price of ground beef increases, the new cost is entered into the menu management system and all recipe costs in which ground beef is an ingredient are automatically adjusted to reflect the price increase.

Exhibit 6 presents an example of how the recipe shown in Exhibit 1 would be pre-costed to yield the standard portion cost. It is impractical to cost some ingredients, especially a small amount of an inexpensive item. For example, no costs are included for salt and pepper. (The symbol "TT" means "to taste.") The cost per purchase unit is recorded in column 3.

To arrive at the total cost of each ingredient (column 4), the amount of the ingredient (column 2) is multiplied by the cost per unit (column 3). For example, the total cost of fish fillets is calculated as follows:

$$\text{Amount} \times \text{Cost/Unit} = \text{Total Cost}$$
$$\text{22 lb, 8 oz} \times \$4.85 = \$109.13 \text{ (rounded)}$$

The total ingredient cost for the recipe is indicated at the bottom of column 4. The total ingredient cost for preparing 60 portions of fish fillet amandine according to the recipe is $119.50. The portion cost for this menu item is calculated at the bottom of the worksheet:

$$\frac{\text{Total Cost}}{\text{Number of Portions}} = \text{Standard Portion Cost}$$

$$\frac{\$119.50}{60} = \$1.99$$

Therefore, the standard portion cost—the cost to prepare one portion according to the recipe—is $1.99. Changes in the yield of a standard recipe that occur because of a change in the portion size will affect the standard portion cost. Anytime the portion size is altered, a new standard portion cost must be calculated.

Calculating Standard Dinner Costs

Many food service operations combine individual menu items to create dinners or other meals that are costed, priced, and sold as one selection (although some operations such as cafeterias offer items à la carte—each item individually priced). The worksheet presented in Exhibit 7 provides a format which a restaurant manager might use to determine standard dinner costs for an entree and its component costs. The cost of each item listed on the **standard dinner cost worksheet** is obtained from pre-costed standard recipes for each menu item. The costs of items offered as part of the dinner are totaled to arrive at the dinner cost of $4.14.

Because the vegetable varies from day to day (the term "du jour" for vegetable in Exhibit 6 means "of the day," and because guests have choices in the potato, dressing, and juice categories, it would take an impractical amount of time to determine the standard dinner cost for all the different dinner combinations that are possible. For the categories in which the guests have a choice, managers can choose the cost of the most popular item in the category to determine the dinner cost. For example, if baked potatoes are chosen most often by guests, then the portion cost of baked potatoes might be used when calculating the standard dinner cost. It is also possible to select the item with the highest portion cost in a category and use this when determining the standard dinner cost. In addition, managers can track the actual number of each item chosen for several days, and then calculate an average cost that can be used when determining the standard dinner cost. Regardless of the method used, planners should be aware of the item cost which is

Exhibit 7   Standard Dinner Cost Worksheet

					Date of Last Cost
					8/1/00

Name of Dinner *Fish Fillet Amandine*

	Item		Portion Cost			
Entree	*Fish Amandine*	*$1.99*				
Vegetable	*du Jour*	*.32*				
Potato	*Choice*	*.40*				
Salad	*Tossed Green*	*.60*				
Dressing	*Choice*	*.15*				
Juice	*Tomato/Pineapple*	*.25*				
Bread	*Loaf*	*.15*				
Butter	*Butter*	*.06*				
Other						
Garnish	*Orange/Lemon/Parsley*	*.10*				
Condiment	*Cocktail Sauce*	*.12*				
		$4.14				

used in calculating the standard dinner cost. Then, when additional items are considered, they can better assure that the per portion cost of the new item will be in line with that used in earlier cost calculations.

The worksheet provides four more columns for calculating the standard dinner cost when the standard portion costs of items change (due to a change in an ingredient's price on the item's standard recipe). When this occurs, the new standard portion cost is added to the unchanged costs of the other dinner items to arrive at a revised standard dinner cost. Increasingly, computerized menu management systems are used to update the costs of menu items. These systems are also used to calculate possible food costs when managers consider changing menu prices.

Calculating Standard Portion Cost: Beverage

Establishing a standard drink cost for beverages is relatively simple because usually there are few ingredients. A standard recipe form, such as the one shown in Exhibit 8 for a Manhattan, can provide space for listing ingredient costs and calculating the standard drink cost.

Ingredients are listed in column 1 of the standard recipe. The bottle size for each liquor ingredient is noted in column 2. Most alcoholic beverages are sold by the liter rather than by the ounce. Therefore, because recipes and bar equipment typically use ounces as a unit of measure, it is usually necessary to convert liters to ounces before making recipe extensions or costing calculations.

The cost of the bottle of liquor is recorded in column 3. Since there are four columns in this section, three ingredient price changes can be noted before a new standard form must be used in this manual system. As with the food-costing

Exhibit 8   Sample Standard Beverage Recipe

ITEM: Manhattan

						Date 6/19/—		Date		Date		Date	
A) Drink Sales Price						$4.00	$		$		$		
B) Drink Cost						.530	$		$		$		
C) Drink Cost Percentage						13.3%		%		%		%	

		Bottle Data				Drink Data					
		6/19—									
Ingredients	**Size**	**Cost**	**Cost**	**Cost**	**Cost**	**Size**	**6/19**				
1	2	3	3	3	3	4	5	5	5	5	
Whiskey, Rye	L (33.8 oz)	9.65				1.50 oz	.430				
Vermouth, Sweet	750 ML (25.4 oz)	2.69				.75 oz	.080				
Angostura Bitters	16 oz	4.56				dash	.010				
Cherry (stem maraschino)						1 ea.	.010				
Water (Ice)						.75 oz	—				
TOTALS						3 oz	.530				

PREPARATION PROCEDURE:
Place ingredients into a mixing glass. Add ice and stir long enough to chill. Strain into cocktail glass. Garnish with a stem Maraschino cherry.

GLASS USED: $3^1/_2$ oz Line Cocktail.

procedures noted above, computerized systems make this process quick and easy. The amount of each ingredient is listed in column 4. Column 5 shows the cost of each ingredient for one drink.

How are ingredient costs calculated? To determine the cost of the rye whiskey used in the Manhattan, for example, the price of the bottle of rye whiskey first must be divided by the number of ounces in the bottle to obtain the cost per ounce:

$$\text{Cost per Ounce} = \frac{\$9.65 \text{ (price per liter bottle)}}{33.8 \text{ (ounces per liter bottle)}} = \$.286 \text{ (rounded)}$$

When calculating a bottle's cost per ounce, some beverage managers deduct an ounce or so before dividing to allow for evaporation or spillage. This will increase the cost per ounce.

Since 1.5 ounces of rye whiskey are used in a Manhattan, the ingredient cost for rye whiskey is $.43: $.286 × 1.5 ounces = $.429, or $.43 (rounded).

The costs of the rye whiskey and the other ingredients used to make the Manhattan are added together and the total drink cost ($.530) is recorded at the bottom of column 5. This figure is then transferred to Line B at the top of the recipe.

Line C at the top of the recipe indicates the drink cost percentage. The drink cost percentage expresses how much of the drink sales price (recorded on line A) the drink cost represents. The drink cost percentage is calculated by dividing the cost of the drink by the drink's selling price and multiplying by 100. The drink cost percentage for the Manhattan in the sample recipe is calculated as follows:

$$\text{Drink Cost Percentage} = \frac{\$.530 \text{ (drink cost)}}{\$4.00 \text{ (selling price)}} = .133 \text{ (rounded)} \times 100 = 13.3\%$$

Special Standard Cost Tools for Beverage Control

The five standard cost tools—standard purchase specifications, standard recipes, standard yields, standard portion sizes, and standard portion costs—are necessary to establish performance standards for both food and beverages. However, two additional standard cost tools are important to the beverage operation: standard glassware and standard ice size.

Standard Glassware. Glassware obviously affects portion size, quality, and perceived value. In too small a glass, highballs made with mixers such as soda, tonic, or water will be too strong since less mixer can be added to the standard portion of liquor. Conversely, in too large a glass, the drink will taste weak since the greater amount of mixer dilutes the standard portion of liquor. Therefore, the standard drink recipe should specify a standard glass size, which should be determined when the beverage recipe is standardized. A standard glassware review sheet, such as the one shown in Exhibit 9, should be posted in the work area. The same style and size of glass should be used every time the drink is prepared. This means, of course, that sufficient quantities of all necessary glassware must be available at all times.

Glassware is also important in marketing to help carry out an atmosphere theme and to influence the appearance and presentation of the drink. However, while glassware affects presentation (marketing) concerns, it is wise to limit the number of different glasses in inventory. For example, the same glass might be used for ice water, soft drinks, milk, and highballs. If this can be done, problems with the costs of glassware, storage space behind the bar, and training time for bartenders and servers may be reduced.

Standard Ice Size. It is easy to ignore the effect of ice size on drink quality. Although any size ice is suitable for most food service purposes, drink standardization must

Exhibit 9   Sample Review Sheet for Standard Beverage Glassware

Line Cocktail
(4½ oz. lines at 3 oz.)

Collins
(12 oz.)

Champagne
(5½ oz.)

Highball
(8 oz.)

Old Fashioned
(6 oz.)

Line Whiskey
(1½ oz. line at 1¼ oz.)

Red and White
Table Wine
and Champagne
(8½ oz.)

Aperitif or
Dessert Wine
(3 to 5 oz.)

Line Brandy
(2 oz.)

Cordial
(1 oz.)

Whiskey Sour
(6 oz.)

On-the-Rocks
(7 oz.)

Port Wine
(4 oz.)

Brandy Snifter
(5 oz.)

Beer Pilsner
(8 oz.)

consider ice cube size. Bigger cubes leave more empty space in the glass because they do not clump together as smaller cubes do. This space must be filled with something. In a liquor-only drink, such as a martini, the amount of beverage appears smaller, unless a larger portion is served. In a mixed drink, the drink will be diluted by adding more mix. On the other hand, small cubes or shaved ice fill up a glass more completely before a beverage is added, but both melt more quickly. Therefore, a delay in serving or consuming the drink may create a diluted taste. Management must therefore consider its operating procedures to determine the proper size of ice cubes for the operation.

Exhibit 10   Sample Ingredient Cost List

01 - CHICKEN DELICIOUS, INC.		INGREDIENT COST LIST					SA1222
001 - CHICKEN DELICIOUS #1							10.35.19

EXPENSE CATAGORY	INGRED. NUMBER	INGREDIENT DESCRIPTION	PURCHASE UNIT	PURCHASE COST	RECIPE YIELD	RECIPE UNIT	RECIPE COST
01	1	Chicken	Case	51.00	32.00	Head	1.5937
02	41	Shortening	50 lb	19.12	50.00	lb	.3824
03	42	Milk & Egg Dip	24 lb/cs	28.51	24.00	lb	1.1879
03	43	Fine Salt	80 lb	7.98	80.00	lb	.0097
03	44	Seasoning	24 lb/10	61.38	24.00	Pkts	2.5575
03	45	Flour	25 lb	3.89	1.00	Bag	3.8900
04	2	Roll	80/cs	6.76	180.00	Each	.0375
05	3	Potato Mix	6 #10 Cans	31.88	34.80	lb	.9160
06	49	Cabbage	50 lb	11.75	50.00	lb	.2350
06	50	Onions	lb	1.70	50.00	lb	.0340
06	52	Mayonnaise	4 Gal.	17.81	40.00	Gal.	.4452
06	53	Salad Oil	4 Gal.	16.43	32.00	Pint	.5134
06	54	Vinegar	4 Gal.	11.92	32.00	Pint	.3725
06	55	Sugar	25 lb	8.98	25.00	lb	.3592
06	56	Salt	80 lb	4.90	80.00	lb	.0612
07	6	Gravy Mix	24 lb/cs	16.07	24.00	lb	.6695
07	65	Pepper	1 lb	4.41	1.00	lb	4.4100
07	66	Margarine Qtrs	30 lb	11.22	30.00	lb	.3740
09	12	Bucket	100 cs	20.72	100.00	Each	.2072
09	15	Dinner Box	250 cs	13.32	250.00	Each	.0532
09	16	Snack Box	300 cs	12.54	300.00	Each	.0418
09	17	Plastic Forks	6000 cs	37.47	6000.00	Each	.0062
09	19	Napkins	6000 cs	31.68	6000.00	Each	.0052
09	28	3.5 oz cup	2000 cs	29.10	2000.00	Each	.0145
09	29	3.5 oz lid	2000 cs	14.20	2000.00	Each	.0071
09	69	Labels	1000 cs	2.71	1000.00	Each	.0027
10	75	Milk	1/2 Pint	.19	1.00	Each	.1900
15	21	Chicken Livers	Case	72.00	72.00	1/2 lb	1.0000
15	22	Breading	25 lb	25.00	650.00	1 Cup	.0384

Source: Tridata, Inc., Atlanta, Georgia.

Computer Applications: Recipe Management Software

Recipe management software maintains three of the most important files used by an integrated food service computer system: an ingredient file, a standard recipe file, and a menu item file. Most other management software programs must be able to access data contained within these files to produce special reports for management.[1]

Ingredient File

An **ingredient file** contains important data about each purchased ingredient. Ingredient file data generally include ingredient code numbers and descriptions, as well as each ingredient's:

- Purchase unit and cost per purchase unit
- Issue unit and cost per issue unit
- Recipe unit and cost per recipe unit

Exhibit 10 illustrates a sample ingredient cost list produced from some of the data contained in an ingredient file. This report is useful for detailing unit expenditures at current costs and monitoring relationships among various product units (such as purchase, issue, and recipe units of the same ingredient). Some ingredient files may specify more than one recipe unit. For example, the recipe unit for bread used for French toast is by the slice; the recipe unit for bread used for stuffing may be by the ounce.

The initial creation of an ingredient file and the subsequent file updates (daily, weekly, monthly, etc.) are often challenging tasks for many food service managers. However, the benefits of an ingredient file often outweigh the cost of creating and maintaining the file. When the ingredient file can be accessed by other management software programs (especially by inventory software), ingredient data can easily be transferred (rather than re-inputted) to appropriate management software programs.

Since other management software programs rely on data maintained by the ingredient file, it is important that data contained in the file are accurate. If errors are made when initially entering data, all subsequent processing will be unreliable and system reports will be relatively worthless.

Standard Recipe File

Computers can assist in generating standard recipes by simplifying many of the calculations needed. Numerous software programs that calculate recipe quantities based upon estimated unit sales and then print the standard recipe are available. Exhibit 11 illustrates a standard recipe generated by computer.

Exhibit 12 illustrates standard recipe conversion information generated by recipe management software. The software converts recipe ingredient amounts to weights and then to ingredient costs. It can also determine nutritional information for an entire meal (or other period) and define applicable preparation areas (for example, whether ingredients are to be issued or delivered to specific workstations).

Some recipe management software programs provide space within standard recipe records for preparation instructions (also referred to as assembly instructions) that are typically found on standard recipe cards. This can be a useful feature when the number of portions yielded by a particular standard recipe has to be expanded or contracted to accommodate forecasted needs. For example, if a standard recipe is designed to yield 100 portions but 530 portions are needed, it may be possible (depending on the particular menu item) to instruct the system to proportionately adjust the ingredient quantities. A recipe for 530 portions can be printed that includes preparation information, thus providing a complete plan for the new recipe's production.

Few restaurants purchase all menu item ingredients in ready-to-use or pre-portioned form. Some ingredients are made on the premises. This means that the ingredients within a **standard recipe file** may be either inventory items or references to other recipe files. Recipes that are included as ingredients within a standard recipe record are called **sub-recipes**. For example, in Exhibit 11, enchilada sauce is listed as "subr 2643" (sub-recipe 2643). Exhibit 13 presents the sub-recipe for enchilada sauce. (Note that the recipe is also identified as 2643 in Exhibit 13.)

Exhibit 11 Computer-Generated Standard Recipe

```
REPORT#: 90    * * * CBORD FOODSERVICE MANAGEMENT SYSTEMS * * *      PAGE:   4
OPTION : 3.5.8.         MENU MANAGEMENT SYSTEM - V6.23                MAY 09
USER#  : 28          MSU Residence Halls Fall - LCode 1              1540 HOURS
                PRODUCTION RECIPE

FUNCTION NAME:
        UNIT:
        DATE: FRIDAY    05/09
=================================================================================
0084  BURRITO WET MEAT (BEEF & TURKEY)
                                            YIELD    :    1.80 SCP
---------------------------------------------------------------------------------
PORTIONS :      30.00    8.30 OZ   COOKING TIME : 25MIN
PORTION DESC : 1 BURRITO           COOKING TEMP : 350F
PREP TIME:                         COOKING EQUIP: Oven
                                   SERVING PAN  : SHALLOW COUNTER PAN
PREPARE MAIN BATCH  1 TIME(S)      SERVING UTEN : SPATULA
---------------------------------------------------------------------------------
      INGREDIENT          ------- MAIN BATCH -------- ------ PARTIAL BATCH ------
                                  QUANTITY                  QUANTITY
---------------------------------------------------------------------------------
      REVISED 12-20

GROUND TURKEY             2 LBS    8      OZS
GROUND BEEF              1 LBS     4      OZS
ONIONS                            4 3/4  OZS
TACO SEASONING                    1 3/4  OZS
SALT                              1 1/4  OZS
REFRIED BEANS            1 QT      3 1/2  CUP
10" DIE CUT TORTILLA             30      EACH
ENCHILADA SAUCE SUBR 2643         3 3/4  CUP
    **GARNISH**
LETTUCE SHREDDED                  7 1/4  OZS
TOMATOES DICED                   14 1/2  OZS
MILD SHREDDED CHEDDAR             7 1/4  OZS

    1. BROWN BOTH GROUND MEATS TOGETHER (BE SURE THEY ARE WELL MIXED.)
       WITH ONIONS.
    2. DRAIN OFF FAT.  ADD TACO SEASONING AND SALT, MIX WELL.
       ADJUST SEASONING IF NECESSARY.
    3. ADD BEANS TO SEASONED MEAT AND MIX WELL.
    4. MAKE SAUCE AND HOLD AT A MINIMUM INTERNAL TEMP OF 145.
    5. TO ASSEMBLE BURRITOS: PLACE A #12 SCOOP OF FILLING (4OZ)
       ON LOWER 1/3 OF TORTILLA.  FOLD IN SIDES FIRST, THEN ROLL STARTING
       AT THE BOTTOM TO COVER FILLING.
    6. PLACE 16 IN EACH SCP.
    7. COVER PANS WITH PLASTIC WRAP AND FOIL.  BAKE IN A 350 DEG OVEN
   CCP>FOR 25 MINUTES OR UNTIL AN INTERNAL TEMP OF 155 IS REACHED.
    8. UNCOVER AND LADLE 16 OZS. OF SAUCE OVER EACH PAN OF BURRITOS.
    9. JUST BEFORE SERVICE SPRINKLE ON 4OZ SHREDDED LETTUCE, 4OZ CHEESE
       AND 8OZ DICED TOMATOES.

    NOTE:  HEAT FLOUR TORTILLAS ON A 300F GRILL FOR APPROX. 30 SECONDS.
           THIS WILL MAKE THE TORTILLAS FLEXIBLE AND EASY TO FOLD.
```

Source: Michigan State University, Division of Housing and Food Services, East Lansing, Michigan.

Including sub-recipes as ingredients for a particular standard recipe is called **chaining recipes**. Chaining recipes enables the food service computer system to maintain a single record for a particular menu item that includes a number of sub-recipes. When ingredient costs change, recipe management software programs must be capable of automatically updating not only the costs of standard recipes, but also the costs of sub-recipes that are used as ingredients in other standard recipes.

Menu Item File

A menu item file contains data for all meal periods and menu items sold. Important data maintained by this file may include the menu's identification number,

Exhibit 12   Standard Recipe Conversion Information

FIDF Nmbr	Ingredient Name (Instruction -->)		Quantity Unit		Wgt in lbs	Ext Flg	Cost Yld	Nutr Yld	Nutr ID	R F	I C	Prp Area	Adv FOW Prp	Item Cost
1														
1														
16	GROUND TURKEY		2.080 LBS	*	2.080	_	1	0.750	1215	_	_	_·_	_	1.747
123	GROUND BEEF		1.050 LB	*	1.050	_	1	0.750	550	_	_	_·_	_	1.281
1079	ONIONS		0.250 LBS	*	0.250	_	1	1	3633	_	_	_·_	_	0.250
566	TACO SEASONING		1.500 OZS	*	0.094	_	1	1	5059	_	_	_·_	_	0.183
283	SALT		1.000 OZ	*	0.063	_	1	1	5096	_	_	_·_	_	0.006
222	REFRIED BEANS		1.560 QTS	*	3.640	_	1	1	3202	_	_	_·_	_	1.585
2652	10" DIE CUT TORTILLA		25.000 EACH	*	2.083	_	1	1	5041	_	_	_·_	_	1.543
2670	ENCHILADA SAUCE SUBR 2643		0.195 GALLONS	*	1.978	_	1	1	.	___	_	_	_·_	0.455
1	**GARNISH**													
1076	LETTUCE SHREDDED	*	0.380 LBS	*	0.380	_	1	1	3538	_	_	_·	_	0.194
948	TOMATOES DICED	*	0.750 LBS	*	0.750	_	1	1	7127	_	_	_·_	_	0.647
886	MILD SHREDDED CHEDDAR		0.380 LBS	*	0.380	_	1	1	347	_	_	_·_	_	0.724

Source: Michigan State University, Division of Housing and Food Services, East Lansing, Michigan.

Exhibit 13   Computer-Generated Sub-Recipe

```
REPORT#: 90     * * * CBORD FOODSERVICE MANAGEMENT SYSTEMS * * *      PAGE:    5
OPTION : 3.5.8.           MENU MANAGEMENT SYSTEM - V6.23              MAY 09
USER#  : 28               MSU Residence Halls Fall - LCode 1          1540 HOURS
               PRODUCTION RECIPE

FUNCTION NAME:
         UNIT:
         DATE: FRIDAY    05/09
==============================================================================
2643  SAUCE ENCHILADA HOMEMADE
                                            YIELD    :      0.23 GALLONS

PORTIONS :      9.98    3.00 OZ    COOKING TIME :
PORTION DESC : SERVING             COOKING TEMP :
PREP TIME:                         COOKING EQUIP:
                                   SERVING PAN  :
PREPARE MAIN BATCH  1 TIME(S)      SERVING UTEN :

        INGREDIENT         ------- MAIN BATCH -------- ------ PARTIAL BATCH ------
                                   QUANTITY                   QUANTITY

      NEW RECIPE 2-29

MARGARINE                             1 1/4 OZS
ALL PURPOSE FLOUR-GOLDMED             1 1/4 OZS
VEGETARIAN CHICKEN BASE                 3/4 OZS
LAWREY SEASONING SALT                   1/2 TSP
GROUND CHILI POWDER         1 TBSP      3/4 TSP
GROUND CUMIN SEED                2      TSP
GARLIC POWDER                           1/2 TSP
GROUND RED PEPPER                       1/8 TSP
TOMATO PUREE                            1/8 #10 CAN
WATER                                 3     CUP

      1. MELT MARGARINE IN KETTLE.  ADD FLOUR TO MAKE ROUX.
      2. COOL SLIGHTLY, ADD WATER AND SPICES. WHIP UNTIL SMOOTH.   SIMMER
         10 MINUTES.
      3. ADD PUREE AND SIMMER 5 MINUTES.
      4. ADJUST SEASONING IF NEEDED.
      5. SERVE ON WET BURRITOS.
```

Source: Michigan State University, Division of Housing and Food Services, East Lansing, Michigan.

descriptor, recipe code number, selling price, ingredient quantities for inventory reporting, and sales totals (by unit).

This file also stores historical information about the actual number of items sold. Generally, after a meal period, the actual number of menu items served is manually entered into the menu item file, or automatically transferred from an electronic cash register (ECR) or point-of-sale (POS) system through an interface to the restaurant management system. This data can be accessed by management or by sophisticated forecasting programs to project future unit sales, determine the number of ingredient quantities to purchase, and schedule needed personnel. In addition, computer-based sales analysis applications access data in the menu item file to produce various sales analysis reports for management. When menu items, prices, or tax tables need to be changed, the menu item file is accessed and appropriate changes are entered according to procedures indicated in the user's manual provided by the system's vendor.

Standard Food Costs

The best sources of information to use as the basis for establishing standards are the property's operating budgets developed for a current fiscal period and in-house measurements that consider potential costs matched with anticipated revenue. The remainder of this chapter discusses this second method of establishing standard costs. Standard costs can be implemented after the standard cost control tools for the food and beverage operation discussed earlier in this chapter have been developed.

When standard food costs are known, management is able to compare the cost of food with the revenue it generates. There are several ways to measure food cost. One way expresses costs in terms of total dollars spent on food per day, week, or year. The more common method of measuring food cost in commercial food and beverage operations is the **food cost percentage**. This expresses cost as a percentage of food revenue and is calculated by dividing food costs by food revenue and multiplying by 100. In institutional, non-pricing operations, the food cost percentage often measures food cost differently by expressing it as a percentage of total operating expenses rather than as a percentage of revenue. In all cases, the **standard food cost percentage** represents the planned food cost percentage against which actual food costs are measured.

The procedure to calculate food cost percentage begins by first establishing all standard cost tools: standard purchase specifications, recipes, yields, portion sizes, and portion costs. With these tools, the standard food cost for each item is developed following the process discussed earlier.

Next, a time period for a trial study must be selected. Over this trial period, accurate sales information for each menu item is collected to calculate an overall standard food cost. The longer the time period for the analysis, the more accurate the information. A practical and reasonably accurate method for calculating standard food costs involves the use of the worksheet illustrated in Exhibit 14.

Each menu item is listed on the left side of the form. If an item is offered for sale individually, such as soup or eggplant appetizer, it is listed separately on the

Exhibit 14　Worksheet for Determining Standard Food Cost

| | 8/1 | 8/2 | 8/3 | 8/4 | 8/5 | 8/6 | 8/7 | 8/8 | 8/9 | 8/10 | 8/11 | 8/12 | 8/13 | 8/14 | 8/15 | 8/16 | Total Items Sold | Item Sales Price | Total Food Revenue | Item Food Cost | Total Food Cost | Food Cost Percentage |
| | Date | Date | Date | Date | Date | Date | Date | Date | Date | Date | Date | Date | Date | Date | Date | Date | | | | | | |
Items																						
Soup	12	18	14	20	15	18	0	14	16	17	19	14	18	0	12	16	223	0.90	200.70	0.32	71.36	35.56%
Eggplant	15	21	23	16	15	18	0	17	19	26	15	14	18	0	14	21	252	1.15	289.80	0.35	88.20	30.43%
Hamburger	35	41	38	42	30	37	0	37	39	41	41	29	37	37	33	40	520	2.35	1222.00	0.95	494.00	40.43%
Fish	20	18	16	24	26	18	0	22	16	19	23	26	18	0	20	15	281	2.95	828.95	0.85	238.85	28.81%
Steak	27	25	29	27	26	30	0	29	23	32	26	26	31	0	26	24	381	3.95	1504.95	1.15	438.15	29.11%
Stew	30	35	40	37	39	30	0	32	33	43	36	38	31	0	30	35	489	3.85	1882.65	1.10	537.90	28.57%
Diet Platter	11	15	17	12	15	14	0	13	13	20	11	13	14	0	10	15	193	2.95	569.35	0.80	154.40	27.12%
Sea Platter	30	31	35	29	34	30	0	32	29	38	28	32	31	0	30	30	439	4.25	1865.75	1.35	592.65	31.76%
Plum Pie	12	10	18	12	11	15	0	14	8	19	11	11	16	0	12	9	178	1.95	347.10	0.80	142.40	41.03%
C. Eclair	15	11	21	13	14	11	0	17	9	24	12	13	12	0	14	10	196	2.15	421.40	0.75	147.00	34.88%
S. Remo	30	28	25	37	29	40	29	32	26	29	36	27	51	26	28	21	494	3.25	1605.50	0.95	469.30	29.23%
Oysters	29	30	31	27	26	48	31	31	28	34	26	27	49	28	27	30	502	2.90	1455.80	1.20	602.40	41.38%
Gumbo	50	48	52	57	45	67	51	52	46	55	56	44	66	48	50	46	833	2.50	2082.50	0.85	708.05	34.00%
F. Amandine	70	65	63	67	70	78	40	72	63	66	66	68	77	37	65	66	1033	4.95	5113.35	2.45	2530.85	49.49%
F. Shrimp	60	54	55	57	62	64	38	62	52	58	56	61	62	35	55	52	883	5.95	5253.85	2.01	1774.83	33.78%
Sea Shrimp	45	45	35	38	41	47	25	47	43	38	37	39	45	22	40	43	630	6.25	3937.50	1.85	1165.50	29.60%
N.Y. Strip	10	8	9	9	12	18	0	12	6	12	8	11	11	2	8	8	144	8.15	1173.60	3.45	496.80	42.33%
Oyster Pie	19	17	18	18	20	23	10	21	15	21	17	21	22	8	19	17	286	5.95	1701.70	2.25	643.50	37.82%
Pecan Pie	28	30	26	41	29	40	20	30	28	29	40	28	40	18	29	30	486	2.25	1093.50	0.80	388.80	35.56%
Brulot	15	14	15	16	10	25	5	17	12	18	15	11	25	3	14	16	231	3.55	820.05	0.90	207.90	25.35%
																Totals	8674		33370.00		11892.84	
																			Standard Food Cost Percentage = 35.64%			

worksheet. If it is sold as a dinner or in combination with other items, such as seafood or steak, it is combined with the dinner. Since actual food cost is calculated across all meal periods (properties do not determine actual food cost separately for breakfast, lunch, and dinner) the worksheet should list all menu items. (Because of space considerations, the worksheet in Exhibit 14 shows only a partial list of available menu items in a restaurant.)

Sales History Information

The information necessary to determine standard food cost may come from actual sales records citing the number of each menu item sold during one or more prior periods. If a sales history has been kept, the total number of each item sold can easily be transferred to the worksheet. (In the sample sales history form, Exhibit 15, note that the last column compiles total item sales.)

If there is no record of past item sales (for example, if an entirely new menu is introduced), items sold must be tallied daily during the study period. An accurate tally of the number of each à la carte and complete meal item sold during the trial period must be made. The information may come from an analysis of the guest checks created each day during the study period or from a management report generated by most electronic cash registers or point-of-sale systems. The worksheet in Exhibit 14 has space for only 16 days. Because accuracy increases as the number of days increases, two or more forms can be used to tally item sales for at least one month.

By recording this information on a worksheet, total sales (number of units) and total food costs for the trial period can be easily tracked. With this information, an overall food cost percentage can be figured. Because each food item is likely to have a different food cost percentage, calculating the overall food cost involves determining a weighted average food cost. Items with a high food cost raise the average food cost percentage; items with a low food cost reduce it. It is this weighted average food cost that will be used as the standard against which to measure actual food costs. Note the following points about Exhibit 14:

1. The item sales price (column 19) is the actual selling price of each menu item as printed on the menu.

2. Total food revenue (column 20 [column 18 times column 19]) represents the total revenue expected from sales of the individual menu items. In the first example, 223 servings of soup were sold at 90 cents each, resulting in a total revenue of $200.70. Actual revenue may be less than expected revenue. Differences could be due to theft, to errors in processing sales information, or to inaccurate counts of the number of items sold.

3. Item food cost (column 21) is the standard portion cost. If the item is sold individually, this figure can be taken from the pre-costed standard recipe (Exhibit 6). If the item is a grouping of menu items, such as a New York strip steak dinner, then the figure can be transferred from the standard dinner cost worksheet (Exhibit 7).

Exhibit 15 Sample Sales History Form

Date	1	2	3	4	5	6	7	8	9	10	11	12	13	14	15	16	17	18	19	20	21	22	23	24	25	26	27	28	29	30	31	Total Item Sales
Day	SU	M	TU	W																												
Weather	Rain	Clear	Clear	Clear																												
Meals Served	386	391	379	397																												
Special Events	—	—	Sale	Sale																												

Number of Portions Served

	1	2	3	4	5	6	7	8	9	10	11	12	13	14	15	16	17	18	19	20	21	22	23	24	25	26	27	28	29	30	31	Total Item Sales
Soup	12	18	14	20																												
Eggplant	15	21	23	16																												
Hamburger	35	41	38	42																												
Fish	20	18	16	24																												
Steak	27	25	29	27																												
Stew	30	35	40	37																												
Diet Platter	11	15	17	12																												
Sea Platter	30	31	35	29																												
Plum Pie	12	10	18	12																												
C. Eclair	15	11	21	13																												
S. Remo	30	28	25	37																												
Oysters	29	30	31	27																												
Gumbo	50	48	52	57																												
F. Amandine	70	65	63	67																												
F. Shrimp	60	54	55	57																												
Sea Shrimp	45	45	35	38																												
N.Y. Strip	10	8	9	9																												
Oyster Pie	19	17	18	18																												
Pecan Pie	28	30	26	41																												
Brulot	15	14	15	16																												

4. Total food cost (column 22 [column 18 times column 21]) is the total cost of all food used to produce the number of items sold. For example, the 223 servings of soup each had a standard food cost of 32 cents (column 21). The total food cost, then, is:

$$223 \text{ servings} \quad \times \quad \$.32 \quad = \quad \$71.36$$

5. The food cost percentage (column 23 [column 21 divided by column 19]) is calculated by dividing the food cost (column 21) by the sales price (column 19) and multiplying by 100. The standard food cost percentage for the soup is:

$$\frac{\$.32}{\$.90} \quad \times \quad 100 \quad = \quad 35.6\% \text{ (rounded)}$$

While the standard food cost percentage for each individual item is of some interest, one more step is needed to arrive at the overall standard food cost percentage.

6. To calculate the standard food cost percentage against which to compare actual food costs, the sum of the total food cost column is divided by the sum of the total food revenue column and multiplied by 100. In the example in Exhibit 14 the standard food cost percentage is calculated as:

$$\frac{\$11,892.84}{\$33,370} \quad \times \quad 100 \quad = \quad 35.64\% \text{ (rounded)}$$

The effort needed to calculate an overall standard food cost percentage can be simplified by using one of the many electronic spreadsheet programs available for a personal computer. The number of each menu item sold can be entered on a daily basis. The computer can calculate total revenue and total costs along with the item's standard food cost percentage and the overall standard food cost percentage.

Calculating Standard Costs per Meal

One final comment about developing standard food costs must be made. Properties offering more than one menu, such as lunch and dinner, must decide whether to develop standard food costs by meal or across all meals. If by-meal food costs are desired, calculations for each meal must be done on a separate worksheet. There are two advantages to a separate listing. First, when food cost standards are separated by meals, it is easier to compare any differences between standard and actual costs. Second, since corrective action can focus specifically upon the meal period contributing higher than expected food costs, the reasons for losses can more quickly be identified and brought under control.

There is, however, one serious disadvantage to overcome when standards are established for each separate meal period. To effect control, actual food costs must also be assessed separately for each meal. Even with the use of point-of-sale equipment, the process of determining how much of each food item is used for breakfast, lunch, or dinner is very time-consuming. For example, a manager might know the cost of food that should have been used during a meal period (number of items sold times each item's standard food cost). But if some food was wasted or improperly portioned during preparation, the *actual* cost of food used would be greater than that determined from the tally of sales. Many food and beverage managers, therefore, find it more helpful to spend time identifying problems common to all meal periods, such as ineffective purchasing, receiving, storing, and issuing, or problems in production and service, rather than searching for problems applicable to a specific meal period.

Defining Expected Food Costs

The standard food cost percentage is one of the most important tools of the control process. It becomes the manager's goal since it defines expected food costs. If actual food costs are close to this goal, the management team is probably doing a good job. If, on the other hand, actual food costs are greater than standard food costs, there may be problems within the operation. The manager should first check to see if the sales mix has changed since the information was collected to determine the standard food cost. For example, it may be that more items with higher food cost percentages are being sold. This is a common reason that total food costs and food cost percentages are higher than expected. If this is not the cause, the manager must analyze the food service operation to determine where corrective action is needed.

Ideal Costs Based Upon Actual Sales Mix

To this point, we have discussed the development of standard food costs that are based upon historical sales mix. We have noted that when actual costs do not approach standard costs, one reason may be that the sales mix for the period under study is different from the sales mix at the time the standard food cost was calculated.

The concept of ideal cost addresses this problem. An **ideal cost** is based on the actual number of each menu item sold. After each meal period or at the end of a day, the actual number of each item sold can be multiplied by its per-portion standard food cost to arrive at the expected cost for serving that number of the item. When this process is completed for all menu items and the expected costs are added together, an ideal cost for the meal period or day can be determined. This data is, in turn, summed for each successive meal period or day to generate an ideal food cost for the entire time period (such as month) for which actual costs will be assessed.

Because an ideal cost is based on the actual number sold, it provides a more accurate basis of comparison against actual food cost. This gives management an opportunity to effect control closer to the time of production and service.

For an ideal cost system to be effective, standard recipe costs must be kept current. This means that management must maintain up-to-date information about ingredient purchase costs and continually recalculate (pre-cost) standard recipes. The need for a large amount of computation suggests that ideal cost may be best implemented using a computer-based system. To that end, system manufacturers often include software to generate an ideal cost as part of their ECR or POS systems. With computerized systems, the process of determining ideal costs is relatively simple.

Standard Beverage Costs

Standard beverage costs are calculated for exactly the same reason as standard food costs. The manager wants to establish a goal—a base of comparison—against which to measure actual results of the beverage operation. The standard beverage cost becomes the goal. The steps in calculating standard beverage costs are:

1. Establish all standard cost tools: standard purchase specifications, recipes, yields, portion sizes, portion costs, glassware, and ice.

2. Select a time period for the analysis. As with standard food costs, more time and effort spent on determining standard beverage costs will generally produce more accurate cost calculations. However, no system can provide data with 100 percent accuracy. The best time schedule will allow observation of all phases of the beverage operation, including both slow and busy times, or shifts with high, low, and/or regular prices. At a minimum, the review should cover two or three weeks in succession. Operations with several beverage outlets need a longer observation period for sales to reflect an average volume and a variety of drinks served.

3. Inform all affected staff members—bartenders, food and beverage servers, and others—about the study. They will want to know:

   a. The reason for the study—to determine cost expectations for accounting, recordkeeping, management, and control purposes.

   b. Why the study is important—management wants to assess how well the beverage program is operating.

   c. What's in it for them—the results of the study will help staff members know what's expected of them, and cost savings may be shared with the staff.

   d. Implications of the study—results of the analysis have no bearing on employment status; no one's honesty or competency is being reviewed or questioned.

   e. Procedures for the study—there will be minimal, if any, disruption in ongoing operations.

4. Set rules for the study period, emphasizing that during the trial study employees must very carefully follow all standard procedures. The purpose is to ensure that accurate and reliable information is collected.

   a. Standard beverage recipes are to be used whenever drinks are prepared.

   b. Portion control tools (shot glasses, jiggers) and standard glassware are to be used in preparing every drink.

   c. Management personnel might work behind the bar whenever possible during the study to better assure that required procedures are followed consistently. When not working the bar, managers should carefully

Exhibit 16   Calculation of Beverage Cost Percentage

> Value of Inventory Behind Bar at the Beginning of Trial Period
> + Value of Issues to the Bar During the Trial Period
> − Value of Inventory Behind Bar at the End of Trial Period
> = Gross Beverage Cost
>
> + Value of Transfers to Bar During the Trial Period
> − Value of Transfers from Bar During the Trial Period
> − Cost of Complimentary Drinks (if any)
> = Net Beverage Cost
>
> $$\frac{\text{Net Beverage Cost}}{\text{Beverage Revenue During Trial Period}} \times 100 = \text{Standard Beverage Cost Percent}$$

supervise operations to ensure compliance with all standard operating procedures.

    d. At the beginning of each shift, the manager should remind personnel that the property is involved in the beverage study and that careful compliance with all procedures is important.

    e. Revenue from all drinks served must be collected. Management must approve all complimentary drinks. Personnel must save all drinks returned because of mistakes. Special precautions to minimize the possibility of guest "walkouts" and errors in guest checks should be used.

5. Before the study begins, take careful inventory of the quantity of liquor behind the bar.

6. Maintain a record of the cost of all liquor issued to the bar during the trial study.

7. Record any beverages transferred from the bar and any food transferred to the bar.

8. Calculate the standard beverage cost. Close supervision and efficient operations during the study period should yield a reasonably accurate standard beverage cost. That is, with continued use of the standard cost tools, a lower beverage cost percentage most likely could not be achieved without measures such as raising prices, reducing portion sizes, or revising basic operating procedures.

Exhibit 16 shows how the beverage cost is calculated for the trial period—the standard against which costs of actual beverage operation will be compared.

As with the standard food cost percentage, the standard beverage cost percentage is a goal that managers of the beverage operation should work toward. There are, of course, many factors that affect actual practice. For example, errors may occur, control of the beverage operation may gradually become looser, or changes in policy may require revised procedures. These and similar factors reinforce the value of recalling the standard beverage cost percentage when examining actual operating results. The beverage manager should understand that when actual beverage costs exceed standard beverage costs, a problem may exist.

Endnotes

1. The reader interested in a detailed explanation of computer applications and recipe management software should read Michael L. Kasavana and John J. Cahill's *Managing Computers in the Hospitality Industry*, 3d ed. (Lansing, Mich.: Educational Institute of the American Hotel & Lodging Association, 1997).

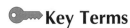 ## Key Terms

adjustment factor—The number by which the amount of each ingredient indicated in a standard recipe is multiplied in order to increase or decrease the recipe's yield, determined by dividing the desired yield by the original yield.

chaining recipes—Including sub-recipes as ingredients for a particular standard recipe. This enables the food service computer system to maintain a single record for a particular menu item that includes a number of sub-recipes.

cost factor—A constant value that may be used to convert new "as purchased" (AP) prices into a revised cost per servable pound, assuming that the standard purchase specifications, standard recipe, and standard yield remain the same. The cost factor is determined by dividing the cost per servable pound by the original "as purchased" (AP) cost per pound.

cost per servable pound—Information needed to calculate standard portion costs, determined by dividing the "as purchased" (AP) price by the yield percentage as a decimal.

food cost percentage—In relation to commercial food and beverage operations, food cost percentage expresses cost as a percentage of revenue and is calculated by dividing food costs by food revenue and multiplying by 100; in relation to institutional food and beverage operations, the food cost percentage expresses cost as a percentage of expenses and is calculated by dividing food costs by total operating expenses and multiplying by 100.

ideal cost—A method of calculating standard food costs based on the actual number (sales mix) of each menu item sold during a day or meal period; the actual count of each item sold is multiplied by its per-portion standard food cost to arrive at the expected cost for serving all portions of the item.

ingredient file—An electronic record that contains important data on each purchased ingredient, such as ingredient code number, description, purchase unit, purchase unit cost, issue unit, issue unit cost, and recipe unit cost.

portion control tools—Items such as weighing and measuring equipment, ladles and scoops to portion food, jiggers and shot glasses for beverages, or automated beverage-dispensing equipment. These tools must be available and used every time a recipe or beverage is prepared.

pre-costing—The process of determining the costs of ingredients used in a standard recipe to arrive at a standard portion cost for one item yielded by the recipe.

production loss—The difference between the raw or "as purchased" (AP) weight and the prepared or "edible portion" (EP) weight.

purchase specification—A concise description of the quality, size, weight, count, and other quality factors desired for a particular item.

standard dinner cost worksheet—A format for determining standard food costs for all items that are combined in a menu selection.

standard food cost percentage—The planned food cost percentage against which actual food costs are measured.

standard portion cost—The cost of preparing and serving one portion of food or one drink item according to the standard recipe.

standard portion size—The quantity (for example, weight, number of ounces or cost) of a menu item to be derived from a standard recipe.

standard recipe—A formula for producing a food or beverage item. The formula provides a summary of ingredients, the required quantity of each, specific preparation procedures, portion size and portioning equipment, garnish information, and any other information necessary to prepare the item.

standard recipe file—An electronic record that contains recipes for menu items. Important data included are recipe code number, recipe name, ingredients, preparation instructions, number of portions, portion size, cost of ingredients, menu selling price, and food cost percentage.

standard yield—Results when an item is produced according to established standard production procedures outlined in the standard recipe; for example, if the standard purchase specifications are followed and a meat item is properly trimmed, cooked, and portioned, the actual yield should closely approximate the standard yield.

sub-recipe—A recipe that yields an "ingredient" such as sauce which is used for another recipe.

yield—The net weight or volume of a food item after it has been processed and made ready for sale to the guest.

yield factor—See yield percentage.

yield percentage—The ratio of servable weight to original weight, calculated by dividing the servable weight by the original weight and multiplying by 100 to change the decimal to a percentage.

**Review Questions** ————————————————————————————

1. What problems arise when standard food purchase specifications are not used?

2. How can existing procedures for preparing foods be incorporated into standard recipes?

3. How can knowledge of standard yields assist food buyers in determining which products are the "best" buy?

4. What is a standard portion size? What are advantages to its use?

5. Why are standard portion costs important?

6. How are standard portion costs developed?

7. What purpose does a "high warning flag" serve in a standard recipe file which is part of recipe management software?

8. What is meant by "chaining recipes"?

9. What can (should) be done if ingredient costs for standard recipes increase significantly? How does this increase affect standard portion costs?

10. How are the standard food costs for a complete dinner developed?

11. What is the primary advantage of using ideal costs for calculating standard food costs?

**Internet Sites** ——————————————————————————————————

For more information, visit the following Internet sites. Remember that Internet addresses can change without notice. If the site is no longer there, you can use a search engine to look for additional sites.

Associations

American Culinary Federation (ACF)
http://www.acfchefs.org

American Hotel & Lodging Association (AH&LA)
http://www.ahlaonline.org

American School Food Service Association (ASFSA)
http://www.asfsa.org

Club Managers Association of America (CMAA)
http://www.cmaa.org

The Educational Foundation of NRA
http://www.edfound.org

The Educational Institute of AH&LA
http://www.ei-ahla.org

Hospitality Financial and Technology Professionals
http://www.hftp.org

Institute of Food Technologies
http://www.ift.org

International Hotel and Restaurant Association
http://www.ih-ra.com

National Association of College and
University Food Services
http://www.nacufs.org

National Restaurant Association (NRA)
http://www.restaurant.org

Food and Beverage Resources

Club Management Online
http://www.club–mgmt.com/dining/
index.html

Cookbooks Online
http://www.cookbooks.com

CuisineNet
http://www.cuisinenet.com

Microbrewery and brewpub guide
http://www.realbeer.com

Prepared Foods. Product development,
ingredients, suppliers
http://www.preparedfoods.com

Management Companies

ARAMARK
http://www.aramark.com

Bon Appétit Management Company
http://www.bamco.com

Compass Group
http://www.compass–na.com

Sodexho Marriott
http://www.sodexhomarriott.com

The Wood Company
http://www.woodco.com

Publications—Online and Printed

Bon Appétit
http://food.epicurious.com

Club Management Magazine
http://www.club–mgmt.com

Electronic Gourmet Guide
http://www.foodwine.com

Food and Hospitality Magazine
http://www.foodserviceworld.com

Food Management
http://www.foodservicesearch.com

Food Network: CyberKitchen
http://www.foodtv.com

Food Processing: The Magazine of
Strategy, Technology and Trends
http://www.foodprocessing.com

Gourmet
http://food.epicurious.com

Internet Food Channel
http://www.foodchannel.com

International Hotel and Restaurant
Association journal
www.hotelsmag.com

International Journal of Hospitality
Management
http://www.mcb.co.uk/ijchm.htm

Journal of the American Dietetic
Association
http://www.eatright.org/
journaltoc.html

Journal of Nutrition, publication of American Society of Nutritional Sciences
http://nutrition.org

Lodging Food and Beverage
http://www.lodgingnews.com/lodgingfnb/

Lodging Hospitality Online
http://www.lhonline.com

Lodging News, journal of the American Hotel & Lodging Association
http://www.ei-ahla.org/webs/lodging/index.html

Nation's Restaurant News
http://www.nrn.com

On the Rail—News for Food Professionals
http://www.ontherail.com

Restaurants and Institutions magazine
http://www.rimag.com

Restaurant Business, Food Service, and ID magazines
http://www.foodservicetoday.com

Restaurant Hospitality
www.foodservicesearch.com

Restaurants and Institutions
http://www.rimag.com

Restaurants USA, publication of National Restaurant Association
http://www.restaurant.org/rusa

World Hospitality, management magazine for hotel executives.
http://www.worldhospitality.com

Problems

Problem 1

Several yield tests for roasting steamship rounds have been carefully undertaken. A summary of results (average per round) follows:

$$
\begin{aligned}
\text{As purchased (AP) weigh} &= \text{22 lb 7 oz} \\
\text{Servable Weight} &= \text{17 lb 10 oz} \\
\text{Cost (AP)} &= \text{\$6.95 per lb}
\end{aligned}
$$

a. What is the cost per servable pound?

b. Use the above information to determine the number of pounds of steamship rounds to purchase for a weekend buffet being planned for 275 guests (six [EP—on the plate] ounces will be served to each guest)

c. Use the above information to calculate a cost factor and then use the cost factor to determine the revised cost per servable pound when the AP price of the round rises to $7.45 per pound.

d. Using the revised cost per servable pound, calculate the per portion cost for the six-ounce portion which will be provided on the buffet.

Problem 2

A yield test is done on three beef rounds. The as-purchased (AP) and edible portion (EP) data is shown below:

	AP (Original) Weight	EP (Servable) Weight
round #1	19lb-12 oz	16lb-20z
round #2	21lb-13oz	17lb-15oz
round #3	20lb-9oz	16lb-14oz

a. What is the yield ratio (ratio of servable weight to original weight) for each round?

b. What do the percentage numbers generated in the above calculations mean?

c. What is the *average* yield ratio (ratio of servable weight to original weight) for the three rounds calculated above?

d. What is the cost per servable pound for each of the above rounds if the purchase (AP) cost is $6.15 per pound?

e. What do the costs per servable pound for the 3 rounds in Question D actually represent?

f. What is the *average* cost per servable pound in Question D?

g. How many pounds of round must be purchased to serve 5 ounces (edible portion—on the plate) to 300 guests using the average yield ratio calculated in Question C?

h. How many steamship rounds must be purchased to prepare the required number of portions needed for the banquet?

Problem 3

Following is cost per servable pound and AP price information for steamship rounds purchased by three restaurants.

Restaurant	Cost per Servable Pound	AP Price
A	$8.95	$5.95
B	$10.12	$6.10
C	$11.70	$6.20

a. What is the cost factor for each restaurant?

b. How can a restaurant manager use the cost factor?

Problem 4

What is the new cost per servable pound using cost factors in Problem 3 above when the AP price changes in each restaurant?

Restaurant	New AP Price	Cost Factor
A	$6.20	1.50
B	$6.35	1.66
C	$6.75	1.89

Problem 5

The original recipe yields 75 five–ounce servings; the chef desires 100 six-ounce servings. What is the new quantity for each of the following ingredients in the recipe? (Note: Express the revised quantities in amounts which are easiest for the cooks to weigh/measure)

Ingredient	Original Quantity
Brown Sugar	2 pounds
Fluid Milk	3 quarts
Dry Mustard	1 tablespoon

Problem 6

What is the easiest way to express each of the following in a standard recipe?

_____	=	4 cups
_____	=	16 oz
_____	=	7 tsp
_____	=	4 tbs
_____	=	10 cups
_____	=	10 tsp
_____	=	18 qts
_____	=	31 ounces

Problem 7

What is the adjustment factor in each of the following situations?

Original Recipe	New Recipe (Desired Yield)
60 3-oz servings	80 3-oz servings
70 5-oz servings	45 5-oz servings
80 $^{1}/_{2}$-cup servings	100 $^{1}/_{2}$-cup servings
50 $^{3}/_{4}$-cup servings	35 $^{3}/_{4}$-cup servings

Problem 8

What is the adjustment factor in each of the following situations?

Original Recipe	New Recipe (Desired Yield)
60 1-cup servings	75 $^{3}/_{4}$-cup servings
45 $^{3}/_{4}$-cup servings	30 $^{1}/_{2}$-cup servings
90 4-oz servings	80 6-oz servings
125 3-oz servings	200 4-oz servings

Problem 9

What is the quantity of each ingredient which is required to produce the desired recipes?

Ingredient	Original Quantity	Desired Recipe Adjustment Factor
Brown Sugar	3 pounds 12 oz	1.4
Fluid Whole Milk	2 quarts	1.4
Salt	1 $^1/_2$ tablespoons	1.4

Problem 10

Cost the following recipe and calculate the per portion cost:

Recipe: Baked Lasagna
Yield: 30 servings

Ingredient	Amount Needed	Purchase Unit	Cost/ Purchase Unit
Lasagna Noodles	3 lb	10 lb box	$11.71
Garlic Cloves	6 cloves	Lb	1.01
Olive Oil	$^3/_4$ cups	4-1 gal case	62.09
Onion, diced	3 cups	20 lb	14.33
Ground Beef	3 lb	10 lb poly bag	22.17
Tomato Sauce	3 qts	6# 10/case	16.25
Oregano	1 $^1/_2$ tsp	5 oz can	1.93
Ricotta cheese	3 cup	2-5 lb/case	13.70
Mozzarella cheese	2 $^1/_4$ lb	5 lb	14.55
Romano cheese	$^3/_4$ cup	5 lb	22.97

Hints:

Conversions are available from: Francis T. Lynch, *The Book of Yields,* 5th ed. (Sonora, Calif.: Chef's Desk, 2000).

Onion   3.72 cups per pound
Garlic   15 cloves per head; 1.85 ounces per head
Oregano   one tablespoon = $^1/_{10}$ ounce
Ricotta cheese   8.68 ounces per cup
Romano cheese (assume similar to parmesan)   4.7 cups per pound

Chapter Appendix

These weight and measurement conversions can be used for chapter problems and for questions that arise in food and beverage operations.

Weight & Measurement Conversions

kilogram × 2.204 = pounds (1 kg = 2.2 lb)

grams × 0.035 = ounces (100 g = 3.5 oz)

ounce × 28 = grams (1 oz = 28 g)

liter × 2.1 = pints (1 liter = 2.1 pt)

liter × 1.06 = quarts (1 liter = 1.06 qts)

cups × 0.24 = liter (5 c = 1.05 liter)

gallons × 3.8 = liter (1 gal = 3.8 liter)

Celsius temperature × 9/5, add 32 = ° Fahrenheit   Note: $9/5 = 1.8$

Fahrenheit temperature minus 32, × 5/9 = ° Celsius   Note: $5/9 = .55$

0° Celsius = 32° Fahrenheit

100° Celsius = 212° Fahrenheit

---

3 teaspoons = 1 tablespoon	2 cups = 1 pint
4 tablespoons = $1/4$ cup	4 cups = 1 quart
8 tablespoons = $1/2$ cup	4 quarts = 1 U.S. gallon
16 tablespoons = 1 cup	8 quarts = 1 peck (dry)
1 cup = 8 fluid ounces	16 ounces = 1 pound

200°F. to 205°F.	= 95°C.
220°F. to 225°F.	= 105°C.
245°F. to 250°F.	= 120°C.
275°F. to 275°F.	= 135°C.
300°F. to 305°F.	= 150°C.
325°F. to 330°F.	= 165°C.
345°F. to 350°F.	= 175°C.
370°F. to 375°F.	= 190°C.
400°F. to 405°F.	= 205°C.
425°F. to 430°F.	= 220°C.
445°F. to 450°F.	= 230°C.
470°F. to 475°F.	= 260°C.
500°F.	= 175°C.

(continued)

WEIGHT	VOLUME
grams/pounds/ounces	liters/gallons/quarts/pints/cups/ounces

1 kilogram = 2.204 pounds	1 milliliter = 0.03 ounces
1 gram = 0.035 ounces	1 liter = 4.4 cups
1 pound = 0.454 kilograms	1 liter = 2.1 pints
1 ounce = 28 grams	1 liter = 1.06 quarts
	1 liter = 0.26 gallons
	1 teaspoon = 5 milliliter
	1 tablespoon = 15 milliliter
	1 fluid ounce = 28 millilitre
	1 cup = 0.24 liter
	1 pint = 0.47 liter
	1 quart = 0.95 liter
	1 gallon = 3.8 liter

$1/4$ tsp = 1.25 ml	1 c = .24 liter
$1/2$ tsp = 2.5 ml	1 $1/4$ c = .3 liter
$3/4$ tsp = 3.75 m	I $1/2$ c = .36 liter
1 tsp = 5 ml	1 pints (pt) = .47 liter
1 $1/2$ tsp = 7.5 ml	2 c = .48 liter
1 $1/4$ tsp = 6.25 ml	2 $1/2$ c = .6 liter
1 $3/4$ tsp = 8.75 ml	3 c = .72 liter
2 tsp = 10 ml	3 $1/2$ c = .84 liter
1 tablespoon (tbs) = 15 ml	1 quart (qt) = 0.95 liter
2 tbs = 30 ml	4 c = .96 liter
1 fluid ounces (fl oz) = 30 ml	4 $1/2$ c = 1.08 liter
$1/4$ cup (c) = .06 liter	5 c = 1.2 liter
$1/2$ c = .12 liter	5 $1/2$ c = 1.32 liter
$3/4$ c = .18 liter	1 ounce (oz) = 28 grams (g)
	1 lb = 0.45 kg

Chapter 4 Outline

The Budget Process: An Overview
    Budgeting in Multi-Unit Operations
    Budget Reforecasting
Three Steps of Budget Development
    Step 1: Calculate Projected Revenue
        Levels
    Step 2: Determine Profit Requirements
    Step 3: Calculate Projected Expense
        Levels
Budget Development: An Example
    Step 1: Calculate Projected Revenue
        Levels
    Step 2: Determine Profit Requirements
    Step 3: Calculate Projected Expense
        Levels
    The Operating Budget as a Control
        Tool
Computers and the Budget Process
    Electronic Spreadsheets
    Cell Contents
    Recalculation Feature
Cost-Volume-Profit Analysis
    CVP Assumptions and Limitations
    The Basic CVP Equation
    CVP Example: The Lumberjack Cafe
    CVP Example: The Plantation Grill

Competencies

1. Describe the importance and function of an operating budget as a planning and control tool. (pp. 95–96)

2. Distinguish bottom-up budgeting from top-down budgeting. (pp. 96–97)

3. Identify factors that managers consider when projecting revenues in the budgeting process. (pp. 97–98)

4. Identify how fixed, variable, and mixed costs change in response to changes in the sales volume of a food and beverage operation. (p. 101)

5. Distinguish the mark-up method from the percentage method of estimating expenses in the budgeting process. (p. 102)

6. Calculate and interpret variances for revenue and expense items for food and beverage operations. (pp. 103–112)

7. Given relevant cost factors, use a cost-volume-profit equation to calculate the revenues required to reach desired profit levels. (pp. 115–121)

Operations Budgeting and Cost-Volume-Profit Analysis

In COMMERCIAL food and beverage operations, budgets are planning and control tools because they forecast future revenues, expenses, and profits. In non-commercial food and beverage operations, budgets are just as important. They help to ensure that planned expenses do not exceed anticipated revenues and, if required, that an operating surplus ("profit") can be generated. An operating budget is not an obstacle to efficient performance to be prepared and followed only when top management insists. In fact, operating budgets are critical for planning the profit requirements of food and beverage operations. The budget is your best forecast for the future.

Operating budgets are an excellent source of estimated revenue and cost information which can represent planned performance standards. Actual operating data can be compared against budgeted information to determine the extent to which financial plans are attained.

Establishing cost standards is only one use of this important control tool, and in this chapter we will see that an operating budget must be developed for many other purposes. This chapter also examines an important financial planning tool—cost-volume-profit (CVP) analysis. Managers can use CVP analysis to determine the revenues required at any desired profit level. Sometimes referred to as "break-even analysis," CVP reviews the relationships among costs, revenue, and profits associated with alternative plans.

The Budget Process: An Overview

An **operating budget** is a plan that estimates how much revenue will be generated and what expenses will be incurred to meet financial requirements and goals. There are several different types of budgets—for example: long- and short-term, capital, and cash. The type of budget most useful to a food and beverage operation is a short-term, (one-year) operating budget, which covers items affecting the income statement. The budget is a constant reminder of the amount of revenue planned. And, just as crucial for purposes of control, information stemming from the budget limits the amount of allowable expenses. If these limits are exceeded, budgeted profits decrease unless expenses are reduced in other areas and/or revenue increases beyond the anticipated level.

Once developed, the budget becomes an important part of the control process. The budget plan tells managers how much money can be spent in each expense category. When actual revenue falls below forecasted levels and/or when actual expenses exceed budget estimates, managers know there may be problems. Corrective action can then be implemented on a timely basis. A current period's budget is used to develop the budgets for the next fiscal period. Information from the current budget is the basis for beginning the budget process for the next fiscal year.

Because the budget provides anticipated revenue and cost figures, it enables the calculation of a budgeted food cost percentage (budgeted food cost divided by budgeted food revenue multiplied by 100) and a budgeted beverage cost percentage (budgeted beverage cost divided by budgeted beverage revenue multiplied by 100). In a similar way, benchmarks for all other expenses—such as labor and energy costs—can also be calculated. These budget percentages can later be compared with percentages representing actual operating results to measure the food and beverage manager's effectiveness in meeting budget goals.

Managers have two special concerns when they establish operating budget standards. The goals set for revenue, profit requirements, and operating expenses must be attainable and must not compromise established quality requirements. If standards are impossible to attain, personnel may get frustrated and the operation could deteriorate. For example, if food costs have averaged 45 percent, achieving a budgeted goal of 38 percent may not be possible, at least within a single fiscal period. Furthermore, food and beverage managers are concerned about quality standards. In our example, the 38 percent projected food cost could be achieved by raising prices, reducing portion sizes, or purchasing lower quality products. However, these procedures may be unacceptable because they will reduce quality and perceived value for the operation's guests. Management should set minimum quality standards based upon the expectations of the target markets. This helps ensure that standards will not be compromised as the budget plan is developed and implemented.

When necessary, management can use the budget not only to evaluate past efforts but also to plan corrective action for the future. Since the budget helps define responsibilities, management personnel can be held responsible for meeting revenue goals and keeping all operating costs within budgeted limits. When budget figures are exceeded or underspent, responsibility can correctly be assigned to the manager in charge.

In small food and beverage operations, the owner/manager generally develops the budget. In larger operations, other staff members provide important help. For example, department heads, whose performance will be judged by the extent to which they attain budget goals, might be assigned to plan expense levels for their areas of responsibility, in consultation with senior management personnel. In still larger operations, a budget committee may review department revenue and expense plans before a final property-wide budget is approved.

Budgeting in Multi-Unit Operations

The budget development process described later in this chapter works well in a single-unit operation where all profit must be generated by a single property. But how should budgets be developed in multi-unit operations where ownership is concerned about total profits from all operations?

There are basically two methods used to develop operating budgets in multi-unit operations. The most common method uses a **bottom-up budgeting** approach in which operating budgets are assembled at the unit level and are "rolled" up the organization. Another approach is referred to as **top-down budgeting**. With this plan, budgets are developed at the corporate level and are then passed down to lower organizational levels, with each successively lower level becoming responsible for a specific segment of the budget.

The main advantage of using bottom-up budgeting is that budget plans are specifically geared to the individual operation. When budgets are developed for a specific operation by the unit manager, the lower level participation yields a budget that is "our plan," not a plan thrust upon lower management by higher organizational levels. The "ownership" this creates helps the unit manager recognize the importance—and feasibility—of the operating budget. Likewise, bottom-up budgeting enables budget planners to focus on specific units and special problems that are likely to be encountered.

Unfortunately, corporate-level managers encounter a problem when the sum of profits anticipated by individual units, generating their own operating budgets, does not equal the profit requirements of the corporation. For example, a restaurant company may be owned by a parent organization that mandates a profit contribution larger than that which is planned to be generated by the individual units. This points to an advantage of top-down budgeting.

In addition to helping plan for corporate-level profit expectations, top-down budgeting has other potential advantages. For example, unit managers in specific properties may not be aware of marketing commitments, advertising campaigns, menu changes, and other factors that can have a significant impact upon operating budgets within an individual unit.

In actual practice, budget planners in multi-unit organizations use a give-and-take method that first develops tentative budget plans and then modifies them to be realistic expectations for individual properties. Psychological aspects of budget development must also be considered and incorporated into budget development strategies. For example, unit managers may wish to send conservative estimates "up the organization," and, conversely, top-level managers may wish to suggest more aggressive budget goals.

Budget Reforecasting

Budgets are developed several months before the start of the food and beverage operation's fiscal year. As such, future events that affect revenue and expense levels cannot be accurately forecasted. Since the operating budget is a critical control tool, it is important to have updated information against which to compare actual operating results.

Many food and beverage operations use a method of reforecasting to update budgets. For example, if revenue trends are significantly different than expected, revised revenue estimates for the budget may be developed. This same approach is used to consider realistic expense estimates based upon actual performance during the earlier parts of the budget year.

Reforecasting is most easily accomplished when all expenses are expressed as a percentage of revenue. Then, as revenue estimates increase or decrease, affected operating expenses can be adjusted accordingly.

When reforecasting is done, food and beverage managers can use information from income statements to compare actual operating results with:

- Budgeted revenue and expense levels—both for the current period and for cumulative to-date results during the operating year.

- Reforecasted revenue and expense information—both for the month and fiscal year-to-date.

Three Steps of Budget Development

There are three major steps in the process of developing a budget. First, forecasts of expected revenue are determined. Second, required profit levels for the food and beverage operation are calculated. Third, an appropriate method is used to calculate projected costs incurred in generating the forecasted revenue. Although it is useful to divide the process of budget development into these three steps, the last two steps really belong to the same phase of budget development because the profit requirement can be regarded as one of the "costs" assessed in calculating expenses. This concept of treating profit as a cost is explained later in this chapter.

Step 1: Calculate Projected Revenue Levels

The first step in the budget development process is to estimate revenue levels. In hotel and restaurant operations, forecasts are normally made separately for food and beverage revenues. This helps managers pinpoint operating problems during the budget period. When budgets are based on combined food and beverage revenues, managers may not be able to easily identify operating problems during the budget period. However, when accurate guest check averages are available, some managers combine food and beverage revenues when developing budgets. In this case, revenue forecasts are based on the number of guests anticipated for the period covered by the budget. Revenue forecasts are determined by multiplying the number of anticipated guests by the amount of the average guest check. Depending on a number of other factors, this forecast may be increased (for example, if selling prices are planned to increase during the period covered by the budget) or decreased (for example, if fewer guests are anticipated because of major road construction in front of the restaurant).

Projected revenue calculations should be made at least monthly. Calculating revenue projections on a weekly basis would provide even more specific information and perhaps increased accuracy. Individual estimates can then be combined into an annual revenue forecast. By using either monthly or weekly projections, actual revenue can later be compared with budgeted revenue—and actual expenses with budgeted expenses—in time for corrective action, if necessary. Generally, figures for past revenue levels can be obtained from monthly income statements. Collecting revenue figures is made relatively easy by today's common use of computerized systems that list monthly cumulative "to-date" statistics. This also makes it easy to notice trends between fiscal periods.

There are many factors that affect the development of revenue forecasts. In fact, anything that can influence revenue levels also affects the development of revenue forecasts. For instance, internal sales promotion plans or scheduled remodeling could have a strong impact on revenue. Consequently, projected revenue for the coming fiscal period may need to be adjusted to account for these plans. Important factors to consider in determining revenue estimates include revenue histories, current factors, economic variables, and other factors.

Revenue Histories. Useful forecasts for the new budget period can be developed by analyzing past revenue levels and identifying trends. For example, if examining revenue histories shows that food and beverage revenue has increased by an average of eight percent for each of the past five years, then revenue for the upcoming period could be estimated by simply adding eight percent to the current revenue level. This assumes that the revenue growth of the past will continue in the future.

Current Factors. There are many factors over which the property has little or no control that may affect revenue during the new budget period. For example, new competition, street improvement projects, or even the weather may have a strong impact on revenue levels. Social issues, such as liability laws regarding the sale and service of alcoholic beverages, may affect alcoholic beverage revenue.[1] Budgeted revenue figures that are based on revenue histories and trend studies would need to be adjusted if any of these factors currently affect the property.

Economic Variables. As costs increase during periods of high inflation, selling prices for food and beverage products must also be increased. At the same time, the public's habits and lifestyles are affected by economic conditions. When inflation rises, guests may demand greater value for their money. Some guests may "trade down" and replace their usual dining experiences with less expensive meals in lower-priced restaurants. Other guests may simply "trade out" and enjoy more meals at home with their families.

Other Factors. Properties offering both food and beverages must estimate total revenue levels for both services. As noted previously, when making projections for food and beverage operations, revenue and expenses should normally be kept separate so that, subsequently, each can be controlled separately. Many lodging properties use the concept of **derived demand**, in which estimates of room revenue are used to help project revenue from food, beverages, and other revenue centers based upon guest spending patterns that have been developed from in-house studies. The hotel food and beverage manager must still calculate the impact of banquet operations and local community spending patterns separately to determine the total operating budget for the food and beverage department.

Special Concerns in Forecasting Beverage Revenue. Few small beverage operations develop specific budget revenue estimates for individual beverage products such as beer, wine, liquor, and soft drinks. Rather, they assume that each beverage product will generate the same percentage of total beverage revenue in each budget period. For example, if liquor has been responsible for 70 percent of beverage revenue in past years, beverage managers may assume that it will continue to contribute 70 percent of future beverage revenue. However, beverage managers should carefully review trends in these percentage-of-revenue statistics. Wine, sparkling water, and non-alcoholic specialty drinks are generating an increased proportion of beverage revenue in many places. Where this is true, other products, such as liquor, will contribute a reduced percentage of revenue.

Decisions regarding the percentage of total beverage revenue applicable to each product are relatively easy to make when electronic cash registers or other point-of-sale devices are used to record information about beverage revenue by category. In operations that do not use computerized equipment or keep records on this basis, it may be necessary to base product revenue percentages on administrative judgment. In this case, perhaps a trial period for keeping careful product revenue records may provide some hard data to back up estimates of product revenue percentages.

Step 2: Determine Profit Requirements

There are two basic ways to treat profit when budgets are developed: (1) regarding profit as "what is left over from revenue after subtracting expenses," and (2) treating profit as if it were a "cost." The traditional approach determines profit by deducting estimated expenses from forecasted revenue:

$$\text{Profit} = \text{Revenue} - \text{Expenses}$$

A better approach treats profit as a "cost." This approach determines profit requirements before estimating expenses so that, in effect, the property pays itself first. Money remaining after profit requirements have been deducted from revenue is then used to pay for the operation's expenses. While the traditional method uses estimated expense levels to determine profit, this approach uses forecasted revenue and required profit levels to determine allowable expenses:

$$\text{Revenue} - \text{Required Profit} = \text{Allowable Operating Expenses}$$

With this formula, the food and beverage manager is concerned about achieving budgeted profit levels while at the same time assuring sufficient revenue to meet expenses. Using this plan for developing a budget, the food and beverage manager wants to (a) generate revenue, (b) plan for the desired operating profit, (c) have sufficient money remaining to meet the expenses required to generate the revenue, and (d) achieve all this without sacrificing quality requirements.

The "profit as cost" approach to budget development requires that profit levels be assessed after revenue is determined. How should profit levels be determined? The answer to this question depends on the specific nature of each food and beverage operation.

For a freestanding restaurant or other food service operation, the principles behind the determination of profit can be understood in terms of the accounting concepts of "return on investment" and/or "return on assets." Investors require that the property provide them with a reasonable return on their investment and that management safeguard the assets they have invested in the operation. This entitles investors to require additional profit to help compensate for the risk of their investment. In light of the high rate of restaurant failures, this risk is often great and, therefore, required returns are often high.

In lodging operations, investment requirements can be generated from the rooms department, food and beverage department, and perhaps other revenue centers as well. The owner, working with the general manager, must first determine the amount of profit required from the lodging operation. Then, the staff must allocate profit responsibilities among the different departments based on expected levels of departmental revenue. The food and beverage manager will ultimately be responsible for generating a required amount of profit and will spread this responsibility between revenue-producing centers such as dining rooms, banquets, beverage operations, and room service.

What happens when it is not possible to generate the required profit levels given the amount of estimated revenue? Does this mean that this method of treating profit is incorrect? On the contrary, this situation proves that the method works very well! Instead of waiting until the budget year is almost over, food and beverage managers using this method are able to determine at the time the budget is being developed whether required profit levels can be generated. If they cannot, alternatives can be considered early in the planning process. If profit requirements are known at the time the budget is developed, plans to generate required profit (such as increasing revenue and/or reducing expenses) can be formulated.

Step 3: Calculate Projected Expense Levels

Once revenue volumes are estimated and profit requirements are determined, expenses required to generate the projected level of revenue can be estimated. These expenses include: cost of food sold, labor expense, supplies expense, utilities, marketing expense, rent expense, depreciation expense, insurance expense, and many other expenses as well. Budget planning requires that management examine how these expenses are affected by changes in revenue volume. In this context, costs can be seen as fixed, variable, or mixed (partly fixed and partly variable).

Fixed costs are costs that remain constant in the short run, even though revenue volume may vary. Common examples of fixed costs are: management salaries, rent expense, insurance expense, property taxes, depreciation expense, and interest expense.

Variable costs are costs that vary in relation to changes in the volume of business. If variable costs are strictly defined as costs that vary in exact proportion to total revenue, then few costs, if any, are truly variable. However, several costs come close to this definition and may legitimately be considered variable costs. For example, food and beverage costs increase as revenue volume increases simply because more food and beverage products must be purchased to prepare and serve the additional meals and drinks. Other examples of variable costs are labor costs for waged personnel and the cost of some supplies used in food production and service areas.

Mixed costs are costs that contain both fixed and variable cost elements. These costs are also referred to as semi-variable or semi-fixed costs. Although, in practice, the variable element of a mixed cost may not be directly proportional to usage or revenue volume, this assumption is generally accepted. An example of a mixed cost is telephone expense. One portion of this expense would be the fixed cost of the system; the other portion would be the variable cost of calls made during a specified period.[2]

Managers must consider each of these types of expenses as the budget is developed. The best method for estimating expense levels is, of course, the one that is most useful to the individual operation. Several widely used methods are described in the following sections.

Simple Mark-Up Method. Perhaps the most common method of estimating food and beverage operating expenses is the **mark-up** method, which is based on the current expense level. This amount is then increased (or perhaps decreased, though this is rare) to arrive at the expense level for the new operating budget. For example, if the current month's food cost is $135,000, and a 12 percent cost (.12, as a decimal) increase is anticipated for the next budget period, the adjusted food cost for the new budget period is:

Current Month's Food Cost $\times$ Cost Increase = Anticipated Cost Increase

$135,000 $\times$ .12 = $16,200

Current Month's Food Cost + Anticipated Cost Increase = Adjusted Food Cost

$135,000 + $16,200 = $151,200

Note: the above calculations are the same as estimating a 112 percent food cut for the new period (current month's cost [$135,000] ($\times$) anticipated cost [112%] = $151,200).

Budgeted food costs for each month are totaled to arrive at the estimated food cost for the new budget year. Total projected costs for the entire food and beverage operation are then determined by combining similar calculations for beverage and all other expense categories.

One problem with this method is that, by basing projections on current expense levels, it assumes all costs were reasonable during the current year. If, in fact, some costs were too high—because of waste, theft, or some other reason—that inefficiency is extended into the new budget.

Percentage Method. Another frequently used method of estimating food and beverage operating expenses is the **percentage method**, which is based on the current percentage of each expense relative to revenue. Food and beverage cost percentages are calculated by dividing food or beverage cost by food or beverage revenue and multiplying by 100. The percentage method for forecasting food and beverage expenses assumes that the same cost percentages from the current period will continue to apply to the projected revenue for the new budget period. For example, if the current beverage cost percentage is 24 percent, when the new budget is developed, 24 percent of the estimated beverage revenue is allocated for beverage costs.

Like the mark-up method, the percentage method assumes that the current cost percentage is reasonable. This has the potential disadvantage of continuing an inefficient operation if the current budgeted cost percentage is higher than it should be. Close analysis to ensure that the budget allows for the planned profit goal can offset this disadvantage.

Zero-Based Budget Calculations. A third method, **zero-based budgeting**, avoids the disadvantages of the other two by starting over from zero instead of extending costs or cost percentages transferred from the current period. This method takes more time and involves starting at a zero expense level for each category of cost and building up to new budgeted expense levels, justifying each step along the way. As a result, it yields expense information designed specifically for the period covered by the new operating budget. Forecasting costs in this way provides a very useful control tool for later comparing budgeted costs with actual costs. However, because it requires a significant commitment of time to justify each cost estimate, the zero-based budget is not frequently used in commercial food and beverage operations.

Special Concerns in Estimating Beverage Expenses. Separate costs for different beverage products may be considered in budget development. For example, suppose 70 percent (.70) of beverage revenue is estimated to be from liquor, and the beverage cost for liquor is 28 percent (.28) of its revenue. If beverage revenue equals $100,000, the total cost of liquor is:

% of Beverage Revenue (Liquor)		Total Beverage Revenue		Beverage Cost (Liquor)		Total Cost
	×		×		=	
.70	×	$100,000	×	.28	=	$19,600

The same process is used for estimating costs of beer, wine, and soft drinks. The sum of the costs for the separate beverage products will be the total beverage cost to be used for budget calculations.

Estimating Other Expenses. So far, our discussion of budget development has emphasized calculating the allowable food and beverage costs based upon forecasted revenue. However, management must also consider the impact of other expenses—such as labor, supplies, and advertising—on the entire budget.

The same basic procedures can be used to estimate costs for all other expenses allocated to the food and beverage department. For example, labor costs represent a significant expense for all types of food service operations. Managers must take the time to objectively assess likely labor cost levels based on estimated revenue. Energy and advertising expenses are other examples of costs that are generally significant and, therefore, demand attention during budget development. However, some categories of expense, such as office supplies, may have little financial impact on the food and beverage operation. Simple mark-ups are likely to be a fast and reasonably accurate way to budget for these expenses.

Budget Development: An Example

The following example illustrates a step-by-step process for developing a budget. Although the example focuses on developing a budget for the food operation, the same procedures can be used to plan a beverage budget. Where applicable, the example includes completed sample budget worksheets accompanied by a discussion reviewing the role of the worksheets in developing operating budget information.

Exhibit 1　Budget Worksheet A: Food Revenue History Analysis

	YEAR 1			YEAR 2			YEAR 3 (Current Year)		
Month	**Revenue**	**Difference (Previous Year)**	**%**	**Revenue**	**Difference (Previous Year)**	**%**	**Revenue**	**Difference (Previous Year)**	**%**
	1	2	3	4	5	6	7	8	9
Jan.	$112,550			$118,420	$5,870	5%	$129,600	$11,180	9%
Feb.	112,430			116,550	4,120	4	125,400	8,850	8
Mar.	112,220			121,375	9,155	8	126,350	4,975	4
Apr.	113,050			119,000	5,950	5	127,450	8,450	7
May	112,975			119,800	6,825	6	126,575	6,775	6
June	112,490			117,550	5,060	4	124,300	6,750	6
July	112,200			122,400	10,200	9	128,500	6,100	5
Aug.	112,950			119,900	6,950	6	124,375	4,475	4
Sept.	112,490			121,540	9,050	8	129,500	7,960	7
Oct.	112,420			122,410	9,990	9	124,650*	2,240	2
Nov.	112,310			121,450	9,140	8	131,150*	9,700	8
Dec.	112,300			120,400	8,100	7	129,200*	8,800	7
Totals	**$1,350,385**			**$1,440,795**	**$90,410**	**7%****	**$1,527,050**	**$86,255**	**6%****

* Estimates (the operating budget is being developed in October for the coming calendar year).
** Percents are rounded.

Step 1: Calculate Projected Revenue Levels

The first step of the budget development process is to forecast revenue levels for the new budget period. As explained earlier in this chapter, these projections can be based initially on the operation's past history.

Assume that the food and beverage operation in this example is currently in its third year. Further assume that this operation keeps revenue history records in its electronic register system. The monthly food revenue information is copied to Budget Worksheet A: Food Revenue History Analysis, which is shown in Exhibit 1. Notice that since next year's budget is being developed in October of the current year, revenue figures for October, November, and December are estimates. The worksheet not only reports revenue for each month, but also indicates the amount of change in dollars and percentages over the same month in the previous year.

Determining Monthly Revenue Differences. To calculate the amount of change in January revenue from Year 2 to Year 3, subtract January revenue for Year 2 (column 4) from the January revenue for Year 3 (column 7):

$$\underset{\text{(column 7)}}{\text{Year 3—January}} - \underset{\text{(column 4)}}{\text{Year 2—January}} = \underset{\text{(column 8)}}{\text{Change in Revenue Dollars}}$$

$$\$129,600 \quad - \quad \$118,420 \quad = \quad \$11,180$$

Note that column 8 shows that January revenue has increased by $11,180.

To calculate the monthly percentage of revenue increase, divide the $11,180 increase (column 8) by January revenue for Year 2, $118,420 (column 4), and multiply by 100. This percentage (column 9) is:

Increase in January Revenue:

$$\frac{\text{Year 2 to Year 3 (col. 8)}}{\underset{\text{(column 4)}}{\text{Year 2—January Revenue}}} \times 100 = \underset{\text{(column 9)}}{\text{Monthly \% of Revenue Increase}}$$

$$\frac{\$11,180}{\$118,420} = .09 \text{ (rounded)} \times 100 = 9\%$$

Determining Annual Revenue Differences. To calculate the annual percentage of revenue differences, perform the same type of calculation using totals at the bottom of the columns. To calculate the current year increase over the previous year:

$$\frac{\underset{\text{Year 2 to Year 3 (col. 8)}}{\text{Increase in Revenue from}}}{\text{Year 2—Revenue (col. 4)}} \times 100 = \underset{\text{(column 9)}}{\text{Annual \% of Revenue Increase}}$$

$$\frac{\$86,255}{\$1,440,745} = .06 \text{ (rounded)} \times 100 = 6\%$$

To calculate the percentage revenue increase in the second year over the first year:

$$\frac{\underset{\text{Year 1 to Year 2 (col. 5)}}{\text{Increase in Revenue from}}}{\text{Year 1—Revenue (col. 1)}} \times 100 = \underset{\text{(column 6)}}{\text{Annual \% of Revenue Increase}}$$

$$\frac{\$90,410}{\$1,350,385} = .07 \text{ (rounded)} \times 100 = 7\%$$

Revenue History Analysis. Analysis of the revenue history shows that food revenue in Year 2 increased 7 percent over Year 1, while food revenue in the current year (Year 3) increased only 6 percent over Year 2. With this knowledge the food service manager should study current economic and other factors to estimate revenue for the next year. Suppose the manager believes the downward trend can be reversed and that revenue will increase by 10 percent during the coming year. The manager can then distribute monthly food revenue projections on Budget Worksheet B: Estimated Monthly Food Revenue for Operating Budget (Exhibit 2) by adding 10 percent to each month's revenue.

While using Worksheet B to distribute revenue, the budget planner can analyze monthly trends and operations. The manager of the food and beverage operation in this example should consider why the increase in percentage of revenue declined in some months, such as March, July, and especially October. The manager can also ask what can be done to continue the high revenue growth in January, February, and November. Furthermore, the manager must determine how much of the revenue increase is real growth and how much is due only to an increase in selling prices.

The total estimated revenue of $1,679,756 for the operating budget in Budget Worksheet B is a 10 percent increase in food revenue over the current year. This revenue of $1,679,756 is the base by which to generate required profits and to meet expenses incurred in producing that revenue from food operations. The next two steps show how to estimate profits and expenses.

Exhibit 2   Budget Worksheet B: Estimated Monthly Food Revenue for Operating Budget

Estimated Monthly Food Revenue for Operating Budget			
Month	Revenue in Current Year	Increase by 10%	Estimated Revenue: New Operating Budget
January	$ 129,600	$ 12,960	$ 142,560
February	125,400	12,540	137,940
March	126,350	12,635	138,985
April	127,450	12,745	140,195
May	126,575	12,658	139,233
June	124,300	12,430	136,730
July	128,500	12,850	141,350
August	124,375	12,438	136,813
September	129,500	12,950	142,450
October	124,650*	12,465	137,115
November	131,150*	13,115	144,265
December	129,200*	12,920	142,120
Totals	**$ 1,527,050**	**$152,706**	**$ 1,679,756**

* Estimates

Step 2: Determine Profit Requirements

Determining the amount of profit expected from the food and beverage operation involves calculating the total profit required from food and beverage revenue. It also involves separating required profit levels for the food operation from the profit required from the beverage operation.

To understand how profit is determined, you need to know how costs are allocated within a food and beverage operation. Although details of cost allocation are beyond the scope of this chapter, some basic principles of cost allocation are discussed in the following section.[3]

Cost Allocation Principles. Food and beverage costs are charged to food and beverage departments, respectively. The application of this principle requires correct assigning of food transfers to the beverage department and beverage transfers to the kitchen.

Other large expenses are divided between the food and beverage departments and prorated according to how much expense each incurs. For example, wages for employees involved in both food and beverage operations—the bookkeeper and purchasing agent—can be prorated based on the percentage of revenue. If 75 percent of the total food and beverage revenue comes from food, then 75 percent of these indirect labor costs could be allocated to the food department. Smaller expenses, such as supplies or equipment, can also be allocated on the basis of a simple revenue percentage.

Budget Worksheet C: Recap and Allocation of Current Costs Between Food and Beverage Operations (Exhibit 3) indicates the total amount (column 2) of each cost (column 1) identified in the restaurant's accounting system. Each cost is then

Exhibit 3   Budget Worksheet C: Recap and Allocation of Current Costs Between Food and Beverage Operations

		Amount Prorated To			
	Total Annual Current Cost	Food		Beverage	
Type of Cost		Revenue = $1,527,050	Percent of Revenue	Revenue = $381,760	Percent of Revenue
1	2	3	4	5	6
Food	$ 534,468	$ 534,468	35%	—	—
Beverage	99,258	—	—	$99,258	26%
Payroll	419,938	366,492	24	53,446	14
Payroll Taxes and Employee Benefits	34,359	30,541	2	3,818	1
Direct Operating Expenses	95,441	76,353	5	19,088	5
Music/Entertainment	61,082	—	—	61,082	16
Advertising	38,176	30,541	2	7,635	2
Utilities	83,988	76,353	5	7,635	2
Administration/General	76,352	61,082	4	15,270	4
Repairs/Maintenance	22,906	15,271	1	7,635	2
Rent	141,252	106,894	7	34,358	9
Real Estate/Property Taxes	22,906	15,271	1	7,635	2
Insurance	38,176	30,541	2	7,635	2
Interest Expense	68,717	61,082	4	7,635	2
Depreciation	57,265	45,812	3	11,453	3
Totals	**$1,794,284**	**$1,450,701**	**95%**	**$343,583**	**90%**

Recap	Total	Food Operation	Beverage Operation
Revenue	$1,908,810	$1,527,050	$ 381,760
Product Cost	633,726	534,468	99,258
Non-Product Cost	1,160,558	916,233	244,325
Total Cost	1,794,284	1,450,701	343,583
Profit Before Tax (Revenue minus Total Cost)	$ 114,526	$ 76,349	$ 38,177

divided between the food and beverage operations according to the applicable revenue percentages. (To simplify the example, no allocations based upon transfers to and from the food and beverage operation are included.)

The figures at the top of columns 3 and 5 on Worksheet C are the current food revenue and beverage revenue, respectively. The current food revenue total of $1,527,050 is transferred from Budget Worksheet B (Exhibit 2). Percentage of revenue (columns 4 and 6) is calculated for each cost by dividing the amount of cost allocated to the operation in the current budget by the total revenue for the operation and multiplying by 100.

Calculating Profit. Profit before taxes for the current year of the food and beverage operation is calculated as follows: total revenue of $1,908,810 minus total costs of $1,794,284 equals $114,526. The profit percentage for the current year is determined by dividing the profit before taxes by total revenue and multiplying by 100:

$114,526 divided by $1,908,810 = .06 (rounded) × 100 = 6 percent. This means that profit before taxes for the current year is 6 percent of total revenue.

Let's suppose that, for next year, the owner wants to realize a before-tax profit of 10 percent of total revenue. Worksheet B (Exhibit 2) calculates food revenue for the next year at $1,679,756. Let's assume that a similar worksheet was prepared for beverage revenue and it estimates next year's beverage revenue at $385,580. Total projected revenue amounts to $2,065,336 ($1,679,756 + $385,580). The dollar amount of the owner's required profit for the next year would then be calculated as $206,534 ($2,065,336 × .10).

To reach this new profit requirement, the food and beverage manager will have to operate the food and beverage program more effectively. The manager will have to increase revenue from the current year and also work to reduce operating costs. Moreover, the manager will have to take the needed steps to achieve the required profit goal without sacrificing quality requirements. This is the control process in action.

Two points should be made about the required profit level. First, determining profit requirements on the basis of revenue alone is not always appropriate. As stated earlier in this chapter, it may be better to express profit requirements as a specified percentage of return on investments or assets. Second, although the required amount of profit can be generated by either food or beverages or both, normally the beverage operation yields a higher profit per dollar of revenue. One approach to spreading required profit between food and beverage operations includes the following:

1. Charge the food operation for direct product costs (food costs).

2. Allocate non-product costs between the food and beverage operations by percentage, as was done for the current year in Budget Worksheet C.

3. Calculate profit required from food revenue:

$$\text{Food Revenue} - \left[\text{Food Costs} + \frac{\text{Allocated Share of}}{\text{Non-Product Costs}}\right] = \frac{\text{Profit Required}}{\text{from Food Revenue}}$$

4. Calculate profit required from beverage revenue:

$$\text{Total Required Profit} - \text{Profit from Food Revenue} = \frac{\text{Profit Required from}}{\text{Beverage Revenue}}$$

Step 3: Calculate Projected Expense Levels

The next step in the budget development process is to estimate the expenses that the food and beverage operation will incur in generating the estimated revenue. Some of these expenses—such as food, beverage, and labor costs, can be considered "variable" in that the amount of the expense changes proportionately with the level of revenue. To project these costs, the planner multiplies each cost's current percentage of revenue, as listed in Budget Worksheet C, by the estimated revenue for the new budget period.

Other expenses such as interest and depreciation are considered fixed because they do not vary with the level of revenue. These expenses are estimated for the

Exhibit 4 Budget Worksheet D: Calculation of Food Operation Costs for Budget

Calculation of Food Operation Costs for Budget			
Category of Cost	**Percent of Food Revenue**	**Estimated Revenue: Budget Year**	**Estimated Cost: Budget Year**
1	2	3	4
Food Cost	35%		$587,915
Payroll	24		403,141
Payroll Taxes/Employee Benefits	2		33,595
Direct Operating Expenses	5		83,988
Music/Entertainment	—		—
Advertising	2		33,595
Utilities	5		83,988
Administration/General	4		67,190
Repairs/Maintenance	1		16,798
Rent	6*		106,894
Real Estate/Property Taxes	1*		15,271
Insurance	2*		30,541
Interest Expense	4*		61,082
Depreciation	3*		45,812
Other (Specify):		$1,679,756	
_____			
_____			
_____			
		Total Estimated Cost:	**$1,569,810**

*These percentages are for fixed costs and are calculated by dividing cost (see Exhibit 3) by estimated food revenue for the new budget year. All percentages are rounded.

budget year using the actual dollar amount for the current year. The estimated cost is then divided by the estimated revenue to determine the budgeted percentage.

The calculations for both variable and fixed budgeted costs are done on Budget Worksheet D: Calculation of Food Operation Costs for Budget (Exhibit 4). Note that the dollar amounts for rent, real estate/property taxes, insurance, interest, and depreciation did not change from the current year's expenses, shown on Budget Worksheet C.

The Operating Budget as a Control Tool

For the operating budget to be a meaningful and workable control tool, it must be in an easy-to-use format, such as Budget Worksheet E: Food Operation Budget (Exhibit 5). Worksheet E is generated each month. The sample is for January—the first month of the new budget year.

1. Column 1 lists food revenue, cost of goods sold (food cost), individual operating expenses, total operating expenses, and profit before taxes in a format similar to an income statement.

2. Column 2 indicates the percentage of food revenue represented by each item as indicated in Budget Worksheet D.

Exhibit 5   Budget Worksheet E: Food Operation Budget

		Budget		Actual			
Item	Budget Percent	Month	Year	Month	Year	Variance	Actual Percent
1	2	3	4	5	6	7	8
Food Revenue	100%	$142,560	$1,679,756	$155,440	$155,440	$12,880	100%
Cost of Goods Sold Food Cost	35	49,896	587,915	51,750	51,750	-1,854	33
Operating Expenses Payroll	24	34,214	403,141	36,400	36,400	-2,186	23
Payroll Tax/Benefits	2	2,851	33,595	3,000	3,000	-149	2
Direct Operating Expenses	5	7,128	83,988	7,900	7,900	-772	5
Music/Entertainment	—	—	—	—	—	—	—
Advertising	2	2,851	33,595	2,851	2,851	0	2
Utilities	5	7,128	83,988	7,190	7,190	-62	5
Administration/General	4	5,702	67,190	5,800	5,800	-98	4
Repairs/Maintenance	1	1,426	16,798	1,400	1,400	26	1
Rent	6	8,908	106,894	8,908	8,908	0	6
Real Estate/Property Taxes	1	1,273	15,271	1,273	1,273	0	1
Insurance	2	2,545	30,541	2,545	2,545	0	2
Interest Expense	4	5,090	61,082	5,090	5,090	0	3
Depreciation	3	3,818	45,812	3,818	3,818	0	2
Other (Specify)	—	—	—	—	—	—	—
Total Operating Expenses	60%*	$82,934	$981,895	$86,175	$86,175	$-3,241	55%*
Profit (Before Tax)	7%	$9,730	$109,946	$17,515	$17,515	$7,785	11%

Food Operation Budget — Month: January

*Because of the rounding of percentages for fixed costs (see Exhibit 4), the sum of the percentages for individual operating expenses is one percentage point higher than this figure.

3. Column 3 lists budgeted revenue, expenses, and the before-tax profit goal of the month. Total food revenue of $142,560 is obtained directly from Budget Worksheet B. To calculate the amount for each variable expense listed in column 1, multiply the budget percentage (column 2) as a decimal by the total monthly revenue of $142,560 (column 3). For example, the monthly payroll expense is:

$$\text{Budget Percentage} \times \text{Food Revenue} = \text{Monthly Payroll Expense}$$
$$.24 \times \$142,560 = \$34,214 \text{ (rounded)}$$

To calculate the monthly amount for fixed expenses, divide the budgeted amount for the entire year (column 4) by 12. For example, the monthly interest expense is calculated as follows:

$$\frac{\$61,082}{12} = \$5,090$$

To find the monthly profit before taxes, subtract food and operating costs from revenue:

$ 142,560	Budgeted Monthly Revenue	
− 49,896	Budgeted Monthly Food Costs	
− 82,934	Budgeted Monthly Operating Costs	
$ 9,730	Budgeted Monthly Profit Before Taxes	

4. Column 4 lists budgeted revenue, expenses, and the before-tax profit goal for the entire year. Total food revenue of $1,679,756 is obtained directly from Budget Worksheet B. Each operating expense—for example, payroll of $403,141—is obtained directly from Budget Worksheet D.

5. Column 5 lists the actual revenue, expenses, and the before-tax profit for the month. Information in this column is entered every month during the time covered by the operating budget. Data is obtained from the same source documents used to develop information for monthly accounting statements.

6. Column 6 tallies information about actual revenue, expenses, and before-tax profit on a cumulative, year-to-date basis. Since January is the first month of the new budget period, the figures in column 6 are the same as those recorded in column 5.

7. Column 7 shows the variance between budgeted and actual amounts. To calculate the variance for a revenue item, subtract budget from actual. Classify the variance as favorable if it is positive or unfavorable if it is negative. For example, the variance in food revenue for January is:

$$\text{Actual} \quad - \quad \text{Budget} \quad = \quad \text{Revenue Variance}$$
$$\$155,440 \quad - \quad \$142,560 \quad = \quad +\$12,880 \text{ (favorable)}$$

The variance for an expense item is determined by subtracting actual from budget. A favorable variance is positive; an unfavorable variance is negative. For example, the variance for direct operating expenses is:

$$\text{Budget} \quad - \quad \text{Actual} \quad = \quad \text{Expense Variance}$$
$$\$7,128 \quad - \quad \$7,900 \quad = \quad -\$772 \text{ (unfavorable)}$$

8. Column 8 provides information about each expense as a percentage of actual food revenue. For example, the actual food cost percentage for January is:

$$\frac{\text{Food Cost}}{\text{Food Revenue}} \times 100 = \text{Food Cost Percentage}$$

$$\frac{\$51,750}{\$155,440} = .33 \times 100 = 33\%$$

Assessing Results. Information in Budget Worksheet E tells the food manager:

- What food revenue, costs, and profits *should be*

- What food revenue, costs, and profits *actually are*

A simple analysis of the variance column on Budget Worksheet E yields important information:

1. The actual food revenue for January was much greater than anticipated. The favorable variance, actual food revenue of $155,440 minus $142,560 planned food revenue, represents an increase in revenue of $12,880.

2. Food costs were $1,854 greater than planned ($49,896 budgeted food cost minus $51,750 actual food cost). This is an unfavorable variance.

3. Although the dollar amount for food costs is expected to be greater since food revenue was also greater than planned, the actual food cost percentage (33 percent as shown in column 8) is less than the planned food cost percentage (35 percent as shown in column 2). This indicates that there is a potential problem with food quality, portion control, or another area; it is unlikely that food cost percentage could be reduced this much unless there were an obvious reason (such as a much lower purchase cost for a high-volume entree).

4. Operating expenses were $3,241 greater than planned ($82,934 budgeted operating expenses minus $86,175 actual operating expenses). This is an unfavorable variance, but it might be explained, at least in part, by the much higher revenue volume.

5. Profit was $7,785 more than planned ($17,515 actual profit minus $9,730 planned profit). This variance is favorable.

In reviewing these results of operations, the most important feature is that actual profit is higher than expected. Not only are the dollars greater, but so is the percentage of profit to total revenue. This means that, while total expenses were higher due to increased revenue, they increased at a smaller percentage of revenue than was budgeted.

A word of caution must be expressed. Just because it appears that expenses are in line, you might want to question the increases in the budgeted expenses. Can higher revenue alone explain the higher-than-budgeted costs, or are there other explanations? Recall that food costs were slightly greater than anticipated. Some further analysis may be appropriate here.

Finally, recognize that it is difficult to generalize about variances after only one month. More accurate and meaningful analysis becomes possible with data from several months.

Computers and the Budget Process

Computers are now in common use for both routine and advanced budgeting applications in all but the smallest operations.[4] The programs designed to best perform these activities are termed electronic spreadsheet software. Electronic spreadsheets are simple in concept, but possess powerful computation capabilities.

Electronic Spreadsheets

Electronic spreadsheets resemble a traditional accounting worksheet since they are organized by rows and columns. The border along the worksheet's left margin typically contains numbers to designate row locations while the top margin contains letters depicting column locations. The intersection of a row and column

Exhibit 6   Electronic Spreadsheet Format

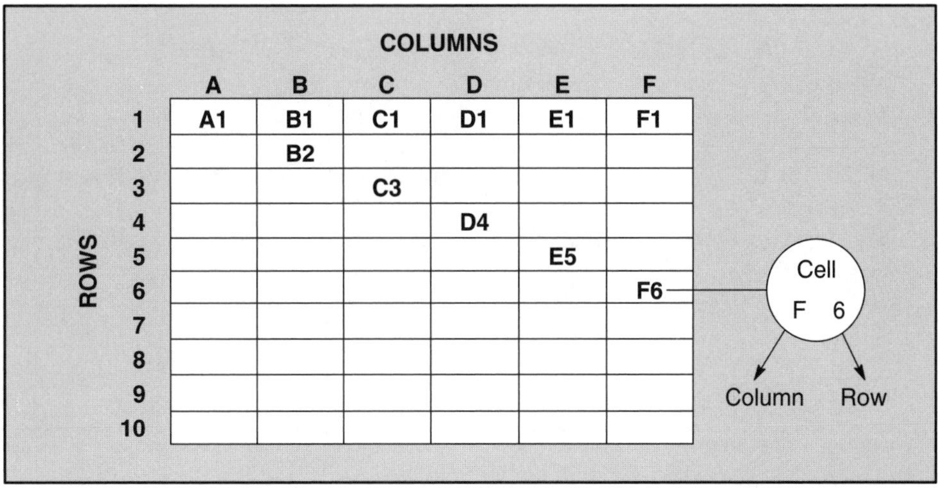

forms a **cell**. A cell address is defined by its respective row and column indicators (see Exhibit 6).

It is important to note that unlike an accountant's worksheet, which is very limited in size, electronic spreadsheets are stored in the computer's extensive memory. Spreadsheets are often so large that their size prohibits them from being displayed in their entirety on a display screen or monitor. At any point in time, the user views only a section, referred to as a window, of an otherwise enormous spreadsheet. The terminal keyboard contains cursor (arrow) keys enabling the user to move from cell to cell and from window to window.

Cell Contents

The food and beverage manager customizes a generic spreadsheet by defining the content of its cells. Electronic spreadsheet cells can contain a label, a number, or a formula. When textual information is entered into a cell it is referred to as a label. Spreadsheet software automatically identifies labels since they are entered from the terminal's typewriter keyboard. Labels assist in the organization of data input and in the comprehensibility of output information. Headings, titles, chart of account lists, and the like typify budgeting labels.

Numeric values, used to produce calculated results, are entered into cells from the keyboard's number keys. The software is capable of identifying numeric input (coming from the numeric keys) similar to the manner in which it recognizes text characters for labels.

Formulas are preceded by special characters (for example, +) or words (for example, sum). These are used so that only the results and not the formula will appear in the addressed cell.

Perhaps the most important benefit of spreadsheet software is its ability to maintain a formula that relates specific cells. For example, consider the spreadsheet in Exhibit 7. Exhibit 7 contains labels in rows 3, 4, 5, 7, and 9. Numeric values appear

Exhibit 7   Sample Food Cost Spreadsheet

	A	B	C	D	E
		Food Cost Spreadsheet			
1					
2					
3		Week 1	Week 2	Week 3	Week 4
4	Food Cost	2500	3000	2750	3275
5	Food Revenue	6500	8000	7775	8400
6					
7	Food Cost %	0.3846	0.3750	0.3537	0.3899
8					
9	Average FC%	0.3758			
10					

in cells B4, C4, D4, E4, B5, C5, D5, and E5. The results of stored formulas are presented in cells B7, C7, D7, E7, and B9. The formula used to produce the output in B7 is + B4/B5. Cell C7 is generated from formula + C4/C5 (note: D7 and E7 are similarly derived). The calculated average food cost percentage found in B9 is computed from this formula: + B7+C7+D7+E7/4.

Formulas, capable of referencing various cells and constants, illustrate the usefulness of spreadsheet programs. They enable someone who has only basic computer skills to direct the computational efforts of a powerful machine.

Recalculation Feature

The budgeting process generally requires many calculations. Moreover, whenever data is altered or extended, numerous recalculations are necessary. Spreadsheet software significantly enhances and streamlines this process since it contains formulas composed of cell addresses and possesses a unique recalculation feature. Spreadsheets can be configured to automatically recalculate all numeric values whenever one value changes. Recalculations are performed in a chaining fashion. As a cell is modified, any and all cells related to it are also changed. In Exhibit 7, the formulas in cells B7, C7, D7, and E7 relate corresponding row 4 and 5 elements. The formula in cell B9, however, depends on the calculated outputs of B7, C7, D7, and E7. Assume week two's food cost was erroneously entered. The data in cell C4 should have been 3200, not 3000. When the cursor is moved to cell C4 and the figure 3200 is entered (replacing 3000), all subsequent computations dependent on this cell data (C7 and B9) will automatically be recalculated. In a manual process, these recalculations would require a working knowledge of the relationship among all data, and would take considerable time to accomplish. There would also be an increased opportunity for making errors in the recalculations.

As noted earlier in this chapter, budget reforecasting is becoming an increasingly used tool to help the food and beverage manager monitor the operation. The recalculation feature of electronic spreadsheet software enables food and beverage managers in all sizes and types of operations to quickly update budget projections by reforecasting revenue levels or expenses when necessary.

Food and beverage managers tend to appreciate spreadsheet output options as much as they do the usefulness of cell contents and automatic recalculations. Many electronic spreadsheet programs provide both text (worksheet) and graphic output formats for any portion of the spreadsheet. Text output consists of a printed copy of the spreadsheet as it appears on the display screen.

The data on a spreadsheet can also be displayed graphically. Graphic options include bar charts, pie charts, or line drawings. Often, a visual presentation of the same data improves comprehension and understanding.

Cost-Volume-Profit Analysis

Cost-volume-profit (CVP) analysis is an analytical process used to determine the revenues required at any desired profit level. Also referred to as "breakeven analysis," CVP reviews the relationships among costs, revenue, and profits associated with alternative plans. CVP analysis is used to help managers answer such questions as:

- How many guests must the operation serve to meet budgeted profit goals?

- When fixed or variable costs increase, how many additional guests must the operation serve to meet budgeted profit goals?

- How profitable would it be for the restaurant to expand its hours of operation?

- Should the restaurant remain open during predictably slow meal periods?

Graphs or equations can be used to conduct the analysis. Use of equations is likely to be faster and more accurate, and this procedure will be used in the discussion and examples that follow.[5]

CVP Assumptions and Limitations

Like all mathematical tools, CVP analysis is based on several assumptions. If these assumptions are not relevant to the actual situations being analyzed, the results of the analysis may be flawed. Some of the more basic assumptions behind CVP analysis include the following:

1. Fixed costs remain constant during the period being analyzed. Over time, fixed costs do change. However, it is reasonable to assume that fixed costs remain constant over a short time span.

2. Variable costs vary directly with revenue during the period under study. In other words, if variable costs equal a certain percentage of revenue, and revenue increases, the new level of variable expenses will still equal the same percentage of revenue.

3. Revenue relates directly to volume. For example, CVP analysis assumes that as business volume (the number of guests served) increases by a certain percentage, revenue will then increase by that same percentage. This means that decisions made from CVP analyses must be reviewed if, during the time

period in question, the sales mix changes. A change in the sales mix usually affects the amount of the guest check average. A higher average guest check results in higher revenue at the same level of business volume.

4. All costs can be properly divided into two components: fixed costs (which do not change as revenue levels change) and variable costs (which vary directly with revenue).

5. Only quantitative factors are considered by the CVP model. Qualitative factors such as employee morale, guest goodwill, and so forth are not considered. Therefore, food and beverage managers must carefully consider these qualitative factors before making any final decisions.

The Basic CVP Equation

The basic CVP analysis equation expresses the cost-volume-profit relationship at the breakeven point as follows:

Net Income (0)   =   Total Revenues   −   Total Variable Costs   −   Total Fixed Costs

Since there is no net income at breakeven, the value is set at zero when performing a breakeven analysis. However, the same equation can be used when an amount of desired net income is known. In these cases, the amount of desired net income is used as the value instead of zero. Variables within the basic CVP analysis equation can be broken down into the following more basic elements:

Total Revenues   =   Guest Check Average   ×   Number of Guests Served

Total Variable Costs   =   Variable Costs Per Guest   ×   Number of Guests Served

Breaking these variables of the basic CVP equation into more basic elements allows managers the flexibility to rearrange the elements into new equations that address a number of different situations. Exhibit 8 lists a few of these equations.

CVP Example: The Lumberjack Cafe

The following information is taken from the budget being proposed for the next calendar year for the Lumberjack Cafe. The number of guests used to estimate the budgeted revenues is 133,333.

- Total annual revenues $1,000,000
- Total annual fixed costs $110,000
- Total annual variable costs $740,000
- Total annual costs   ($ 850,000)
- Total net income before taxes $ 150,000

Given this information we can calculate the guest check average as follows:

Exhibit 8   Variations of CVP Analysis

PROBLEM TO BE SOLVED	EQUATION TO USE
Number of guests served at breakeven point	$$\dfrac{\text{Total Fixed Costs}}{\text{Guest Check Average} - \text{Variable Costs Per Guest}}$$
Number of guests served at desired net income level	$$\dfrac{\text{Total Fixed Costs} + \text{Desired Net Income}}{\text{Guest Check Average} - \text{Variable Costs Per Guest}}$$
Number of additional guests needed because of new fixed costs	$$\dfrac{\text{New Fixed Costs}}{\text{Guest Check Average} - \text{Variable Costs Per Guest}}$$
Total number of guests needed due to additional variable costs	$$\dfrac{\text{Total Fixed Costs} + \text{Desired Net Income}}{\text{Guest Check Average} - \left[\begin{smallmatrix}\text{Old Variable}\\ \text{Costs Per Guest}\end{smallmatrix} + \begin{smallmatrix}\text{Additional Variable}\\ \text{Costs Per Guest}\end{smallmatrix} \right]}$$
Number of guests needed if operating time is extended to yield a desired increase in net income	$$\dfrac{\text{Total Additional Fixed Costs} + \text{Desired Increase in Net Income}}{\text{Guest Check Average} - \text{Variable Costs Per Guest}}$$

$$\frac{\text{Total Annual Revenues}}{\text{Total Guests}} = \text{Guest Check Average}$$

$$\frac{\$1,000,000}{133,333} = \$7.50$$

Variable costs per guest can also be calculated:

$$\frac{\text{Total Annual Variable Costs}}{\text{Total Guests}} = \text{Variable Costs Per Guest}$$

$$\frac{\$740,000}{133,333} = \$5.55$$

Given this information, we can now determine the number of guests that must be served for the Lumberjack Cafe to break even by using one of the equations shown in Exhibit 8:

$$\begin{array}{ccc}\text{Number of guests served} \\ \text{at breakeven point}\end{array} = \frac{\text{Total Fixed Costs}}{\text{Guest Check Average} - \text{Variable Costs Per Guest}}$$

$$56,410 = \frac{\$110,000}{\$7.50 - \$5.55}$$

The manager does not, of course, want to break even. While the operating budget states a net income goal of $150,000, let's use another equation shown in Exhibit 8 and determine the number of guests that must be served for the Lumberjack Cafe to generate a net income of $100,000:

$$\frac{\text{Number of guests served}}{\text{at desired net income level}} = \frac{\text{Total Fixed Costs} + \text{Desired Net Income}}{\text{Guest Check Average} - \text{Variable Costs Per Guest}}$$

$$107,692 = \frac{\$110,000 + \$100,000}{\$7.50 - \$5.55}$$

In order to generate a $100,000 net income level, the Lumberjack Cafe must serve 51,282 guests more than required at the breakeven point (107,692 − 56,410 = 51,282). This is not an unreasonable goal. In fact, the manager is forecasting to serve approximately 133,333 guests during the calendar year for which planning is being done. The net income with this estimated guest count was given to be $150,000. This can be proven as follows:

Net Income = Total Revenues − Total Variable Costs − Total Fixed Costs

$150,000 =	$1,000,000	−	$740,000	−	$110,000
	(133,333 guests × $7.50 guest check average)		(133,333 × $5.55 Variable Costs Per Guest)		

To conclude this example of the Lumberjack Cafe, assume that the property is considering the need to close for extensive remodeling. Only 32,500 guests (less than the breakeven guest count of 56,410 noted above) are expected to be served. How much of a loss will the property suffer?

Net Income = Total Revenues − Total Variable Costs − Total Fixed Costs

($46,625) =	$243,750	−	$180,375	−	$110,000
	(32,500 guests × $7.50 guest check average)		(32,500 guests × $5.55 Variable Costs Per Guest)		

The Lumberjack Cafe will lose $46,625 during the period in which only 32,500 guests are expected to be served.

CVP Example: The Plantation Grill

The following information is taken from the budget being proposed for the next calendar year for the Plantation Grill, which is a small food and beverage outlet in the Fresh Air Hotel. The number of guests used to estimate the budgeted revenues is 39,000 with a guest check average of $11.

- Total annual revenues $ 429,000
- Total annual fixed costs $ 85,000
- Total annual variable costs $ 300,000
- Total annual costs   ($ 385,000)
- Total net income before taxes $ 44,000

Given this information we can calculate the total variable cost per guest as follows:

$$\frac{\text{Total Variable Costs}}{\text{Total Guests}} \quad = \quad \text{Total Variable Costs Per Guest}$$

$$\frac{\$300,000}{39,000} \quad = \quad \$7.70$$

Variable costs as a percentage of revenue can be calculated as follows:

$$\frac{\text{Total Variable Costs}}{\text{Total Revenue}} \quad = \quad \text{Variable Costs as a Percentage of Revenue}$$

$$\frac{\$300,000}{\$429,000} \quad = \quad .70 \text{ (rounded)} \times 100 \ = \ 70\%$$

The food service manager of the Plantation Grill is considering adding entertainment. The cost of the entertainment and special advertising will be $2,800 for a one-month trial period. How many additional guests will be required to break even on this entertainment test? Using another equation from Exhibit 8, we can calculate the number of additional guests as follows:

$$\begin{array}{c}\text{Number of additional} \\ \text{guests needed because} \\ \text{of new fixed costs}\end{array} \ = \ \frac{\text{New Fixed Costs}}{\text{Guest Check Average} \ - \ \text{Variable Costs Per Guest}}$$

$$848 \text{ Guests} \ = \ \frac{\$2,800}{\$11 \ - \ (\$7.70)}$$

Almost 850 additional guests will be required during the month to generate additional revenue required to break even on the entertainment test. Is this reasonable? The food service manager must consider this information when the entertainment decision is made.

Let's assume that the manager of the Plantation Grill is confronted by a 10 percent increase in variable costs. How many guests will be required if fixed costs do not change and the profit goal remains the same? Using another equation from Exhibit 8, we can calculate the number of additional guests as follows:

$$\begin{array}{c}\text{Total number of guests} \\ \text{needed due to additional} \\ \text{variable costs}\end{array} \ = \ \frac{\text{Total Fixed Costs} \ + \ \text{Desired Net Income}}{\text{Guest Check Average} \ - \ \left[\begin{array}{c}\text{Old Variable Costs} \\ \text{Per Guest}\end{array} + \begin{array}{c}\text{Additional} \\ \text{Variable} \\ \text{Costs Per} \\ \text{Guest}\end{array}\right]}$$

$$50,988 \text{ Guests} \ = \ \frac{\$85,000 \ + \ \$44,000}{\$11 \ - \ [\$7.70 \ + \ (.10 \times \$7.70)]}$$

As seen in the preceding example, 50,988 guests spending an average of $11.00 each will be necessary to generate revenue needed to cover fixed costs, variable costs (including increases), and profit requirements.

Can the manager find ways to increase the check average and/or number of guests served? Are there methods to reduce variable costs (or at least the variable cost *increase*)? Will profit expectations have to be reduced? These are some of the options the manager must evaluate—and CVP analysis will provide input as decisions are made.

Let's assume that the Plantation Grill is currently closed on Monday nights. How many guests will be required to generate a $500 net income level if it were to open for Monday night business? The net income goal of $500 is judged to be the minimum required to compensate for the operating problems associated with keeping the facility open. Assume that additional fixed costs of $275 will be incurred to compensate for production, service, and management labor to staff the operation and to pay for other costs such as advertising that are directly incurred by the decision to open. Using an equation from Exhibit 8, we can determine the number of guests that must be served as follows:

$$\begin{array}{l}\text{Number of guests needed} \\ \text{if operating time is} \\ \text{extended to yield a desired} \\ \text{increase in net income}\end{array} = \frac{\text{Total Additional Fixed Costs} + \text{Desired Increase in Net Income}}{\text{Guest Check Average} - \text{Variable Costs Per Guest}}$$

$$235 \text{ Guests} = \frac{\$275 + \$500}{\$11 - (\$7.70)}$$

Can the Plantation Grill generate new business at this volume level? Only the manager can decide. The manager has only a few choices:

- Remain closed on Monday evenings.

- Accept a lower profit requirement (perhaps the "goodwill" and increased possibility of repeat business will be of interest even if there is no or very little profit generated).

- Find a way to reduce additional fixed costs required to remain open.

- Develop procedures to reduce variable costs without reducing quality. If this can be done, variable costs for the other nights of operation will also be affected—and income might be increased significantly.

Let's assume that a new, $6,000 dishwashing machine is being considered for the Plantation Grill. It will be depreciated over 10 years. Annual equipment cost is, therefore, $6,000 divided by 10 years = $600/year. A variation of CVP analysis will allow the manager to determine how much of an increase in revenue will be needed to cover this additional cost without reducing the profit goal. Using an equation from Exhibit 8, we can first calculate the number of guests required and then compute the additional revenue level.

$$\begin{array}{l}\text{Number of additional} \\ \text{guests needed because of} \\ \text{new fixed costs}\end{array} = \frac{\text{New Fixed Costs}}{\text{Guest Check Average} - \text{Variable Costs Per Guest}}$$

$$182 \text{ Guests} = \frac{\$600}{\$11.00 - \$7.70}$$

The additional revenue level can now be determined as $2,002. This is calculated by multiplying the number of additional guests by the guest check average (182 guests × $11).

Endnotes

1. For further information, see *CARE: Controlling Alcohol Risks Effectively* (Lansing, Mich.: Educational Institute of the American Hotel & Lodging Association, 1999).

2. Readers interested in a detailed explanation of determining the fixed and variable elements of mixed costs should read Chapter 6 of Raymond S. Schmidgall's *Hospitality Industry Managerial Accounting*, 4th ed. (Lansing, Mich.: Educational Institute of the American Hotel & Lodging Association, 1997).

3. Readers interested in a detailed explanation of cost allocation should read Chapter 6 of Raymond S. Schmidgall's *Hospitality Industry Managerial Accounting*, 4th ed. (Lansing, Mich.: Educational Institute of the American Hotel & Lodging Association, 1997).

4. Readers interested in a detailed explanation of the use of computers in budgeting and financial planning should read Michael L. Kasavana and John J. Cahill's *Managing Computers in the Hospitality Industry*, 3d ed. (Lansing, Mich.: Educational Institute of the American Hotel & Lodging Association, 1997).

5. Readers interested in a more detailed explanation of cost-volume-profit analysis should read Chapter 7 of Raymond S. Schmidgall's *Hospitality Industry Managerial Accounting*, 4th ed. (Lansing, Mich.: Educational Institute of the American Hotel & Lodging Association, 1997).

 # Key Terms

bottom-up budgeting—A method of budget development in multi-unit organizations in which budgets are assembled at the unit level and then "rolled" up to higher organizational levels.

cell—The intersection of a row and a column on an electronic spreadsheet.

cost-volume-profit (CVP) analysis—An analytical process used by managers to examine the relationships among various costs, revenues, and profit in either graphic or equation form, allowing one to determine the revenue required at any desired profit level. Also called breakeven analysis.

derived demand—A concept of estimating room revenue and then using this information to project revenue from food, beverages, and other revenue centers based upon guest spending patterns that have been developed from in-house studies.

electronic spreadsheets—Computer terminal displays that resemble traditional accounting worksheets but possess powerful computation capabilities.

fixed costs—Costs that remain constant in the short run even though revenue volume may vary; examples of fixed costs include salaries, rent expense, insurance expense, and so on.

guest check average—Total revenue (usually assessed separately for food and beverage) divided by total guests; the average amount of revenue generated from each guest.

mark-up—An approach to pricing goods and services that determines selling prices by adding a certain percentage to the cost of goods sold (food cost); the mark-up is designed to cover all non-product costs (e.g., labor, utilities, supplies, interest expense, taxes, etc.) and also cover the desired profit.

operating budget—Management's detailed plans for generating revenue and incurring expenses to meet profit requirements for each department within the hospitality operation; also referred to as the revenue and expense budget.

percentage method—A method of estimating food and beverage operating expenses based on the current percentage of each expense relative to revenue.

top-down budgeting—A method of budget development in multi-unit organizations in which budgets are developed at the corporate level and are then passed down to lower organizational levels, with each successively lower level becoming responsible for a specific segment of the budget.

variable costs—Costs that change proportionately with the volume of business; examples of variable costs include food costs, beverage costs, labor costs, and the cost of some supplies used in food production and service areas.

zero-based budgeting—A method of estimating food and beverage operating expenses that starts over from zero instead of extending costs or cost percentages transferred from the current budget period; it involves starting at a zero expense level for each category of cost and building up to the new budget expense level, justifying each step along the way.

 Review Questions ——————————————————————

1. What is an operating budget and why is it important?

2. What are the basic procedures necessary to develop a budget plan?

3. Why is it important to compare budget standards with actual operating results? How often should this be done?

4. How should the required level of profit be determined?

5. What advantages does an electronic spreadsheet have over manual methods in the budgeting process?

6. What is meant by a "chained recalculation"?

7. How would you go about incorporating profit requirements into the pricing process?

8. What are the advantages and disadvantages of "top-down" and "bottom-up" budgeting in multi-unit properties?

9. What are the assumptions required for CVP analysis?

10. Give examples of the types of management issues that can be addressed by CVP analysis.

Internet Sites

For more information, visit the following Internet sites. Remember that Internet addresses can change without notice. If the site is no longer there, you can use a search engine to look for additional sites.

Associations

American Culinary Federation (ACF)
http://www.acfchefs.org

American Hotel & Lodging Association (AH&LA)
http://www.ahlaonline.org

American School Food Service Association
(ASFSA)
http://www.asfsa.org

Club Managers Association of America (CMAA)
http://www.cmaa.org

The Educational Foundation of NRA
http://www.edfound.org

The Educational Institute of AH&LA
http://www.ei–ahla.org

Hospitality Financial and Technology Professionals
http://www.hftp.org

Institute of Food Technologies
http://www.ift.org

International Hotel and Restaurant Association
http://www.ih–ra.com

National Association of College and University Food Services
http://www.nacufs.org

National Restaurant Association (NRA)
http://www.restaurant.org

Food and Beverage Resources

Club Management Online
http://www.club–mgmt.com/dining/index.html

Business Owner's Toolkit: Cost / Volume / Profit Analysis
http://www.toolkit.cch.com/text/P06_7500.asp

Prepared Foods. Product development, ingredients, suppliers
http://www.preparedfoods.com

Restaurant Management Resources Network: Food Cost Tips and Strategies
http://www.profitable.com/results/foodcost.html

Schiff's Food Service, Inc.: 99 Sins of Food Cost Control
http://www.schiffs.com/schiffscom/99sins.htm

Management Companies

ARAMARK
http://www.aramark.com

Bon Appétit Management Company
http://www.bamco.com

Compass Group
http://www.compass–na.com

Sodexho Marriott
http://www.sodexhomarriott.com

The Wood Company
http://www.woodco.com

Publications—Online and Printed

Club Management Magazine
http://www.club-mgmt.com

Electronic Gourmet Guide
http://www.foodwine.com

Food and Hospitality Magazine
http://www.foodserviceworld.com

Food Management
http://www.foodservicesearch.com

Food Network: CyberKitchen
http://www.foodtv.com

Food Processing: The Magazine of
Strategy, Technology and Trends
http://www.foodprocessing.com

Internet Food Channel
http://www.foodchannel.com

International Hotel and Restaurant
Association journal
www.hotelsmag.com

International Journal of Hospitality
Management
http://www.mcb.co.uk/ijchm.htm

Journal of Hospitality Financial
Management
http://hrta.fnr.umass.edu/sheel/
ahfme/jhfm/aboutjhfm.html

Lodging Food and Beverage
http://www.lodgingnews.com/
lodgingfnb/

Lodging Hospitality Online
http://www.lhonline.com

Lodging News, journal of the American
Hotel & Lodging Association
http://www.ei-ahla.org/webs/
lodging/index.html

Nation's Restaurant News
http://www.nrn.com

On the Rail—News for Food
Professionals
http://www.ontherail.com

Restaurants and Institutions magazine
http://www.rimag.com

Restaurant Business, Food Service, and
ID magazines
http://www.foodservicetoday.com

Restaurant Hospitality
www.foodservicesearch.com

Restaurants and Institutions
http://www.rimag.com

Restaurants USA, publication of
National Restaurant Association
http://www.restaurant.org/rusa

World Hospitality, management
magazine for hotel executives
http://www.worldhospitality.com

 **Problems** ———————————————————————

Problem 1

a. What is the initial budgeted profit (before tax) being planned by the Spartanland restaurant for the current year given the following information (all data estimated)?

- Revenue (food) $975,000
- Revenue (beverage) $135,000
- Food cost = 31% of food revenue
- Beverage cost = 22% of beverage revenue
- Labor cost (payroll) = 34% of total revenue
- Employee benefits = 18% of labor cost (payroll)
- Other operating expenses = 14% of total revenue
- All fixed costs = 8% of total revenue

b. The owner does not approve of the initial budget. Working together, the owner and manager believe they can accomplish the following:

- Implement marketing plans to increase the number of guests consuming food by an additional 12,000 (guest check average = $22.50)
- Increase beverage revenues by 8% over initial estimates
- Decrease food costs to 30%
- Decrease beverage costs to 20%
- Decrease payroll costs to 32% (but benefit costs will increase by 6% over the initial budget because of new payroll taxes not included in the original budget)
- Decrease operating expenses to 12% of total revenue
- Note: fixed costs will remain at the same *dollar* amount as in the original budget

c. What is the revised estimate of budgeted profit before tax?

Problem 2

The manager of the Spartanland Restaurant is developing the operating budget for next year using finanacial information from the current year as follows:

Item	Current Year's Amount	Next Year's Percentage Increase (Decrease)	Next Year's Amount ($)
A. Food Revenue	$973,000	4%	_____
B. Beverage Revenue	$112,500	2%	_____
C. Food Cost	36%	1%	_____
D. Beverage Cost	23%	(1%)	_____
E. Labor (including benefits)	$298,000	(2%)	_____
F. Other Operating Costs	16%	same	_____
G. Fixed Costs	$70,000	same	_____

a. What is the *current year's* budgeted profit or (loss)?

b. Develop next year's budget: indicate the profit or (loss).

Problem 3

The Blue Ridge Café's budget for next year indicates the following:

• Revenues		$765,000
• Total fixed costs	$91,000	
• Total variable costs	$512,000	
Total Costs		$603,000
Net Income Before tax		$162,000

Revenue estimates assume 89,470 guests will be served.

a. What is the guest check average?

b. What are the variable costs per guests?

c. How many guests must be served for the Blue Ridge Café to break even?

d. If the owner needed a net income of at least $114,000, how many guests would need to be served?

e. How many more guests are needed to generate a net income of $114,000 than are needed to break even?

f. If the Blue Ridge Café decides to close during two months that traditionally generate slow business it will lose about 18,000 guests. If the owner chooses to do this, what will be the new net income or loss?

g. The manager is considering a kitchen renovation which will add $7,500 in new fixed costs (depreciation and interest) each year. How much will the café's net income or (loss) be if it does this during the first year that it closes for two months? (See Question F above)

h. The Blue Ridge Café closes for two months (Question F), incurs the additional fixed costs (Question G) *and* is the "victim" of a problem in the economy that results in a 14 percent increase in variable costs. How many additional guests are needed for it to maintain its net income level (Question G)?

Problem 4

The Anytown Restaurant has the following financial information available:

• Food Costs	$365,000
• Labor Costs	$315,000
• All other costs (including fixed costs)	$224,000
• Net income (profit)	$76,000
• Number of guests served	89,000

a. What is its revenue?

b. What is the Anytown Restaurant's guest check average?

c. Assume the Anytown Restaurant has fixed costs of $95,000; what are its variable costs? (Hint: all costs − fixed costs = variable costs)

d. What is the variable cost per guest?

e. How many guests must the restaurant serve to break even?

f. How many guests must be served to have a net income (profit) of $105,000?

g. Assume the Anytown Restaurant serves only 84,000 guests. What will be its net income (loss)?

Chapter 5 Outline

Competencies

1. Explain how a system of food service control points helps managers carry out critical functions on a daily basis. (pp. 129–130)

2. Describe factors that influence menu planning strategies and identify internal and external factors that influence menu changes. (pp. 130–138)

3. Calculate a base selling price for menu items using simple mark-up pricing methods. (pp. 138–144)

4. Calculate a base selling price for menu items using the contribution margin pricing method. (p. 144)

5. Calculate a base selling price for menu items using the ratio pricing method. (p. 145)

6. Calculate a base selling price for menu items using prime costs pricing methods. (pp. 146–149)

7. Describe important pricing considerations that affect the final selling price of menu items. (pp. 149–159)

8. Explain the menu engineering method for pricing food and beverage items. (pp. 159–163)

5

The Menu:
The Foundation for Control

THE MENU IS THE FOUNDATION for the control process in a food and beverage operation. The menu planning control point begins the control process. This chapter focuses on the menu and presents an overview of other control points that play crucial roles in determining the success or failure of a food and beverage operation. The chapter contains practical, objective techniques for effective menu planning, pricing, and evaluation. The final sections of the chapter examine computer-based menu management applications.

Food Service Control Points

Control points are basic operating activities that must be performed in any food service establishment. Exhibit 1 illustrates the nine main control points. The flow chart begins with the menu planning control point at the base, since menu planning is the foundation for control. The flow chart uses boxes to illustrate each of the control points. The arrows between boxes indicate a flow of products and, in some cases, a transfer of paperwork and/or a movement of personnel. For example, the arrow between the holding and serving control points represents the flow of food products from the production staff to the service staff. It also depicts the movement of servers from the kitchen to the dining room and the flow of food products from service staff to guests. (It is sometimes helpful to think of serving [moving the product from production staff to service staff] and service [moving products from service staff to guests] as separate tasks. But for purposes of our discussion, we will refer to them as one step in the control process, and we will use the terms *serving* and *service* interchangeably.) Notice that three control points—preparing, cooking, and holding—are grouped together and identified as production activities. They take place in the kitchen.

Beginning with menu planning, each control point plays a crucial role in determining the success or failure of a food and beverage operation. Each control point is a miniature system with its own structure and functions. Each basic operating activity has specific objectives, guidelines, standards, and internal processes that contribute to the success of the operation and the ultimate goal: guest satisfaction.

When a food and beverage operation is seen as a system of control points, the control activities associated with each function are easier to identify and carry out on a daily basis. This systems approach permits the manager to establish an audit

Exhibit 1   Flow Chart of Basic Operating Activities or Control Points in a Food and Beverage Operation

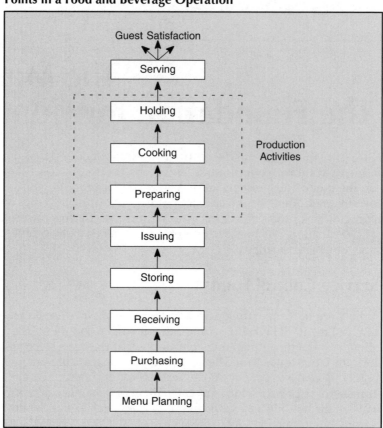

Source: Adapted from Ronald F. Cichy, *Quality Sanitation Management* (Lansing, Mich.: Educational Institute of the American Hotel & Lodging Association, 1994), p. 3.

trail of control activities. It is then easier to separate, identify, and take corrective action to resolve problems that are identified. In short, the manager becomes proactive instead of reactive; that is, the manager takes time for short and long-range planning in the hope of controlling future events, rather than waiting for crises to develop and then taking a "fire fighting" approach.

The Menu's Influence

The process of planning a menu never ends; the final menu is never achieved. Rather, the process is ongoing, dynamic, and based on the expectations of the operation's present and potential guests—its target markets. From creating an image to communicating a plan for satisfying the guests, influencing the guests' purchase decisions, merchandising the correct products, and more, the menu has a continuous impact on all aspects of an operation. A properly planned and well designed menu stimulates revenue and increases the guest check average, because whenever a menu is presented to a guest, a sales transaction begins. And the menu not only creates but reflects the operation's image. The image may be elegant, businesslike, fun, ethnic, or trendy, depending on what the target market(s) desire.

The menu has an impact on every aspect of a food and beverage manager's job as well as the operation itself. The following sections identify some of the more important areas of a food service operation that are directly affected by the menu.

Product Control Procedures. The food and beverage products must be controlled. If an operation needs shrimp to produce a menu item, shrimp will need to be purchased, received, stored, issued, prepared, cooked, served and accounted for.

Cost Control Procedures. Careful cost control procedures must be followed as more expensive products are served, as service styles dictated by the menu become more complex, and as guests desire a "dining experience," not just a "meal."

Production Requirements. Food items required by the menu must be produced consistently. Product quality, staff productivity and skills, timing and scheduling, and other kitchen (back- or heart-of-the-house) functions are all dictated by the menu.

Nutritional Content of Meals. Non-commercial food service programs and, increasingly, commercial food service operations are concerned about the nutritional content of food served to consumers. The menu can have an impact on the health and well-being of those to whom it is offered.

Equipment Needs. Equipment must be available to prepare products required by the menu. The menu must be balanced based on available equipment resources so that no one station is overloaded or underutilized.

Sanitation Management. Since the menu sets the stage for the remaining control points, management must consider menu items in light of possible sanitation hazards. Once the potential hazards are identified, the risks can be reduced.

Layout and Space Requirements. There must be adequate facilities for the staff and equipment required to produce items listed on the menu. The layout and design of facilities establish the physical space within which food production and service take place. The physical facilities must be adequate for the purchasing, receiving, storing, issuing, production, and serving of every item on the menu.

Staffing Needs. Employees must be available to produce and serve all items required by the menu. As a menu becomes more complex, greater demands may be placed upon the staff. Staffing needs are also influenced by the degree to which the menu uses convenience food items (food items the operation purchases that have some or all of the labor built into them which otherwise would need to be added on-site).

Service Requirements. The food and beverage manager must carefully plan how products will be served to the guest. The menu affects the skill levels required for service personnel along with equipment, inventory, and facilities needed in the front of the house.

Revenue Control Procedures. For example, when a simple menu is served in a fast-food operation, the potential for revenue control problems is not as great as the problem potential in a table service restaurant offering an elaborate menu.

Menu Planning

The menu is not only an important control tool, it is also a sales, advertising, merchandising, and marketing tool. In this respect, the menu addresses both control- and marketing-related concerns and blends them into a workable system.

Marketing Implications of the Menu

Because it lists the items an operation is offering for sale, a menu, in effect, communicates a property's food and beverage marketing plans. In developing its marketing plans, a property needs to assess the products, service, **ambience** (theme and atmosphere), and perceived value that its target market(s) expect. Items selected for inclusion in the menu should be based on the needs and desires of the operation's target market(s). In carrying out its marketing plans, the food and beverage operation must strive to meet or exceed the expectations of the guests being served.

Management must never forget the marketing implications of the menu planning process. Exhibit 2 illustrates factors to consider in planning the menu. Notice that the most important and numerous concerns involve the guest and the quality of menu items. These are also the most complex concerns. Others include cost, availability, and production/operation concerns.

In addition, menu planners should study the competition and the types of menu items offered by both direct and indirect competitors in the area. It is especially necessary to consider items offered by competitors who are trying to attract the same target market(s). What are guests of other properties purchasing? Why? What are the selling prices? What can be done to make the property's own products and services special—and more attractive to guests? These and related questions with marketing implications constitute a primary source of information for menu planners in all types of food and beverage operations.

Theme and Atmosphere

The complexity of menu planning in commercial properties depends upon the ambience of the food and beverage operation. Menu planning for table service restaurants is different from menu planning for banquet or buffet service operations. Ambience, the guest check average, and marketing concerns are prime examples of these differences.

Many food and beverage operations have a specific theme and atmosphere. French, Italian, and Chinese restaurants are examples of operations with ethnic themes. Others feature the cuisine of the American Southwest (for example, chili rellenos, tortillas, enchiladas) or Cajun cuisine (for example, jambalaya, gumbo, blackened redfish). Still others create a healthy ambience by capitalizing on an atmosphere and theme built on open, airy, plant-filled facilities that serve high

Exhibit 2   Priority Concerns of the Menu Planner

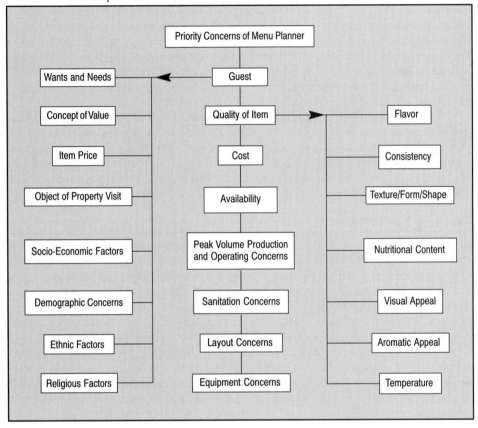

quality, light, fresh foods. In any case, menu items offered must be compatible with the theme and atmosphere of the operation.

Menu Planning Strategies

In the past, food service managers often attempted to diversify their menus by adding many new menu items. Since most items were made from scratch, the number and variety of raw ingredients increased correspondingly.

Another strategy, called "rationalization," limits the menu to those items that best enhance the operation's image. Its objective is simplification for the sake of operational efficiency. An operation can offer several menu items that use the same raw ingredients. This cross-utilization enables an operation to prepare and serve many menu selections with a limited number of raw ingredients.

When the menu is carefully planned to ensure a balance of menu selections in each category, the results of these new strategies can be a streamlining of the purchasing, receiving, storing, issuing, production, and serving control points.

Today, as in the past, food service managers are searching for new menu item alternatives. The increasing number of high-quality convenience foods has made it easier to offer new items without having to buy additional raw ingredients or elaborate equipment. High-quality convenience products can be purchased in semi-prepared or fully prepared forms. Because they have built-in labor, they also reduce in-house labor requirements. Of course, convenience food products usually have a higher AP (as purchased) price than the raw ingredients from which they are made.

It is always best to base initial menu plans on the needs and desires of the target market(s). However, several other factors may influence the menu selection. Among these factors are the recommended storage conditions (time and temperature); personnel skill levels; the product's availability and seasonality; the stability of quality and price levels; and the operation's ability to purchase, produce, and serve the menu items in a safe, sanitary, and cost-effective way.

Building the Menu

Entrées are typically selected first in the menu planning process. It is important to consider not only the types of entrées, but also their costs, preparation methods, and compatibility with theme and atmosphere. A basic decision in planning the entrée base concerns the number of entrées to offer. How many menu items should the operation provide? Some managers feel they should have something for everyone and, therefore, provide a wide range of entrées. This approach creates a number of problems that require careful planning and control to resolve.

The variety of entrées also affects the types and quantities of ingredients (each with its own standard purchase specifications) that must be received, stored, issued, produced, and served. A corresponding amount of preparation equipment and number of skilled personnel must also be available, and production/service problems are more likely to occur. In summary, control is more complex.

The reverse approach of making available only a limited number of entrées reduces these types of problems considerably. In the United States there are many specialty/theme restaurants that offer relatively few entrées. By focusing on a specific segment of the market, this type of operation not only simplifies marketing techniques, but also minimizes many in-house production, serving and control problems.

After selecting entrées, menu planners must choose menu items to complement the entrées. A common procedure is to plan appetizers and/or soups, followed by high-starch items and/or vegetables (if not part of the entrée), then accompanying salads, and, finally, other menu components such as breads, desserts, and beverages. Trends in entrée consumption affect the other items added to the menu.

Dining Trends

One dining trend compatible with many lifestyles is "grazing." Grazers are unlikely to select a full meal, but rather choose appetizers, salads, and desserts to complete their menu selections. Grazers are more likely to choose smaller portions of more menu items than to select a larger portion single entrée. Therefore, menus featuring a wide selection of appetizers, salads, and desserts are popular with grazers. Menus are being designed with interchangeable courses, sometimes referred to as "modular cuisine."

The grazing trend is expected to continue and grow as guests change their eating habits and focus on the perceived high value of making multiple menu selections to "build their own" meals. The grazing trend seems to be particularly popular with the health- and fitness-conscious baby boomers, whose lifestyles reflect their desire for variety.

If a food and beverage operation's business is transient and the clientele changes frequently, the menu may be static (remain the same). Generally, menus that change—dynamic menus—are preferable to static menus. However, menu variability depends on the seasonal availability of raw ingredients at reasonable costs, the number and types of courses offered, the potential for using leftovers and local ingredients, the preferences of the guests, the operation's image, and the desires of the target market(s).

When the business is highly repetitive and involves regular guests such as businesspeople and others who reside in the local area, there is a greater need for daily specials that regularly change. Often, daily specials feature local or regional fresh ingredients and permit the menu planner to take advantage of reduced costs and increased availability to add interest to a menu. A trend today in daily specials is to announce their availability on attractive, eye-catching iridescent or colorfully lighted menu boards and suggestively merchandise them to guests.

Menu Design

As already noted, the design of the menu can influence the guest's purchase decisions, stimulate sales of additional or preferable menu items, and increase the guest check average. Guests are influenced by visual cues provided by the menu. Readability, artwork, type styles, physical design, and layout play an important role in merchandising the food and beverage products that are profitable to the operation and satisfying to the guests.

Exhibits 3, 4, and 5 show the focal points of single-sheet, single-fold, and two-fold menus. Menu items featured in these positions often draw the reader's attention because of their location. Of course, other devices such as art, pictures, and graphics can be used to draw the reader's attention elsewhere.

Menu Changes

Because conditions change, a food service operation's menu must also change. Menu changes are influenced by both external and internal factors.

External Factors External factors include consumer demands, economic conditions, the competition, supply levels, and industry trends. Consumer demands are perhaps the most important factor to consider in changing a menu. Management should first decide which potential market(s) it wants to attract with the modified menu. Then the proposed menu change must be evaluated in light of the negative and positive effects it may have on current guests.

Exhibit 3   Focal Point of Single-Sheet Menu

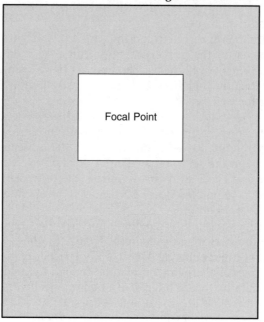

Exhibit 4   Focal Point of Single-Fold Menu

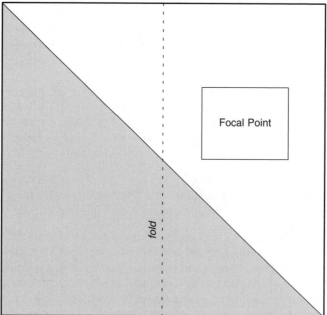

Exhibit 5   Focal Point of Two-Fold Menu

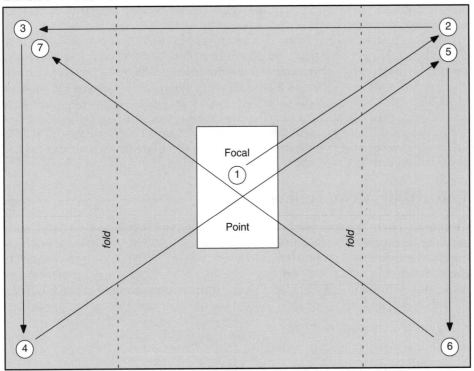

The numbers indicate the order of eye movement, given that no special graphics are used.

Economic conditions include the cost of ingredients and the potential profitability of new menu items. Menu items offered by the competition may dictate choices to be made available. For example, a hotel food service located next to a restaurant offering the "best Chinese food in town" may elect not to serve Chinese cuisine. Supply levels relate the price to the quality and quantity of the proposed menu items. Supply levels are highly variable for some seasonal raw ingredients such as fresh fruits and vegetables. Industry trends provide general information about how the industry is responding to new demands. At present, an overall trend in many areas relates to a more sophisticated guest who is searching for an increasingly higher price-value relationship and who will pay more to receive more.

Internal Factors. Internal factors that may result in a proposed menu change include the facility's meal pattern, concept and theme, operational system, and menu mix. The typical meal pattern is breakfast, lunch, and dinner. Management must decide if existing meal periods should be continued or altered. Expectations of guests have a direct influence on this decision. Any change must fit with the establishment's concept and theme. A restaurant that is known as the best steakhouse in the city may do itself a disservice by adding an extensive variety of fresh fish and shellfish to the menu. An establishment's image may also rule out certain foods that do not blend with its theme and decor. For example, even though ethnic foods are growing in popularity, a hotel restaurant may find it difficult to fit ethnic foods into its projected image.

Menu changes are also modified by the establishment's operational system. For example, if extensive new equipment purchases are crucial to the successful production and service of the menu item, the change may be too costly. Also, the change may raise both food and labor costs to unacceptable levels. Or, in some cases, the skill levels of production and service personnel may not be adequate to successfully produce and present the new menu item. The operation's existing menu has a certain overall combination or mix of items. This menu mix will be affected by any change in individual items. All of these factors should be evaluated before menu changes are finalized and implemented.

Calculating Menu Selling Prices

Commercial food service operations, as well as many institutional facilities, must establish appropriate selling prices for menu items. Objective pricing methods ensure that the property's profit requirements, as well as the value guests attach to the entire dining experience (including service, cleanliness, and ambience), are incorporated into the selling price. Pricing approaches examined in the following sections are:

- Subjective pricing methods
- Simple mark-up pricing methods
- Contribution margin pricing method
- Ratio pricing method
- Simple prime costs method
- Specific prime costs method

Subjective Pricing Methods

Although prices determine to a large extent whether financial goals of the operation are met, many managers use very subjective pricing methods. These methods establish prices, but generally fail to relate them to profit requirements or even costs. When the subject of pricing methods comes up, many managers speak about the "art" of pricing and suggest that intuition and special knowledge about guests' ability to pay are the most important considerations. Consider the following pricing methods and notice that each is based simply upon the manager's assumptions or guesses about what prices should be.

The Reasonable Price Method. This method uses a price that the food service manager thinks will represent a value to the guest. The manager presumes to know—from the guest's perspective—what charge is fair and equitable. In other words, the manager asks, "If I were a guest, what price would I pay for the item being served?" The manager's best guess in answering this question becomes the product's selling price.

The Highest Price Method. Using this plan, a manager sets the highest price that he or she thinks guests are willing to pay. The concept of value is stretched to the maximum and is then "backed off" to provide a margin of error in the manager's estimate.

The Loss Leader Method. With this plan, an unusually low price is set for an item (or items). The manager assumes that guests will be attracted to the property to purchase the low-priced item(s) and that they will then select other items while they are there. Beverage or food prices on some items are set low to bring guests into the property, but purchases of other items are necessary for the operation to meet profit requirements. This pricing method is sometimes used as an "early bird" or senior citizen discount to attract specific segments of the market.

The Intuitive Price Method. When prices are set by intuition alone, the manager takes little more than a wild guess about the selling price. Closely related to this approach is a trial-and-error pricing plan—if one price doesn't work, another is tested. The intuitive price method differs from the reasonable price method in that there is less effort to determine what represents value from the guests' perspective.

These pricing methods are based on assumptions, hunches, and guesses. Such methods are generally ineffective because they do not consider profit requirements and the product costs necessary to put the item on the table.

These subjective pricing methods may be common in the food service industry simply because they have been used in the past, because the manager setting prices has no information about product costs or profit requirements to work with, and/or because the manager is not familiar with more objective methods. In today's market, with increased consumer demands for value in dining, and with higher purchase prices for products needed by the property, these plans seldom work.

Objective Pricing Methods

If the reasonable price, highest price, loss leader, and intuitive price methods are subjective and should not be used, what are better alternatives? Objective methods based upon data in the approved operating budget help the manager transfer budget plans into selling prices which help generate revenue required by the operating budget. Each of the methods which follow, to some extent at least, helps the manager to better assure selling prices incorporate budget requirements.

Before any objective pricing method can be used, however, three basic cost procedures must be in place and consistently used.

- Standard recipes—Standard recipes dictate the type and amount of each ingredient required to produce a menu item. Also, they indicate the portion size to be served. A standard recipe must be available for each item when a selling price is being developed. For example, if the manager is pricing an oyster platter, standard recipes must be available for the oyster entrée, its garnish, salad with dressing choice, potato or other starch, vegetable choice, bread and butter and/or any other items which comprise the "oyster platter."

- Pre-costing with current costs—Each affected recipe must be pre-costed with current market cost data to determine the cost to produce one portion of each component of the menu item being priced.

- Standard recipes must be used—While this may be obvious, many operations have standard recipes available but do not consistently use them. Too often, because of labor turnover and other reasons, production personnel deviate from recipes from which historically have dictated the quantity, methodology and cost of food production. If recipes are not used, there is no reason to have them or to cost them.

Simple Mark-Up By Multiplier Pricing Methods

Some pricing methods use a mark-up by a multiplier based upon food costs for menu items. The methods are designed to cover all costs and to yield the desired profit. The following sections examine ingredients mark-up pricing, prime-ingredient mark-up pricing, and mark-up with accompaniment costs. Advantages and disadvantages of these methods are also discussed.

Ingredients Mark-Up Method. The **ingredients mark-up pricing method** attempts to consider all product costs: food costs when pricing food items, and beverage costs when pricing beverages. The three steps to pricing with this method are as follows:

1. Determine the ingredients' costs.
2. Determine the multiplier to use in marking up the ingredients' costs.
3. Establish a base selling price by multiplying the ingredients' costs by the multiplier to calculate a final selling price.

A **base selling price** is not necessarily the final selling price. The simple output from formulas may not be an appropriate final selling price. Rather, a base selling price is considered a starting point from which other factors must be assessed and the price adjusted accordingly. These other factors are addressed later in this chapter as important pricing considerations.

The multiplier determined in step 2 is generally based on the desired food (or beverage) cost percentage (which might be established by in-house assessment procedures or from budget development). For example, if the desired food cost percentage is 40 percent, the multiplier would be 2.5, determined as follows:

$$\text{Multiplier} = \frac{1}{\text{Desired Food Cost Percentage}}$$

$$2.5 = \frac{1}{.40}$$

Assume that an oyster platter has a standard food cost of $5.32 (the total per portion cost for all items constituting the dinner). If a 40 percent food cost is desired, the price of the oyster platter is determined as follows:

$$\text{Base Selling Price} = \text{Ingredient Cost} \times \text{Multiplier}$$
$$\$13.30 = \$5.32 \times 2.5$$

If this price appears reasonable based on the market for oyster platters, then the item is sold for about $13.30.

Prime-Ingredient Mark-Up Method. The **prime-ingredient mark-up pricing method** differs from the ingredients mark-up method in that only the cost of the prime ingredient is marked up. In addition, the multiplier used must be greater than the multiplier used when considering the total cost of all ingredients.

Using the same oyster platter example, assume the prime ingredient cost is $2.65 (in this case, the prime ingredient is a serving of oysters). If a multiplier of 5.02 is used, the oyster platter is priced at $13.30. The price is calculated as follows:

Base Selling Price   =   Prime Ingredient's Cost × Multiplier

$13.30   = $2.65   ×   5.02

If the cost of the oysters in this example increases to $2.75 for the dinner portion, the new price would be $13.81 ($2.75 × 5.02).

The prime-ingredient approach assumes that the costs of all ingredients change in proportion to the prime ingredient. That is, when the prime ingredient's cost increases 10 percent, then other ingredients' costs are assumed to increase also by 10 percent.

Mark-Up with Accompaniment Costs. Using the **mark-up with accompaniment costs pricing method,** managers determine ingredient costs based only upon entrée items and then add a standard accompaniment or "plate" cost to this amount before multiplying by a multiplier. This plate cost is an average cost for all non-entrée and other relatively inexpensive items including salad, vegetables, bread, butter, and non-alcoholic beverages. For example:

Entrée Costs	$ 3.15
Plate Cost	+ $ 1.25
Estimated Food Cost	$ 4.40
Multiplier	× 3.3
Base Selling Price	$14.52

Note that the "plate" cost, covering the estimated food cost of all items other than the entrée cost, is added to the entrée cost before the multiplier is used.

An advantage of this method is its simplicity. Careful calculations for only the expensive entrée costs are necessary. Time can be saved by combining all other food costs into an estimated plate cost.

A disadvantage may be that plate costs are not truly representative of food costs associated with these other items. How is the plate cost determined? How often is it adjusted? Also, managers must establish a reasonable and objective multiplier that relates to profit requirements. If this is not done, the mark-up with accompaniment costs pricing method is no better than the subjective pricing methods discussed earlier.

Determining the Multiplier. The mark-up pricing methods just discussed are simple to use and, for that reason, are commonly used in the food service industry. A significant disadvantage, however, involves determining the multiplier. How does a manager decide this? For many managers, it is a subjective decision based primarily upon experience and "rule of thumb" (such as the traditional 40 percent food

It's Easy to Calculate Menu Pricing Mark-Ups

How to Establish Multipliers

The Mark-Up by Multiplier Pricing Methods arrive at a Base Selling price by multiplying a factor (multiplier) by the ingredient food cost. How are the multipliers established?

I. Ingredient Mark-Up Method

$$\text{Multiplier} = \frac{1}{\text{Desired (Budgeted) Food Cost Percentage}}$$

Example:
Assume Budgeted
Food Cost Percent $= 33\%: \frac{1}{33} = \underline{3.03}$ (multiplier)

II. Prime Ingredient Mark-Up Method

$$\text{Multiplier} = \frac{\text{Total Food Revenue}}{\text{Total Entrée Costs}}$$

Example:
Assume: Total Food Costs $=$ \$ 1,000,000
Total Entrée Costs $=$ \$ 350,000
Total Revenue $=$ \$ 2,025,000

Multiplier $= \underline{5.79}$ (multiplier)

III. Mark-Up With Accompaniment Method

Step A: Calculate per meal accompaniment costs
Assume: Total Food Costs $=$ \$ 1,000,000
Total Entrée Costs $=$ \$ 350,000
Total accompaniment costs $=$ \$ 650,000
Number of guests $=$ 125,000

$$\frac{\$5.20}{\text{Per meal Accompaniment costs}} = \frac{\$650,000 \text{ (accompaniment costs)}}{125,000 \text{ (guests)}}$$

(continued)

Step B: Calculate Total per meal food costs

Entrée costs	$ 5.75
Accompaniment Costs	$ 5.20
Total per meal Food costs	$ 10.95

Step C: Calculate Multiplier
Use same method as for Method 1

$$\text{Multiplier} = \frac{1}{\text{Desired (Budgeted)}\ \text{Food Cost Percentage}}$$

Example:
Budgeted
Food Cost $= 33\%: \dfrac{1}{33} = \underline{3.03}$ (multiplier; use for all entrees)

cost). Should managers use last year's average food cost percentage? Should they use a statistic supplied by a national, state, or other food service association or consulting firm?

It is, of course, possible to use a multiplier based upon the planned food and other costs from the operating budget. If, on the average, menu items are priced to yield the food cost percentage dictated by the budget, planners have developed a simple foundation for generating revenue sufficient to cover food costs and to yield a **contribution margin** (food revenue minus food costs) sufficient for other expenses and profit requirements. The little time required to generate and use this multiplier based on the operating budget may make it especially cost effective for many small-volume operations.

However, the impact of sales mix cannot be overlooked. If, for example, increased unit sales of a higher food cost percentage item replace sales of its counterparts with lower food cost percentages, the average food cost percentage can be made according to budget—but with undesirable financial results.

There are other potential disadvantages of using simple multiplier pricing methods. For example, these pricing methods do not reflect higher or lower labor, energy, or other costs associated with production of specific menu items. Rather, they either assume that all operating costs relate in some direct way to food costs or that these cost differences can be ignored. These assumptions may not be warranted as one considers the extensive amount of labor required to prepare some items relative to others.

The mark-up pricing methods using a multiplier also assume that all food costs associated with producing a menu item are known. In fact, many other costs may be excluded from the cost of ingredients used as the base for the multiplier. For example, operators not adjusting cost of goods sold by values of transfers to and from the food department would ignore these costs. Also, how are theft, pilferage, overportioning, and spoilage addressed when standard recipe costs alone are used as the base for the multiplier? What about minor costs such as herbs and spices—often ignored in price calculations but relatively expensive when a year's worth of purchases is considered? Problems with calculating costs of "help yourself" salad or dessert bars, and all you can eat buffets also emphasize the point that multipliers applied to partial food costs may not yield accurate base selling prices.

Contribution Margin Pricing Method

The term *contribution margin* refers to the amount left after a menu item's food cost is subtracted from its selling price. The contribution margin is the amount that the sale of a menu item "contributes" to pay for all non-food costs allocated to the food service operation and to help with profit requirements. With a **contribution margin pricing method**, managers can set base selling prices for menu items by following two steps:

1. Determine the average contribution margin required per guest by dividing all non-food costs plus required profit by the number of expected guests.
2. Determine the base selling price for a menu item by adding the average contribution margin required per guest to the item's standard food cost.

Let's assume that the approved operating budget provides the manager with the following data: all non-food costs are $695,000, required profit is set at $74,000, and 135,000 guests are expected to be served. With this information, the manager can calculate a base selling price for a menu item with a standard food cost of $4.60 as follows:

Step #1: Determine the average contribution margin required per guest. This can be accomplished by using the following formula:

$$\frac{\text{Non-Food Costs} + \text{Required Profit}}{\text{Number of Expected Guests}} = \text{Average Contribution Margin Required per Guest}$$

$$\frac{\$695,000 + \$74,000}{135,000} = \$5.70$$

Step #2: Determine the base selling price for a menu item. This is done by adding the average contribution margin required per guest to the item's standard food cost. The base selling price for a menu item with a $4.60 food cost would be $10.30 ($4.60 + $5.70 = $10.30).

Advantages of this method are its ease and practicality when reasonably accurate information is available from the operating budget. It is also useful in those operations where costs associated with serving each guest are basically the same, with the exception of varying food costs. Also, this method tends to reduce the range of selling prices on the menu, since the only difference is reflected in the actual food cost incorporated into the selling price. A potential disadvantage of this method is that it assumes that each guest should pay the same share of the property's non-food costs and profit requirements.

Ratio Pricing Method

The **ratio pricing method** determines the relationship between food costs and all non-food costs plus profit requirements and uses this ratio to develop base selling prices for menu items. The three steps to ratio pricing are as follows:

1. Determine the ratio of food costs to all non-food costs plus required profit by dividing all non-food costs plus profit by food costs.

2. Calculate the amount of non-food costs plus profit required for a menu item by multiplying the standard food cost of the menu item by the ratio calculated in step 1.

3. Determine the base selling price of a menu item by adding the result of step 2 to the standard food cost of the menu item.

Assume that the approved operating budget of a family-style restaurant (with no alcoholic beverage sales) provides the following information: food costs are $435,000, all non-food costs (labor and other costs) are $790,000, and required profit is $95,000. Using the ratio pricing method, the manager establishes a base selling price for a menu item with a standard food cost of $4.75 as follows:

Step #1: Determine the ratio of food costs to all other costs plus profit requirements. This is calculated with the following formula:

$$\frac{\text{All Non-Food Costs} + \text{Required Profit}}{\text{Food Costs}} = \text{Ratio}$$

$$\frac{\$790,000 + \$95,000}{\$435,000} = 2.03$$

This ratio means that for each $1 of revenue required to cover food costs, $2.03 of additional revenue is needed to pay for non-food costs and meet profit requirements.

Step #2: Calculate the amount of non-food costs and profit required for a menu item. This is accomplished by multiplying the standard food cost of the menu item by the ratio calculated in step 1. Therefore, if the standard food cost of the menu item is $4.75, the amount of non-food costs and profit required is $9.64 ($4.75 × 2.03 = $9.64).

Step #3: Determine the base selling price for the menu item. This is done by adding the result of step 2 to the standard food cost of the menu item. The base selling price for the item with a $4.75 food cost would be $14.39 ($4.75 + $9.64 = $14.39).

The ratio method of menu pricing is simple to use and can be based on operating budget requirements. However, it does have several disadvantages. In an operation offering both food and beverages, it is necessary to separate non-food costs and profit requirements between the two revenue centers. Also, under this pricing method, each meal assumes an equal share of non-food costs and profit. The ratio pricing method does not compensate for higher labor costs associated with the preparation of labor-intensive menu items.

Simple Prime Costs Method

The term **prime costs** refers to the most significant costs in a food service operation: product (food and beverage) and labor. A **simple prime costs pricing method** involves assessing the labor costs for the food service operation and factoring these costs into the pricing equation. The three steps to simple prime costs pricing are as follows:

1. Determine the labor cost per guest by dividing labor costs by the number of expected guests.

2. Determine the prime costs per guest by adding the labor cost per guest to the menu item's food cost.

3. Determine the menu item's base selling price by dividing the prime costs per guest by the desired prime costs percentage.

The following example demonstrates the simple prime costs pricing method. Let's assume that the food service manager has obtained the following data:

Menu Item Food Cost	$3.75
Labor Costs	$210,000
Number of Expected Guests	75,000
Desired Prime Costs Percentage	62%

The food cost for the menu item is the standard cost derived by costing the item's standard recipe. Labor costs and estimated guests are obtained from the approved operating budget. The desired prime costs percentage combines projected food and labor cost percentages, also from the operating budget.

Step #1: Determine the labor cost per guest. The labor cost per guest is determined by dividing labor costs by the number of expected guests:

$$\text{Labor Cost per Guest} = \frac{\text{Labor Costs}}{\text{Number of Expected Guests}}$$

$$\$2.80 = \frac{\$210,000}{75,000}$$

Step #2: Determine the prime costs per guest. The labor cost per guest ($2.80) added to the menu item's food cost ($3.75) equals $6.55.

Step #3: Determine the menu item's base selling price. This is calculated by dividing the prime costs per guest (the result of step 2) by the desired prime costs percentage:

$$\text{Base Selling Price} = \frac{\text{Prime Costs per Guest}}{\text{Desired Prime Costs Percentage}}$$

$$\$10.56 = \frac{\$6.55}{.62}$$

Exhibit 6   Calculations for Specific Prime Costs Pricing

Budget Item	Operating Budget Percentage	Category A (Extensive Preparation) Items	Category B (Non-Extensive Preparation) Items
(1)	(2)	(3)	(4)
Food Cost	35%	60% of 35% = 21%	40% of 35% = 14%
Labor Cost	30%	55% of 30% = 17% 60% of 13% = 8%	40% of 13% = 5%
All Other Costs	20%	60% of 20% = 12%	40% of 20% = 8%
Profit	15%	60% of 15% = 9%	40% of 15% = 6%
Total	100%	67%	33%
Multiplier	$\frac{100\%}{35\%}$ = 2.9	$\frac{67\%}{21\%}$ = 3.2	$\frac{33\%}{14\%}$ = 2.4

The food service manager would then adjust this base selling price in relation to other factors, such as the operation's target markets and the competition. Advantages of this method are its focus on both food and labor costs and the fact that it is easy to use. An obvious disadvantage is the need to assign an equal labor cost to each menu item, even though the actual labor costs for menu items mayvary greatly. The specific prime costs pricing method attempts to overcome this problem.

Specific Prime Costs Method

With the **specific prime costs pricing method** the food service manager develops multipliers for menu items so that the base selling prices for the items cover their food costs and their fair share of labor costs. Items with extensive preparation have higher labor costs and should have higher mark-ups. Conversely, items not requiring extensive preparation have lower labor costs that can be reflected in a lower mark-up.

The manager first divides all menu items into two categories: those that do and those that do not involve extensive preparation labor. The definition of extensive preparation labor is left to the manager to determine. For example, perhaps stew made from scratch is considered labor-intensive to prepare, while a steak that only has to be broiled is considered non-labor-intensive. Typically, all items are assumed to require approximately the same amount of labor for service and cleanup; these labor costs are shared by both categories of menu items.

Next, the manager allocates appropriate percentages of total food costs and labor costs to each category of menu items. Let's assume that the manager's analysis of menu items sold during a recent period showed that:

- 60 percent of the total food cost is expended for items requiring extensive preparation (Category A items).

- 40 percent of total food cost is expended for items requiring little preparation (Category B items).

- 55 percent of all labor costs is incurred for preparation of all menu items (both Category A and Category B items).

- 45 percent of all labor costs is incurred for service, cleanup, and other non-preparation activities.

Given this information, Exhibit 6 demonstrates the calculations to be made using the specific prime costs pricing method.

Note that line items from the approved operating budget are listed in column 1. These line items include: food cost, labor cost, all other costs, and profit. Operating budget percentages for each line item are noted in column 2. These figures represent percentages of forecasted revenue. For example, the operating budget specifies a 35 percent food cost—35 percent of expected revenue will go toward paying food costs. These percentages are re-allocated in column 3 for menu items that involve extensive preparation labor (Category A) and in column 4 for items that do not involve extensive preparation labor (Category B).

Recall that the manager's previous analysis of menu items sold during a recent period showed that the food costs required to produce Category A items (involving extensive preparation) equaled 60 percent of the food costs incurred for the period. An adjusted food cost percentage for labor-intensive menu items of 21 percent can be calculated by multiplying the 35 percent total food cost by 60 percent ($.35 \times .6 = .21 \times 100 = 21$ percent). Similarly, an adjusted food cost percentage for non-labor-intensive menu items of 14 percent is calculated by multiplying the 35 percent total food cost by 40 percent ($.35 \times .4 = .14 \times 100 = 14$ percent).

The manager now needs to allocate the total labor cost percentage (30 percent as shown in column 2) between preparation and non-preparation labor activities. In this particular case, the manager decides to allocate all of the preparation labor to Category A menu items because little or no labor expense is incurred for Category B menu items. Recall that the manager's previous analysis showed that 55 percent of all labor cost is incurred for the preparation of menu items. Since all of this labor cost will be allocated to Category A menu items, the manager multiplies 30 percent (the percentage of revenue representing total labor costs) by 55 percent (the percentage of total labor costs for preparing menu items). Exhibit 6 shows that 17 percent [$.30 \times .55 = .17$ (rounded) $\times 100 = 17$ percent] of the total labor cost is charged to menu items involving extensive preparation.

The remaining 13 percent of the total labor costs (30 percent labor costs from the operating budget minus 17 percent labor costs for preparation of menu items) is allocated between both Category A and Category B menu items, since this is the cost of labor incurred for service, cleanup, and other activities that should be shared equally. However, sharing equally does not necessarily mean a 50/50 split. Because food costs have been allocated on the 60/40 basis, this approach is also used to allocate non-preparation labor. Therefore, 8 percent of labor costs are charged to Category A menu items [$.60 \times .13 = .08$ (rounded) $\times 100 = 8$ percent]. This labor cost is identified in column 3. The remaining 5 percent of non-preparation labor cost (13 percent $-$ 8 percent $=$ 5 percent) is allocated to Category B menu items. This labor cost is identified in column 4.

All other costs (20 percent of forecasted revenue as shown in column 2) and profit (15 percent of forecasted revenue as noted in column 2) are also allocated on the 60/40 basis between Category A and Category B menu items.

At this point in the process, the manager can determine several multipliers. Multipliers are set by adding the individual cost percentages (food cost, labor cost, all other costs, and profit) and dividing by the desired food cost percentage.

For example, a multiplier based on the 35 percent desired food cost from the current operating budget (column 2) is 2.9. This is calculated by dividing 100 percent (the total cost and profit percentage shown at the bottom of column 2) by the budgeted food cost percentage of 35 percent [1 divided by .35 equals 2.9 (rounded)].

The multiplier for menu items requiring extensive preparation (column 3) is calculated by dividing 67 percent (the total cost and profit percentage shown at the bottom of column 3) by the desired food cost percentage of 21 percent for this category of menu items [.67 divided by .21 equals 3.2 (rounded)].

The multiplier for menu items requiring little preparation (column 4) is calculated by dividing 33 percent (the total cost and profit percentage shown at the bottom of column 4) by the desired food cost percentage of 14 percent for this category of menu items [.33 divided by .14 equals 2.4 (rounded)].

Note that the multiplier for items involving extensive preparation (3.2) is higher than that for items in the non-extensive preparation category (2.4). Let's assume that the food cost of a menu item involving extensive preparation is $4.75. The food service manager determines a base selling price for that item by multiplying $4.75 by 3.2. This yields a base selling price for the menu item of $15.20. Note that the resulting base selling price ($15.20) is higher than if the item's food cost was marked up by only 2.4 (the mark-up for menu items that require little preparation), which would yield an $11.40 base selling price. This lower price reflects the fact that there is much less labor required to produce the menu item.

While the specific prime costs pricing method establishes base selling prices for the items to cover their fair share of labor costs, there are several disadvantages to this pricing method. Significant time may be spent in classifying menu items into extensive-preparation and non-extensive-preparation categories. Time will also be spent performing the necessary calculations. Also, this pricing method forces managers to assume that the relationships among all other operating costs vary in the same proportion as food costs. While this is often a reasonable assumption, there may be costs, such as higher energy costs, associated with preparing some items that reduce the accuracy of this method.

Important Pricing Considerations

Throughout this section, we have suggested that the result of menu pricing calculations is a base selling price. This is because the simple output of formulas used in the examples may not be an appropriate final selling price for a menu item. Rather, it is a starting point from which other factors must be assessed.

The concept of value (price relative to quality) is always important. Guests pay for more than just the product (food and beverage) when they visit the operation. Quality of service, cleanliness of the facility, and atmosphere are also part of the dining experience and should, even if subjectively, be factored into the selling-price decision.

The basic law of supply and demand is another factor to be considered. Ultimately, the price that can be charged is established by the guests themselves as they decide whether to return to the property.

Volume concerns must also be considered. As fewer guests are served, overhead charges per guest increase; selling prices must be higher. The reverse is also true: more guests may allow the manager to reduce overhead costs in the pricing decision.

The price charged by the competition for a similar product is another concern. The more an operation can differentiate its products from those of the competition, the more freedom the operation has in setting a selling price.

For example, perhaps two properties offer a similar steak dinner. While the price charged for the steak is important, there are other factors that may influence people to visit one property or the other. Perhaps one property provides entertainment, while the other offers an attractive atmosphere. Emphasizing the differences between the property's own products and services and those offered by other businesses is one way to remain competitive.

One technique that can be used to attract guests from competitors is lowering menu prices. This may succeed in bringing more people into an operation, but only if the lower priced items are considered by guests as substitutes for what the competition offers. If there are no significant differences between what one operation offers and what the competition offers, then guests may see price as the determining factor in selecting one property over the others. However, if there are non-price-related differences that are important to guests (such as atmosphere, entertainment, etc.) this technique may not work.

Raising prices is also a way of responding to pressures from the competition. With higher prices, fewer menu items will need to be sold for the operation to meet profit requirements. However, raising a menu item's selling price may be effective only if the increased revenue from the price increase makes up for the revenue lost as demand falls off and current guests begin to buy other menu items as substitutes. In fact, in some cases, a more effective strategy for increasing total revenue may be lowering a menu item's selling price. Lowering prices may increase the volume of unit sales, and this increase may produce an increase in total revenue.

What we are really talking about here is the concept of **elasticity of demand**. Elasticity is a term economists use to describe how the quantity demanded responds to changes in price. If a certain percentage price change creates a larger percentage change in the quantity demanded, the demand is elastic and the item is considered to be price-sensitive. If, on the other hand, the percentage change in quantity demanded is less than the percentage change in price, the demand is inelastic. Before changing the established price of a menu item, it is important to know the elasticity of demand for that item—the extent to which demand changes as the price changes.

Evaluating the Menu

You know the menu is a most important tool influencing the success or failure of a food and beverage operation. But how should menus be evaluated to determine whether the most profitable menu items are being sold? The process of **menu engineering** is an increasingly popular approach to this problem of menu evaluation.

What is a "good" menu item? There are two measures of how good a menu item is: its popularity and its profitability. A popular menu item is ordered frequently by guests. A profitable menu item generates a high contribution margin. Menu items can be evaluated in terms of both their popularity and profitability.

Basically, the menu engineering process uses information readily available to the food and beverage manager to classify menu items into four types:

1. Stars—items that are popular and profitable
2. Plowhorses—items that are not profitable but popular
3. Puzzles—items that are profitable but not popular
4. Dogs—items that are neither profitable nor popular

To classify each menu item into one of the four basic categories, managers must develop a practical way to define and measure the relative profitability and popularity of each menu item. This can be accomplished by using information about standard food costs and frequency of unit sales.

Earlier in this chapter, we noted that the basis of a menu item's profitability is *not* the level of its food cost, but its contribution margin. Some managers assume that the lower a menu item's food cost percentage, the more profitable the sale of the item is to the operation. In other words, the lower the percentage of revenue needed to pay for the food needed for the menu item, the larger the percentage of revenue available for all other expenses and profit. While this theory sounds good, it can be easily disproved. Consider the following example.

Menu Item	Food Cost	Menu Selling Price	Food Cost %	Contribution Margin
Chicken	$2.48	$7.50	33%	$5.02
Steak	$6.02	$14.00	43%	$7.98

In this example, chicken has the lower food cost percentage (33 percent compared to 43 percent cost for steak). According to the traditional view, the sale of chicken should help the operation more than the sale of steak. However, as shown by the contribution margin (menu selling price minus food cost), only $5.02 is left from the sale of chicken to pay for all other costs and to make a contribution to the property's profit requirements. In the case of steak, $7.98 remains.

This example illustrates a very important point: the goal of effective menu planning and evaluation should be to increase the contribution margin of each menu item—not decrease its food cost percentage. There is truth in the old saying, "You can't bank percentages!"

Information about frequency of unit sales for each menu item can be gathered by tallying the number of each item sold during some specified time period (such as two weeks). This information can be abstracted from guest checks or, more frequently, by analysis of unit sales information from the electronic register or production records indicating leftovers, if applicable. Popular items are those with a relatively high menu mix percentage. Accordingly, "star" menu items are those with relatively high contribution margins and high menu mix percentages, while items classified as "dogs" score relatively low on both measures.

In performing a menu engineering analysis, it is not enough to consider menu items individually. Each item's contribution margin and menu mix percentage will provide measures for the item's levels of profitability and popularity, but the problem is to evaluate how high or low these levels are in comparison with all other menu items. What constitutes a "high" level of profitability or popularity? For example, suppose that unit sales of a particular menu item represent 10 percent of total unit sales. Is this a "high" menu mix? Should this item be classified as a "popular" menu item? The answer depends on the menu mix percentages of all other menu items and on the total number of items on the menu. For instance, if the menu in question contains ten different items, 10 percent of total unit sales may be regarded as a high level of popularity, but if there are only four items on the menu, this figure would represent a low level of popularity. Likewise, by itself, a menu item's contribution margin tells us very little about how profitable unit sales of this item are when compared with other menu items.

Defining Profitability

The basis for measuring the degree of profitability of each menu item is the average contribution margin. A "high" contribution margin for an individual menu item would be one that is equal to or greater than the average contribution margin for all menu items. The concept of the menu's average contribution margin provides managers with a precise measure of each menu item's profitability, and it is easily calculated from readily available information. Recall that the contribution margin of a menu item is calculated by subtracting its food cost from its selling price.

Since the manager knows the costs incurred and the revenue generated for each individual menu item, the total menu costs and the total menu revenues generated can be determined by simply summing the figures for each menu item. The total contribution margin for all menu items is calculated by subtracting total menu costs from total menu revenues.

Finally, the average contribution margin is calculated by dividing the total menu contribution margin by the total number of menu items sold during the specified time period in which unit sales data were collected.

$$\text{Average Contribution Margin} = \frac{\text{Total Contribution Margin}}{\text{Total Number of Items Sold}}$$

Individual contribution margins for each menu item can now be compared to the average contribution margin for all menu items to assess each item's level of profitability. A profitable menu item is one whose individual contribution margin equals or exceeds the average contribution margin. The concept of average contribution margin is further illustrated in an example of menu engineering analysis presented later in this chapter.

Defining Popularity

The basis for measuring the degree of popularity of each menu item is called the popularity index. This index is based upon the notion of "expected popularity." For the purpose of analysis, each menu item is assumed to be equally popular. This means that each item is "expected" to contribute an equal share of total menu unit sales. Therefore, the expected popularity of each menu item is calculated by simply dividing 100 percent (i.e., total unit sales) by the number of items on the menu. For example, if there are only four items on a menu and each item is assumed to be equally popular, the unit sales of each item would be expected to represent 25 percent of total unit sales (100 percent divided by 4 equals 25 percent). On the other hand, if there were ten items on the menu, each item would be expected to represent 10 percent of total unit sales (100 percent divided by 10 equals 10 percent).

Menu engineering assumes that an item is popular if its unit sales equal 70 percent of what is expected. Thus, the popularity index for items on a given menu is defined as 70 percent of the expected popularity of each item on that menu. (The popularity index of 70 percent is based upon the experience of the authors of *Menu Engineering*. The popularity index for a specific property can be adjusted to a higher or lower level depending upon the manager's emphasis on selling popular and profitable items.)

For example, a food item on a four-item menu would be considered popular if its unit sales represented 17.5 percent of total unit sales (100 percent ÷ 4 items = 25 percent × 70 percent = 17.5 percent). On the other hand, a food item on a ten-item menu would be considered popular if it accounted for only 7 percent of total unit sales (100 percent ÷ 10 items = 10 percent × 70 percent = 7 percent). This is why the menu item in the previous example, which represented 10 percent of total unit sales, would be considered popular if it were part of a ten-item menu and unpopular if it belonged to a four-item menu. The concept of a popularity index makes it possible to measure the relative degree of popularity of each item on a given menu.

With these tools of menu engineering, managers can evaluate the profitability and popularity of menu items and classify them as either stars, plowhorses, puzzles, or dogs. The results of this evaluation should be used to improve the menu.

Evaluating Menu Items

Exhibit 7 provides an analysis for a food and beverage operation offering only four menu items. Each of these is listed in column A of Exhibit 7. Assume that this operation collected information about the frequency of unit sales for each menu item over a two-week period. This information is recorded in column B. Note at the bottom of column B (box N) that a total of 1,000 entrées were sold during the two-week period.

The menu mix (percentage of unit sales represented by each menu item) is calculated in column C. For example, 42 percent of all items sold were chicken dinners (420 chicken dinners sold divided by 1,000 total dinners sold = .42 × 100 = 42 percent).

Exhibit 7   Menu Engineering Worksheet

Menu Engineering Worksheet

Restaurant: _Terrace Cafe_

Date: _6/10/00_

Meal Period: _Dinner_

(A) Menu Item Name	(B) Number Sold (MM)	(C) Menu Mix %	(D) Item Food Cost	(E) Item Selling Price	(F) Item CM (E – D)	(G) Menu Costs (D × B)	(H) Menu Revenues (E × B)	(L) Menu CM (H – G)	(P) CM Category	(R) MM% Category	(S) Menu Item Classification
Chicken Dinner	420	42%	$5.21	$7.95	$2.74	$ 2,188.20	$3,339.00	$1,150.80	Low	High	Plowhorse
NY Strip Steak	360	36%	8.50	12.50	4.00	3,060.00	4,500.00	1,440.00	High	High	Star
Lobster Tail	150	15%	9.95	14.50	4.55	1,492.50	2,175.00	682.50	High	Low	Puzzle
Tenderloin Tips	70	7%	7.00	9.45	2.45	490.00	661.50	171.50	Low	Low	Dog
Column Totals:	N					I	J	M			
	1,000					$7,230.70	$10,675.50	$3,444.80			

Additional Computations:

O = M/N

$3.44

Q = (100%/items) (70%)

17.5%

(Box O = Average Contribution Margin)

Source: Adapted from Michael L. Kasavana and Donald I. Smith, *Menu Engineering* (Okemos, Mich.: Hospitality Publications, 1982), p. 64.

The item's food cost is recorded in column D. For example, the total ingredient cost of all items comprising the chicken dinner is calculated to be $5.21.

Each item's selling price is listed in column E. This information is taken directly from the menu. You will note that the chicken dinner sells for $7.95.

Column F (*Item CM*) lists the contribution margin of the menu item. To calculate the contribution margin for the chicken dinner, we subtract the item's food cost from the item's selling price. For example, for chicken dinners: $7.95 − $5.21 = $2.74.

The total menu cost (column G) is calculated by multiplying the number of each item sold (column B) by the item's food cost (column D). The total menu cost for the chicken dinner is calculated as follows: 420 chicken dinners × $5.21 food cost = $2,188.20.

Menu revenues (column H) are calculated by multiplying the number of each item sold by the item's selling price. The menu revenue for chicken dinners ($3,339) is calculated by multiplying the number of chicken dinners by the selling price: 420 chicken dinners × $7.95 = $3,339.

The contribution margin for the total sales of the menu item (column L) is calculated by subtracting the menu costs from the menu revenues. For example, the menu contribution for the chicken dinner ($1,150.80) is calculated by deducting the item's menu cost ($2,188.20) in column G, from the menu revenues ($3,339) in column H.

It is now possible to determine the average contribution margin (the basis for profitability) and the popularity index (the basis for popularity). In Exhibit 7, the total menu cost of $7,230.70 is recorded at the bottom of column G (box I) and is calculated by summing the menu costs for each individual item. Likewise, the total menu revenues are calculated by summing the individual revenues for each item in column H. The total revenues of $10,675.50 are noted at the bottom of column H in box J.

The next step is to calculate the total contribution margin for all menu items by subtracting menu costs (box I) from menu revenues (box J). Because 1,000 menu items were sold (box N) and because the total menu contribution margin is $3,444.80 (box M), the average contribution margin is $3.44 (box O):

$$\text{Average Contribution Margin} = \frac{\text{Total Contribution Margin}}{\text{Total Number of Items Sold}}$$

$$\$3.44 = \frac{\$3,444.80}{1,000}$$

Those items that are profitable (i.e., those with a high contribution margin) are those whose contribution margin is equal to or greater than the average contribution margin for all menu items ($3.44). Items with a contribution margin above this amount are, then, those items the property most wishes to sell. Column P shows that the most profitable menu items are New York Strip Steak and Lobster Tail.

Column R in Exhibit 7 indicates the assessment of each item's popularity. The judgment is arrived at by comparing each item's menu mix percentage (percentage of total unit sales indicated in column C) with the popularity index calculated for this particular menu. Because there are only four items, each item has an expected popularity of 25 percent (100 percent divided by 4 equals 25 percent). Assuming that unit sales of a popular item should equal 70 percent of what is expected for it, the popularity index is 17.5 percent (70 percent × 25 percent = 17.5 percent). In Exhibit 7, then, popular items are those whose unit sales represent 17.5 percent or more of total sales (see box Q). For example, because the menu mix percentage (column C) for the chicken dinner is 42 percent, its menu mix category is rated as high (column R). In contrast, consider the tenderloin tips dinner: its menu mix (7 percent) is much lower than the 17.5 percent required for an item to be classified as popular. Therefore, its menu mix category is rated as low (column R).

Given this information, it is possible to classify menu items. Consider the chicken dinner again. We just noted that this is a popular item. Is it also profitable? Its contribution margin is $2.74 (column F). This is less than the average contribution margin and is classified as a relatively low contribution margin item (column P). The chicken dinner is popular but unprofitable. Therefore, this menu item is classified as a plowhorse (column S).

As a second example, consider the lobster tail dinner in Exhibit 7. Its contribution margin category (column P) is rated as high since its individual contribution margin (column F) is $4.55 (which is significantly more than the $3.44 required for an item to be classified as profitable). Its menu mix category (column R) is low. Its menu mix percentage of 15 percent (column C) is lower than the 17.5 percent required for the item to be classified as popular. Therefore, this menu item is classified as a "puzzle" (column S). It is a profitable item that the property wishes to sell, but it is not popular with guests.

Improving the Menu

The benefits of menu engineering can only accrue if information gained from the menu engineering analysis is used to improve the menu. What can a food and beverage manager do with this knowledge about the various food item classifications?

Managing Plowhorses. First, let's consider plowhorses (those items low in contribution margin, but high in popularity). Guests like these items, but, unfortunately, plowhorses do not contribute their fair share of contribution margin. Possible strategies for managing a plowhorse menu item include:

- Increase prices carefully. Perhaps the item is popular because it represents a great value to guests. If prices could be increased, the item may still represent a good value, may remain popular, and may generate a higher contribution margin. This alternative may be most effective when the item is unique to the property and cannot be obtained elsewhere.

- Test for demand. If there is no strong resistance to price increases, it may be useful to complement an increased price with other strategies such as repackaging the item or repositioning it on the menu. These other strategies may be designed to maintain or increase the item's popularity while generating a higher contribution margin through the increase in selling price. If prices are to be increased, this should probably be done in several stages rather than all at once.

- Relocate the item to a lower profile on the menu. Depending upon the menu layout, certain areas of a menu represent a better location than others. A plowhorse can be relocated to a less desirable area of the menu. Since the item is popular, some guests will search it out. Others will be drawn to higher profile areas of the menu that list more profitable items the property wishes to sell.

- Shift demand to more desirable items. Menu engineering allows the manager to determine which items to sell—those high in popularity and high in contribution margin. Servers using suggestive selling techniques, for example, would *not* recommend plowhorses. Table tents and other point of sale tools would, likewise, suggest stars and puzzles (because of their high contribution margins); they would not suggest plowhorses.

- Combine with lower cost products. The contribution margin of a plowhorse can be increased if lower cost meal accompaniments are offered with the entree. Perhaps, for example, higher priced vegetables and dessert accompaniments can be replaced with other, less expensive items without reducing the item's popularity. If this can be done, the contribution margin will increase.

- Assess the direct labor factor. The food and beverage manager should know if there is a significant amount of direct labor required to produce the plowhorse item. If an item with a low contribution margin does not have a significant amount of direct labor involved in production (a convenience food product, for example), the manager may be able to justify the lower contribution margin since fewer revenue dollars will be required to compensate for labor cost.

- Consider portion reduction. If the portion size is reduced, the product cost will be decreased and the contribution margin will increase. This alternative must be viewed with caution, of course, since the guest's perception of value may decrease when the portion size is reduced.

Managing Puzzles. Puzzles are items that are high in contribution margin but low in popularity—items the food and beverage manager desires to sell since their contribution margin is relatively high. The challenge is to find ways to increase the number of guests ordering these items. Alternatives include:

- Shift demand to these items. Techniques include repositioning the items to more visible areas of the menu, renaming them, using suggestive selling techniques, developing advertising campaigns, using table tents, using buttons and badges on server uniforms, highlighting items on menu boards at the entrance to the dining area, and other strategies to increase the item's popularity.

- Consider a price decrease. Perhaps an item is low in popularity because it does not represent a value to guests. If this is the case, the selling price might be decreased with the contribution margin still remaining higher than average. This could lead to increased popularity, since a reduced selling price would represent a greater value to the guest.

- Add value to the item. Offering a larger portion size, adding more expensive meal accompaniments or garnishes, and using higher quality ingredients are among the ways that value can be increased. These techniques may lead to increased popularity and to a contribution margin that is lower, but still higher than the average generated by the menu.

Managing Stars. Stars are items that are high in contribution margin and high in popularity. The best advice for managing stars includes:

- Maintain rigid specifications. Do not attempt to alter the quality of the product being served.

- Place in a highly visible location on the menu. Stars are items that the food and beverage operator wants to sell. Therefore, make sure guests are aware of their availability.

- Test for selling price inelasticity. Perhaps the star is popular because it is a significant value to the guest. Or, perhaps the star is not available in its existing form elsewhere in the marketplace. These might be two instances in which the price could be increased without a decrease in popularity.

- Use suggestive selling techniques. Some of the techniques for shifting demand to puzzles might also be useful for stars.

Managing Dogs. Dogs (items that are low in contribution margin and low in popularity) are obvious candidates for removal from the menu. After all, they do not contribute their fair share of contribution margin and they are not popular. Alternatively, the selling price could be increased, since this would at least generate a higher contribution margin. When a "dog" requires a significant amount of direct labor, does not permit sufficient use of leftovers, and has a relatively short storage life, the reasons for removing the item from the menu become more compelling.

To this point, we have suggested how a menu item classification system lends itself to the development of improved menus by more effective management of individual menu items. Are there other advantages to the use of the menu engineering process? Yes, it can be used to evaluate the worth of the entire menu. Consider, for example, the current practice in the industry when a menu is revised. The manager, guests, employees, and others may offer their opinions about the revisions. They may subjectively assess the menu's "worth" and offer their views about its improvements over earlier versions. If the guests "seem" to like it and if there are no overt employee problems with the revised menu, it is judged to be acceptable.

By contrast, menu engineering can be used to evaluate menu revisions in an objective manner. For example, if the popularity of an individual menu remains stable (or increases) while its contribution margin increases, the revised menu is a good one. With the tools of menu engineering, the worth of a revised menu can be objectively assessed. If, for example, a previous menu generated an average contribution margin of $2.50 and a successive menu generates an average contribution margin of $2.75 without a subsequent decrease in guest count, the new menu is better: the average guest leaves 25 cents more in contribution margin than when the previous menu was in use.

Computer-Based Menu Management

Menu management computer applications help management answer such questions as:

- What is the most profitable price to assign a menu item?
- At what price level and sales mix does a food service operation maximize its profits?
- Which current menu items require repricing, retention, replacement, or repositioning on the menu?
- How should daily specials and new items be priced?
- How can the success of a menu change be evaluated?

As already seen, menu engineering is a menu management model that helps evaluate decisions regarding current and future menu pricing, design, and contents. The following sections examine a computerized application of menu engineering.

Menu Engineering Analysis

Data for analysis can be entered into the program's database manually, automatically (from an integrated restaurant management applications package), or electronically (through an external ECR/POS system interface). A stand-alone version of menu engineering requires that the user input each menu item's product cost, selling price, and sales history. This minimal input is sufficient to generate a complete menu engineering analysis. Food service operators who use computer-based recipe management applications to provide accurate product cost data can program a menu engineering application to read this data from a file, rather than rely upon user input.

Following data input and selection of the analysis option, the menu engineering application begins its work. As the analysis progresses, a menu item's contribution margin and unit sales activity will be categorized as relatively high or low. Procedures performed here are identical to those described for the manual analysis earlier. Eventually, each item will be further classified for both its marketing and pricing success. The menu engineering output is composed of five reports:

- Menu item analysis
- Menu mix analysis

Exhibit 8   Menu Item Analysis

Item Analysis				
Item Name	Item Price	Portion Cost	Contr. Margin	Item Count
Fried Shrimp	7.95	4.85	3.10	210
Fried Chicken	4.95	2.21	2.74	420
Chopped Sirloin	4.50	1.95	2.55	90
Prime Rib	7.95	4.95	3.00	600
King Prime Rib	9.95	5.65	4.30	60
NY Strip Steak	8.50	4.50	4.00	360
Top Sirloin	7.95	4.30	3.65	510
Red Snapper	6.95	3.95	3.00	240
Lobster Tail	9.50	4.95	4.55	150
Tenderloin Tips	6.45	4.00	2.45	360

Source: Adapted from Michael L. Kasavana and Donald I. Smith, *Menu Engineering* (Okemos, Mich.: Hospitality Publications, 1982), p. 77.

- Menu engineering summary
- Four-box analysis
- Menu engineering graph

Menu Item Analysis

Exhibit 8 illustrates the initial report in the menu engineering analysis. This is an item-by-item listing accompanied by selling price, portion cost, contribution margin, and item count (number sold). The primary purpose of this report is to provide the user with a means by which to verify the data that is to be analyzed. This can be helpful when data has been manually entered into the program.

Menu Mix Analysis

Exhibit 9 illustrates a menu mix analysis report. This report evaluates each item's participation in the overall menu's performance. The percentage of menu mix (%MM Share) is based upon each item's count divided by the total number of items sold. Each percentage is then ranked as high or low depending upon its comparison with the menu engineering rule for menu mix sufficiency. The percentage each item has contributed to the menu's total contribution margin is found in the column labeled %CM Share. Each item's contribution margin is then ranked according to how it compares with the menu's weighted average contribution margin (ACM). A menu classification for each item is determined by considering its MM group rank and CM group rank together.

Menu Engineering Summary

Exhibit 10 illustrates a menu engineering summary report. Perhaps the most informative report produced by the menu engineering application, this analysis

Exhibit 9   Menu Mix Analysis

						Menu Mix Analysis	
Item Name	MM Count	% MM Share	Group Rank	% CM Share	Contr. Margin	Group Rank	Menu Class
Fried Shrimp	210	7.00	HIGH	6.73	3.10	LOW	PLOWHORSE
Fried Chicken	420	14.00	HIGH	11.89	2.74	LOW	PLOWHORSE
Chopped Sirloin	90	3.00	LOW	2.37	2.55	LOW	<< DOG >>
Prime Rib	600	20.00	HIGH	18.60	3.00	LOW	PLOWHORSE
King Prime Rib	60	2.00	LOW	2.67	4.30	HIGH	?PUZZLE?
NY Strip Steak	360	12.00	HIGH	14.88	4.00	HIGH	**STAR**
Top Sirloin	510	17.00	HIGH	19.24	3.65	HIGH	**STAR**
Red Snapper	240	8.00	HIGH	7.44	3.00	LOW	PLOWHORSE
Lobster Tail	150	5.00	LOW	7.05	4.55	HIGH	?PUZZLE?
Tenderloin Tips	360	12.00	HIGH	9.12	2.45	LOW	PLOWHORSE

Source: Adapted from Michael L. Kasavana and Donald I. Smith, *Menu Engineering* (Okemos, Mich.: Hospitality Publications, 1982), p. 77.

Exhibit 10   Menu Engineering Summary

	Menu Engineering Summary				
	Total	Average		Low	High
Price	22050.00	7.35		4.50	9.95
Food Cost	12374.70	4.12		1.95	5.65
Contribution Margin	9675.30	3.23		2.45	4.55
Demand Factor	3000	300		60	600
Food Cost Percentage . .	56.12%				
Number of Items	10				

Source: Adapted from Michael L. Kasavana and Donald I. Smith, *Menu Engineering* (Okemos, Mich.: Hospitality Publications, 1982), p. 78.

presents important information in capsule form to produce a concise statement of operations. The row labeled *Price* shows total menu revenue, average item selling price, lowest selling price, and highest selling price. The *Food Cost* row contains total menu costs, average item food cost, lowest cost item, and highest cost item. The *Contribution Margin* row shows total menu CM, average item CM, lowest item CM, and highest item CM. The *Demand Factor* row lists total number of covers (guests), average number of covers, lowest item count, and highest item count. Much of the information in the body of this report is used elsewhere in the overall menu engineering system. For example, the lowest and highest selling prices on the menu are termed price points and can be used to help identify target market success. This report also contains the menu's food cost percentage and number of items sold.

Exhibit 11   Four-Box Analysis

<table>
<tr>
<td>

PLOWHORSE

Fried Shrimp
Fried Chicken
Prime Rib
Red Snapper
Tenderloin Tips

</td>
<td>

STAR

NY Strip
Steak
Top Sirloin

</td>
</tr>
<tr>
<td>

DOG

Chopped Sirloin

</td>
<td>

PUZZLE

King Prime Rib
Lobster Tail

</td>
</tr>
</table>

Source: Adapted from Michael L. Kasavana and Donald I. Smith, *Menu Engineering* (Okemos, Mich.: Hospitality Publications, 1982), p. 78.

Four-Box Analysis

Exhibit 11 illustrates a four-box analysis that indexes the menu classifications developed in the menu mix analysis report. Since menu engineering leads to a series of decision strategies specific to each menu classification, this report provides the user with insight about the number of items found in each category. For example, Exhibit 11 displays a menu composed of five plowhorses, two stars, two puzzles, and one dog. Are five plowhorses too many? This type of evaluation process begins with the four-box matrix and continues through the menu engineering graph.

Menu Engineering Graph

Exhibit 12 illustrates a menu engineering graph, a useful means to evaluate decision strategies. Because it indicates each competing menu item's position relative to all others, the menu engineering graph is the most powerful report produced by a menu engineering application. The vertical axis of the graph positions menu mix and the horizontal axis positions contribution margin. Each item is then graphed according to its CM and MM coordinates. It is especially important to note that not all items in the same classification possess identical characteristics. This technique, therefore, points out that a different menu engineering strategy may be appropriate for items even though they are similarly segmented. Prime rib, for example, presents a very different profile from fried shrimp. Neither item as currently priced generates the average contribution margin. Yet prime rib is the most popular menu item and represents a great value to the guest. Therefore, the food service operator may be more willing to raise the price of prime rib than the price of fried shrimp.

Exhibit 12   Menu Engineering Graph

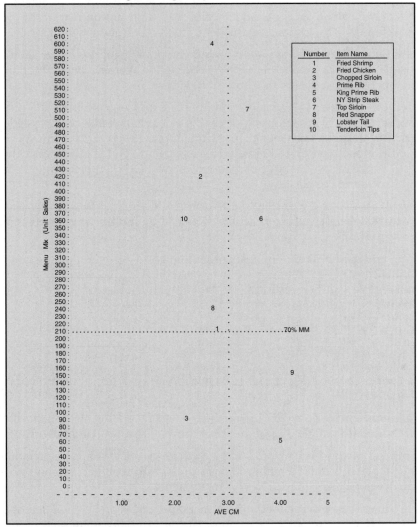

Source: Adapted from Michael L. Kasavana and Donald I. Smith, *Menu Engineering* (Okemos, Mich.: Hospitality Publications, 1982), p. 80.

🔑 Key Terms

ambience—The theme or atmosphere of a food and beverage operation.

base selling price—The result of pricing formulas—not necessarily the final selling price. A base selling price is considered a starting point from which other factors must be assessed and the price adjusted accordingly.

contribution margin—Revenue minus food costs for either an entire operating department or for a given menu item. It represents the amount of revenue that is contributed toward fixed costs and profits. The contribution margin of a menu item is determined by subtracting the item's food cost from its selling price.

contribution margin pricing method—A menu pricing approach that determines the base selling price for a menu item by adding the average contribution margin required per guest to the item's standard food cost.

elasticity of demand—A term economists use to describe how the quantity demanded responds to changes in price. If a price change of a certain percentage creates a larger percentage change in the quantity demanded, the demand is elastic, and the item is considered to be price-sensitive. If, on the other hand, the percentage change in the quantity demanded is less than the percentage change in price, the demand is inelastic.

ingredients mark-up pricing method—A menu pricing approach that considers all food costs. A base selling price is established by multiplying the ingredients' costs by a multiplier.

mark-up with accompaniment costs pricing method—A menu pricing approach that establishes a base selling price by determining ingredient costs based only upon the entrée and then adding a standard accompaniment or "plate" cost to this amount before multiplying by a multiplier.

menu engineering—A manual or computerized method of menu analysis and item pricing that considers both the profitability and popularity of competing menu items.

prime costs—The most significant costs in a food service operation: product costs, (food and beverage) and labor costs.

prime-ingredient mark-up pricing method—A menu pricing method in which the cost of the entrée is marked up rather than the total cost of all ingredients.

ratio pricing method—A menu pricing method that determines the relationship between food costs and all non-food costs plus profit requirements and uses this ratio to develop base selling prices for menu items.

simple prime costs pricing method—A menu pricing approach that determines a menu item's base selling price by dividing the prime costs per guest by the desired prime costs percentage.

specific prime costs pricing method—A menu pricing approach in which multipliers for menu items are determined in such a way that the base selling prices for the items cover their fair share of labor costs.

Review Questions

1. In what ways can a system of control points help the food and beverage manager consistently identify and carry out control functions on a daily basis?

2. What are some of the more important planning and control activities that are directly affected by the menu?

3. What are some marketing implications of menu planning?

4. How are menu changes modified by external and internal factors?

5. How can the multiplier be determined for simple mark-up methods of pricing menu items?

6. In what ways does the contribution margin pricing method differ from the ratio pricing method?

7. In what ways does the simple prime costs pricing method differ from the specific prime costs pricing method?

8. What factors other than the base selling price established by pricing formulas must managers consider when setting menu prices?

9. How does menu engineering define the profitability and popularity of a menu item?

10. What actions can managers take to improve the menu by managing items identified as plowhorses? puzzles? stars? dogs?

 ## Internet Sites

For more information, visit the following Internet sites. Remember that Internet addresses can change without notice. If the site is no longer there, you can use a search engine to look for additional sites.

Associations

American Culinary Federation (ACF)
http://www.acfchefs.org

American Hotel & Lodging Association (AH&LA)
http://www.ahlaonline.org

American School Food Service Association (ASFSA)
http://www.asfsa.org

Club Managers Association of America (CMAA)
http://www.cmaa.org

The Educational Foundation of NRA
http://www.edfound.org

The Educational Institute of AH&LA
http://www.ei–ahla.org

Hospitality Financial and Technology Professionals
http://www.hftp.org

Institute of Food Technologies
http://www.ift.org

International Hotel and Restaurant Association
http://www.ih–ra.com

National Association of College and University Food Services
http://www.nacufs.org

National Restaurant Association (NRA)
http://www.restaurant.org

Food and Beverage Resources

Club Management Online
http://www.club-mgmt.com/dining/index.html

Prepared Foods. Product development, ingredients, suppliers
http://www.preparedfoods.com

Management Companies

ARAMARK
http://www.aramark.com

Sodexho Marriott
http://www.sodexhomarriott.com

Bon Appétit Management Company
http://www.bamco.com

The Wood Company
http://www.woodco.com

Compass Group
http://www.compass-na.com

Publications—Online and Printed

Bon Appétit
http://food.epicurious.com

Club Management Magazine
http://www.club-mgmt.com

Electronic Gourmet Guide
http://www.foodwine.com

Food and Hospitality Magazine
http://www.foodserviceworld.com

Food Management
http://www.foodservicesearch.com

Food Network: CyberKitchen
http://www.foodtv.com

Food Processing: The Magazine of Strategy, Technology and Trends
http://www.foodprocessing.com

Gourmet
http://food.epicurious.com

Internet Food Channel
http://www.foodchannel.com

International Hotel and Restaurant Association journal
www.hotelsmag.com

International Journal of Hospitality Management
http://www.mcb.co.uk/ijchm.htm

Journal of the American Dietetic Association
http://www.eatright.org/journaltoc.html

Journal of Nutrition, publication of American Society of Nutritional Sciences
http://nutrition.org

Lodging Food and Beverage
http://www.lodgingnews.com/lodgingfnb/

Lodging Hospitality Online
http://www.lhonline.com

Lodging News, journal of the American Hotel & Lodging Association
http://www.ei-ahla.org/webs/lodging/index.html

Nation's Restaurant News
http://www.nrn.com

On the Rail—News for Food Professionals
http://www.ontherail.com

Restaurants and Institutions magazine
http://www.rimag.com

Restaurant Business, Food Service, and ID magazines
http://www.foodservicetoday.com

Restaurant Hospitality
www.foodservicesearch.com

Restaurants and Institutions
http://www.rimag.com

Restaurants USA, publication of National Restaurant Association
http://www.restaurant.org/rusa

World Hospitality. Management magazine for hotel executives.
http://www.worldhospitality.com

# Case Study

The Perils of Menu Planning

Until six months ago, the Madison Avenue Grill was a thriving 300-unit casual-dining chain with restaurants stretching from Seattle, Washington, to London, England. But lately the news has not been so good. Karen Seaton, financial officer for the chain, has discovered that customer counts are falling off, with sales down 2.9 percent.

All signs pointed to the menu. Although Madison Avenue Grill has established a strong reputation as a quality restaurant serving upscale burgers, ribs, and fish, the novelty of their offerings has faded. In many markets, fresher, trendier concepts have taken hold. If the Grill is to withstand the competition, the menu has to change. And the sooner the better.

After consulting with COO and company cofounder Marcus Turner, Karen has gained the opportunity to test a new menu concept. To help develop that concept, she has called a 9:00 A.M. meeting with Marcus and three other company leaders: Jorge Estrada, director of marketing; Anne Hudson, director of operations/service; and Chef Charles Gustafsen. Her instructions to each: Come prepared to suggest one new menu item that can be launched immediately to turn the situation around—and be prepared to offer a rationale for the recommendation.

The five met around a large conference table in Marcus Turner's office. Karen made certain there were financial reports at each place.

"Since you're all aware of why we're meeting today, I'll keep the preliminaries brief. In a nutshell, our current numbers do not look good," she said. "The bottom line's in jeopardy, people, and if we don't do something fast, it's going to look even worse. Since the problems all seem to point to our menu, that's where I suggest we look for solutions. You're all here because I think we'll be able to come to some creative solutions if we work together. Input from each of you is important because any change we make to the menu impacts a number of key control points—purchasing, receiving, storing, issuing, production, service, and, of course, guest satisfaction. We need the one solution that will work best for everyone in the operation."

"So what's your new menu idea?" Anne Hudson asked, looking up from her notepad.

"I think we need something that takes relatively little prep time, offers a high margin, and brings people through the doors," Karen said. "A profitable convenience food, if you will."

At the words *convenience food*, Chef Gustafsen's jaw tightened. "And your recommendation?"

"Prime rib."

"Done to death," Jorge Estrada sighed. "And haven't you heard that beef is out?"

"If you want convenience," the chef interjected, "you couldn't pick a more inconvenient cut. It's too easy to overcook. Of course, with the proper slow-cooking equipment, it can be managed, but—"

Karen held up her hands. "Okay, okay. Given the current financials, I'm certainly not going to recommend new equipment in every unit. I know *I* like prime rib and I thought it would be a big hit."

COO Marcus Turner leaned forward, rubbing his hands. "You know what I like? I think—"

"If you want to bring people through the door, you have to give them what they want," Jorge interrupted. "All of my market research is pointing to one thing: pita wraps. They're very hot right now. They capture people's fondness for lighter, healthier food; you can make them any way you want—Tex-Mex, Greek, stir-fry, whatever; and they are guaranteed to pull people into our operations. If you want even more reasons, they're fast and easy to prepare, so we can turn more tables at lunch and dinner."

"Wraps have a very low margin, Jorge," Karen said, frowning.

"But we'll make it up through increased traffic."

"I'm not so sure," Anne said. "I can tell you right now that my servers are not going to be happy pushing $4 or $5 wraps all the time. To bring their tips up, they're going to be recommending higher-priced items. And frankly, wraps can be messy. That may mean my bussers have to spend a little more time cleaning up at each table, and that may cut into your fast-turning tables theory."

"Not to mention the additional prep time," Charles said. "Suddenly we're doing a lot of cutting and chopping we didn't need to do before." He paused before adding, "And for what? So we can jump on the latest sandwich bandwagon. Where's the creativity in that?"

"Speaking of creativity—" Marcus began.

Karen cleared her throat and turned to Anne Hudson. "What's your menu solution?"

Anne flipped through her notepad, searching for her notes. "To be honest, I'm not all that particular about what we decide. I just need something my people can sell easily, that generates a good-size check, and that guests will enjoy. I, uh—" at last she found her notes—"I'm recommending some kind of dessert special, offered either nightly or weekly. I think people will come out to see what the specials are—that addresses your traffic concerns, Jorge—and $4 and $5 desserts represent a good profit for the company while boosting the check average nicely for our servers," she said, nodding at Karen. "We could even make our kitchen staff happy by purchasing brand-name desserts that require minimal prepping and can be easily stored, garnished, and served."

Chef Charles, who had been looking increasingly hopeful as Anne described her idea, suddenly reddened. "Why does the Grill even pay me a salary! Here I am, a classically trained chef who could help turn things around for us, and you recommend that we throw something on a plate that our guests could just as easily pick up at the supermarket. And when do we get to show our customers we know how to prepare food? Oh, I forgot. We get to decide which side of the cheesecake to place our little sprig of mint on."

"Chef—"

"Why not let me do what I am trained to do? Give me the freedom to create true culinary specialties, not serve up some store-bought concoctions. I can create one for every day of the week, signature dishes of the Madison Avenue Grill, and guests will come back day after day to experience them. Besides, if we prepare it ourselves, we can take advantage of special buys and seasonal specials and increase value. I am certain that with my unique creations on the menu, all it would take is a little marketing expertise to bring people through the door and keep them coming back."

"I know what keeps people coming back," Marcus ventured.

"What about quality, chef?" Anne asked. "How are our hundreds of cooks going to maintain quality for a recipe they prepare only once a week? How will servers be able to develop strong product knowledge? And how do we justify purchasing and storing specialized ingredients in all of our locations for seven one-of-a-kind dishes?"

"You talk about marketing like it's some kind of cure-all," Jorge added, feeling his own temper rising. "Even if every one of your recipes was incredible, the fact is, that's not what people are saying they want. What's wrong with giving guests what they want?"

"I have to admit I have some concerns about profitability issues, as well," Karen said.

Then, no longer able to put him off, she glanced up at her boss. Marcus Turner was poised on the edge of his seat, looking suspiciously as if he had something to add.

"Mr. Turner?"

Marcus smiled broadly. "Finally, someone wants to hear my idea." He leaned back in his chair, a faraway look filling his eyes. "As some of you may know, I recently spent a couple weeks fly-fishing in Maine."

Jorge leaned over to Anne. "While we were up to our necks in extra work," he whispered.

Marcus ignored him. "You know what they love in Maine?" he asked the ceiling. "Fresh Maine lobster. Now, I know I've been out of operations for a while, but I can recognize a hit when I see one."

Karen buried her head in her hands. "Fresh Maine lobster."

"Exactly. Now, I hate to just jump in and give you the *answer* like this, but my instincts are telling me—"

"How do you suggest we get fresh Maine lobster to our units in Montana?" Anne asked. "Or, say, North Dakota?"

"Airplanes."

"And do you know what air delivery adds to the final price? We'd be talking 25 to 35 dollars for a lobster—"

"Well, the servers would love it," Marcus interjected.

"—in restaurants with a check average of $6 for lunch and $12 for dinner. Who's going to buy them?"

"Well, now, if marketing just did their job," Marcus said, his voice trailing off.

"Marketing?" Jorge said, incredulous. "Marketing's been telling you what people want, and it isn't Maine lobster. Not in Las Vegas, not in Louisiana, and certainly not in London."

"And what about storage? We'd need lobster tanks in every store."

"We'd have to buy bibs, cookers, crackers ..."

"We'd need to establish receiving procedures to process live animals."

"Okay, okay," Marcus said, his smile fading fast. "But if lobster's definitely out of the question, where does that leave us? Assuming we have some truly workable ideas already on the table, how do we determine which is the right one for Madison Avenue Grill?"

Discussion Questions

1. What rationale did each member of the management team present in support of the menu item he or she recommended?

2. What are some of the advantages and disadvantages of each suggested menu item based on the control points of purchasing, receiving/storing/issuing, production, and service?

3. Use the information you gathered in answering Discussion Question #2 to complete the following decision matrix. Place a "+" in the appropriate column/row intersection if the advantages seem to outweigh the disadvantages, place a "–" if the disadvantages seem to outweigh the advantages, and place a "?" if you cannot decide which outweighs the other.

Menu Item	Purchasing	Receiving/Storing/Issuing	Production	Service
Prime Rib				
Pita Wraps				
Dessert Specials				
Signature Items				
Maine Lobster				
Other				
Other				

Of all the suggested menu items, which would you choose as the best solution to the Madison Avenue Grill's declining customer base? Why?

4. Keeping in mind the chain's desire for a new high-profit, popular, convenient menu item, what item would you suggest? What would be the advantages and disadvantages of your suggested item in terms of the control points of purchasing, receiving/storing/issuing, production, and service? Add your suggested menu item to the decision matrix you completed above, and, of all the suggested menu items, which would you now choose as the best solution to the chain's declining customer base? Why?

Case Number: 4655CA

The following industry experts helped generate and develop this case: Timothy J. Pugh, Regional Manager, Damon's—The Place for Ribs (Steve Montanye Enterprises, East Lansing, Michigan); and Lawrence E. Ross, Assistant Professor, Florida Southern College, and owner of Sago Grill, Lakeland, Florida.

 **Problems** ─────────────────────────

Problem 1

The total ingredient cost in a recipe is $4.73; the manager desires a 37.5% food cost. What is the base selling price of the item using the ingredients mark-up method? Should the manager price the item in the above example at the base selling price you calculated? Why or why not?

Problem 2

The chef has pre-costed the recipe for an entrée and a sauce which is one item on the menu; the food cost is $6.34. A prime ingredient multiplier of 3.72 has been established. What is the base selling price when the prime ingredient mark-up method is used?

Problem 3

The Prairie Town Grill does not serve alcoholic beverages. Its operating budget reveals the following:

- Revenue $1,375,000
- Food Cost $585,000
- Non-food costs $710,000
- Profit $80,000
- Number of guests   161,580
- Guest check average $8.51
- Contribution margin $790,000 (revenue − food costs)

Using the above information, calculate the base selling price of a menu item with a total ingredient cost of $4.85 using the methods below.

a. Use the contribution margin pricing method.

b. Use the ratio pricing method.

c. Use the simple prime costs method (note: the non-food costs *include* $426,250 in labor costs).

Problem 4

The manager uses the mark-up with accompaniment cost method to establish a base selling price. What is that price when the entrée cost is $2.12, the plate cost is $1.70 and the mark-up multiplier is 2.1?

Problem 5

The manager of the University Square Bistro has the following operating data available:

- Revenue $1,187,000
- Food Cost $403,580   (includes entrée costs of $274,434)
- Labor Cost $367,970
- Other non-food costs $316,550   (excludes labor)
- Desired profit $98,900
- Number of guests   107,900

Use the above information to establish the base selling price of a menu item with alternative pricing methods. Note: the item to be priced has a food cost of $4.57 (entrée cost = $3.12; plate cost = $1.45)

a) What is the approximate base selling price using the ingredients mark-up method?

b) What is the approximate base selling price using the prime ingredient mark-up method?

c) What is the approximate base selling price using the mark-up with accompaniment costs method?

d) What is the approximate base selling price using the contribution margin pricing method?

e) What is the approximate base price using the ratio pricing method?

f) What is the approximate base selling price using the simple prime costs method?

g) What is the base selling price using the specific price cost method? (Note: assume that (a) 70% of food cost is for items involving extensive preparation (b) 60% of labor cost is for preparation activities and (c) the item to be priced involves significant preparation.

Problem 6

Complete the Menu Engineering Worksheet on the following page; suggest strategies to effectively manage each item after the worksheet is completed.

Problem 6 Worksheet

Menu Engineering Worksheet

Restaurant: Terry's Overland Grill

Date: _____ 7/10/XX

Meal Period: _____ Dinner

(A) Menu Item Name	(B) Number Sold (MM)	(C) Menu Mix %	(D) Item Food Cost	(E) Item Selling Price	(F) Item CM	(G) Menu Costs	(H) Menu Revenues	(L) Menu CM	(P) CM Category	(R) MM% Category	(S) Menu Item Classification
A	481		4.90	12.50							
B	190		6.50	14.75							
C	205		5.20	10.60							
D	340		7.00	16.80							
Column Totals:	N					I	J	M			

O = M/N

Q = (100%/items) (70%)

Additional Computations:

Part III

Designing Effective Food and Beverage Control Systems

Chapter 6 Outline

Purchasing Objectives and Procedures
Purchasing Responsibilities
Selecting Suppliers
Purchasing the Proper Quality
Purchasing the Proper Quantities
    Perishable Products
    Non-Perishable Products
The Purchase Order System
    Computerized Purchasing Systems
Security Concerns in Purchasing
Reducing the Cost of the Purchasing
    Function
Receiving Controls
    Receiving Personnel
    Receiving Procedures
    Request-for-Credit Memos
    Marking Procedures
    Security Concerns in Receiving
    Computerized Receiving Systems

Competencies

1. Explain how effective purchasing practices affect the bottom line of a food and beverage operation. (pp. 177–178)

2. Describe procedures related to the purchasing cycle and identify purchasing responsibilities within a food and beverage operation. (pp. 178–180)

3. Identify factors that food and beverage managers should consider when selecting a supplier. (pp. 180–181)

4. Identify factors that food and beverage managers should assess when purchasing food products. (pp. 181–186)

5. Calculate the quantities of food products to purchase using the minimum/maximum ordering system. (pp. 186–187)

6. Identify security concerns related to the purchasing function. (pp. 191–193)

7. Describe actions that managers can take to reduce the cost of the purchasing function. (pp. 193–194)

8. Describe receiving control procedures. (pp. 194–200)

Purchasing and Receiving Controls

E<small>VERY ASPECT OF</small> planning for a food and beverage operation begins with the menu. This is true for purchasing and receiving activities as well. The menu determines products that must be purchased. If items are not needed, they should not be purchased. While this seems obvious, the rusty, dusty cans in some storerooms and the pounds of frozen products stored for a year or more in freezers suggest that this principle is not always followed. Likewise, in beverage operations, purchasing needs are determined by the menu. Many managers feel they must offer an extremely large selection of various call brand products, which may spend most of their time on the shelf. A better approach may be to offer a limited range of popular call brands while keeping other call brands on hand for regular guests.

While the menu's impact on the control system is obvious, cost control also depends on the skills and abilities of purchasing personnel and others who work within the food and beverage operation. If ineffective management and staff personnel are employed, no amount of planning and control can ensure success.

Since cost savings in food and beverage purchasing go directly to the bottom line, no hospitality operation can afford inefficient purchasing procedures. Consider the following example.

Let's assume that the profits earned by a food and beverage operation are eight percent of the revenue generated. This means that for every dollar of revenue, the operation earns a profit of eight cents. Let's assume that poor purchasing practices waste $500 every week. How much must the operation generate in additional revenue to pay for the wasted $500?

The answer is *not* $500 dollars. Revenue must also be used to pay for food costs, beverage costs, necessary labor costs, mortgage payments, taxes, and many other types of costs as well. The wasted $500 must come out of the operation's profits. So, to maintain an eight percent profit level, the operation must earn the $500 lost in profit by generating additional weekly revenue of $6,250 ($500 divided by the .08 profit requirement). No operation can afford to allocate its first $6,250 in revenue each week to offset higher-than-necessary costs which could have been reduced by effective purchasing.

Although the control process is affected by decisions made in all areas of the complex food and beverage management system, it is convenient to begin discussing food and beverage cost control where the physical cycle of the operation begins—at the purchasing and receiving control points. However, actual cost control begins

Exhibit 1   The Purchasing Cycle: An Audit Trail

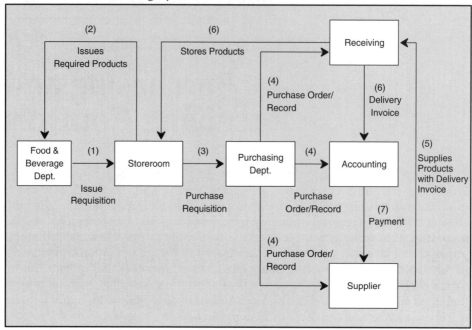

when goals for purchasing and receiving are established. Many plans and procedures are already in place before the physical cycle begins.

Purchasing Objectives and Procedures

Purchasing is the series of activities designed to obtain products of the right quality and quantity, at the right price and time, and from the right source. These simple objectives can be difficult to achieve. Since the purchasing cycle involves a variety of different procedures, many activities must be controlled when designing and managing purchasing tasks. The complexity of purchasing is illustrated in Exhibit 1. Notice that the purchasing cycle involves the following activities:

1. The chef in the food department and the bartender (or bar manager) in the beverage department complete an issue requisition when items are needed.

2. The storeroom responds by issuing required products to the user department.

3. When products in inventory reach a predetermined reorder point, the storeroom forwards a purchase requisition to the purchasing department.

4. The purchasing department orders required products from the proper supplier, perhaps using a purchase order or a purchase record. Increasingly, food service operators place orders with suppliers using e-commerce (business-to-business) technology. Purchasing personnel send or transmit the purchase

order or purchase record information to the receiving and accounting departments. (Purchase orders and purchase records are discussed later in this chapter.)

5. The supplier delivers the products to the receiving department along with a delivery invoice (see Exhibit 8).

6. The receiving clerk places products in the storeroom and forwards the delivery invoice, perhaps with other documents, to the accounting department. In some properties, these forms are reviewed by the food and beverage management staff before being routed to accounting personnel.

7. After further processing of necessary documents, accounting department personnel send payment to the supplier and file copies of the purchasing/receiving forms for accounting and/or control purposes.

This purchasing cycle is repeated every time products are ordered. You can see that purchasing is more than "picking up the phone and calling in an order." It is a complex cycle of activities requiring special planning and control procedures that create an audit trail. An **audit trail** is a series of records, documents, and/or reports that trace the flow of resources through an operation.

Purchasing Responsibilities

Ultimate responsibility for purchasing decisions generally lies with the food and beverage manager. In small operations, the general manager may function as a food and beverage manager. In very small properties, the owner, manager, and food and beverage manager are frequently the same individual.

As properties increase in size, positions become more specialized. In a small hotel, for example, the food and beverage manager (who may perform many duties frequently done by individuals in different positions in larger properties) may be responsible for purchasing. In large food and beverage operations, a staff purchasing agent may be assigned to perform the many activities that may be necessary. When a purchasing agent is employed, it is important to recall the difference between a **line position** and **staff position**. As the name suggests, line managers are in the chain of command. They make the decisions affecting the food and beverage operation. Examples of line positions include the general manager, food and beverage manager, lower-level supervisors, and entry-level employees. By contrast, staff personnel provide specialized technical and advisory assistance to line managers.

The purchasing agent, therefore, is in a staff (advisory) relationship to the food and beverage manager. As such, purchasing agents should not make decisions involving, for example, the definition of required quality, whether items should be purchased in convenience form or be prepared on-site, or whether purchase quantities should be increased or decreased to reflect price trends. These and numerous other decision-making tasks applicable to purchasing should be done by line personnel with suggestions from staff purchasing officials. In this regard, the purchasing agent functions in much the same way as does a personnel officer, accountant, or public relations official; the purchasing agent studies problems and gives advice, but does not make purchasing decisions. Generally, it is the food and beverage manager who bears ultimate responsibility for purchasing decisions.

Selecting Suppliers

Managers of food and beverage operations should choose suppliers carefully. Detailed purchase specifications and objective calculations of quantities to order are ineffective without professional suppliers. Essentially, the food and beverage manager bases supplier evaluations on the consistency of:

- Correct quality products

- Reasonable prices

- Prompt delivery

- Service, including product information

When selecting suppliers, the purchasers must consider a number of factors. Not every supplier who carries the needed product is appropriate for the food and beverage operation. The supplier with the lowest price may not be "right" for the operation, either. The following are important factors to consider when selecting a supplier.

- **Location**. Delivery time, transportation costs, and unexpected delays may be reduced if the supplier's facility is close to the food and beverage operation.

- **Quality of the Supplier's Operation.** Such things as sanitation, in-house processing, handling of orders, and the quantity and quality of items in stock must be assessed.

- **Technical Ability of the Supplier's Staff.** Good salespersons are more than order-takers. They know their products and can help the operation resolve problems involving the products they supply.

- **Value.** The purchaser must carefully assess the supplier's prices in relation to the quality of products needed by the operation.

- **Compatibility**. A good working relationship between the food and beverage purchaser and the supplier requires mutual beliefs about ethics and the fair treatment of both the guests and the supplier.

- **Honesty and Fairness**. These traits must be part of the ongoing business relationship and the supplier's reputation.

- **Delivery Personnel**. Their appearance, attitude, and courtesy contribute to the impression formed by the food and beverage operation.

The purchasing manager should identify all possible sources for all items needed, determine the best suppliers, and choose from among them. While long-standing relationships with suppliers can help in future dealings, managers should be careful not to get too comfortable with their suppliers. There is the danger of allowing standards to slip so that the property is not getting the most from its purchasing dollar. Therefore, it is appropriate to periodically review the selection of suppliers and assess their performance in meeting the operation's expectations.

Purchasing the Proper Quality

In relation to the purchasing function, the term **quality** refers to the suitability of a product for its intended use. The more suitable a product, the higher its quality. For example, a super colossal olive may represent the right quality product for garnish or salad purposes. It may not, however, represent the proper quality if it is to be chopped and used as a salad bar topping.

Decisions about quality requirements are first made when the goals of the business are established and subsequent marketing plans are developed. At that time, the spirit and intent of the food and beverage operation's quality standards are determined. Later, **standard purchase specifications** are documented in detail to indicate the requirements for products suitable for every intended purpose. These specifications provide detailed descriptions of the quality, size, and weight desired for particular items.

The relationship between quality and price is referred to as value. Just as the guest considers value when deciding what to order in the restaurant or lounge, food and beverage managers must also consider value when choosing products to purchase. To purchase products of optimal value for the food and beverage operation, the purchaser must carefully evaluate each product's quality (suitability for intended use) in relation to its cost.

The format for purchase specifications illustrated in Exhibit 2 indicates specific quality requirements. Notice that it not only describes the desired product, but also specifies how the product will be used. In addition, it informs the supplier about the operation's procedures for ensuring that the delivered item does, in fact, meet the required quality specifications. Standard purchase specifications must:

- Accurately describe minimum quality requirements

- Clearly and simply indicate the food and beverage operation's needs

- Realistically define needs, yet not limit the number of acceptable suppliers

Generally, specifications should be developed for all products purchased. However, there is a need to be practical in following this principle. Developing detailed specifications for products such as salt and other seasonings or bar swizzle sticks is often not justified. Instead, managers involved with the purchasing function should first develop specifications for expensive, high-volume items and then formalize quality requirements for other products as time permits. These items are often called "A" items; the relatively few products which required the largest expenditure of food purchase dollars. For example, in some operations 75 percent of all product dollars buy only 25 percent of all products.

When items are purchased by brand, such as liquor or ketchup, the brand itself becomes the specification. However, it is still necessary to specify container size and special instructions.

Exhibit 2   Purchase Specification Format

(name of food and beverage operation)

1. Product name: _____

2. Product used for:

> Clearly indicate product use (such as olive garnish for beverage, hamburger patty for grill frying for sandwich, etc.)

3. Product general description:

> Provide general quality information about desired product. For example, "iceberg lettuce; heads to be green, firm without spoilage, excessive dirt or damage. No more than 10 outer leaves; packed 24 heads per case."

4. Detailed description:

> Purchaser should state other factors which help to clearly identify desired product. Examples of specific factors, which vary by product being described, may include:
>
> - Geographic origin
> - Variety
> - Type
> - Style
> - Grade
>
> - Product size
> - Portion size
> - Brand name
> - Density
>
> - Medium of pack
> - Specific gravity
> - Container size
> - Edible yield, trim

5. Product test procedures:

> Test procedures occur at time product is received and as/after product is prepared/used. Thus, for example, products to be at a refrigerated temperature upon delivery can be tested with a thermometer. Portion-cut meat patties can be randomly weighed. Lettuce packed 24 heads per case can be counted.

6. Special instructions and requirements:

> Any additional information needed to clearly indicate quality expectations can be included here. Examples include bidding procedures, if applicable, labeling and/or packaging requirements and special delivery and service requirements.

Quality concerns are important when purchasing alcoholic beverages as well as when purchasing foods. However, liquor, wines and beers are generally purchased by brand name and, as noted above, the brand then becomes the specification. Many food and beverage operations feature a range of quality, and therefore, a range of prices for the alcoholic beverages being served. Liquor may be available in a **house brand** (also called pour brand or speed rail brand [named after the shelf which is normally located close to the bartender for quick access]) and a **call brand**. Other properties offer very high brands referred to as **premium** brands. Many beverage consumers prefer a specific brand, and the manager must make a marketing decision to determine the call and premium brands to be offered. In addition, many guests judge the overall quality of the restaurant, in part, by the quality of house brands available. For example, a high-check restaurant will not likely offer a low quality house brand. In fact, some food and beverage operations offer only call or premium brands as a statement about the quality of all products offered by the property.

Wine is also purchased with the same types of concerns. Many properties offer a house brand and numerous better known and higher quality wines on their list. House brands may be available by the glass or carafe (sometimes in different sizes). Today, a wide number of microbreweries produce beers which are very popular with many guests. Food and beverage managers may offer several brands at different prices. The history of the label, the guest's experience with the brand and the significant amount of advertising done by beverage manufacturers and distributors all impact the perceived quality and popularity of alcoholic beverages offered by the food service operation.

Another purchasing tool is the **food sample data sheet** (Exhibit 3). This sheet helps standardize the evaluation of a product. It can be used to record purchasing, storing, preparing, and serving information about products that the operation is sampling and considering for purchase. The food sample data sheet makes product selection more objective.

Purchasing the Proper Quantities

Purchasing the proper quantities of items is just as important as developing correct quality specifications. Problems that can arise when too much of a product is ordered include:

- Cash flow problems resulting from excessive money tied up in inventory

- Increased storage costs such as interest, insurance, and, sometimes, rented storage space

- Deterioration in quality, or damaged products

- Increased chance of theft and pilferage

Purchasing insufficient quantities also has potential disadvantages such as dissatisfied guests due to stockouts, emergency and rush orders which are frequently expensive and time-consuming, and lost discounts from volume purchases.

To avoid these problems, food and beverage managers must periodically assess a number of factors that affect the purchase of proper quantities. These factors include the following:

Popularity of Menu Items. As unit sales of menu items increase, additional quantities of ingredients are obviously needed.

Exhibit 3   Food Sample Data Sheet

1. Product: _____

2. Brand Name: _____

3. Presented By: _____   Date: _____

4. Varieties Available: _____

5. Shelf Life: (Frozen) _____ (Thawed, Refrigerated, Dry) _____

6. Preparation and Sanitation Considerations: _____

   _____

   _____

   _____

7. Menu Suggestions: _____

8. Merchandising Help Available (Poster, Table Tents, etc.): _____

9. Case Size (Number of Portions): _____

10. Portion Size: _____

11. Distributed By: _____

12. Minimum Order: _____

13. Any Additional Ordering Information: _____

    _____

14. Lead Time: _____

15. Approximate Price Per Serving: _____

NOTE: Were the following information sheets received with products?

   a. Nutritional and Ingredient Analysis: Yes _____   No _____

   b. Specification Sheet: Yes _____   No _____

Source: Ronald F. Cichy, *Quality Sanitation Management* (Lansing, Mich.: Educational Institute of the American Hotel & Lodging Association, 1994), p. 181.

Product Cost Concerns. Higher product costs may result in increased selling prices, which, in turn, may result in decreased sales levels. In this case, the need for continued purchase of the product should be evaluated. Also, management may make judgments about future prices and buy more if prices are expected to increase or less if prices are expected to decrease. This is called **speculative purchasing** and should only be done by management based upon information provided by the purchaser.

Available Storage Space. Available space may limit quantities purchased. Storage space in dry, frozen, and refrigerated areas may not be adequate to accommodate quantity purchases.

Safety Level. Maintaining a safety level of products in inventory may require buying a quantity above that actually needed to allow for delivery delays, increased usage, or other unexpected developments.

Supplier Constraints. For example, suppliers may specify minimum dollar and/or poundage requirements for delivery. Also, some suppliers may not break cases, bags, or other packing containers to meet overly specific order quantities. Therefore, the standard commercial units of the packaging influence quantities purchased.

Perishable Products

Perishable items (such as fresh produce, bakery, and dairy products) should be used as soon as possible. These types of products are normally purchased several times weekly according to the following formula:

$$\text{Quantity Needed} - \text{Quantity Available} = \begin{array}{l}\text{Quantity to Purchase for}\\ \text{Immediate Use}\end{array}$$

Sample procedures for purchasing perishable products are as follows:

1. Determine normal usage rates. For example, assess, for a normal two-day purchasing period, the specific number of cases of selected produce items, pounds of fresh meat, fresh poultry fryers, and other perishable products the property typically uses.

2. Assess the amount of each item currently in inventory.

3. Calculate the quantity to purchase by subtracting the quantity available (step 2) from the quantity needed (step 1).

4. Adjust routine quantities as necessary for special functions, holidays, or other unique circumstances.

When purchasing items for immediate use, some properties use a form such as the one illustrated in Exhibit 4. When reviewing the perishable product quotation/call sheet, notice that the perishable items needed are listed in column 1; the quantity of each item needed for the time covered by the order is in column 2. The inventory amount noted in column 3 is determined by an actual physical count of the quantity on hand. The amount to order (column 4) is determined by subtracting the amount on hand (column 3) from the amount needed (column 2). In the first example, only $3^{1}/_{2}$ cases of spinach are needed (6 cases minus $2^{1}/_{2}$ cases equals $3^{1}/_{2}$ cases), but 4 cases should be purchased if suppliers will not break cases or if the increased broken case price is judged excessive.

The prices quoted by eligible suppliers are listed in columns 5, 6, and 7. Each supplier has copies of the food and beverage operation's quality specifications on which to base the price for each item. The buyer can either select the supplier with the lowest total price for everything required or use several suppliers, depending upon who has the lowest price item by item. However, minimum delivery requirements may limit this purchasing option. Also, the processing cost for each order

Exhibit 4   Perishable Product Quotation/Call Sheet

Item	Needed	On Hand	Order	A & B Co.	Green Produce	Local Supplier
		Amount			Supplier	
1	2	3	4	5	6	7
Spinach	6 cs	2^{1}/2 cs	4 cs	22^{00}/cs = $88.00	14^{85}/cs = $59.40	21^{70}/cs = $86.80
Ice Lettuce	8 cs	1 cs	7 cs	17^{00}/cs = $119.00	16^{75}/cs = $117.25	18^{10}/cs = $126.70
Carrots	3-20#	20#	2-20#	14^{70}/bag = $29.40	13^{90}/bag = $27.80	13^{80}/bag = $27.60
Tomatoes	2 lugs	^{1}/2 lug	2 lugs	18^{60}/lug = $37.20	18^{00}/lug = $36.00	18^{10}/lug = $36.20
			Totals	$861.40	$799.25	$842.15

(often unassessed but frequently expensive) should be considered. E-commerce, discussed earlier in this chapter, can reduce the "paperwork" required to collect the required information. In addition, large operations may subscribe to electronic "newspapers" providing real-time price information.

Non-Perishable Products

To determine the quantity of non-perishable products to purchase, it is often practical to use a minimum/maximum system of inventory management. This system is based upon the concept of "A" items discussed earlier; only a few of all items purchased represent high-cost or high-frequency items. Minimum/maximum ordering systems give first attention to these high-priority items and help managers determine when products must be purchased and how much of each product to order.

For each purchase item, the **minimum/maximum ordering system** assesses the minimum quantity below which inventory levels should not fall and the maximum quantity above which inventory levels should not rise. The **minimum inventory level** is the safety level—the number of purchase units that must always remain in inventory. The **maximum inventory level** is the greatest number of purchase units permitted in storage. The maximum inventory level of purchase units permitted in storage is the usage rate plus the minimum (safety) level.

The most important factor for determining when more purchase units must be ordered is, of course, the rate at which they are used by the operation. The **usage rate** is the number of purchase units used per order period. Purchase units are counted in terms of the number of shipping containers of normal size for each product. For example, if ten cases (six number-10 cans) of green peas are normally used between deliveries, the usage rate for green peas is ten cases.

In addition to usage rates, managers must determine a lead-time quantity for each purchase item. The **lead-time quantity** is the number of purchase units withdrawn from inventory between the time an order is placed and when it is delivered. Again, purchase units are counted in terms of normal size shipping containers. For example, if two cases of green peas are used between ordering and receiving, the lead-time quantity is two cases. This lead-time quantity is separate from the safety (minimum) level of purchase units kept in inventory. The safety level must allow for such things as late deliveries and greater than normal usage.

The **order point** is the number of purchase units in stock when an order is placed. The order point is reached when the number of purchase units in inventory equals the lead-time quantity plus the safety level:

$$\text{Purchase Units at Order Point} = \text{Purchase Units in Lead Time} + \text{Purchase Units in Safety Level}$$

If products are ordered at the order point, the quantity in inventory will be reduced to the safety (minimum) level by the time products are received. When the order arrives, the inventory level for the product will again be brought back to the maximum level. Examples of the minimum/maximum order inventory system are found in Exhibit 5.

The Purchase Order System

So far, we have been discussing control procedures that apply prior to the actual purchasing task. Before the purchasing process begins, the food and beverage operation should have specified minimum quality standards, calculated quantities of products to be purchased, determined order points for each purchase item, and considered eligible suppliers. It is important that control procedures be built into the actual purchasing process as well. For this purpose, large food and beverage operations use a purchase order system.

With a **purchase order system**, a purchase order is sent (by mail, fax, or email) to the supplier awarded the order. Information about the order is retained in the purchasing department and is also circulated internally among the receiving and accounting departments. The purchase order formally identifies the product, quantity, unit cost, and total cost that both the supplier and purchaser have agreed upon. In addition, the purchase order may include guarantees, warranties, payment requirements, inspection rights, "hold harmless" provisions, and other legal, contractual concerns.

A purchase order, such as the sample form shown in Exhibit 6, is the food and beverage operation's record of the specifics of all incoming shipments. The property must pay the agreed-upon price for no less than the agreed-upon quality for the amount ordered. Higher than necessary food and beverage costs are frequently traced to communication and coordination problems among the several

Exhibit 5   Minimum/Maximum Order System

Example 1. Assume:
  Purchase unit = case (6 number-10 cans)
  Usage rate = 2 cases per day
  Order period = monthly (30 days)
  Monthly usage rate = 2 cases/day × 30 days = 60 cases
  Lead time = 4 days
  Lead-time usage rate = 4 days at 2 cases/day = 8 cases
  Safety level = 4 days at 2 cases/day = 8 cases
  Order point = lead time + safety level
    16 cases = 8 cases + 8 cases
  Maximum level = usage rate + safety level
    68 cases = 60 cases + 8 cases
  When ordering at the order point, the quantity to order is monthly usage rate.
This is shown by the following calculation:
  Order point   16 cases
  Monthly usage rate   60 cases
  Total cases available   76
  Lead-time usage rate   − 8
  Maximum level   68 cases
So the maximum level is maintained.

Example 2. When placing an order before the order point is reached, such as when putting together an order for price quotations from suppliers, first determine the number of cases in storage, then subtract the order point from the amount in storage.
  Amount in storage   25 cases
  Order point   − 16 cases
  Excess over order point   9 cases

The amount to order is the usage rate minus the number of cases in excess of the order point:
  51 cases = 60 cases − 9 cases

The decision to order 51 cases can be proved:
  Cases ordered   51
  Amount available   25
  Total   76
  Lead-time usage rate   − 8
  Maximum level   68

Again, the maximum inventory level is maintained.

---

departments or personnel involved in purchasing. Properly used, the purchase order minimizes these problems.

Rather than using a purchase order system, smaller food and beverage operations may simply summarize purchase order information by using an in-house purchase record form, such as that shown in Exhibit 7. The **purchase record** performs the same functions as the purchase order. It provides the food and beverage operation with a detailed record of all incoming shipments. Affected personnel

Exhibit 6 Purchase Order

Purchase Order
Number: _____

Order Date: _____

Payment Terms: _____

To: _____
    (supplier)

From/
Ship to: _____
    (name of food service operation)

_____

_____
(address)

_____
(address)

Delivery Date: _____

Please Ship:

Quantity Ordered	Description	✓	Units Shipped	Unit Cost	Total Cost

Total Cost _____

Important: This Purchase Order expressly limits acceptance to the terms and conditions stated above, noted on the reverse side hereof, and any additional terms and conditions affixed hereto or otherwise referenced. Any additional terms and conditions proposed by seller are objected to and rejected.

_____
Authorized Signature

and departments must know all the specifics about incoming food and beverage products. Without a written record, busy management staff may forget the details. Properly used, the purchase record helps to control higher than necessary food and beverage costs.

Exhibit 7   Purchase Record

				(supplier)			
Date Ordered	Item Description	Unit	Price	No. of Units	Total Cost	Invoice No.	Comments

Computerized Purchasing Systems

Some computer-generated purchase orders are produced by an integrated software package composed of numerous modules, one of which is the purchasing module. To generate accurate purchase orders, the purchasing module accesses data from other modules that maintain ingredient files, recipe files, menu item files, and inventory files.

Purchase orders can also be generated by a purchasing module that accesses and analyzes unit sales forecast data. This method assumes a zero-based inventory system for developing purchasing orders. Rather than referencing existing inventory levels, the purchasing module forecasts anticipated unit sales, projects needed inventory items, and automatically generates the necessary purchase orders.

Regardless of the method used to produce purchase orders, purchasing modules typically provide override options that enable management to alter items and quantities prior to the final preparation and distribution of purchase orders.

Properties dealing with more than one supplier may receive competitive bids and store them in a bid specification file that typically contains the specific characteristics of purchased items. Suppliers are asked to quote prices for products that meet or exceed stated specifications. Normally, a bid specification form can be printed at any time upon demand. Once bids are obtained, they can be entered into the computer system, and the purchasing module can sort items to be purchased by supplier and lowest bid.

Telephone communication links between food service operations and suppliers are on the increase and have a significant impact on the ordering process. A growing trend among computer system vendors and food service suppliers is to install order entry telephone lines for telecommunicating purchase orders directly from customer properties. The property must first develop its own purchase order file and then use communications software to send purchase orders to the supplier's computer system. Purchase order filing is usually sorted by vendor and maintained by purchase order number and date.

Some suppliers allow clients to use autodial modems. An **autodial modem** functions without user intervention, enabling late-night transmission of purchase orders for next-day processing. Some sophisticated purchase order telecommunication links provide for two-way communication (duplex) between the supplier and the property. This linkage allows the food and beverage purchaser to make online inquiries about current prices and/or stock availability. It also permits the supplier to send information about featured items, price specials, and close-out sales to the purchaser.

Today, some large food and beverage operations are developing computerized Just-In-Time (JIT) purchasing systems. Managers at such operations realize that excess inventory ties up cash and valuable storage space, so they work with **prime suppliers** to develop JIT systems. Prime suppliers are suppliers who receive all—or a significant amount—of an operation's purchase orders for selected products during a specified time period. Prime suppliers are selected by comparing price quotations for the volume of estimated product quantities for specific time periods that are submitted by eligible suppliers.

In one JIT plan, individual outlets within a property can calculate ingredients needed for daily production and electronically transmit those needs to the purchasing office, where totals of all ingredients required for the following day's preparation needs are assessed. These totals are then transmitted to the prime supplier, who delivers the needed products in time for preparation. Properties that use JIT systems require a relatively small amount of storage space for back-up supplies because products are supplied according to need. As purchasing processes become increasingly computerized, implementation of JIT systems becomes more practical all the time.

Security Concerns in Purchasing

In small food and beverage operations, where owners/managers may purchase and receive the products themselves, control procedures are less concerned with theft than with obtaining the best value. In larger operations, where other personnel take on purchasing tasks, security becomes an increasingly important concern. The control process must guard against several types of theft that are possible during the purchasing process.

Kickbacks. In several common types of kickbacks, the buyer works in collusion with someone from the supplier's company. The kickback can be money or gifts. Either way, the owner of the operation is the loser. In one kickback scheme, products are purchased at prices higher than necessary. The two thieves then split the difference between the real and inflated prices. To best control this type of theft, the owner/manager can routinely review invoices and ask such questions as, "Why are so many products purchased from the same supplier?" The manager can also periodically review the selection of suppliers and solicit price quotations randomly to ensure that prices paid are the best—or, at least, competitive—for the quality and quantity of products being purchased.

In another kickback procedure, the delivery invoice is padded by adding items that were not received, or it is increased by adding unreasonable charges for handling or some other service. This scheme works well when the same employee receives as well as purchases. Therefore, designing a system that separates the purchasing and receiving tasks can help prevent this type of kickback.

You have learned that, in large hotels, purchasing may be the responsibility of a staff purchasing department. Receiving and storing activities may be performed by the accounting department. Under this system, products do not come under the control of production staff until they are issued. This system helps reduce the possibility that one person, working alone, can implement a kickback scheme.

Fictitious Companies. Purchasing personnel can steal by setting up a nonexistent company that then submits invoices for products never received. Managers can periodically review the selection of suppliers by examining the names of payees on company checks. Unless the manager is familiar with the supplier, checks should never be sent to companies with only post office box addresses.

Reprocessing. Suppliers may try to send an invoice to the food and beverage operation for processing a second time. To avoid this type of theft, operations need an internal system to verify which invoices have not been paid and to cancel invoices when they are paid.

Delivery Invoice Errors. Intentional arithmetic errors, short weight or counts, wrong quality, and similar "mistakes" can cost the operation money. Management or secretarial personnel must check all arithmetic on invoices and statements—even when they are computer-generated—and follow proper receiving practices (reviewed later in this chapter) to catch these mistakes. Whether they are innocent mistakes or fraud, the bottom line is the same: the operation loses money.

Credit Memo Problems. When products are not delivered or when deliveries are short of the quantities ordered, a request-for-credit memo should be issued to reduce the original delivery invoice by the value of the items not delivered. The supplier should then issue a credit memo to adjust the account. Managers and receiving staff should never accept a "we'll deliver it later and not charge you" comment from the truck driver. A request-for-credit memo should be written and attached to the delivery invoice. The manager should also alert the property's accounting department to ensure that the supplier properly processes the credit to the buyer's account.

Quality Substitutions. Quality substitutions occur when a price is quoted for the proper quality item but a lower quality item is delivered. Proper receiving practices can prevent paying more for a lower quality product. Brand or label substitutions are also possible if receiving personnel are not familiar with products ordered. If alert staff do recognize product problems, the supplier can "allege" a mistake and exchange the products for those of proper quality. This problem occurs more frequently than some purchasers may suspect and requires close attention to both purchasing and receiving duties.

Purchaser Theft. Purchasers might practice a variety of other thefts: purchasing for their own use, reciprocal purchasing for their own benefit, purchasing products wholesale with the intention of reselling them to selected employees or to others. Using an effectively designed purchasing system can help reduce these types of potential problems.

There is a gray area of purchasing ethics in which purchasing personnel may be offered gifts or free meals, invitations to parties, or other inducements designed to increase the supplier's business. Buyers must put the property first and make decisions based on what is best for the property rather than for themselves.

Reducing the Cost of the Purchasing Function

Professional food and beverage managers adopt a number of techniques to make certain that purchase dollars are spent wisely. The following sections examine a number of these techniques.

Negotiate Prices. Some food and beverage managers mistakenly believe that an initial price quoted by the supplier is "fixed" and that purchasing involves simply soliciting price quotations and then accepting the lowest price quoted for the specified quality. In fact, discussions with sales managers (not the distributor sales representative who calls on the buyer) may yield lower prices.

Review Quality Standards. Be sure that the proper quality of products is being purchased. If, for example, products of higher than necessary quality are being used, purchase prices can be reduced by purchasing items of the correct quality.

Evaluate the Need to Purchase Convenience Products. Sometimes, employees can prepare products of acceptable quality at a lower cost than that required for purchasing the products in a convenience form.

Discontinue Unnecessary Supplier Services. Costs incurred by suppliers for such services as storage, handling, delivery, and "grace" periods for the payment of bills may all be included in the product purchase cost. Purchasing staff should carefully consider exactly what services are desired and assess whether purchase prices can be reduced if other undesired services are discontinued.

Combine Orders. Sometimes purchase costs can be reduced if a larger order is placed with a supplier. The concept of "one-stop" shopping, which involves buying a wide range of products from one supplier, recognizes this principle.

Purchase in Larger Quantities. If practical, a larger number of units of required products can be purchased. It is necessary, of course, to weigh potential savings from volume purchases against costs incurred in tying up money and inventory space. With large volume purchases, there is also an increased possibility of theft and a potential increase in spoilage and other quality problems.

Pay Cash. Some suppliers will quote a lower price if products are paid for at the time of delivery.

Change Purchase Unit Size. For example, if flour is purchased in a 50-pound bag rather than a 10-pound bag, the cost per pound is likely to be less.

Consider Cooperative Purchasing. Consider the use of cooperative (pool) purchasing, in which several properties combine orders to increase the volume of items ordered.

Consider Promotional Discounts. "Opportunity buys" (for example, items that a supplier plans to discontinue or has overstocked) sometimes arise, and, if the products can be used by the operation, these can represent significant savings over regular prices.

Receiving Controls

The planning and control that goes into the purchasing process is wasted if no one ensures that products delivered meet the operation's standard purchase specifications. In too many operations, whoever happens to be "close to the back door" when a delivery is made signs the invoice. Great care must be taken to ensure an effective receiving process. Receiving is an important part of the product cost control system. Except as noted, food and beverage controls related to receiving discussed in this section are applicable to both food and beverage products.

Receiving Personnel

Effective receiving requires knowledgeable receiving personnel. Staff must be trained to receive properly. They must know product quality standards and be able to recognize them when products are delivered. They must also understand all receiving procedures and know how to complete internal receiving records.[1]

The number of persons who receive products varies among food service operations. In a relatively small operation, the manager or the assistant manager may be in charge of receiving. In a larger operation, full-time or part-time staff typically handle the receiving function, and the person in charge of receiving may be called a receiving or storeroom clerk, or steward. This individual usually reports to either the food controller, the assistant manager, or the food and beverage manager.

Regardless of how many individuals are assigned to the receiving function, the general requirements are the same. Naturally, good health and personal cleanliness are essential for the receiver, as well as for all other personnel in the food service business. To protect the health of guests and employees alike, strict sanitation standards should be part of every aspect of food handling.

Receiving personnel should be able to use all required equipment, facilities, and forms. Increasingly, computerized receiving systems require someone who is able to work with highly-technical equipment and systems. Because of the volume of written information to be processed, receiving staff must be able to read and write. Among other things, they must be able to check the actual products delivered against the written purchase specifications, written purchase orders, and the invoice itself.

Receiving personnel must be committed to protecting the interests of the operation. While food production experience is invaluable, this does not imply that any kitchen worker in the operation is qualified to perform the receiving function. Only selected and trained employees should be permitted to receive food and beverage products.

Properly trained receivers know what to do when there is a problem with product deliveries. In this respect, the receiving function is just as important as the purchasing function; as soon as the receiver signs the invoice, the merchandise legally becomes the property of the food and beverage operation and is no longer the responsibility of the supplier.

Finally, receiving personnel need cooperation from other departments in the food service property or hotel. They must coordinate purchase requisitions from the departments with the delivery schedules of suppliers. Ideally, receiving should take place during slow periods in the operation's daily business cycle. By scheduling deliveries at these times, the receiver's undivided attention can be given to the receiving duties. The property's delivery hours should be posted on the back door, and the receiver should always be available when deliveries are expected. A supplier's ability to accommodate an operation's delivery hours should be a major consideration in the supplier selection process.

The receiving area should be near the delivery door. Delivery personnel should be allowed only in restricted back-of-the-house areas and should not be permitted in food production areas, access corridors, or other off-limits areas. Since proper receiving requires that most items be weighed or counted, accurate, conveniently located scales are necessary along with other equipment such as calculators, marking pens, rulers, files, thermometers, and transportation equipment.

Receiving Procedures

Control procedures adopted by food and beverage operations include the following:

Check Incoming Products against Purchase Orders or Purchase Records. Obviously, the property does not want to accept items it did not order, receive partial or no deliveries of required products, receive items of unacceptable quality, or pay a price higher than that agreed upon. These problems can be prevented by comparing incoming products against an in-house record of the purchase agreement.

Check Incoming Products against Standard Purchase Specifications. This requires knowledgeable and skilled receiving personnel. They should not allow themselves to be rushed by delivery persons. Sometimes the suppliers will agree to deliver products at their risk, allowing the buyer to sign and send invoices after inspecting deliveries. Cooperation in receiving is an important item to consider when selecting suppliers. Whether receiving 96-count (to the case) lemons, chilled poultry, or fresh seafood, receiving staff must know how to confirm that the correct product is, in fact, being delivered and that the food and beverage operation is getting what it pays for.

Check Incoming Products against Delivery Invoices. The supplier provides the delivery invoice, which becomes the basis for subsequent payment claims. A

Exhibit 8   Sample Delivery Invoice

Delivery Invoice

ABC Club, Restaurant, Institution, and Hotel Supplier

Route: _____

Invoice No.: _____

Customer No.: _____

Stop: _____

Sold To: XYZ Hotel
Street Address
City/State/Zip

Ship To: XYZ Hotel
Street Address
City/State/Zip

Salesperson	Terms	Customer P.O.	Our Order #	Order Date	Invoice Date

Ordered	Shipped	Item Description	Pack	Weight (lb.)	Unit Price	Amount
6/15	x	L.O. Bacon 18/22	15#	90.00	2.0700LB	186.30
2/6	x	Link Sausage 8/1	6#	12.00	1.5300LB	18.36
1/12	x	Sausage Patties 1.5 oz	12#	12.00	2.3900LB	28.68
1cs	x	Crepe Cheese Blintz 3 oz	24#	1.00	77.860CS	77.86
2 bxs	x	Franks in a Blanket	100PC	2.00	34.500BX	69.00
2/10	x	AB Franks 4/1	10#	10.00	1.8200LB	18.20

Total Items:	Total Boxes:		Total Weight:	Total Due: $398.40

Received On Account:		Date:	

Delivered By		Received By

Before signing this receipt, be sure all items are accounted for and are in satisfactory condition. ABC will not be responsible for any shortages or damages after the delivery driver leaves. Service Charge: 1.5 Percent Per Month on Unpaid Balance—18 Percent Annual Rate.

definite policy must be developed, implemented, and enforced for the measuring, weighing, or counting of incoming products to ensure that the proper quantity of product is delivered and billed. Typically, it is not practical to weigh or count every case of product being delivered. It is helpful, however, to routinely weigh/count selected cases on a random basis. Suppliers or delivery persons are less likely to short-weigh a count if they expect random inspections. Likewise, price information on the invoice should be verified by reviewing the purchase order or purchase record. Any discrepancies should be handled by a request-for-credit memo (a sample delivery invoice is shown in Exhibit 8).

Exhibit 9   Daily Receiving Report

| Date: _8/1/00_ | | | | | | | | | | | | | Page _1_ of _2_ |

Supplier	Invoice No.	Item	Purchase Unit	No. of Purchase Units	Purchase Unit Price	Total Cost	Distribution						Transfer to Storage
							Food		Beverages				
							Directs	Stores	Liquor	Beer	Wine	Soda	
1	2	3	4	5	6	7	8	9	10	11	12	13	14
AJAX	10111	Gr. Beef	10#	6	$ 28.50	$171.00		$171.00					Bill
ABC Liquor	6281	B. Scotch	cs (750)	2	$ 71.80	$143.60			$143.60				Bill
		XYZ Chablis	cs (750)	1	$ 95.00	$ 95.00					$ 95.00		Bill
B/E Produce	70666	Lettuce	cs	2	$ 21.00	$ 42.00	$ 42.00						
						Totals	$351.00	$475.00	$683.50	—	$275.00		

Accept Incoming Products. This is normally done by signing the delivery invoice. At this point, ownership of the products is transferred to the property, and the products become the responsibility of the food and beverage operation.

Move Accepted Products to Storage Immediately. Security to minimize employee theft is a concern here. Likewise, the quality of products needing low-temperature storage will deteriorate if they are left at room temperatures, which are frequently very warm in back-of-the-house production areas. Use a stock rotation process; incoming items should be placed behind and/or under items already in inventory.

Complete Necessary Receiving Documents. A typical receiving document is a daily receiving report such as the sample shown in Exhibit 9. The daily receiving report is used for several purposes:

- To separate beverage costs—liquor, beer, wine, soda—from food costs. This information is needed for income statements that isolate revenue and "costs of goods sold" categories for these items.

- To add up the value of "directs" in a daily food cost assessment system.

- To transfer responsibility for product control from receiving to storeroom personnel (in large operations with different receiving and storeroom personnel).

In examining the daily receiving report, note the following points. Information about all incoming products received during the shift can be recorded on one form with additional pages as necessary. Columns 1 to 3, respectively, list the supplier's name, invoice number, and items received.

Columns 4 to 7 indicate for each item the purchase unit, which is the size of the shipping container (ground beef comes in 10-pound bags); number of purchase

Exhibit 10   Request-for-Credit Memo

Request-for-Credit Memo

(prepare in duplicate)   Number: _____

From: _____   To: _____
_____   (supplier)
_____   _____
_____   _____
                                                             _____

Credit should be given on the following:

Invoice Number: _____   Invoice Date: _____

Product	Unit	Number	Price/Unit	Total Price

Reason: Total: _____

_____   _____
(delivery person)   (authorizing signature)

units (the property received six 10-pound bags of ground beef); cost per unit (a 10-pound bag of ground beef costs $28.50—or $2.85 per pound); and total cost of the item (six 10-pound bags of ground beef at $28.50 equals $171.00). In the distribution columns 8 to 13, the total cost in column 7 of each item is carried over by category. Food items are classified as "directs" or "stores." ("Directs" are charged to food costs on the day of receipt; "stores" enter storage records, such as perpetual inventory forms, and are charged to food costs when issued.) Each beverage item is classified as liquor, beer, wine, or soda. For example, columns in the sample forms note bar Scotch and house Chablis wine.

Column 14—transfer to storage—is used in larger operations with separate receiving and storage staff to indicate that all products received actually enter storeroom areas.

Request-for-Credit Memos

Every time a delivery invoice is modified at the time of receiving, a request-for-credit memo becomes necessary (Exhibit 10). For example, if deliveries do not include the full quantity specified on the delivery invoice, are refused because of quality problems, or are rejected for any other reason, this is noted on the request-for-credit memo. Never permit the delivery person to leave off items on the invoice and deliver them "free" next time. The following procedures should be used to process a request-for-credit memo.

1. Note problems with items on the invoice.

2. Complete the request-for-credit memo, have the delivery person sign it, and return a copy to the supplier along with the delivery invoice.

3. Attach the property's copy of the memo to its copy of the delivery invoice. Note the correct amount of the invoice on the face of the invoice.

4. Call the supplier to advise that the original invoice has been amended by a request-for-credit memo.

5. If short or refused products are subsequently delivered, a separate invoice can accompany the items. The new invoice is processed in the usual manner.

6. Do not file any problem invoices. Hold them in a separate file until all problems, such as a supplier's confirmation of a credit, are resolved.

Marking Procedures

Marking and tagging puts invoice information directly on items. For example, marking case goods or bottles of liquor with the delivery date and price makes it easier to judge whether stock rotation plans are effective. Also, when valuing inventory, cost data can be taken directly from the cases or bottles; this saves the time needed to look up the information on the daily receiving report, delivery invoice, or in the computerized database. Recording the unit price on products makes it more likely that the operation's staff members will think about them as alternative forms of cash. Therefore, they may be more careful in handling, portioning, and controlling waste.

Security Concerns in Receiving

Examples of supplier theft possibilities when products are received include the following:

- The supplier may deliver lesser quality items, such as inexpensive domestic wines instead of higher quality wines, or 30 percent fat content ground beef instead of 20 percent, and the operation pays the price for the higher quality.

- Short-weight or short-count products may be delivered so the food service operation pays for more products than it receives.

- Thawed products may be represented as fresh, while the operation pays the higher price for fresh.

- Ice may be ground into ground meat products, fillers such as soy products or non-fat dry milk extenders may be added, and meat may be sold with excess fat trim.

- Weight of ice and/or packaging may be included in the product weight on which price is based.

- "Slacked out" seafood—frozen fish, thawed and packed in ice—may be sold as fresh.

- Expensive steaks and inexpensive meat may be combined in one container, and when the entire container is weighed, the operation may be billed for more expensive steaks than are actually in the container.

- One empty liquor bottle may be included in a case of 12 bottles.

These are just a few of the many ways that suppliers can steal from the property by overcharging for amount and/or quality. To help guard against theft at receiving, some basic principles should be followed:

1. Have different people receive and purchase, unless the owner/manager performs both duties.

2. Train employees to receive properly. Receiving is too important to leave to whomever happens to be handy.

3. To the maximum extent possible, schedule product deliveries at slow times so that receiving personnel, who may have other duties, have time to receive correctly.

4. Have deliveries made to a specified area of the facility, and be sure receiving scales and other equipment are available and are used.

5. After receipt, immediately move products to storage. Chances for employee theft increase the longer products remain unattended.

6. Do not permit salespersons or delivery/route persons access to back-of-the-house production or storage areas. To the maximum extent possible, the receiving area should be close to an outside exit and visible to management personnel.

7. Lock the outside door. Install an audio signal so delivery persons can ring when they arrive. With this plan, receiving personnel have delivery persons in sight during their entire visit.

Computerized Receiving Systems

Computer technology is now helping some food and beverage operations with the receiving task. Over time, many additional properties will take advantage of technology as products are received. Packing cases containing food and beverage products often have universal product codes/bar code information attached. Data indicates product code (name), purchase/delivery date, product price and, perhaps, other information. An optical scanner is used to "read" this information and, at the same time, update perpetual inventory levels and develop daily receiving and other reports desired by the operation. This process allows for rapid generation of important control information with minimal chances of error.

Endnotes ————————————————————————————————

1. Materials presented in this section are based on Ronald F. Cichy's *Quality Sanitation Management* (Lansing, Mich.: Educational Institute of the American Hotel & Lodging Association, 1994).

Key Terms ————————————————————————————————

audit trail—A series of records, documents, and/or reports that traces the flow of resources through an operation.

autodial modem—An electronic communications device that functions without user intervention, enabling late-night transmission of purchase orders for next-day processing.

call brand—A brand of liquor offered which is of higher quality and price than the property's house brand liquor.

food sample data sheet—A form that helps standardize the evaluation of a product by recording purchasing, storing, preparing, and serving information about products the operation is sampling and considering for purchase.

house brand—A brand of liquor which is provided to guests when a call brand is not specified (also called pour brand or speed rail brand).

lead-time quantity—The number of purchase units withdrawn from inventory between the time the order is placed and when it is delivered.

line position—A decision maker in the chain of command within an organiztion.

maximum inventory level—The greatest number of purchase units permitted in storage; calculated by adding the minimum (safety) level to the usage rate.

minimum inventory level—The number of purchase units that must always remain in inventory; also referred to as the safety level.

minimum/maximum ordering system—A system to help managers determine when products must be purchased and how much of each to order by assessing the minimum quantity below which inventory levels should not fall and the maximum quantity above which inventory levels should not rise.

order point—The number of purchase units in stock when an order is placed.

premium brand—A liquor of very high quality which is sold at a higher price than a property's call brand.

prime supplier—A vendor who receives the order to supply all or much of a property's need for specific product(s) for a specified period of time.

purchase order system—An ordering system requiring that formal purchase orders be sent to suppliers awarded orders. Purchase orders identify the products, quantities, unit costs, and total costs that both the suppliers and the purchaser have agreed upon. In addition, the purchase order may include guarantees, warranties, payment requirements, inspection rights, "hold harmless" provisions, and other legal, contractual concerns. The purchase order is the food and beverage operation's record of the specifics of all incoming shipments; copies are retained in the purchasing department and are also circulated internally among the receiving and accounting departments.

purchase record—Provides a small food and beverage operation with an in-house, detailed record of all incoming shipments and performs the same functions as a purchase order.

purchasing—The series of activities designed to obtain products of the right quality and quantity, at the right price and time, and from the right source.

quality—In regard to the purchasing function, the suitability of a product for its intended use; the more suitable a product, the greater its quality.

speculative purchasing—A system whereby management makes judgments about future prices of products and buys more if prices are expected to increase or less if prices are expected to decrease.

staff position—An advisory or technical specialist who provides advice to but does not make decisions for a line official. A purchasing agent is normally in a staff position.

standard purchase specifications—Provide detailed descriptions of the quality, size, and weight desired for particular items that are to be purchased.

usage rate—The number of purchase units used per order period.

Review Questions

1. What are the purposes of an effective purchasing system?

2. What forms are necessary for an effective purchasing system? Why are they important? How are they used?

3. What are standard purchase specifications? Why are they important?

4. Why should a purchaser not order larger quantities than necessary?

5. What factors should be considered when selecting suppliers?

6. What are some of the ways in which theft can occur at the time of purchase?

7. What are the basic steps in the receiving process?

8. Why is the daily receiving report important?

9. When should a request-for-credit memo be used?

10. What are common examples of theft during receiving, and what can be done to reduce the opportunities for these problems to occur?

11. How has technology simplified the purchasing and receiving processes?

Internet Sites

For more information, visit the following Internet sites. Remember that Internet addresses can change without notice. If the site is no longer there, you can use a search engine to look for additional sites.

Associations

American Culinary Federation (ACF)
http://www.acfchefs.org

American Hotel & Lodging Association (AH&LA)
http://www.ahlaonline.org

American School Food Service Association
(ASFSA)
http://www.asfsa.org

Club Managers Association of America (CMAA)
http://www.cmaa.org

The Educational Foundation of NRA
http://www.edfound.org

The Educational Institute of AH&LA
http://www.ei–ahla.org

Hospitality Financial and Technology Professionals
http://www.hftp.org

Institute of Food Technologies
http://www.ift.org

International Hotel and Restaurant Association
http://www.ih–ra.com

National Association of College and University Food Services
http://www.nacufs.org

National Restaurant Association (NRA)
http://www.restaurant.org

Food and Beverage Resources

Club Management Online
http://www.club–mgmt.com/dining/index.html

Food and Beverage Network
http://www.foodtrends.com

Food Purchasing, Preparation, and Storage (beef)
http://www.beeftips.org/purch-prep.html

Net Grocer
http://www.netgrocer.com

Prepared Foods. Product development, ingredients, suppliers
http://www.preparedfoods.com

Thomas Food Industry Register
http://www.tfir.com

Food Service Software

Adaco Sevices, Inc.
http://www.adacoservices.com

CMS Hospitality
http://www.cmshosp.com.au

Computrition, Inc.
http://www.computrition.com

Comtrex Systems Corporation
http://www.comtrex.com

Comus Restaurant Systems
http://www.comus.com

Cost Guard
http://www.costguard.com

Culinary Software
http://www.culinarysoftware.com

Eatec Corporation
http://www.eatec.com

Integrated Restaurant Software
http://www.rmstouch.com

MAI Systems Corporation
http://www.maisystems.com

Micros Systems, Inc.
http://www.micros.com

Sulcus Computer Corporation
http://www2.sulcus.nl

Management Companies

ARAMARK
http://www.aramark.com

Bon Appétit Management Company
http://www.bamco.com

Compass Group
http://www.compass–na.com

MSI Solutions
http://www.msisolutions.com

Sodexho Marriott
http://www.sodexhomarriott.com

The Wood Company
http://www.woodco.com

Publications—Online and Printed

Club Management Magazine
http://www.club–mgmt.com

Electronic Gourmet Guide
http://www.foodwine.com

Food and Hospitality Magazine
http://www.foodserviceworld.com

Food Management
http://www.foodservicesearch.com

Food Network: CyberKitchen
http://www.foodtv.com

Food Processing: The Magazine of
Strategy, Technology and Trends
http://www.foodprocessing.com

Internet Food Channel
http://www.foodchannel.com

International Hotel and Restaurant
Association journal
www.hotelsmag.com

International Journal of Hospitality
Management
http://www.mcb.co.uk/ijchm.htm

Journal of Hospitality Financial
Management
http://hrta.fnr.umass.edu/sheel/
ahfme/jhfm/aboutjhfm.html

Lodging Food and Beverage
http://www.lodgingnews.com/
lodgingfnb/

Lodging Hospitality Online
http://www.lhonline.com

Lodging News, journal of the
American Hotel & Lodging Association
http://www.ei–ahla.org/webs/
lodging/index.html

Nation's Restaurant News
http://www.nrn.com

Restaurant Hospitality
www.foodservicesearch.com

On the Rail—News for Food
Professionals
http://www.ontherail.com

Restaurants and Institutions
http://www.rimag.com

Restaurants and Institutions magazine
http://www.rimag.com

Restaurants USA, publication of
National Restaurant Association
http://www.restaurant.org/rusa

Restaurant Business, Food Service, and
ID magazines
http://www.foodservicetoday.com

World Hospitality, management
magazine for hotel executives.
http://www.worldhospitality.com

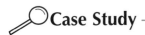 **Case Study** ——————————————————————————

When Life Hands You Lemons…Better Check the Specs

Thursday, 4 P.M.

Sue, the kitchen manager at the Wagon Wheel Restaurant, glanced at the clock. Pierson's Produce would be calling soon for the weekend order. She pulled out a notepad and began to make a quick list. It was going to be a busy weekend—the homecoming game at the college would be bringing in lots of business. She'd better order an extra case of lemons for iced tea, and lettuce for salads.

Sue didn't have time to take inventory, so she tried to picture the storeroom as it looked when she last peeked in. She was sure they had lettuce—or was that cabbage she saw? No, it had to be lettuce. Maybe she'd only order one case for the weekend. They were fine on parsley; no need to order that. But kiwis—that new fruit salad on the menu was popular, so she added kiwis to the list.

Sue was putting the final items on her list when George, the general manager, tapped at her office door. He carried a report in his hand and he didn't look happy.

"Have you seen this report, Sue?" he asked. "Our food costs are on the high side, and it looks like produce is the culprit. It's up to 9.5 percent, and it should be down around 7.5 percent. We really need to do something about that."

"I'll take care of it," she said.

Just then the phone rang. It was Alan from Pierson's Produce, calling for the order.

"Just the man I wanted to talk to," said Sue. She explained George's concern about the produce costs and wondered what Alan could do to help. She could hear him tapping away at his computer keyboard.

"Well, you know, it's the end of the season and prices are higher now, Sue," he said. "But, looking at your past orders, I see you've been paying $22 a case for fancy lemons. If you like, I can get you lemons for … how does $14 a case sound?"

Sue didn't even stop to ask what she might be getting for that price. Saving $8 a case was just what she wanted to hear. She agreed and ordered three cases of lemons, a case of lettuce—yes, only one, she told him—and two cases of kiwis. She checked the items off on her notepad as Alan read back her order. She thanked him and hung up the phone. Then she turned her attention to other matters.

Monday, 4 P.M.

Sue looked up in surprise as George came into her office. He looked even more unhappy than he had last week, if that was possible. He shook a report under her nose.

"I thought you were going to take care of these produce costs," he said. "These figures are even higher—11 percent! How could that happen?"

Sue looked confused. "I don't know," she stammered.

At that moment, Adrian, the chef, who had happened to hear George's question as he was walking by, stuck his head in the door.

"I know how it happened," Adrian said. "We ran out of lemons, lettuce, and parsley this past weekend and I had to send my people down to the grocery store to pick up produce—at retail prices! That's what drove our costs up."

"But I ordered lemons and lettuce on Thursday afternoon," Sue replied. She showed him the torn-off page from her notepad. "Didn't they get delivered?"

Adrian thought back. Yes, three cases of lemons had been received, but they were small and unattractive, obviously not the fancy lemons that the restaurant used to garnish its drinks. "I told the receiving clerk that the produce company must have sent us the wrong lemons and told him to send them back," Adrian said. "They definitely weren't the lemons on our specifications."

Sue groaned. So much for the $8 a case savings on lemons. She guessed she should have told the receiving clerk what to expect.

Adrian continued. "As for the rest of the order, the restaurant got only half the lettuce it needed, and no parsley at all. We had to garnish the Eggs Benedict with scallions until someone could get to the market and buy some parsley." He laughed. "But boy, do we have kiwis to spare. We already had one case. I don't know how we're going to use up two more cases before they go bad."

George looked at Sue for an explanation. "I'm sure this is an isolated incident," he began.

Adrian laughed again and said, "It happens more often than you think. Why don't you ask her about the time we ended up with Florida oranges for our garnishes instead of California oranges?"

Sue glared at Adrian, and George looked at both of them.

"I think it's time we sat down and reviewed some purchasing procedures around here," he said.

Discussion Questions

1. What standard purchasing control practices could Sue have followed that would have prevented the high produce costs?

2. What was right or wrong about the chef's actions to remedy the situation?

3. What steps can Sue take to reduce produce costs in the future?

Case Number: 4656CA

The following industry experts helped generate and develop this case: Timothy J. Pugh, Regional Manager, Damon's—The Place for Ribs (Steve Montanye Enterprises, East Lansing, Michigan); and Lawrence E. Ross, Assistant Professor, Florida Southern College, and owner of Sago Grill, Lakeland, Florida.

 **Problems** ————————————————————

Problem 1

Complete the following perishable product quotation/call sheet; indicate the preferred supplier:

a) if each item is purchased from the supplier quoting the lowest price for that item

b) if all items are purchased from the supplier submitting the lowest total price quotation (Note: suppliers A and B will provide a three percent discount if all products are purchased from them.)

c) explain any special concerns you may have about the price quotations

	Amount			Supplier		
Item	Needed	On Hand	Order	1	2	3
Lettuce	12 cases	4$^{1}/_{2}$ cases		$19.90 cs =	$21.10 cs =	$18.90 cs =
Spinach	6 cases	1$^{1}/_{2}$ cases		$23.40 cs =	$20.10 cs =	$ 24.10 cs =
Cabbage	4 cases	1 case		$12.90 cs =	$9.80 cs =	$11.15 cs =
Escarole	7 cases	3 cases		$27.50 cs =	$21.00 cs =	$29.50 cs =
			Total			

Problem 2

Use the information below to answer the following questions:

- Purchase unit   = 10 lb poly bag (ground beef)
- Usage rate   = 170lb per day
- Order period   = 4 days
- Lead time   = 1 day
- Safety level   = 1 day

a) How many *pounds* should be ordered at the order point? How many 10 lb poly bags should be purchased?

b) The order is placed when there are 390 lbs available. How many *purchase* units should be ordered?

c) What is the usage rate in the four-day order period?

d) How many 10 lb poly bags are used daily and during the order period?

e) How many purchase units are included in the lead time and safety level factors?

f) What is the maximum number of lbs to be available?

g) How many purchase units should be purchased at the order point?

Problem 3

The following information is provided on a delivery invoice. Use this information to answer the following questions:

Item	Ordered	Pack	Weight (lb)	Unit Price	Amount
Ground Beef	25	10 lb	250 lb	$2.30	
Green Beans	12	6 #10 cs		$28.10	
Tomato Sauce	6	6 #10 cs		$26.75	
Shrimp	6	10 5-lb cs	300 lb	$8.45	

a) What is the total amount due?

b) The sharp-eyed employee who received the order noticed the following:
   - Only 23 10-lb bags of ground beef were received
   - One case of green beans appeared damaged (the corner of the case was crushed; the cardboard case looked like it had been wet and then had dried)
   - There were 7 cases of tomato sauce
   - There were only 5 cases (10 5-lb) of shrimp

c) The supplier will give a 10 percent discount if the invoice is paid within 10 days. What is the total amount of the invoice to be paid assuming that this discount is taken?

Chapter 7 Outline

Storing Control: General Procedures
    Inventory Control Policy
    Separating Directs from Stores
    Defining Storage Areas
Security Concerns in Storage Areas
    Limited Access
    Lockable Storage Areas
    Behind-the-Bar Storage
    Storeroom Key Control
Maintaining Quality during Storage
    Product Rotation
    Properly Controlled Environment
    Sanitation Practices
    Proper Storage
Inventory Control Procedures
    Inventory Turnover
    Inventory Recordkeeping Systems
    Physical Inventory System
    Perpetual Inventory System
Computerized Inventory Management
A Special Note about Beverage Inventory
    Behind-the-Bar Inventory Costs
    Computerized Scales
Issuing Control: General Procedures
    Issuing Procedures
    The Food Requisition/Issue Process
    Computer-Generated Issue Quantities
The Beverage Requisition/Issue Process
    Establishing Bar Par Inventory Levels
    Beverage Issuing Steps
    Bottle Marking
    Additional Concerns for Beverage
    Control

Competencies

1. Identify the objectives of a storage system for food service operations. (pp. 210–211)

2. Explain how an inventory classification system helps food service managers design cost-effective inventory control procedures. (pp. 211–212)

3. Distinguish between "directs" and "stores" in relation to the inventory systems of food and beverage operations. (p. 212)

4. Describe procedures for maintaining product quality during storage. (pp. 214–216)

5. Calculate an inventory turnover rate. (pp. 216–217)

6. Distinguish a physical inventory system from a perpetual inventory system. (pp. 217–221)

7. Identify the objectives of issuing systems for food service operations and describe issuing-control procedures. (pp. 226–231)

7

Storing and Issuing Controls

THE STORING AND ISSUING control points play an important role in linking receiving and production. Food and beverage managers must recognize that product costs and quality are affected by storing and issuing systems. Unfortunately, many food and beverage operations lack adequate control procedures for these functions. Products are simply put in the storeroom when received and taken out when needed.

Actually, food and beverage managers would do well to think of the storeroom as a bank vault. Products in storage represent money. If the storeroom contains, for example, $5,000 worth of food and beverage products, think of it as having 5,000 one-dollar bills in storage. Stored products represent money in terms of both their initial cost as well as the cost to replace them if they are stolen, spoiled, or damaged because of improper storage practices. The same care and concern that go into procedures for controlling stored cash should also go into the procedures for controlling stored foods and beverages.

There are many reasons why strict storage and issuing controls are needed in food and beverage operations. Products can be stolen when issued from storage to production areas. Also, mistakes in issuing can result in more products being used in production than are necessary. This, in turn, can result in waste and unnecessarily high food or beverage costs. Moreover, since systems of assessing daily food and beverage costs are based, in part, on the value of daily issues, it is essential to know exactly how much of each product leaves storage areas.

In the first part of this chapter, we will discuss principles of control that should be incorporated into an effective storage system designed for the specific needs of the food and beverage operation. In the remainder of the chapter, we will review control practices relating to issuing products from storage to production areas.

Storing Control: General Procedures

It is important to move food and beverage products into storage areas as soon as they are received. In addition, delivery personnel should have only limited access to back-of-the-house areas. This means that staff from the property—not the delivery persons—should be responsible for this transfer to storage. If deliveries are left unattended in receiving areas, refrigerated and frozen products can easily deteriorate in quality, and dishonest employees may have opportunities to steal. As soon as received products are moved to and placed in storage areas, their quality and security can be better ensured by the control procedures built into the property's storage system. The principles of effective storage systems for both food and beverage products focus on three primary concerns:

Exhibit 1   ABCD Classification Scheme for Foods in Inventory

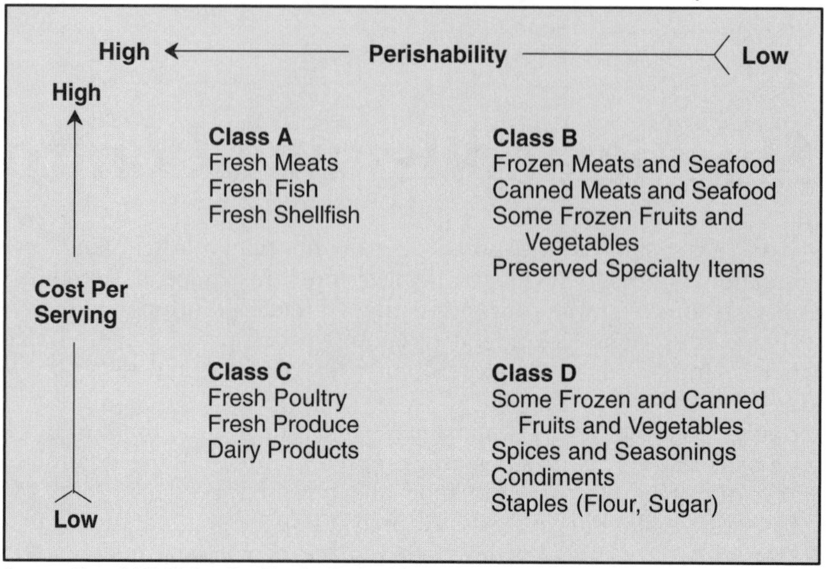

High ← ——————— Perishability ——————— ⟨ Low

High ↑

Class A
Fresh Meats
Fresh Fish
Fresh Shellfish

Class B
Frozen Meats and Seafood
Canned Meats and Seafood
Some Frozen Fruits and
    Vegetables
Preserved Specialty Items

**Cost Per
Serving**

Class C
Fresh Poultry
Fresh Produce
Dairy Products

Class D
Some Frozen and Canned
    Fruits and Vegetables
Spices and Seasonings
Condiments
Staples (Flour, Sugar)

Low ↓

Source: Ronald F. Cichy, *Quality Sanitation Management* (Lansing, Mich.: Educational Institute of the American Hotel & Lodging Association, 1994), p. 224.

- Keeping products secure from theft
- Retaining product quality
- Providing information necessary for the financial accounting system

Inventory Control Policy

When designing storage systems, every control procedure must be cost-effective. It is generally not practical for managers to attempt to regulate all food and beverage products under a strict system of tight controls. Some properties, for example, may not be able to justify a perpetual inventory system for any but the most expensive items. (Perpetual inventory systems are discussed later in this chapter.) As a result, many food and beverage operations, especially smaller ones, maintain tight control over meats, seafood, liquor, and wine, but not as much control over less expensive and less theft-prone products. Others may expand the list of items needing special controls because of specific concerns. The point is that each property is different, and managers must develop basic control procedures that recognize their operation's unique situation.

One approach that has been useful is based on an **ABCD inventory classification system** which categorizes products according to their perishability and cost per serving. Category A items, for example, include those products that are high in both perishability and cost per serving, while category B items are relatively high in cost but low in perishability. Exhibit 1 presents the ABCD approach, indicating the categories and showing examples of inventory items in each category.

One advantage of using this system is the ability to regulate the products needing the tightest control—usually those in categories A and B. Storage systems for these products should be designed and implemented first. Then as time permits and practices require, other products in lower priority categories can be brought under tighter control.

Separating Directs from Stores

For inventory purposes, food products are often separated into two categories: directs and stores.

Directs are usually relatively inexpensive, perishable products generally purchased several times a week for more or less immediate use. Examples are fresh produce, baked goods, and dairy products. Directs may be received and transferred immediately to production areas for preparation or may be held in workstation storage areas. Alternatively, they can be received and placed in central storage areas for withdrawal as needed. However, in either case, directs are not entered into any storage records; they are not considered part of the inventory system. Instead, if daily food costs information is being collected, they are considered part of food costs for the day on which they are received. The primary recordkeeping concern associated with these products lies with receiving, rather than storage, procedures.

Stores are relatively expensive items, may be purchased less often than directs, and are procured in quantities necessary to rebuild inventory levels. Examples are meats, seafood, frozen and canned products, and staples such as flour, sugar, and cereals. Food and beverage operations may purchase stores as often as once a week or as seldom as once every several months, depending on usage rates, inventory levels, and type of product. A minimum/maximum purchasing and inventory system for these items should be in place. Stores must be tightly controlled, usually by recording them in inventory records and using an issuing system to remove them from inventory. These procedures are discussed later in this chapter.

Defining Storage Areas

When products are "in storage" they have been entered into inventory records and should be under tight storage control. Each food and beverage operation must define its storage areas. For example, central storerooms and walk-in refrigerators and freezers are obviously storage areas. However, are items still "in storage" when they are in workstation storage areas such as reach-in refrigerators, pantry shelves, broken-case storage areas, and behind the bar? Managers must designate:

- What locations are considered storage areas
- What items are to be tightly controlled
- What specific procedures will be employed for keeping items secure, maintaining proper quality, taking inventory, and other accounting activities

Security Concerns in Storage Areas

After management determines what items are to be tightly controlled and what locations are to be considered storage areas, security procedures can be designed to ensure that those items stay in those locations—until they are issued to production areas. The following types of procedures help keep storage areas secure.

Limited Access

Only authorized staff members should be permitted in storerooms. In addition to management, authorized staff in larger properties may include receiving and/or storage personnel. Smaller operations can keep storage areas locked and involve management directly in receiving and issuing activities. When a manager is present to unlock the storeroom door, employee theft is less likely. This procedure is more easily implemented if issuing is done only at specified times.

Lockable Storage Areas

The storeroom, freezer, and beverage storage areas should be completely lockable. Depending upon available equipment, one section of a walk-in or reach-in refrigerator might be used to secure expensive refrigerated items. Or, a lockable shelving unit (or cage) can be kept in the walk-in refrigerator. In this way, expensive refrigerated products, such as fresh meats and seafood, or wines being chilled for service, can be kept secure from theft. At the same time, personnel can still have access to produce, dairy, and similar products that are less likely to be stolen.

Refrigerator/freezer units should be lockable with reasonably strong lock clasps and door hinges. Storeroom walls should extend to the ceiling, and there should be no way to enter through the ceiling from another room. If there are windows, they should at least be made secure and unopenable. The point is to design, within practical limits, storage areas that are difficult for unauthorized employees to enter without being detected.

Some properties maintain a "precious room." A precious room is a locked storage area within a locked storage area. For example, liquor and expensive buffet chafing dishes might be kept locked in a closet inside a locked storeroom.

The goal of all of these procedures is to reduce opportunities for employee pilferage. The answers to commonsense questions such as "How would I steal from my storage areas if I were a dishonest employee?" may point to security loopholes in storage areas.

Behind-the-Bar Storage

The quantity of beverage products kept behind the bar should be minimal since storage space is limited and this area is less secure than the central storage area. Liquor should be locked behind the bar when the bar is closed. Lockable cabinets, roll-down screens, or similar devices can keep beverages out of the reach of cleaning staff and other employees when the bar is closed.

Storeroom Key Control

Only staff members who need keys should have them. Manual locks or combinations should be changed routinely and each time an employee with access to keys leaves the property's employment. An excellent policy is that all keys remain at the property at all times, securely locked in the manager's office when not in use. Some food and beverage managers may feel key control procedures are unnecessary.

However, a significant number of dollars can be lost because of inadequate key control. This fact should convince managers to emphasize this aspect of the operation's control system.

Newer locking systems eliminate the need for traditional keys. For example, pins correlating with a "combination code" can be depressed by authorized personnel who have memorized the code. When these individuals no longer need access to lockable areas, combinations can be quickly (and inexpensively) changed. Other systems may use plastic cards, similar to credit cards, with coded information designed to operate locks. These systems are in common use for hotel guest rooms and are increasingly being used in back-of-house areas as well. Either of these or related systems may yield information about the identity of persons entering lockable areas, time of entry, and length of time that the individual was in the area.

Increasingly, these and related systems provide more specific control information to help ensure that only persons authorized to enter storage areas do, in fact, gain access to these locations.

Maintaining Quality during Storage

Improper storage practices can reduce the quality of products in storage. In fact, most food products—including frozen foods—experience a loss in quality if stored too long. While this is especially true for foods, it also applies to some wines and most beers. It is important that control procedures designed to minimize the loss of quality of products in storage be strictly followed. Food costs increase as items judged unfit for use are discarded and replaced. If, because of pressure to keep food costs down, lower quality products are served to guests, there may be serious marketing implications. The following sections present several procedures for maintaining quality during storage.

Product Rotation

The **first-in, first-out (FIFO) inventory rotation** method is a good rule. The products held in inventory the longest should be the first to be issued to production areas. To facilitate this, when newly received products enter storage areas they should be placed under or behind products already in storage. Marking the date of receipt on every item makes it possible to compare dates of products used in production with those of items in storage areas. Those items in production should have been received earlier than those remaining in storage. This method will help management ensure that stock rotation practices are followed.

Properly Controlled Environment

Maintain proper temperature, humidity, and ventilation. Use accurate thermometers and check them routinely. Proper temperatures are (unless otherwise regulated by government sources):

- Dry storage temperature—50° to 70°F (10° to 21°C)
- Refrigerated storage temperature—40°F (4°C) or lower
- Freezer storage temperature—0°F (-18°C) or lower

Require management's permission to discard spoiled items. This way, managers can judge the effectiveness of its quality control methods and also assess the costs of failing to comply with proper storage procedures.

Sanitation Practices

Establish and follow regular cleaning times for all storage facilities, in contrast with cleaning them only when extra time becomes available.[1] This applies not only to storerooms and storage spaces, but also to walk-in and reach-in refrigerators and storage equipment. Facilities and equipment should be made of nonporous, easily cleaned materials. Shelving units should be louvered or slotted to permit air circulation. They should not be covered with aluminum foil or any other material that impedes air flow. Lower shelves, drainage racks, and similar storage equipment should be at least two inches from walls and at least six inches off the floor to permit mop and broom cleaning and to discourage rodent and insect nesting.

In following proper sanitation practices, it is important to use professional pest control services. Faced with the many exotic chemicals and poisons on the market, probably very few food and beverage managers are qualified to plan and manage rodent and insect control programs. It is too dangerous for a well-intentioned but untrained person to spray and spread chemicals in food production and service areas.

Proper Storage

Store products properly. For example, store products in their original packaging, away from the wall, to allow air circulation. Store items that absorb odors, such as flour, away from products that give off odors, such as onions. Store opened products in clean, labeled, covered containers designed for food storage, rather than using empty glass jars (which can break) or empty number-10 cans (which cannot be properly cleaned).

Generally, products should be stored in quantities that can be used within a reasonable time period. There are exceptions to this rule, such as investments in wines and volume purchases made as hedges against price increases, but these decisions should be made by top management, not by purchasing staff. Beverage products are generally stored for less than one month. Food items classified as stores are usually used within an even shorter time period. Perishable products are purchased two or more times weekly.

Inventory Control Procedures

The third major concern in storage, after security and minimizing quality losses, is recordkeeping. We have already mentioned that inventory procedures play an important role in the security concerns of the control system. There are several other reasons for designing and implementing effective inventory recordkeeping systems:

- Financial accounting systems need inventory values to generate monthly statements. The value of products in inventory is considered part of the property's current assets (for the balance sheet) and is also used to assess costs (for the income statement).

- Daily control procedures may require knowing the quantity of products currently available. For example, a food and beverage manager may wish to keep a perpetual inventory record of selected expensive items to allow frequent and quick assessment of any differences between the quantity that should be in storage and how much is actually there.

- Inventory records help managers determine not only when to order new products, but also how much of each product to order.

Inventory Turnover

One important function of keeping accurate inventory records is to allow managers to assess how much money is being invested in non-productive inventory. The value of goods in inventory is typically calculated on a monthly basis to provide information for financial accounting systems. **Non-productive inventory** refers to products in storage that are not issued to production areas during the time period (usually monthly) covered by financial records. In order to determine how much money is tied up in non-productive inventory, managers measure the inventory turnover rate. The **inventory turnover rate** shows the number of times in a given period that inventory is converted or turned into revenue. In financial terms, it measures the rate at which inventory is turned into food or beverage costs required to generate food or beverage revenue.

Inventory turnover rates can be determined for food or beverage products in storage. The inventory turnover is calculated by dividing the cost of food (or beverages) used by the average food (or beverage) inventory (in dollars). The **average inventory** value is determined by adding the value of inventory at the beginning of the time period in question (usually a month) to the value of inventory at the end of that period and then dividing the sum by two.

For example, to calculate the inventory turnover rate for food products for a month, assume the following data:

- Food Inventory Value at Beginning of Month = $18,500
- Food Inventory Value at End of Month = $19,500
- Cost of Food Used = $122, 750

$$\frac{\text{Average Food Inventory}}{\text{for Month}} = \frac{\text{Beginning Inventory} + \text{Ending Inventory}}{2}$$

$$\frac{\text{Average Food Inventory}}{\text{for Month}} = \frac{\$18,500 + \$19,500}{2} = \$19,000$$

$$\text{Food Inventory Turnover} = \frac{\text{Cost of Food Used for Month}}{\text{Average Food Inventory for Month}}$$

$$\text{Food Inventory Turnover} = \frac{\$122,750}{\$19,000} = 6.46 \text{ times}$$

In this example, the cost of inventory is turned into revenue on an average of 6.46 times during the month. This means that 6.46 times the average amount of daily inventory must be purchased sometime during the month to keep the operation supplied.

The inventory turnover rate is an important tool to use in managing inventory levels. As this rate decreases, more money is being invested in inventory. If too much of the property's funds are being used to purchase excess products for inventory, cash flow problems may result and create other difficulties for the operation. Also, products may spoil or otherwise deteriorate in quality because of excessive inventory levels. On the other hand, as the turnover rate increases, less money is being invested in inventory. As average inventory levels are reduced, however, a point will be reached at which stock-outs begin to occur and guest dissatisfaction and operating problems can result.

Therefore, to properly control the property's investment in inventory, food and beverage managers must determine the best turnover rate for their particular operations. This process requires monitoring. If the turnover rate is calculated monthly, the food and beverage manager can learn of any increases or decreases in inventory turnover and respond accordingly. It may also be a good idea to calculate turnover rates for specific product categories. One would normally expect highly perishable items (such as fresh meats and seafood, fruits, and vegetables) to turn over more rapidly than less perishable items (such as spices, staples, and frozen or canned products).

Inventory Recordkeeping Systems

There are two basic kinds of recordkeeping systems for products in storage: physical inventory and perpetual inventory. A **physical inventory system** involves actual observation and counting of stored products on a periodic basis. A **perpetual inventory system** involves keeping a running balance of the quantity of stored products by recording all newly purchased items as they enter storage areas and all quantities issued from storage to production areas.

Physical Inventory System

A physical inventory system is used to periodically assess the value of food and beverage products in inventory. This is done at least monthly to develop information needed for the balance sheet and income statement. Inventory value is counted as a current asset, and inventory values, both at the beginning and end of the financial period, are a factor in assessing food and beverage costs.

Before a physical inventory of stored products can be taken, the food and beverage manager must make several decisions about the design of the physical inventory system.

- *What products should be considered in making an inventory count?* This decision is partially related to the question of which areas are to be considered storage areas under the control of the inventory system. For example, does inventoryinclude products in broken-case and workstation storage areas? What about products in process, such as frozen poultry thawing in the refrigerator? What items are "stores" and included in inventory, and what items are "directs" and excluded from inventory?

- *How should monetary value be assigned to products in inventory?* One method is to calculate the actual cost of stored products at the time the physical inventory is made. Another method is to use the average costs of stored products over several inventory counts. Others include the **last-in, first-out (LIFO) inventory valuation** system and the **first-in, first-out (FIFO) inventory valuation** system.[2] Under the LIFO system, the costs of the products most recently added to inventory (last in) are the costs assigned when products are issued (first out). This leads to cost of sales figures that more accurately reflect current replacement costs. It also tends to create a smaller total inventory value. That is, since the most recent (and usually most expensive) costs are the first to be "issued," the remaining inventory is made up of the earlier (and usually lower) costs. Conversely, under the FIFO system, the oldest (and usually lowest) costs are "issued" first, leaving the more recent (and usually higher) costs remaining in inventory. This creates a higher total inventory value and a lower cost of sales. (Note, however, that seasonal price variations—for example, for fresh fruit—will sometimes cause recent purchases to cost *less* than earlier purchases.) Typically, an accountant helps determine the best inventory valuation system for the property. This is because inventory values affect food costs which impact profitability and, therefore, taxes.

- *How should costs of such items as opened containers of spices in production areas and opened bottles of liquor at the bar be handled?* Often, the cost of such opened, unused items is assumed to average out. In other words, their value is thought to remain approximately the same from month to month. So, once an estimated cost is established, it can be used monthly.

- *What procedures should be used in counting the products in inventory?* Persons involved in managing storage areas should not take inventory counts alone. Perhaps the food inventory can be taken by the food manager, while the beverage manager takes the beverage inventory. In both situations, a representative from the accounting office can assist in conducting the physical inventory.

As stored products are observed and counted, a physical inventory form (Exhibit 2) can be used to record inventory information. When reviewing the form, note:

1. Products (column 1) can be listed in the same order as they are found in the storage area (or on the perpetual inventory form). Listing products in this sequence makes the task of locating items on the form easier when taking the inventory count. It also reduces the likelihood that products will be missed when inventory is taken.

2. The storage unit (column 2) is the basis on which products are purchased and costs are assessed. For example, in the inventory shown in Exhibit 2, applesauce is purchased and stored in cases containing six number-10 cans each, while flour comes in 25-pound bags.

Exhibit 2   Physical Inventory Form

		Amount in Storage	Purchase Price	Total Price	Amount in Storage	Purchase Price	Total Price
Physical Inventory							
Type of Product: _____		**Month** _____			**Month** _____		
Product	**Unit**	**Amount in Storage**	**Purchase Price**	**Total Price**	**Amount in Storage**	**Purchase Price**	**Total Price**
Col. 1	Col. 2	Col. 3	Col. 4	Col. 5	Col. 6	Col. 7	Col. 8
Applesauce	6 #10	4 ⅓	$15.85	$68.63			
Green Beans	6 #10	3 ⅚	18.95	72.58			
Flour	25# bag	3	4.85	14.55			
Rice	50# bag	1	12.50	12.50			
			Total	$486.55			

3. The amount in storage (column 3) is determined by actually counting all items in storage. With one technique, one person counts while a second person records the quantities on the inventory form. In another, two people can make independent counts and compare results before entering information on the inventory form.

4. Purchase price (column 4) is the cost per storage unit (column 2) of the product. Price information is easier to record if products are marked with their unit prices at the time they are stored.

5. Total price (column 5) is the total cost of the amount of each product in inventory, and is calculated by multiplying the number of stored items (column 3) by the purchase price per storage unit (column 4).

6. Columns 6 through 8 are used to repeat the above inventory valuation procedures for a second month.

7. The total food and beverage costs (recorded at the bottom of column 5) calculated by the physical inventory are given to accounting personnel to use in developing financial statements. They can also be used by food and beverage managers to calculate inventory turnover rates.

A physical inventory indicates only how much of each product is in inventory and the actual value of all stored products. Two limitations of a physical inventory system are that it does not indicate how much of each product should be available and what the value of products in inventory should be. A perpetual inventory system compensates for these problems.

Exhibit 3   Perpetual Inventory Form

Perpetual Inventory

| Product Name: | P.D.Q. Shrimp | | | Purchase Unit Size: | 5 lb bag | | |

Date	In Carried Forward	Out	Balance 15	Date	In Carried Forward	Out	Balance
Col. 1	Col. 2	Col. 3	Col. 4	Col. 1	Col. 2	Col. 3	Col. 4
5/16		3	12				
5/17		3	9				
5/18	6		15				
5/19		2	13				

Perpetual Inventory System

A perpetual inventory system keeps a running balance of the quantity of food and beverage products in inventory. It operates like a bank checking account. When more food or beverages are put in the bank (the storage area), the balance is increased. As products are removed (issued), the balance decreases. At any time, then, the amount of products that should be currently available is known.

Large properties with specialized storage and accounting personnel may use a perpetual inventory system for all, or almost all, products in storage. Small food and beverage operations may find it more practical to use perpetual inventory control only for expensive items and those purchased in large quantities.

A sample perpetual inventory form is shown in Exhibit 3. Note the following when studying the form:

1. Information about each product under perpetual inventory control is recorded on a separate form.

2. Each time a product enters inventory (column 2) or is removed from inventory (column 3), the balance in inventory (column 4) is adjusted.

3. Columns are repeated on the right so the form can be used for a longer time period.

4. The form does not have information about product cost. With this system, control is based on the number of units, not their cost. Costs can be assessed when taking physical inventories and recording on the form in Exhibit 2, as discussed earlier.

A physical count is still necessary with a perpetual inventory system to verify the accuracy of the inventory balances. When using a perpetual inventory system, staff members who maintain the perpetual inventory records should not perform the physical inventory used for verification.

When the physical count of a product differs from the quantity indicated on the perpetual record, a control problem may exist, and management must determine the reason for the variance. Perhaps products are not being recorded at the time of receipt or issue, or perhaps theft is occurring. The purpose of control procedures is to indicate when such problems exist. Management's task is to discover why a problem exists and, of course, to correct it.

Computerized Inventory Management

Despite its obvious importance, inventory control is one of the least uniform software applications. Systems differ in file capacity and report capability. Moreover, the food and beverage business, with its unique inventory characteristics, usually does not lend itself to using software developed for another industry. In other words, if an automobile manufacturer, a bicycle repair shop, and a retail clothing chain can successfully use the same inventory control package, this does not mean that the software can be used successfully in a food and beverage operation.

Ideally, the software will feature an integrated package containing an ingredient file (for food and non-food items) and an inventory file. The ingredient file contains all necessary information to define the ingredients. The inventory file deals with inventory stock levels and reorder points and is used for computing usage, variances, and product valuations.

The initial creation of a food and beverage ingredient file and subsequent file updates (daily, weekly, monthly, etc.) can be an overwhelming task for some food service operations. For example, a restaurant may offer 30 (or more) food items and 50 (or more) beverage products. An inventory of 1,500 ingredients may need to be purchased. If errors are made when data is initially entered, all subsequent processing will be unreliable and system reports will be relatively worthless. In addition, computer applications that do not support integrated files can be extremely cumbersome because users must re-input data from several files to run a particular program.

Some inventory applications provide file space for more than one ingredient designation, such as item file code number, inventory sequence number, internal customer code, and so on. The ability to work with additional designations can increase the efficiency of the inventory control system. For example, a user may be able to print ingredients on a physical inventory worksheet according to the order in which they are shelved.

Another concern is how usage is charted by the inventory application—by unit, by cost, or by both unit and cost. A system that charts items by unit may be able to report changes in stock levels, but may not be able to provide financial data necessary for food costing. The most effective inventory applications are those that track items in terms of both unit and cost. Exhibit 4 illustrates a sample inventory usage report that details usage in terms of both units and dollar amounts.

Exhibit 4   Sample Inventory Usage Report

Your Place
MANAGEMENT SUMMARY
1/22/98 11:59:00 PM – 1/31/98 11:59:00 PM

General Information:

Act. Cost of Goods:	$13,062.10	43.39%	Sales Reported	$30,101.55	100.00%
Ideal Cost of Goods:	$11,626.98	38.63%	Sales Calculated	$31,070.35	103.22%
Net Variance:	$1,435.12	4.77%	Sales Variance	($968.80)	-3.22%

Customer Count	2508
Inventory Value	$9,856.43
Year-To-Date Sales	$60,203.10

ITEM USAGE RANKINGS:

Item		Usage		Variance			Activity			Inventory		
Abbreviation	Unit	Actual	Ideal	Units	Dollars	% Sales	Begin	Purch	End	Days Left	Cost	Value
Top 15 Overused:												
Shrimp U15	lb	477.00	456.49	20.51	$167	0.6	310.00	465.00	298.00	14.0	$8.150	$2,428.70
Oyster	bushel	15.00	12.25	2.75	$124	0.4	6.50	16.00	7.50	8.5	$45.000	$337.50
Pot 80 Ct	case	27.50	13.51	13.99	$114	0.4	4.50	32.00	9.00	3.0	$8.180	$73.62
Coffee ns	lb	60.00	41.88	18.13	$85	0.3	220.00	190.00	350.00	38.7	$4.670	$1,634.50
Turkey	lb	331.25	300.07	31.18	$76	0.3	160.00	206.25	35.00	16.3	$2.450	$85.75
Tomato 5x6	case	34.50	26.32	8.18	$74	0.2	5.00	30.00	0.50	3.5	$9.100	$4.55
Chili Sc	#10	55.00	29.48	25.52	$73	0.2	76.00	84.00	105.00	26.3	$2.850	$299.25
Bl Chz Drs	gal	15.00	5.57	9.43	$62	0.2	0.00	68.00	53.00	16.4	$6.525	$345.83
Garl Crtns	lb	95.00	29.72	65.28	$60	0.2	25.00	300.00	230.00	16.1	$0.925	$212.75
1000 Isle	gal	11.00	1.86	9.14	$60	0.2	16.00	36.00	41.00	23.9	$6.525	$267.52
Filet 10 oz	each	623.00	612.00	11.00	$58	0.2	22.00	630.00	29.00	0.7	$5.250	$152.25
Lemon	case	8.50	4.37	4.13	$43	0.1	4.00	10.00	5.50	2.8	$10.300	$56.65
Ketchup Cn	#10	50.00	29.48	20.52	$41	0.1	80.00	66.00	96.00	30.5	$1.980	$190.08
Equal	case	2.40	0.15	2.25	$38	0.1	3.60	6.00	7.20	25.2	$17.100	$123.12
Fry Shortn	lb	190.00	100.84	89.16	$36	0.1	715.00	175.00	700.00	84.0	$0.403	$282.00
					$1,110	3.7						
Top 5 Underused:												
Wheat Brd	loaf	173.00	201.50	-28.50	($40)	-0.1	7.00	200.00	34.00	0.7	$1.390	$47.26
Strawberry	pint	294.12	309.75	-15.63	($19)	-0.1	6.00	288.12	0.00	0.0	$1.208	$0.00
Srdo Roll	doz	185.00	191.75	-6.75	($13)	0.0	27.00	200.00	42.00	2.8	$1.890	$79.38
Strawb Glz	pkg	138.00	154.50	-16.50	($8)	0.0	1.00	144.00	7.00	1.0	$0.483	$3.38
Horseradsh	qt	12.50	14.74	-2.24	($8)	0.0	20.50	12.00	20.00	35.0	$3.430	$68.60
					($87)	-0.3						

Source: FOOD-TRAK® System. ©1998, System Concepts, Inc.

When reviewing Exhibit 4, note the following; the management summary indicates:

1. Items in which actual usage exceeds ideal usage ("Top 15 Overused")

2. Items in which actual usage is less than ideal usage ("Top 5 Underused")

3. The variance in units, dollars, and percent of sales between ideal and actual usage

4. Item activity: beginning inventory, purchases, and ending inventory (in purchase units; i.e., pounds [lb] of shrimp)

5. The status of current inventory level: number of days left and value based upon ending inventory [in units] times the unit cost; for example, the value of ending inventory of shrimp is $2,428.70 [298 pounds in ending inventory times per pound cost of $8.15]

Conversion tables can be maintained by which to track ingredients (by unit and by cost) as they pass through purchasing/receiving, storing/issuing, and production/service control points. To efficiently maintain a perpetual inventory rec-ord, a computerized inventory management system must be able to automatically convert purchase units into issue units and recipe units (also referred to as usable units). Inventory data must be specific to each of these control points because purchase units (i.e., case, drum, etc.) may differ from storeroom inventory units (i.e., #10 can, pound, etc.). Storeroom inventory units, in turn, differ from standard recipe units (i.e., ounce, cup, etc.). Some systems are not able to support the number of conversion tables necessary to track menu items through ingredient purchase, storage, and use (standard recipe).

For example, assume that an ingredient is purchased, issued, and used in different units. When a shipment of the ingredient arrives, it should be easy to update the inventory record by simply entering the purchase unit received. The computer should then automatically convert this entry into issue units. Without this conversion capability, it would be necessary to manually calculate the number of units that will be stored and increase the inventory record accordingly. Similarly, at the end of a meal period, the computer system should be capable of updating the inventory record by entering the standard recipe units that should have been used to prepare menu items. If the restaurant management system cannot convert issue units into recipe units, these calculations may also have to be performed manually and the inventory record decreased accordingly.

Similarly, the computer-based system should also be able to track the costs associated with these various ingredient units. For example, assume that ketchup is purchased by the case (six number-10 cans), issued from the storeroom to the kitchen by the can, and used in recipes by the ounce. Given the information about the purchase unit's net weight and cost, the computer should be able to automatically extend costs for issue and recipe unit(s). To arrive at these costs through manual calculations, an employee must compute the price per ounce of the purchase unit. Performing these calculations manually for every ingredient purchased can be a tedious, error-prone, time-consuming process. A food service management applications package can perform these calculations in fractions of a second. Care must be taken to ensure that the ingredient file contains the necessary data and conversion definitions.

Management should clarify how basic food service concepts are defined within the inventory application design. While the terms "inventory usage," "inventory variance," and "inventory valuation" are common, they do not have the same meaning in all computer systems. For example, inventory usage attempts to identify changes in inventory level (depletion of stock on hand) from one point in time to another. However, is an inventory item considered "used" (for costing purposes) at the time it is received, or when it is issued to the kitchen, or at the time of service? Each of these time frames presents a different usage result and subsequent cost computation. The point in time that is most desirable for a particular restaurant operation may not be the time frame that is built into the application's design. Also, since methods of inventory valuation vary, management must be careful to clarify which methods a particular food service inventory package should support.

Technology can also assist in the inventory valuation process through optical scanning. Universal product code (UPC) information on product packages can be scanned to quickly and accurately assess the quantity of unopened product packages in inventory. Scanning results can provide helpful information for verifying perpetual inventories and for calculating cost-of-goods-sold data when actual food and beverage costs are calculated.

A Special Note about Beverage Inventory

The basic control procedures already noted apply to both food and beverage products. However, since beverages, especially liquor and wine, are expensive and popular targets of theft, they require some special control precautions.

Even small food and beverage operations normally use a perpetual inventory system for alcoholic beverages. While important for many stored food products, control procedures such as locked storage areas, controlled access, and management of storeroom access are especially critical to the control of alcoholic beverages. The inventory task is easier if prices are marked on the bottles or cases when they are originally placed in storage.

An important consideration in designing inventory control procedures for beverages is whether beverage inventory values will include items currently behind the bar as well as beverage items in the central storeroom. Consistency is the key here. Items behind the bar should either always be included or never be included in inventory recordkeeping procedures. Some beverage managers believe it is unnecessary to include items behind the bar in inventories because the bar quantities will average out. Others believe that the increased accuracy gained from including behind-the-bar items in inventory records, and the tighter control this provides, is worthwhile.

If only central storeroom beverage products are to be counted, the physical inventory form (Exhibit 2) is sufficient for recording information about quantities and costs. This inventory form can, then, be used for both food and beverage items.

Exhibit 5   Beverage Inventory Cost Card

		Quantity Available					
		Bottles Behind Bar		In Central Storage	Total	Cost Per Storage Unit	Total Cost
Beverage Item	Storage Unit	Open	Unopened	In Central Storage	Total	Cost Per Storage Unit	Total Cost
Col. 1	Col. 2	Col. 3	Col. 4	Col. 5	Col. 6	Col. 7	Col. 8
Bar Scotch	750 ml	¾	3	12	15 ¾	$12.50	$196.88
Bar Gin	750 ml	½	3	24	27 ½	11.75	323.13

However, when both central storeroom and behind-the-bar inventory costs are assessed, a beverage inventory cost card (Exhibit 5) can be used.

Behind-the-Bar Inventory Costs

When beverage items behind the bar are valued for inventory purposes, the following procedures can be used to manually assess costs:

1. Count the number of unopened bottles of each type of beverage product.

2. Determine the quantity of beverage products in opened bottles. This can be done either by visually estimating (for example, to the nearest tenth of a bottle), by weighing, or by using dipsticks.

3. Add the number of unopened bottles of each type of beverage to the amount remaining in opened bottles to assess the total volume of product available behind the bar.

4. Add the amount in the central storeroom to the behind-the-bar amount to determine the total beverage inventory.

5. Calculate the total cost of beverage items in inventory.

Computerized Scales

Computerized scales are now available to accurately weigh open bottles of alcoholic beverages behind the bar when taking beverage inventories. The process is simple: each type of liquor (for example, a 750 ml bottle of house Scotch or a specific size bottle of a call brand) is given a code. This code indicates the empty bottle weight. The person taking inventory places an opened bottle on the scale and enters the code into the computer. The computer then (a) deducts the empty bottle weight from the total open bottle weight, (b) determines the quantity of liquor available in the bottle, and (c) calculates the cost of liquor and sales value of each type of liquor in behind-the-bar storage areas. Use of a computerized scale improves the speed and accuracy of taking inventory.

Issuing Control: General Procedures

At some point, products are removed from storage and transferred to production areas—the kitchen and bar. Unfortunately, some properties have very informal, if any, issuing procedures and exert little control over this process. An open-door policy may even be in effect: whenever anyone needs something, they simply walk into the storage area and take it. However, if a food and beverage operation does not limit access to storage areas and keep records of items removed, it is not possible to compare the quantity of products removed from storage with the quantity of items produced or the levels of revenue generated. Limited access to storage areas and special procedures for issuing products from storage to production are essential for effective food and beverage controls. When designing basic control procedures for a food and beverage operation, it is important to consider this aspect of the management system.

The objectives of an effective issuing system can be met by using techniques available to food and beverage operations of all sizes. A well-designed issuing system has the following objectives:

- To limit access to storage areas to authorized staff members only.

- To match items removed from storage with actual production requirements.

- To assess quantities and costs of products removed from storage. This record keeping becomes important when updating perpetual inventory records and assessing costs of issues to calculate daily food and beverage costs.

Issuing Procedures

Any food and beverage operation, regardless of size, can make use of requisition forms. Large hotels and restaurants often have full-time storeroom staff who assemble products included on requisitions and sign them over to production unit employees. Smaller properties may assign issuing responsibilities to employees who work in storerooms at specified times only. If the ABCD approach is used, requisition forms should be used, at least, for the priority items. All of these methods succeed in limiting access to storage areas and assigning responsibility for issuing to a specific person. In addition, the requisition forms can be used to provide information for daily cost calculations or to update perpetual inventory records. Thus, there are reasonable procedures that any food and beverage operation can develop to properly control issuing procedures.

By planning ahead, issuing can be limited to specified times. For example, products for making breakfast might be issued from 6:00 to 6:30 A.M. Items needed for lunch could be issued from 10:30 to 11:00 A.M., and similarly for dinner or late evening shifts. Normally, beverages to replenish bar inventories are issued either

Exhibit 6   Food Requisition Form

Food Requisition

Storage Type (check one):   Date: _____

Refrigerated _____

Frozen _____   Work Unit: _____

Dry _____✓_____   Approved for Withdrawal: _____

Item	Purchase Unit	No. of Units	Unit Price	Total Cost	Employee Initials	
					Received By	Withdrawn By
Col. 1	Col. 2	Col. 3	Col. 4	Col. 5	Col. 6	Col. 7
Tomato Paste	CS-6 #10	2 ½	$28.50	$71.25	JC	Ken
Green Beans	CS-6 #10	1 ½	22.75	34.13	JC	Ken
				Total	$596.17	

at the beginning or end of each bar shift. (Beverage issuing is discussed later in this chapter.) By limiting issuing to specified times, even the smallest food and beverage operation can use many of the control procedures described in this chapter.

The Food Requisition/Issue Process

The food requisition form (Exhibit 6) identifies the type and amount of each food item necessary for production during a given shift or other time period.

1. The form identifies each item to be withdrawn from storage in column 1. Studying the standard recipes to be prepared helps ensure that nothing is forgotten.

2. The purchase unit size of each item needed is entered in column 2, while the quantity needed is entered in column 3. The quantity of each item needed is based upon the recipes to be used during the shift (or other time period) minus any products already withdrawn from inventory and available in production, broken-case storage, or other storage areas. If the production employee completing the form does not know the purchase unit available in storage, the total quantity needed should be noted in column 3, and the storeroom employee or management staff member responsible for issuing can then complete column 2.

3. After production personnel complete the form, it then goes to the chef, kitchen manager, or other responsible employee who should approve the products for withdrawal from inventory.

4. Next, the form goes to the appropriate storage area. The food requisition form can be designed to distinguish whether products are from refrigerated, frozen, or dry storage areas. Smaller properties may not need this classification system. Completing the unit price (column 4) is simple if costs from the delivery invoice are marked on cases and packages when they are received and placed in storage. Alternatively, costs may be transferred from the daily receiving report to containers as the items are shelved. To complete total cost (column 5), the number of purchase units (column 3) is multiplied by the cost per unit (column 4). It is not necessary to calculate total cost at the time of issuing, nor does the storeroom employee have to do so before signing products over to production areas.

5. The storage or management employee responsible for issuing verifies that items listed were indeed withdrawn by initialing column 7. The employee accepting the issued products can also initial the requisition form (in column 6). This transfers responsibility for the products from whomever did the issuing to the production employee withdrawing the products. If there is a discrepancy between the amount taken from storage and the amount delivered to production areas, documentation helps determine who is responsible and where and when the problem occurred.

6. After issuing is completed, the items should be transferred promptly to the appropriate production areas.

Depending upon the specific operation, requisition forms may be processed in several ways. When all daily issues are finished, the manager, the storeroom clerk, or secretarial/bookkeeping personnel may use the forms to update perpetual inventory records. Since the perpetual inventory form (Exhibit 3) does not carry cost information, column 5 need not be completed for this task.

The food requisition forms for the day can be forwarded to the manager or secretary/bookkeeper to review and to use in calculating the daily food cost information. If total cost (column 5) is not yet completed, it is calculated now. If it was calculated by storage personnel, other personnel should verify the calculation before completing daily food cost records.

Computer-Generated Issue Quantities

Precost computer software enables management to apply a projected sales mix across a standard recipe file to produce a "prior to service" cost report. A byproduct of this costing scheme is a complete list of all ingredient quantities required to satisfy the demand for a planned menu. In other words, if four items on a given menu each require ketchup as a recipe ingredient, the quantity of ketchup to be issued would be the total amount for the entire meal period. Ingredient totals are typically contained in a breakout quantities report. The computer system lists all items (by issue unit) requiring requisition to produce a projected sales mix.

Requisition information is electronically transferred from user departments to the storage area(s). No "paperwork" is required.

Some software packages go a step further and split breakout quantities by preparation area. In this case, ingredients are summed by preparation area only (found in each recipe record) and reported accordingly. Therefore, although the fryer, broiler, and pantry stations may all use the same ingredient, individual breakout lists will contain only the appropriate total for each workstation. This approach helps tighten inventory control and, over time, may provide a basis for a highly reliable forecasting system. Projected sales mixes, which yield breakout quantities, are easily assessed based on whether sufficient quantities were issued. If secondary requisitioning is necessary, the forecasting formulas must be refined.

The Beverage Requisition/Issue Process

The basic procedures for issuing food also apply to beverages. However, since beverages, by their nature, are very susceptible to employee theft, there are several additional concerns in transferring beverages from storage to production areas. Special procedures incorporated into beverage issuing can reduce the possibility or frequency of employee theft.

Establishing Bar Par Inventory Levels

Beverages should be issued only in quantities needed to re-establish bar par inventory levels. A **bar par** is an established number of bottles of each type of beverage that is always kept in behind-the-bar storage areas. A bar par is established for each type of liquor and wine kept behind the bar. Some food and beverage operations also set pars for bottled beer. Bar pars are established on the basis of the number of bottles of each beverage type used during a busy shift. For example, if an average busy shift uses four bottles of house brand Scotch, the beverage manager may be conservative and set the bar par at five bottles—four full bottles in behind-the-bar storage and one opened bottle in the speedrail or back-bar display area.

The number of empty bottles at the beginning or end of each shift—preferably the end—determines the number of full bottles needed to replenish the bar par. If, for example, the bar par is five bottles for house Scotch and two bottles are empty, then two bottles will be issued to maintain the bar par. An important rule is that empty bottles must be presented before full bottles are issued.

Beverage Issuing Steps

The beverage issuing process typically includes the following steps:

1. At the end of each shift, the bartender places the bottles emptied during the shift on top of the bar.

2. The bartender completes a beverage requisition form (Exhibit 7), recording the name of each type of liquor or wine emptied (column 1), the number of empty bottles (column 2), and the size of the bottle (column 3). Depending upon the specific property, the bartender may also record the unit cost

Exhibit 7   Beverage Requisition Form

		Beverage Requisition		

Shift: _A.M. (Lunch)_   **Date:** _8/1/XX_

Bar: _Main_   **Bartender:** _John Smith_

Liquor	Number of Bottles	Size	Unit Cost	Total Cost
Col. 1	Col. 2	Col. 3	Col. 4	Col. 5
B. Scotch	3	750 ml	$12.50	$37.50
B. Gin	2	750 ml	11.75	23.50

Total Bottles: _12_   Total Cost: _$118.75_

Check one:

OK to Issue: _JN_   ☐ low price

Issued by: _GC_   ☑ reg. price

Received by: _JS_   ☐ high price

$118.75 ÷ $593.75 = 20%
(cost)   (revenue)   (beverage percent)

(column 4). Information for this column comes from the invoice cost marked on the bottle at the time it was placed in storage.

3. The beverage manager checks the number and type of empty bottles on the bar against the information on the beverage requisition form. If there are no problems, he or she signs or initials the "OK to Issue" section of the sheet.

4. The bartender or manager takes the empty bottles and the beverage requisition to the beverage storage area. The person responsible for issuing: (a) compares empty bottles with the data on the issue requisition, (b) bottle-for bottle, replaces empty bottles with full ones, and (c) signs or initials the "issued by" section of the sheet. At the same time, the bartender or manager, who returns full bottles to the bar, signs or initials the "received by" section.

5. Empty bottles are broken or otherwise disposed of according to local or state laws, or as specified by the property's control requirements designed to prevent re-use.

6. Total cost calculations (column 5) and the beverage cost percent calculations at the bottom of the requisition form are normally completed by management or secretarial/bookkeeping personnel, not the bartender or storeroom issuing staff. Except in large properties with storeroom personnel, management office staff should maintain perpetual inventory records for beverage products.

Bottle Marking

Bottle marking identifies a bottle before it is issued. It may simply identify the bottle as house property, or it may also contain information about the bottle's cost and/or date of issue. If a property has only one bar, the bottle can be marked when it is placed in storage. If, however, there is more than one bar in a property, bottles should additionally be marked with the site to which it is issued.

Frequently, the bottle mark is an adhesive-backed label or hard-to-remove ink stamp, with a logo or symbol difficult to duplicate. Since the **bottle mark** identifies the bottle as house property, it helps supervisory staff ensure that all bottles behind the bar belong to the property. There is less likelihood that bartenders can bring in bottles and steal from the operation by selling their own liquor and keeping the revenue.

Bottle marking is important for two other reasons. First, if the cost, from the daily receiving report or delivery invoice, is recorded on the bottle, it is easier to complete the issue requisition form. Second, if the date of issue is recorded on the bottle, it is easier to keep track of the rotation of bottles behind the bar.

The bottle mark, or at least the cost and date of issue, should not be easy to notice. Sometimes special situations require making exceptions to bottle-marking practices. Bottles going to the table, such as liquor for flaming and wine, might be marked on the bottom.

Additional Concerns for Beverage Control

Finally, several additional control concerns about issuing beverages should be noted. When beverages behind the bar frequently run out, bar par levels must be re-examined and increased. Guests do not want to wait while another bottle is brought from the storeroom. Similarly, there may not be time to complete a beverage issue requisition in the middle of a rush period, so information about beverage costs and reduced perpetual inventory balances is lost. To avoid these problems, managers should carefully assess the need for behind-the-bar inventories during the operation's busy periods, and issuing times and bar par quantities should be planned accordingly.

When the bar is not in operation, all bar par inventories should be locked to discourage employee theft. In addition, keys to beverage storeroom areas should not be left with bartenders. In small operations, the key can be sealed in an envelope placed behind the bar. If it must be used when a manager is not immediately available, it will be available. However, the opened envelope will show that the storeroom has been entered. An immediate comparison of perpetual inventory records with physical count may then be in order.

Endnotes

1. The reader interested in further information should read Ronald F. Cichy's *Quality Sanitation Management* (Lansing, Mich.: Educational Institute of the American Hotel & Lodging Association, 1994).

2. The reader interested in more information about inventory valuation techniques should read Raymond S. Schmidgall's *Hospitality Industry Managerial Accounting*, 4th ed. (Lansing, Mich.: Educational Institute of the American Hotel & Lodging Association, 1995).

Key Terms

ABCD inventory classification system—A system of categorizing products according to their perishability and cost per serving; category A includes those products that are high in both perishability and cost per serving; category B items are relatively high in cost but low in perishability; category C items are relatively low in cost but high in perishability; category D items are those that are low in both perishability and cost per serving.

average inventory—Determined by adding the value of inventory at the beginning of the time period in question (usually a month) to the value of inventory at the end of that period and then dividing the sum by two; this value is used when calculating the inventory turnover rate.

bar par—An established number of bottles of each type of beverage that is always kept in behind-the-bar storage areas.

bottle mark—An adhesive-backed label or hard-to-remove ink stamp, with a logo or symbol that is difficult to duplicate; the bottle mark identifies the bottle as house property and helps supervisory staff ensure that all bottles behind the bar belong to the property.

directs—Usually relatively inexpensive, perishable products purchased several times a week for more or less immediate use; examples include fresh produce, baked goods, and dairy products.

first-in, first-out (FIFO) inventory rotation—Products held in inventory the longest are the first to be issued to production areas; when newly received products enter storage areas, they are placed under or behind products already in storage.

first-in, first-out (FIFO) inventory valuation—The earliest inventory costs incurred are assigned when products are issued.

inventory turnover rate—Shows the number of times in a given period that inventory is converted or turned into revenue; calculated by dividing the cost of food (or beverages) used by the average food (or beverage) inventory (in dollars).

last-in, first-out (LIFO) inventory valuation—The most recent inventory costs incurred are assigned when products are issued.

non-productive inventory—Products in storage that are not issued to production areas during the time period (usually monthly) covered by financial records.

perpetual inventory system—A running balance of the quantity of stored products is kept by recording all newly purchased items as they enter storage areas and all quantities issued from storage to production areas.

physical inventory system—The practice of physically counting stored products on a periodic basis.

stores—Generally, relatively expensive items that are purchased less often than directs and in quantities necessary to rebuild inventory levels; examples include meats, seafood, frozen and canned products, and staples such as flour, sugar, and cereals.

 Review Questions

1. Why is effective management of products in storage important?

2. What is the difference between "directs" and "stores"?

3. What are some of the ways to help ensure proper security during storage?

4. What are the key sanitation concerns during storage?

5. What records should be kept of products during storage?

6. How do you calculate inventory turnover? Why is the resulting ratio important?

7. What special procedures should be used to control the most expensive and most frequently used products in inventory?

8. How are purchase units, issue units, and recipe units related in a computer system?

9. What is a bar par? Why is it important?

10. What might be gained by using computerized issuing reports that show breakout quantities by preparation area?

 **Internet Sites**

For more information, visit the following Internet sites. Remember that Internet addresses can change without notice. If the site is no longer there, you can use a search engine to look for additional sites.

Associations

American Culinary Federation (ACF)
http://www.acfchefs.org

American Hotel & Lodging Association (AH&LA)
http://www.ahlaonline.org

American School Food Service
Association (ASFSA)
http://www.asfsa.org

Club Managers Association of America
(CMAA)
http://www.cmaa.org

The Educational Foundation of NRA
http://www.edfound.org

The Educational Institute of AH&LA
http://www.ei–ahla.org

Hospitality Financial and Technology
Professionals
http://www.hftp.org

Institute of Food Technologies
http://www.ift.org

International Hotel and Restaurant
Association
http://www.ih–ra.com

National Association of College and
University Food Services
http://www.nacufs.org

National Restaurant Association (NRA)
http://www.restaurant.org

Food and Beverage Resources

Beverage Controls
http://www.restaurantreport.com/
features/ft_bevcost.html

Club Management Online
http://www.club–mgmt.com/dining/
index.html

Food Trak
http://www.foodtrak.com

Inventory Turnover
http://www.cba.uri.edu/Faculty/
Comerford/Text/Chapter2.html

Microbrewery and brewpub guilde
http://www.realbeer.com

Prepared Foods. Product development,
ingredients, suppliers
http://www.preparedfoods.com

Foodservice Software

Adaco Services, Inc.
http://www.adacoservices.com

CMS Hospitality
http://www.cmshosp.com.au

Computrition, Inc.
http://www.computrition.com

Comtrex Systems Corporation
http://www.comtrex.com

Comus Restaurant Systems
http://www.comus.com

Cost Guard
http://www.costguard.com

Culinary Software
http://www.culinarysoftware.com

Eatec Corporation
http://www.eatec.com

Integrated Restaurant Software
http://www.rmstouch.com

MAI Systems Corporation
http://www.maisystems.com

Micros Systems, Inc.
http://www.micros.com

MSI Solutions
http://www.msisolutions.com

Sulcus Computer Corporation
http://www2.sulcus.nl

Management Companies

ARAMARK
http://www.aramark.com

Bon Appétit Management Company
http://www.bamco.com

Compass Group
http://www.compass-na.com

Sodexho Marriott
http://www.sodexhomarriott.com

The Wood Company
http://www.woodco.com

Publications—Online and Printed

Club Management Magazine
http://www.club-mgmt.com

Electronic Gourmet Guide
http://www.foodwine.com

Food and Hospitality Magazine
http://www.foodserviceworld.com

Food Management
http://www.foodservicesearch.com

Food Network: CyberKitchen
http://www.foodtv.com

Food Processing: The Magazine of
Strategy, Technology and Trends
http://www.foodprocessing.com

Internet Food Channel
http://www.foodchannel.com

International Hotel and Restaurant
Association journal
www.hotelsmag.com

International Journal of Hospitality
Management
http://www.mcb.co.uk/ijchm.htm

Journal of Hospitality Financial
Management
http://hrta.fnr.umass.edu/sheel/
ahfme/jhfm/aboutjhfm.html

Lodging Food and Beverage
http://www.lodgingnews.com/
lodgingfnb/

Lodging Hospitality Online
http://www.lhonline.com

Lodging News, journal of the American
Hotel & Lodging Association
http://www.ei-ahla.org/webs/
lodging/index.html

Nation's Restaurant News
http://www.nrn.com

On the Rail—News for Food
Professionals
http://www.ontherail.com

Restaurant Business, Food Service, and
ID magazines
http://www.foodservicetoday.com

Restaurant Hospitality
www.foodservicesearch.com

Restaurants and Institutions
http://www.rimag.com

Restaurants USA, publication of
National Restaurant Association
http://www.restaurant.org/rusa

World Hospitality, management
magazine for hotel executives
http://www.worldhospitality.com

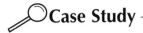**Case Study** ————————————————————————————

Pushing the Envelope on Settings and Supplies

Reuben Diaz was feeling good. It was a hot Saturday night, and things were starting to heat up inside the 125-seat Fiesta Grill. The Grill had experienced an upturn in business the past couple of months, and this was the busiest night Reuben had seen since becoming the general manager four years ago.

A wedding reception was in full swing in the banquet room. The dining room was full, with people waiting in the lobby for tables. And Ted, the Fiesta Grill's new catering manager, had left 30 minutes ago with food and supplies for an off-premises catering event 20 miles away. This was the Grill's first venture into off-premises catering, and Reuben just knew it was going to be a great boon to business.

Reuben walked through the dining room, encouraging his staff. They seemed hurried, but Reuben didn't think that was so unusual under the circumstances. He decided to chat with some of the guests.

"How are you folks tonight?" Reuben asked a couple sitting at a table nearby. "I'm Reuben Diaz, the general manager here at the Fiesta Grill."

There was a long pause. "Actually, we're not doing too well, Mr. Diaz," the man said icily.

Reuben was taken aback. "I'm sorry to hear that," he said. "What's the problem?"

"To start off, our salad plates were warm," the man began. "And coincidentally, so was the *iceberg* lettuce in the salads. Then we were told we couldn't get any wine because there weren't any clean wine glasses. To top it off, we waited 20 minutes for a cup of coffee."

"That's not all, Bob," the woman added, turning to her husband. "Even after our coffee came, we weren't given any cream. And then when our waitress finally brought us some, she forgot to bring spoons to stir it with."

"Let's just say it hasn't been our best night out to eat," Bob said with a forced smile.

Reuben felt his energy draining. He knew this couple was looking to him to solve their problem. "Please accept my apologies Bob, and—"

"Helen," the woman offered her name.

"—and Helen. Your dinners tonight are compliments of the Fiesta Grill. Although that won't change what happened, I hope it can be some consolation," Reu-ben said, trying to ease the tension a little.

"That's very nice of you," said Bob. "We appreciate it."

"Yes. Thank you very much," Helen added.

"You're welcome," Reuben said. "And please come again. I don't think you'll be disappointed."

"Yeah, we'll be back," Bob said. "But maybe next time on a slower night." He smiled.

"Well, I hope to see you again soon. Have a good night, now."

"Thanks," Bob said. "You too."

Before Reuben left Bob and Helen's table, he saw that none of their plates or smallwares had been cleared, even though they were now eating dessert. On his way back to the kitchen, he noticed that several other tables hadn't been pre-bussed, either. "No wonder there weren't any spoons for their coffee," Reuben thought. He decided to ask the buspersons and Sylvia—Bob and Helen's server—about this, but as he reached the kitchen, Kevin, one of the Grill's dishwashers, raced past him toward the exit, pulling off his apron. He had a look of disgust on his face.

"Kevin, whoa—what's wrong?" Reuben stopped him.

"I'm sorry, Mr. Diaz, but it's a mess back there, and I'm sick of it," Kevin said. "Someone just asked me for the fourth time to run two coffee cups through the dishwasher, and they're getting on my case because they don't have any plates. Hey, it's not my fault. I'm outta here."

Reuben began to realize the problem wasn't confined to just Sylvia or Bob and Helen. "Kevin, it looks like we're having some problems tonight with our supply of dishes, cups, and silverware. But could you just stick it out? I'm going to talk to the servers and ask them to take it easy on you. I promise this won't happen again."

Kevin thought a moment. "I don't know..."

"Trust me, I'm going to take care of this," Reuben assured him.

"Well, all right," Kevin said. "You know, if you ask me, one thing you should do is tell the bussers to stop hoarding before their shifts."

"Hoarding? What do you mean?" Reuben asked.

"Hoarding—you know, bussers make a bunch of sets of rolled silverware and stash them in their areas so they don't run out," Kevin replied. "It's great for some servers, but a big pain for others. I don't think they should do it."

"Hoarding causes a lot of problems. Thanks for bringing it to my attention, Kevin," said Reuben.

"OK," Kevin said, and headed back to the kitchen.

Reuben followed him and found Sylvia in the kitchen.

"Sylvia, hi."

"Hi, Reuben," Sylvia said as she garnished some plates.

"I just talked to Bob and Helen."

"Who?" Sylvia quickly placed the plates on a serving tray, hoisted the tray onto her shoulder, and started walking briskly toward the door to the dining room.

"Uh, Bob and Helen, the couple at table... let's see... A2," Reuben said as he followed Sylvia into the dining room.

Sylvia stopped and thought a moment. "Oh, yeah, A2," she said, rolling her eyes.

"What do you mean? Were they giving you a problem?" asked Reuben.

"Back in a minute," Sylvia said as she hurried off to her table.

Reuben waited until Sylvia returned.

"What was the problem with A2?" Reuben asked her when she came back.

"Oh, they were just kinda rude when they didn't get their coffee or their spoons."

"Has there been a shortage of glasses and smallwares tonight?" Reuben asked.

"Glasses have been running low, but we have plenty of smallwares," Sylvia said.

"Oh yeah, why's that?" Reuben asked.

"The bussers made plenty of extras for their stations," Sylvia replied.

"I see," Reuben said. ("Hoarding…" he thought to himself.) "But glasses are low, you say?"

"Yes."

Reuben was dumbfounded. How could this have happened? "Thanks, Sylvia," he said. "Oh, by the way, comp the meals at A2, OK?"

"Sure," Sylvia said.

"Thanks."

Reuben started to recount the events of the past week: On Monday he got the call about Saturday's off-premises event. Sixty settings were needed. He checked inventory and determined that even with the banquet and a full dining room Saturday night, the Grill would be able to handle the off-premises event. But he knew it was going to be tight; there weren't going to be any spare settings lying around. But still, they should have had enough. Then he preset the banquet room three days ago and double-checked the inventory. Again, there were enough settings. So what was the problem?

Reuben decided to check inventory again. He was shocked when he found that the dish staff was struggling just to keep glasses, plates, cups—everything—in rotation. He shook his head. What was going on? He remembered that Ted took a cellular phone with him to the off-premises event, so Reuben went to his office, closed the door behind him, and called Ted.

"Ted? Hi. This is Reuben. How is everything?"

"Reuben—hey, everything's going great here, just great."

"Well, I'm glad to hear it. Unfortunately, I can't say the same."

"Why? What's up?"

"We don't have any settings; servers are running out of cups and plates; guests are becoming irate… I just don't understand it. I figured all this out earlier in the week. It was gonna be close, but we were going to make it."

"I'm sorry to hear you're having problems there, but we took a hundred settings, and it looks like we have just enough—"

"A hundred?" Reuben interrupted.

"Yeah. One hundred."

"But that event was only scheduled for 60."

"Well, that was before they added 40. I told you about that."

"No, you didn't."

"I must have. I told Frank, and he made sure I got the extra food. I didn't tell you?"

"No, you didn't. There's nothing we can do about it now. We'll just have to make do here."

"I'm sorry, Reuben."

"That's OK. These things happen. Keep up the good work. I'll talk to you later."

But of course Reuben knew everything *wasn't* OK. Somehow he had to solve this problem for his guests and his staff—and fast. And he had to make sure the Fiesta Grill wouldn't face this problem in two months—at which time they were again booked for a banquet and an off-premises event on the same night.

Reuben grabbed a bottle of aspirin from his desk and bravely entered the kitchen. "Here we go," he thought to himself.

Discussion Questions

1. What steps could have been taken to prevent the shortage problems at the Fiesta Grill?

2. Assuming the continued success of off-premises catering, what options does the management team have in relation to securing the stock necessary to accommodate increased business? List the advantages and disadvantages of each option.

Case Number: 4657CA

The following industry experts helped generate and develop this case: Timothy J. Pugh, Regional Manager, Damon's—The Place for Ribs (Steve Montanye Enterprises, East Lansing, Michigan); and Lawrence E. Ross, Assistant Professor, Florida Southern College, and owner of Sago Grill, Lakeland, Florida.

 **Problems** —————————————————————————————

Problem 1

The following information applies to the City View Restaurant.

May 1   Food inventory value: $73,480

May 31 Food inventory value: $77,550

Cost of food used during May $386,410

a) What is the inventory turnover rate for food products for the City View Restaurant?

b) What does the answer (inventory turnover ratio) in Question A mean?

Problem 2

What is the total inventory value of the following products?

Physical Inventory				
Type of Product: _____		Month _____		
Product	Unit	Amount in Storage	Purchase Cost	Total Cost
Ground Beef	10 lb bag	6 bag	$2.10/lb	
Canned Peaches	6-6 # 10/cs	3-5/6 cs	$39.40/cs	
Flour	50 lb	2 bag	$22.10 bag	
Shrimp	10/5 lb per case	3-8/10 cs	$7.50/lb	
			Total	

Problem 3

Complete the following perpetual inventory form.

Perpetual Inventory			
Product Name: House Bourbon			
Purchase Unit Size: 750 ml			

		Carried Forward	4
Date	**In**	**Out**	**Balance**
1/7	3		
1/9		2	
1/10		1	
1/12	5	1	
1/15		2	

Problem 4

What is the value of inventory for the following products given the following information:

Beverage Inventory Cost Card (2 Work Stations)							
		Quantity Available					
		Bottles Behind Bar					
Beverage Item	**Storage Unit**	**Open**	**Unopened**	**In Central Storage**	**Total**	**Cost Per Storage Unit**	**Total Cost**
	Col. 1	Col. 2	Col. 3	Col. 4	Col. 5	Col. 6	Col. 7
Bar Vodka	750 ml	$3/4 + 3/4$	3	5		$8.45	
Bar Scotch	750 ml	$3/4 + 1/2$	2	4		$9.90	
Bar Gin	750 ml	$1/4 + 1/4$	2	6		$8.70	
Bar Rum	750 ml	$3/4 + 3/4$	3	5		$7.40	

Problem 5

What is the inventory value of each of the following items at the end of the day? Assume (a) all items are "A" items, (b) leftovers are returned to central inventory at the end of the work day and (c) no products were received.

Item	Unit	Cost/ Unit	Begin Inventory	Amount Issued	Amount Used	Ending Inventory	Cost
Shrimp	lb	$7.35	73 lb	22 lb	18 lb		
Ground Beef	lb	$2.45	60 lb	10 lb	10 lb		
Veal Patty	each	$1.12	29 ea	12 ea	10 ea		
Pork Chops	8 oz	$2.90	51 chops	15 chops 7 chops	16 chops		

Problem 6

What is the total cost of food requisition given the following:

Item	Begin Inventory	Unit Cost	No. Units Issued	Total Cost
Tomato Paste	cs-6 / #10	$39.95	1-5/6	
Canned Peaches	cs- 6 / #10	$28.40	2-4/6	
Canned Green Beans	cs-6 / #10	$21.70	3	
Tomato Juice	cs-12 / 303	$42.50	7/12	

Chapter 8 Outline

Competencies

1. Analyze trends to estimate food production requirements. (pp. 245–248)

2. Use the weighted time series method to estimate food production requirements. (p. 248)

3. Describe the importance and function of food production planning. (pp. 250–254)

4. Identify important control procedures for food and beverage production areas. (pp. 254–259)

5. Identify important control procedures for food and beverage service areas. (pp. 259–265)

6. Describe the features and functions of keyboards, monitors, and printers used by point-of-sale systems. (pp. 265–273)

7. Describe the features and functions of an automated beverage control system. (pp. 274–278)

8

Production and Serving Controls

Because guest satisfaction depends directly on production and serving, these control points are in many ways the most important and complex. Production, for example, must ensure quality while complying with cost limitations. And serving—an art much like acting—requires proper timing, accuracy, and a host of other talents to provide a dining experience that will please guests.

Production and serving involve many more activities—and many more employees—than other control points. The production and serving activities reviewed in this chapter demonstrate the extent to which food and beverage operations do depend on labor. Labor-saving equipment has not replaced people in many hospitality tasks. In food production and serving, the tasks of managing and controlling are hard to separate from personnel supervision.

As control procedures for production and serving are being developed, the guest must be at the forefront of the decision-making process. As the food and beverage manager plans control procedures for purchasing, receiving, storing, and issuing, it is sometimes easy to forget about the guests being served. However, production and serving activities require the manager to focus on guest-related concerns and to match these with other priorities about back-of-the-house control procedures. Therefore, in addition to controlling the operation's resources, such as products, labor, and revenue, the food and beverage manager must consider the impact that operating/control problems will likely have on guests. The professional food and beverage manager consistently incorporates marketing and production concerns into the decision-making process. The manager who controls without considering the guest will not be effective.

Production Planning

Production planning is the first step toward ensuring quality products and dining experiences that meet or exceed guest expectations. Production actually comprises three control points: preparing, cooking, and holding. Personnel assigned to these areas are responsible for the wholesomeness, goodness, and attractiveness of the foods and beverages that will be presented to the guests. Even though the cost and quality of foods and beverages may have been expertly controlled before their arrival at production centers, all gains will be lost if there are no control procedures to guide management and staff through production and serving.

Production planning is simply getting ready for production. Operations of all sizes must plan for production if they are to have food and beverage products, personnel, and equipment available when needed. Planned coordination among departments also prevents under- or over-utilization of resources. While planning does not guarantee that all problems will be eliminated, it certainly heads off many which may have serious economic and marketing consequences. Success, in most instances, correlates with successful planning.

Each food and beverage operation must develop specific procedures for production planning that are suited to its own unique needs. However, a typical strategy is to first forecast production requirements and then translate those requirements into production plans.

Forecasting Production Requirements

Quantities of products required for expected production activities during the upcoming week must be estimated. These projections may be based on sales history records. A careful analysis of previous unit sales can help control production quantities and reduce leftovers. Seasons, weather, special events within the community, and similar factors also affect production estimates. These must be taken into consideration in forecasting production requirements during planning sessions.[1]

Sales history records can be used to estimate production requirements. A common technique, shown in Exhibit 1, makes use of a separate sales history sheet for each day of the week. Data can be derived from guest check tallies (manual system) or from cumulative sales from ECR/POS systems (daily sales summed for a specified fiscal period such as week or month). The sales history record provides space for recording the total of each item sold on a specific day of the week over a five-week period. In addition to recording the number sold, the planner computes the percentage of all guests ordering each item. With this form, trends can be identified and used to predict future sales.

Note that column 1 of Exhibit 1 lists the average number of each menu item ordered daily over the past 80 days. Column 2 lists the percentage total, calculated by dividing the number sold by the total number of guests served and multiplying by 100. For example, in the previous 80 days, an average of 46 shrimp cocktails were served, or 27.4 percent of 168 guests ordered shrimp cocktails.

$$\frac{\text{Number Sold}}{\text{Total Guests}} \quad \times \quad 100 \quad = \quad \text{Percentage of Guests Ordering Item}$$

$$\frac{46}{168} \quad \times \quad 100 \quad = \quad 27.4\%$$

Information from the most recent Tuesday (4/13/XX) is listed in columns 3 and 4. Forty-nine guests of the 177 total ordered the shrimp cocktail appetizer. This amounts to 27.7 percent.

$$\frac{49}{177} \quad \times \quad 100 \quad = \quad 27.7\%$$

Exhibit 1   Sales History Record

Sales History Record

Day ____Tuesday____

Items	Previous 80 Day Average No. Sold	% of Total	4/13/XX No. Sold	% of Total	4/20/XX No. Sold	% of Total	4/27/XX No. Sold	% of Total	5/4/XX No. Sold	% of Total	5/11/XX No. Sold	% of Total
	1	2	3	4	5	6	7	8	9	10	11	12
Appetizers												
Shrimp Cocktail	46	27.4	49	27.7								
Fruit Cup	17	10.1	18	10.2								
Marinated Herring	16	9.5	15	8.5								
Half Grapefruit	6	3.6	8	4.5								
Soup du Jour	27	16.1	31	17.5								
Total Appetizers	112	66.7	121	68.4								
Entrées												
Sirloin Steak	26	15.5	29	16.4								
Prime Rib	58	34.5	62	35.0								
Lobster	28	16.7	26	14.7								
Ragout of Lamb	22	13.1	21	11.9								
Half Chicken	34	20.2	39	22.0								
Total Entrées	168	100.0	177	100.0								
Vegetables & Salads												
Whipped Potatoes	51	30.4	57	32.2								
Baked Potatoes	108	64.3	119	67.2								
Asparagus Spears	111	66.1	108	61.0								
Half Tomato	48	28.6	49	27.7								
Tossed Salad	102	60.7	107	60.5								
Hearts of Lettuce	57	33.9	64	36.2								
Total Veg. & Salad	477	283.9	504	284.7								
Desserts												
Brownie	19	11.3	21	11.9								
Fresh Fruits	9	5.4	10	5.6								
Ice Cream	33	19.6	36	20.3								
Apple Pie	19	11.3	25	14.1								
Devil's Food Cake	14	8.3	10	5.6								
Total Desserts	94	56.0	102	57.6								
Total Guests Served	168	100.0	177	100.0								

Once the total number of guests for the next Tuesday is estimated, the percentage trend can be used to estimate the number of portions of each menu item required. For example, assume that a total of 200 guests is estimated for the next Tuesday. If the manager assumes that the same percentage of guests will order this appetizer, the estimated number of shrimp cocktails needed for next Tuesday can be calculated as follows:

Estimated Guests × Percent as a Decimal = Estimated Servings

200 × .277 = 55

This process is repeated to estimate production requirements for all other menu items and for all other days in the forecast period. Another forecasting technique involves comparing unit sales data for the past month and six months from the past month. As shown in Exhibit 2, the total number of each appetizer (selected items for illustrative purposes only) sold in January (top line) and July (second line), February (top line) and August (second line) etc. is shown. The total unit sales and sales mix (last two columns) are also shown. Note that appetizer 1 (cup of the day [soup]) represents unit sales of 1793 (15.85% of all appetizers sold) for January-June (current year) plus January-March (previous year). Using sales data applicable to a six month period allows many variables to "average out" for production forecasting purposes. In addition, this data is very helpful input for menu revisions; managers wish to sell popular and remove unpopular items.

Computers can be very useful in the projection of production requirements. Electronic files can store historic data, and computer software can be developed to apply these records for future use. While the formulations described above are popular for manual forecasting, computer systems tend to employ time series analysis.

Time series analysis allows for weighting of historic data with respect to its recency. This forecasting method assigns more importance (weight) to recent occurrences (trends). In other words, if we are attempting to forecast how many prime rib dinners will be ordered this Saturday night, we could base our projection on data from five previous Saturdays. For purposes of this example, assume weights of 5, 4, 3, 2, and 1 for the prior Saturdays, with 5 representing the most recent Saturday. Last Saturday 220 portions were sold; the previous week, 200; before that, 110; before that, 200; and prior to that, 150. To project this Saturday's portions, the following steps are taken:

1. Multiply each week's number of portions sold by its respective weight and total the values:

$$(220)(5) + (200)(4) + (110)(3) + (200)(2) + (150)(1) = 2,780$$

2. Divide the computed total by the sum of its weights. This will yield the weighted projection:

$$\frac{2,780}{5 + 4 + 3 + 2 + 1} = \frac{2,780}{15} = 185.3$$

Time series analysis projects that approximately 185 portions will be consumed this Saturday. The computer may develop its forecasted projections based upon stored data, manually inputted data, or data transferred from electronic cash registers. Its output can also be helpful in developing purchase order requirements and labor needs and for providing additional assistance to management. Computer forecasts are performed quickly and accurately, which increases their value to the operation.

Exhibit 2   Gross Sales Analysis: Six-Month Period

RUN DATE 10/30/XX   PAGE 1
TIME 14:09   GROSS SALES ANALYSIS   VERSION 3.22d
STORE # 1   Volume Detail for All Depts
                                            SEP25–30 20XX   SALES REPORT 12

MENU ITEMS	JAN/ JULY	FEB/ AUG	MAR/ SEP	APR/ OCT	MAY/ NOV	JUNE/ DEC	TOTAL	MIX%
Apps								
1 Cup of day	242.00	244.00	237.00	174.00	188.00	157.00		
	168.00	215.00	168.00				1793.00	15.85
2 Bowl of day	38.00	30.00	26.00	21.00	25.00	25.00		
	25.00	30.00	25.00				245.00	2.17
5 Sbakd fr. onion	57.00	37.00	4300	38.00	49.00	58.00		
	51.00	67.00	49.00				449.00	3.97
7 Lgbakd fr. onion	14.00	9.00	13.00	15.00	10.00	9.00		
	14.00	22.00	10.00				116.00	1.03
11 Cupsoup subst	38.00	23.00	33.00	17.00	28.00	24.00		
	14.00	37.00	24.00				238.00	2.10
12 Bowlsoup subst	3.00	1.00		1.00				
		1.00	2.00				8.00	0.07
26 Portobello stix				1.00				
							1.00	0.01
27 Smked salmon				2.00				
							2.00	0.02
28 Hamburger								
		100.00	24.00				124.00	1.10
30 Cup soup		2.00		2.00				
							4.00	0.04
31 Calamari		2.00		2.00				
							4.00	0.04
40 Bowl soup					1.00			
							1.00	0.01
41 Shrmp cktl		1.00		1.00	1.00			
							3.00	0.03
50 Portobello stix								
		1.00	1.00				2.00	0.02
51 Shrimp cocktail								
	3.00	6.00	5.00				14.00	0.12
56 Shrimp cocktail			6.00	6.00	5.00	25.00		
	27.00	17.00	6.00				92.00	0.81
60 Fruit cup								
		1.00					1.00	0.01
65 Chicken skewers	8.00	7.00	5.00	6.00	6.00	11.00		
	8.00	12.00	7.00				70.00	0.62
67 Coleslaw						3.00		
	3.00	2.00					8.00	0.07
68 Portobello stick	5.00	5.00	20.00	11.00	8.00	8.00		
	17.00	1.00					75.00	.66
104 Smked salmon	11.00	17.00	10.00	5.00	5.00	9.00		
	20.00	14.00	9.00				100.00	0.88

Courtesy of the University Club, Michigan State University, East Lansing, Michigan

Formulating Production Plans

Regularly scheduled planning meetings should be held. Personnel most directly involved with production activities should attend these planning sessions. For example, in a small operation the manager and head cook may meet every Wednesday to review production plans for the week beginning on Friday or Saturday.

During these meetings, estimates of production needs, derived from a study of sales history and similar information, must be adjusted and converted into production plans. Sales history records using data from manual or computer tallies may be used to produce a master food production planning worksheet, such as the sample shown in Exhibit 3.

Food production personnel can use this form to determine the amount of menu item ingredients to purchase. The form also allows recording of actual results of each day's operation, including the number of leftovers. This information can be used to modify and update sales history information. Revised counts can then be used in estimating production needs in subsequent weeks.

Other matters must be considered at the production planning meeting. Based upon the estimated production needs, labor and equipment can be scheduled at this meeting. For example, perhaps a special catered event requires items to be produced in especially large quantities. The sample equipment schedule shown in Exhibit 4 relates how to use existing equipment to produce a large quantity of bread products for a special banquet.

After the production planning meeting, the required number of each menu item for the forecast period is known. Therefore, issue requisition forms for some days or items may also be partially completed. These requisition forms might be completely prepared for catered events if these costs are charged to a separate revenue center.

Production Planning and Food Purchasing

Typically, food purchase decisions are not made during production planning sessions. Perishable products, "directs," are normally purchased several times weekly according to forecasted needs. Non-perishable items, "stores," can be purchased according to a minimum/maximum inventory system that takes into account normal usage rates.

When these types of inventory/ordering systems are used, specific purchase decisions need not be based on normal fluctuations in the number of guests expected. Since these purchase decisions are based on typical usage rates, the experience factor is built into the procedures for estimating quantities to purchase.

However, the number of guests estimated during production planning meetings is important when making purchase decisions for special banquet functions. These activities may greatly increase the quantity of items needed, or may require special products not normally carried in inventory. In these cases, it is very important that there be effective communication between planners and purchasers. Although specific procedures will vary, a good policy is to provide purchasing staff with two weeks' notice of special events that will significantly increase the

Exhibit 3 Master Food Production Planning Worksheet

Day Tuesday
Date 8/1/XX

Master Food Production Planning Worksheet

Local Weather Forecast Cloudy & mild
Special Plans: Party of 15 — steaks

Items	Standard Portion Size	Forecasted Portions			Adjusted Forecast	Requisitioning Guide Data		Remarks	Number of Portions Left Over	Actual Number Served
		Guests	Officers*	Total Forecast		Raw Materials Requested	State of Preparation			
Appetizers										
Shrimp Cocktail	5 ea	48	—	48	51	12 lbs of 21–25 count	RTC		—	53
Fruit Cup	5 oz	15	1	19	20	See Recipe for 20 Portions			—	19
Marinated Herring	2 1/2 oz	15	1	16	16	2 1/2 lbs	RTE		—	14
Half Grapefruit	1/2 ea	8	—	8	8	4 Grapefruit			—	9
Soup	6 oz	30	3	33	36	Prepare 2 Gallons			5	32
Entrées										
Sirloin Steak	14 oz	28	—	28	29	29 Sirloin Steaks (Btchr.)	RTC		—	28
Prime Ribs	9 oz	61	1	62	64	3 Ribs of Beef	RTC	Use Re-heat if necessary	out at 10:45 P.M.	62
Lobster	1 1/2 lb	26	—	26	28	28 Lobsters (check stock)			—	26
Ragout of Lamb	4 oz	24	2	26	26	12 lbs lamb fore (3/4" pcs)		Recipe No. E. 402	1 +	25
Half Chicken	1/2 ea	34	2	36	38	38 halves (check stock)			—	39
Vegetables & Salads										
Whipped Potatoes	3 oz	55	1	56	58	13 lbs	AP		2–3	56
Baked Potatoes	1 ea	112	3	115	120	120 Idahos			out at 11:10 P.M.	120
Asparagus Spears	3 ea	108	—	108	113	8 No. 2 cans			2	110
Half Tomato	1/2 ea	48	4	52	54	27 Tomatoes			2	52
Tossed Salad	2 1/2 oz	105	3	108	112	See Recipe No. S.302			—	114
Hearts of Lettuce	1/4 hd	63	2	65	67	18 heads			—	69
Desserts										
Brownie w/Ice cream	1 sq /1 1/2 oz	21	2	23	26	1 pan brownies				24
Fresh Fruits	3 oz	10	—	10	11	See Recipe No. D.113			—	10
Ice Cream	2 1/2 oz	35	3	38	40	Check stock				43
Apple Pie	1/7 cut	21	—	21	21	3 Pies			out at 10:50 P.M.	21
Devils Food Cake	1/8 cut	8	—	8	8	1 cake			1	7
Total No. of Persons		173	5	178	185					180

Abbreviations: AP—as purchased; RTC—ready-to-cook; RTE—ready-to-eat.

*Officers are management staff permitted free meals from menus.

Exhibit 4   Sample Equipment Schedule

Equipment Schedule: Banquet

Time: Equipment Available:	2:00	2:15	2:30	2:45	3:00	3:15	3:30	3:45	4:00	4:15	4:30	4:45	5:00	5:15	5:30
Convection Oven															
1							Bake Batch #1				Bake Batch #2		Buns		
2							Bake Batch #1				Bake Batch #2		Buns		
Electric Oven															
1								Bake Batch #1				Bake Batch #2		Buns	
2								Bake Batch #1				Bake Batch #2		Buns	
3								Bake Batch #1				Bake Batch #2		Buns	
Gas Range													Buns*		
60 Qt. Mixer (2 Bowls)	Mix Batch #2				Mix Buns										
Proof Box															
1		Pan, Proof Batch #1						Pan, Proof Buns							
2				Pan, Proof Batch #2											
Dough Divider						Hamburger Buns									

*Depending upon the number of buns per 18" × 26" pans, there may be as many as four pans that cannot be baked by 5:30. Should this occur, they are panned, stacked, and refrigerated. The following morning they can be proofed and baked before ovens are in full use. Desserts prepared on the prior day may need to be baked at this time also.

number of meals served or that have special purchase requirements. A special event notice (Exhibit 6) can be used to inform purchasing personnel about special purchasing requirements.

Production Planning: Convenience Foods

Convenience foods can be defined as items which have some or all of the labor built into them which would otherwise need to be provided on-site. Typically, the use of convenience foods is not an "all or nothing" decision. Rather, it is necessary to conduct a make-by analysis on a by-item basis to determine whether items should be produced on-site or should be purchased in a readily available convenience food alternative. Let's look, for example, at the Apple Jack Restaurant which offers bread on its menu. Exhibit 5 indicates how bread can be purchased. It can be made from "scratch"; the operation can purchase the flour, shortening, yeast, sugar, salt and other ingredients which are needed to bake the bread on-site. Alternatively, frozen dough can be purchased and can be pre-portioned before proofing and baking. As a third alternative, frozen dough which is already pre-portioned in the correct weight is available. Bread can also be purchased fresh-baked or fresh-baked and sliced. How should an operation needing bread make this decision?

Exhibit 5   Financial Impact of Convenience Food

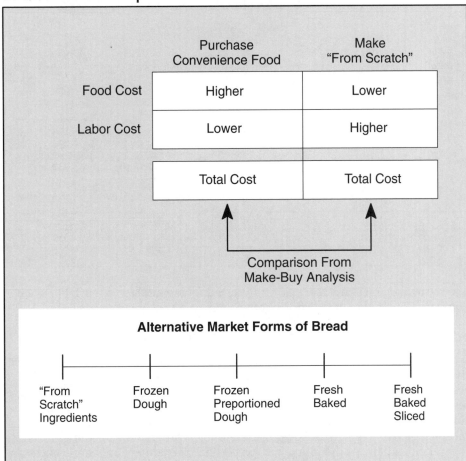

A make-buy analysis allows the operator to first assess the quality of each alternative and consider the costs associated with acceptable alternatives. Quality should always be the first consideration; if a convenience food in the necessary quality is not available there are only two alternatives: prepare the item on-site or do not offer it on the menu.

Exhibit 5 reviews another concern managers must address when evaluating the use of convenience foods. Suppose the manager decides that significant labor savings are possible if hamburger patties are purchased preportioned rather than in the current bulk package which requires on-site portioning. A careful study may determine that the labor hours saved more than offset the higher cost of the preportioned patties; savings can result if preportioned products are purchased. However, unless the production hours that will be saved are actually eliminated from the schedule the labor cost will actually remain the same; food costs will increase,

Exhibit 6   Special Event Notice

Special Event Notice			
Event: _____			
Date: _____	Date of Notice: _____		
No. of Guests _____			
Special Requirements: _____			
Authorizing Official: _____			
The following items are needed for the above event:			

Item	Purchase Unit	Quantity	Estimated Price

and the manager will not realize the forecasted savings. All too often, labor savings "on paper" are not realized and negative financial consequences arise.

Special Beverage Production Planning Requirements

It is important to maintain adequate bar par inventory levels and establish an effective minimum/maximum purchase and inventory system for central storage areas. When these inventory systems are used, little production planning is normally needed for beverage products. Therefore, much of the preceding discussion of production planning procedures does not relate specifically to beverage production. With regard to beverage operations, production planning generally focuses on employee scheduling and expediting. The latter is frequently necessary to maintain constant supplies of some brand liquors and required wines. A special event notice (Exhibit 6) may be used whenever circumstances are judged to affect purchase and inventory beverage requirements.

Production Control

We have learned that food and beverage control begins with the menu. The menu not only dictates what items are to be prepared, but it also is a major marketing tool that describes the plan for meeting or exceeding guests' expectations.

Many books have been written about managing food and beverage products during production. In these books you can find discussions about the details of menu planning, equipment, layout, and design; personnel management; principles of food production; and other topics related to production activities. At some level, all these discussions deal with controlling products during production. In this chapter, we will focus on several of the basic concerns of management that are at the core of controlling the production process.

Quality Requirements

Managers must consider quality requirements in several different ways. These range from the detailed quality requirements of specific operating standards to the general perspectives of management policy and guest expectations. It is important to remember that control procedures must help—not hinder—the operation's ability to meet its required standards.

Control during production begins with adhering to established operating standards. These include standard purchase specifications, standard recipes, standard yields, standard portion sizes, standard portion costs for food production, and standard glass and ice size for beverage production. These control tools provide procedures for uniformly purchasing, producing, and serving products of the required quality. Food purchase specifications also incorporate quality requirements. They dictate the minimum quality and other requirements that all products must meet. Likewise, standard operating procedures (SOPs) dictate quality standards when, for example, they describe how to thaw frozen products, evaluate convenience foods, and develop production plans.

In more general terms, quality requirements are reflected in the property's marketing plans and strategies. Some properties may wish, for example, to serve an inexpensive hamburger of minimal quality. Others offer an inexpensive but high-quality hamburger. Still others attempt to meet a need for "a hamburger dining experience" and offer gourmet hamburgers. Marketing position statements, operating goals, and management philosophies all express at least minimum requirements that must be built into the control system. Management must use control procedures to ensure that the property's plans, based on guests' needs and desires, are attained.

Even though operators may not have formally evaluated marketing concerns or established written operating standards, their properties do have quality requirements. For example, many chefs are concerned that only the finest products be served. Managers want to be proud of all items being served. Over time, these implicit standards are revealed to observant and returning guests.

Even without specific marketing plans, a property's history shapes the level of quality that guests will perceive as adequate and come to expect. The status quo—"how we've always done things"—often influences how things will be done in the future. In this situation it is difficult either to reduce quality standards or to increase quality requirements. Quality is not a fixed standard; it evolves as expectations change. Quality is relative to market perceptions about its adequacy. Guests have expectations of the food and beverage operation. Successful food and beverage managers know their guests' quality standards. They train and **empower** their staff to address and, hopefully, to exceed the guests' wants and needs.

Maintaining Standards

As mentioned earlier, control during production starts with adhering to established operating standards. Food and beverage cost standards—guides to planned or expected results—cannot be developed until standard cost control tools are in use. Cost standards are useless if the tools needed to attain them are not used in production areas. Several conditions make it possible for personnel to comply with production standards.

Training. Employees must understand the standards. Training programs for new staff and refresher sessions for experienced employees are needed. Seasoned employees often forget about, or find shortcuts to, operating procedures. New menu items, new equipment, and revised procedures are among the numerous everyday changes that point to the need for ongoing training for all staff members.

Information. Information must be available in workstations. For example, standard recipes can be put together into readily available files or books for reference. When computerized systems are in place, recipes can be printed out and placed in workstations daily. Portion sizes should also be posted in production areas.

Tools and Equipment. Tools and equipment needed for production staff to follow standards must be available. For example, it does little good for a standard recipe to require six ounces of an ingredient unless an accurate portion scale is available and used. Likewise, when a recipe requires portioning with a number 8 scoop, compliance is impossible unless the operation has the portion tool on hand (a number 8 scoop yields 8 servings per quart). Operating and control problems will result if proper equipment is unavailable or is improperly used. Suppose a bar recipe specifies a certain glass for a highball. What does the bartender do when, during a rush, there are not enough of the specified glasses available? Incorrect substitutions can jeopardize the control system.

Supervision. Management must routinely supervise personnel to ensure compliance with all requirements. They must be alert and watchful of production practices. Food and beverage managers must be able to perform more than one task at a time. For example, when walking past the bar on the way to the office, the manager can observe whether the bartender is using a shot glass or jigger in preparing a drink. When passing a table in the dining room or the serving line in the kitchen, the manager can quickly judge the portion size of an entrée—even though there may be other important concerns at the moment.

Standard Recipes as Production Tools

Standard recipes play an important role in the overall control system of a food and beverage operation. When standard recipes are developed and consistently followed, product costs can be estimated realistically. Standard recipes are the foundation for establishing budgeting and menu pricing procedures.

Standard recipes are basic food and beverage production tools. They not only specify the ingredients and applicable quantities, but also help determine the required amount of production time. If an employee closely follows the procedures outlined in a standard recipe, it should be possible to predict the time required to produce a given number of menu items.

Properly developed standard recipes can also help define effective work practices. Standard recipes can remind cooks to select all necessary pots, pans, and other utensils on one trip to the pot and pan rack; they can suggest when production equipment should be turned on and off, which can yield energy savings.

Safety considerations can also be built into standard recipes. For example, recipes can warn employees not to open a vertical cutter mixer until the blade has stopped or remind them to set the wheel brakes on mobile equipment.

Planners should have standard recipes readily available during planning sessions, and supervisors should confirm that standard recipes are consistently used by all food and beverage production personnel. Standard recipes must be used to ensure consistency in meeting guests' desires and in attaining cost/profit goals. They are at the heart of a food and beverage production control system.

Production Cost Control Procedures

Food production involves preparing, cooking, and holding. The purpose of production controls is to ensure quality while complying with cost limitations. Earlier in this chapter, we discussed quality control and the need to meet quality standards. Here, we present some general cost control procedures:

- Require that all standard cost control tools be used consistently.

- Issue food items only in those amounts needed to meet production requirements forecasted on the basis of past unit sales records and scheduled special events.

- Through supervision, ensure that all personnel are trained in and constantly comply with food production procedures.

- Minimize food waste. How are salad greens processed? How is meat trimmed and cut?

- Use proper quality items. For example, if the property purchases both canned whole and diced tomatoes, select the correct type for the recipe being prepared.

- Monitor employee eating and drinking practices. If a long-stem maraschino cherry costs 6 cents and each shrimp costs 20 cents, an employee working with one hand and eating with the other can quickly raise food costs.

- Put unused items withdrawn from storage back in storage (where there will be tighter control) and re-issue the products when necessary. Make sure that inventory and requisition forms are properly adjusted.

- Require that no item be discarded without prior approval of management. This applies to items spoiled in storage as well as items improperly prepared.

- Match issue and production records with unit sales records to assess the extent to which issued products generate revenue. For example, portion-controlled steaks can be issued to the workstation on the basis of the master food production planning worksheet (Exhibit 3). At the end of the work shift, compare the number of steaks sold (from the electronic register's sales journal tape) with the number of steaks available in the workstation. After adjusting for any over-cooked or returned steaks, the remaining steaks can be accounted for and returned to secure storage. (Perpetual inventory records, if used, can then be adjusted accordingly.)

- Look for production bottlenecks during busy periods and resolve them. Often the staff involved will have ideas about how to improve procedures and reduce costs.

- Be sure measuring and weighing tools and equipment are always used to prepare food and beverage items. Make sure staff use portion-control tools—scoops, ladles, and so on—when portioning food items for service.

- Carefully study the systems used to manage equipment, facility layout and design, and energy usage. Management of these resources is important and has a definite impact on the property's overall profitability.

- Recognize the importance of communication and coordination between work sections and departments when drawing up plans and implementing them.

- Keep records during production to help guide further planning and for accounting use. The design of recordkeeping systems, their accuracy, and the timeliness of information and reports all have control implications.

- Be sure labor-saving convenience food or labor-saving equipment is actually saving labor. Labor costs must decrease at least enough to cover the increased food or equipment costs. If this is not the case, food or equipment costs will be higher, labor costs will remain the same, and profits will be lower than before the labor-saving food or equipment was purchased.

- Be sure production employees understand the principles of food preparation and can apply or modify them to meet quantity food production needs of the operation. Food preparation principles and resulting quality control are basically the same, whatever the quantity of food prepared. However, procedures for handling and processing large volumes of food are different.

- The cooks and managers must have a genuine concern for and appreciation of good food to apply quality control principles. Look for personnel genuinely concerned about preparing and offering the highest quality food products possible within the property's standards.

- Accurately complete leftover reports and use them to fine-tune the quantities of items prepared. Also, use leftovers creatively when possible in future production. However, remember that quality decreases over time, such as when hot items are held for service, cooled, stored, and then reheated. In addition, there are sanitation concerns that override the cost control considerations. For example, potentially hazardous leftovers can create sanitation problems if improperly handled and re-served. Balance controlling food costs with maintaining established food quality levels.

Special Beverage Cost Control Procedures

Many control concerns in food production also apply to beverage production. Certainly, maintaining quality and cost standards is just as important. However, there are specific cost control procedures for beverage production:

- Use standard beverage recipes. Through supervision, ensure that required beverage production procedures are consistently followed. Make sure that the proper amounts of preparation ingredients are put into the proper glass with the proper amount and size of ice.

- Use portion-control tools such as shot glasses and jiggers. Automated beverage systems, which dispense measured quantities of alcoholic beverages, offer more control, but serious study is necessary to cost-justify the equipment's use. This is reviewed in more detail later in this chapter.

- Supervise to ensure that all beverage control procedures are being followed.

- Train beverage staff to produce drinks according to the property's quality and cost requirements.

- Bartenders, especially during rush periods, must be able to work quickly. Knowledge of work simplification principles and a properly designed bar significantly affect production volume.

- Encourage an attitude of concern for guests among beverage staff.

- Control of employee eating and drinking practices requires special emphasis for the bar. Employees should not accept drinks from guests—or from other staff members. Establish and enforce policies for employee conduct "on and off the clock" while at the property.

- Have returned drinks or "mistakes" saved for management review. An excessive number of such drinks is probably a sign that more training or a change in procedures is required.

- Lock bar par inventories when the bar is not in use.

- Match the amount of beverages used (based on issues to replace empty bottles) with revenue generated and develop an actual beverage cost percentage.

- Hold the bartender responsible for cash.

- Hold the bartender responsible for behind-the-bar inventory. At the start of the shift, count all bottles to ensure that the required number of each type of beverage is available in inventory. A similar count of full and empty bottles at the end of the shift should show the bar par still complete.

- Ensure adequate supplies of garnishes, drink mixes, paper supplies, and glassware to enhance production speed and efficiency. Establish procedures to estimate necessary quantities of these and related items according to the forecast of sales.

Serving Controls

After food and beverage products are produced, they must be served to the guest. For purposes of our discussion we will refer to serving (which means moving the product from production staff to service staff) and service (moving products from service staff to guests) as one step in the control process, and we will use the terms *serving* and *service* interchangeably.

The serving activity is critical from a cost control standpoint because the responsibility for menu items changes from the kitchen/bar to the dining room/lounge or other service area. This activity may enhance or detract from the quality of food and beverage products. Many factors affect the quality of service in a food and beverage operation. They include the communication and cooperation between kitchen, bar, and dining room personnel; the flow of products; the menu; the design and layout of the kitchen, bar, and dining room; and the style of service. Standards of service vary greatly with the type of establishment. Management is responsible for standardizing ordering procedures, serving procedures, sanitation practices, and personnel requirements. As with the other control points, the serving function requires sanitation, quality, and cost controls.

Food service assumes many forms today. Besides the traditional forms of table service found in many lodging and food service operations, other types of service are becoming more popular in hospitality establishments. Each requires slightly different standards. For example, special functions and banquets are served differently than cooked-to-order meals. Also, when food products are prepared and transported to a catered event off the premises, product holding becomes a critical control point. Similarly, hotel room service and carry-out service can be profitable and safe if designed properly.

The Server and the Guest

Control procedures are important in the relationship between the server and the guest. Fundamentally, guests' concerns lead the way to control procedures. The server must realize that the guest has needs, wants, desires, and expectations that must be addressed during the dining experience. Important components of dining—including timing, accuracy, merchandising, and work practices—affect guests' experience and satisfaction.

What do guests want? Among other things, they want courteous and attentive service, the right order, cleanliness, and no problems. They do not want to know about the server's or the property's problems.

- The serving process must be adequate; products must be delivered.

- Serving must be properly timed. At breakfast and lunch, this may mean faster service. At a leisurely dinner, timing means a proper flow of products and services throughout the meal, without awkward waits for courses or other server responsibilities.

- Service staff must know the menu, the daily specials, the brands of beverages in stock, and the ingredients and production methods for the food and beverage products offered.

- Service staff must know how to properly serve—match guests with orders, and use standardized procedures for serving and removing food and beverages.

- Service staff must deal with people in a tactful, courteous manner—friendly but professional, helpful but not overbearing.

Ironically, service personnel are often the lowest paid and most poorly trained of all employees in a food and beverage operation. The high turnover rates among servers at many properties illustrate these points. However, from the guest's perspective, servers represent the property. For most guests, the servers are the only employees of the food and beverage operation with whom they come in contact. They represent management to the guests. The best plans and goals of management are often met—or not met—according to how the guest feels about the property, and this feeling is in large measure influenced by the service staff.

As with most other phases of food and beverage management, staff would do well to think about how they would like to be treated if they visited the property as guests. The answer to this question may establish the parameters within which food and beverage service should operate.

Server Responsibilities

Food servers must meet and greet the guests. They are really the property's salespersons, using the most powerful in-house marketing tool—the menu—to please the guests and, simultaneously, to generate revenue for the property and, perhaps, for themselves (in the form of tips). Following are several procedures that are basic to the control of the food and beverage service system.

Accuracy. The correct order must be taken and served. Poor communication between service personnel and guests has the same consequences as poor communication between production and service staff—higher costs and guest dissatisfaction. Effective communication can be helped by such techniques as reviewing orders with guests and using the bin number, if available, rather than pronouncing difficult names of foreign wines. As already noted, servers must be prompt, courteous, and tactful in all dealings with guests. Invariably, guests expect a certain quality of service relative to cost. If they are disappointed, revenues will be lost, guests will not return, and word-of-mouth reports will be negative.

Suggestive Selling. Servers should know which menu items to recommend—generally those with the higher contribution margins. These items are the more profitable ones for the property. Managers should try to maximize the amount of revenue left after product cost is deducted from the selling price. The contribution margin represents money used to cover other costs and to contribute to required profit levels.

Suggestive selling techniques also help generate additional revenue and therefore affect operating control. If a server sells a bottle of wine, an appetizer, or a dessert that guests would not have purchased otherwise, then all three parties benefit:

- Guests have enjoyed products that they otherwise might not have ordered.

- The server has increased the check size and, probably, the tip.

- The food and beverage operation has generated increased revenue.

General Service Procedures

Control procedures designed for food and beverage service systems not only must be correlated with the property's priorities, but they also must constantly focus on the guest's concerns. Two brief examples illustrate this point. As the manager designs systems to ensure that all revenue is collected from all sales, lengthy procedures may result. Reducing the quality of guest service (speed, in this case) is not acceptable. Another example is a beverage charge transfer system that transfers pre-meal beverage charges in the lounge to the dining room for payment at the end of the meal. This system is often cumbersome and awkward. However, such a system might be implemented because guests appreciate the convenience it affords.[2]

How should the property handle these and similar situations involving concerns of both the property and the guest? Each property will find its own answer to this question, and the answer—the resulting procedures—will reflect the extent to which the guest's perspective of service is built into operating plans.

Since servers greatly influence guests' perceptions of the property, rules for service personnel must be developed and used. This information can be included in employee handbooks and may also be the basis for employee training sessions.

The food and beverage server must be alert to the guest's needs. If the guest seems in a hurry or wants a more leisurely dining experience, the server should react accordingly. Likewise, the server must know when to present the check (bill). If servers remain alert and cooperate, they can reduce the possibility of guests leaving without paying.

Simplifying work practices can reduce labor costs and increase guest satisfaction. Many servers waste steps by walking to or from the dining room empty-handed or by not using trays. When refilling water glasses or coffee cups at one table, servers should do so for other guests who, invariably, will also ask for water or coffee refills a few moments later. Similarly, a server removing an empty glass from one table can remove used dishes from other tables on the way to the dish return area.

Servers, including the bartender, should be sure to enter all orders onto guest checks or into electronic register systems for each food and beverage order, to write or print clearly, and to comply with all in-house rules governing ordering of product and revenue collection.

After guests leave, the tables must be cleared and reset quickly for other guests. Revenue is lost when tables are not occupied. Reservation systems depend upon the ability to get tables ready quickly. Guests sitting next to soiled tables throughout their meal do not enjoy the atmosphere that management intends. For this and similar reasons, the front-of-the-house control system must pay close attention to ways that servers and dining room attendants prepare tables for reuse.

Service Control Factors

Serving includes the activities of transferring products from production personnel to serving staff and delivering the products to the guests. In the case of food, this involves getting food from the kitchen personnel to the food servers. For the bar, this involves getting beverages from the bartender to the food and/or beverage servers or to the guests themselves. In a **public bar**, guests may order beverages directly from the bartender while they are sitting or standing at the bar. In a **service bar**, the bartender prepares drinks ordered by serving staff, who then serve the drinks to guests. In bars that function as both public and service bars, the bartender prepares drinks directly for guests as well as for servers to deliver to guests. The following sections examine factors managers should consider when establishing service control procedures.

Timing of Service. Many aspects of food and beverage service must be taken into account when designing service control systems. Timing systems for placing orders are needed. At the same table, one guest may want a well-done filet mignon, while another wants a rare portion of prime rib. When should the order be turned in? What if these guests are in a hurry or, conversely, are lingering over a salad? Many things can happen here to increase costs. For example, if the prime rib comes out medium instead of rare, it must be replaced. Complimentary meals or portions of meals may have to be given ("comped") to dissatisfied guests. Other guests may leave without paying because they are in a hurry and servers do not present the check in time. Therefore, procedures specifying time limits for specific orders, the sequence for turning in orders, and other server-related concerns are needed.

Staff Communication. Production and service staff must communicate effectively. Does "SP" on a guest check mean shrimp platter or seafood platter? Does the notation "martini" tell whether it is to be served with ice or "straight up"? Do service personnel know an item is sold out before placing an order for it? Communication problems increase costs and create dissatisfied guests. Such problems can be resolved, however, by requiring the use of specified abbreviations for food and beverage orders and constantly updating portions left and items sold out. Remote printers help to avoid communication difficulties if order information is entered correctly.

Effects of Favoritism. Favoritism may disrupt service. For example, a production person (bartender or cook) may show favoritism toward a service employee out of affection or because of a bigger share of tips. If one server receives orders before others, guests are affected; they are not concerned or interested in these inter-staff relationships.

Adequate Supplies. Backup supplies must be sufficient. Service, cost, and guest satisfaction are affected by the availability of food items or beverage mixes made in advance of actual production orders. Likewise, plates and glassware, disposable or washable guest supplies, and other materials must be available in the correct quantities. The common production term *"mise en place"* refers to the need to get ready; it applies to the front- and back-of-house. Serving plans must include supplying service areas such as buffet lines, banquet setups, and/or portable bars. Consider both speed and costs involved in using service areas. Excess labor may be needed to continually keep them supplied.

Temperature and Holding Time. Foods must be kept hot (above 140°F/60°C) or cold (below 40°F/-5°C), as appropriate, until served. Not only is palatability—taste and appearance—affected, but poor sanitation practices can create other

Exhibit 7   Sample Job Description for a Coffee Shop Server

JOB TITLE: Coffee Shop Server

IMMEDIATE SUPERVISOR: Coffee Shop Manager

JOB SUMMARY:

Waits on coffee shop guests, takes their orders, and serves them immediately when orders are prepared. When guests have departed, quickly cleans and resets tables. Responsible for knowing the menu items, prices, and daily specials. Must perform side work as required.

DUTIES:

Greets guests at assigned tables, gives them menus, and pours water for them. When guests are ready, takes order. Places food order with kitchen personnel; portions and serves nonalcoholic beverage orders. Serves food orders immediately when prepared.

Watches every assigned table carefully to anticipate guests' needs; checks back with guests regularly for additional orders or requests. When guests complete courses, removes used cutlery and dishes. Presents menu so that guests may order dessert; presents check when guests have been served their final orders.

Places dishes and cutlery that have been removed from the guests' tables in proper bus trays.

Wipes table clean and dries it; decrumbs chair seats; resets table with placemats, cutlery wrapped in a napkin, and glassware; places condiments in proper place. In smoking section, cleans and replaces ashtray and matchbook.

Side work such as stocking condiments, filling salt and pepper shakers, and organizing side stands should be done as needed by server during shift. At end of shift all condiments should be completely full.

SPECIFICATIONS AND PREREQUISITES:

Requires a basic knowledge of composition of food and beverage items on menu as well as menu prices.

Requires familiarity with daily specials and proper table cleaning and setting procedures. Must be able to speak and write basic English.

SKILLS:

Must have the special skills necessary to make guests feel welcome, must have legible handwriting and basic mathematical skills, must be able to operate the electronic cash register, and must be able to give courteous, efficient service.

PHYSICAL:

Must be neat in appearance, possess a pleasant personality, have correct posture, and be able to carry loaded service trays.

problems. Excessive holding times can result in reduced product quality to the point where the food item becomes unservable. What could hurt a food and beverage operation more than an outbreak of food-borne illness because proper food-holding equipment is not available or staff are not trained to work safely and maintain cleanliness around foods?

Updated Job Descriptions. All staff members must clearly understand the exact duties of service personnel. Job descriptions listing required tasks, responsibilities, and other concerns for each position can accomplish this. Job descriptions are helpful management tools. Exhibit 7 shows a sample job description for a server in a coffee shop.

Food Appearance. Do not neglect food appearance. To some extent, guests eat with their eyes. Food and beverages should look attractive when served. Creative garnishes, how food is placed upon plates, and wiping plate rims to remove spilled sauce all influence appearance. The product's appearance and presentation influence the guests' perceptions of value and willingness to pay "top dollar" for menu items.

Expediters. Consider using a food expediter during busy serving times. An **expediter** helps communication between production and service personnel. This staff member controls the process of turning in orders and picking up food items. In some properties, the food server turns in the order to the expediter, who enters the order into a time recorder to monitor production times. In other operations, the expediter manages the orders generated by a remote printer. The expediter also resolves disputes about when the order came up and calls out or gives order information to cooks or servers. The expediter can coordinate order pickups to help ensure that the entire order is ready at the same time and that the server picks up the complete order as soon as it is ready. The expediter may also check portion size and appearance, ensure that all items on the server's tray have been entered into the revenue control system, and verify the prices of items on manual guest checks. However, even when an expediter is used, the executive chef or kitchen manager still should have control over and responsibility for the quality and appearance of all food items served.

Food Checkers. Historically, some properties have used a food checker to help control product quality and cost. This staff member examines each tray before it leaves the pickup area. Frequently, food servers must pass the checker's station on the way to the dining room. In addition to reviewing plates for appearance, portion size, and related concerns, the checker also plays an important role in the operation's revenue control system. Depending on the system, the checker may collect a copy of the guest check and compare items on the check with those on the plate. Service personnel may give payments collected from the guests to the checker, who confirms that the amounts are correct.

In today's cost-conscious food and beverage operation, this position is being phased out. Electronic register control systems are helping to reduce problems. Remote printers help to resolve collisions between production and service staff. In addition, both production and service staff are being better trained to note accuracy of food orders.

Computerized Precheck Systems

An effective way to achieve control over the production-to-service link is through the use of a computerized precheck system.[3] Precheck systems are composed of both hardware and software aimed at operational efficiency through sound internal control. Precheck software usually resides in an electronic cash register (ECR) or point-of-sale (POS) terminal that is connected to local and remote printers. These connections form a communication network between production work areas and service stations. Basically, the server enters an order through a precheck terminal which, in turn, relays the recorded items to the proper workstation for preparation.

Computerized precheck systems ensure that no food or beverage items are produced unless they have first been recorded (accounted for) in a precheck file. The elimination of actual orders being physically given to kitchen personnel or bartenders helps assure management that production will not begin without a unit sale being posted. Some automated systems enable managers to randomly review guest checks while they are being processed. This helps managers to verify that items ordered are in fact being served and that revenues from their sale will be collected.

ECR/POS Technology

Electronic cash registers and point-of-sale terminals are the basic hardware components of food service computer systems. An **electronic cash register** is an independent (standalone) computer system. This means that all of the register's required hardware components are located in the same unit. The register's keyboard serves as an input device; the operator display unit provides output; and the storage (memory) unit and central processor are located within the terminal housing. Therefore, an ECR is a complete computer that need not be connected to any other device in order to operate.

A **point-of-sale terminal**, on the other hand, contains its own input/output units and may even possess a small storage (memory) capacity but does not contain its own central processing unit. In order for POS transactions to be processed, the terminal must be connected to a central processing unit that is located outside the terminal's housing. Since the central processing unit is the most expensive component of a computer system, many food service properties reduce the cost of automation by interfacing several POS terminals conveniently located throughout the restaurant and lounge areas to one large central processing unit.

Because ECR or POS devices are generally sold as modular units, everything but the basic terminal is considered optional equipment. The cash drawer is no exception. Management may choose not to have a cash drawer at all, or to have up to four cash drawers connected to a single register. Multiple cash drawers may enhance management's cash control system when several cashiers work at the same register during the same shift. Each cashier can be assigned a separate cash drawer so that, at the end of the shift, cash drawer receipts can be individually accounted for.

A terminal without a cash drawer is commonly referred to as a precheck terminal. Precheck terminals are used to enter orders, not to settle accounts. For example, a server can use a precheck terminal located in the dining room to relay orders to the appropriate kitchen and bar production areas but generally cannot use this device for guest check settlement. An ECR/POS device with a cash drawer is commonly referred to as a cashier terminal. This device can normally handle both prechecking and cashiering functions.

In addition to ECRs and/or POS terminals, food service computer systems generally require hardware components such as:

- Order entry devices

- Display units

- Printers or video display units

Order Entry Devices

Order entry devices include keyboards, touch-screen terminals, hand-held terminals, and magnetic strip readers. The most common order entry device has been the keyboard, but touch-screen terminals are becoming increasingly popular.

Two primary types of keyboard surfaces are micro-motion and reed style. The micro-motion design is characterized by a flat, spill-resistant mask. Reed styling, on the other hand, involves raised key construction. Both keyboard designs are usually capable of supporting interchangeable menu boards.

A menu board overlays the keyboard surface and identifies the function performed by each key during a specific meal period. Different types of keyboard keys identified by a menu board include:

- Preset keys

- Price look-up keys

- Modifier keys

- Function keys

- Settlement keys

- Numeric keypad

A preset key is programmed to access the price, descriptor, department code, tax, and inventory status for a specific menu item. Automatic menu pricing makes faster guest service possible and eliminates price and tax errors by servers during busy meal periods. The term "descriptor" refers to the abbreviated description of a menu item, such as "SHRMPCKT" for shrimp cocktail or "PRIME" for prime rib. A department code refers to the menu category to which the preset item belongs. Typical department codes are appetizer, entrée, dessert, and so on.

Once a preset key is pressed, descriptions of the item and its price are retrieved from the system's memory and appear on the operator's display unit. This data may also be relayed (along with preparation instructions) to the appropriate production station or printed on a guest check. In addition, the sales represented by this transaction are retained for revenue reporting and for tracking inventory levels. Sales data of individual items are important for guest check totaling as well as for producing management reports.

Because terminals generally have a limited number of preset keys, price look-up keys are used to supplement preset keys. Price look-up keys operate similarly to preset keys, except that they require the user to identify a menu item by its reference code number (up to five digits) rather than by its name or descriptor. For example, if a server wants to record the sale of a cheeseburger and there is no preset key for that item, the server must enter the code number for cheeseburgers

Sample menu keyboard. (Courtesy of Validec, Inc., San Carlos, California)

(706, for example) and press the price look-up key. Once activated, price look-up keys perform the same functions as preset keys.

Modifier keys allow servers to relay preparation instructions (such as rare, medium, or well-done for a steak) to remote workstation printers or video display screens located in food production areas. Typically, a server enters the item ordered and then presses the appropriate preparation modifier key.

Modifier keys can also be used to legitimately alter menu item prices. For example, modifier keys may be useful to a restaurant that sells house wine by the carafe and half-carafe. Instead of tying up two preset keys (one for carafe, the other for half-carafe), a single preset key can be designated for house wine by the carafe and a modifier key can be programmed as a half-portion modifier. When a half-carafe is sold, the server simply presses both the carafe preset key and half-portion modifier key to register a half-carafe sale. The system adds the price of a half-carafe to its running total of wine revenues. In addition, the system adjusts its perpetual inventory records accordingly.

While preset and price look-up keys are used for order entry, function keys assist the operator in processing transactions. Sample function keys are: clear, discount, void, and no-sale. These keys are important for error correction (clear

Exhibit 8   Touch-Screen Terminal Activated by Touch or Light Pen

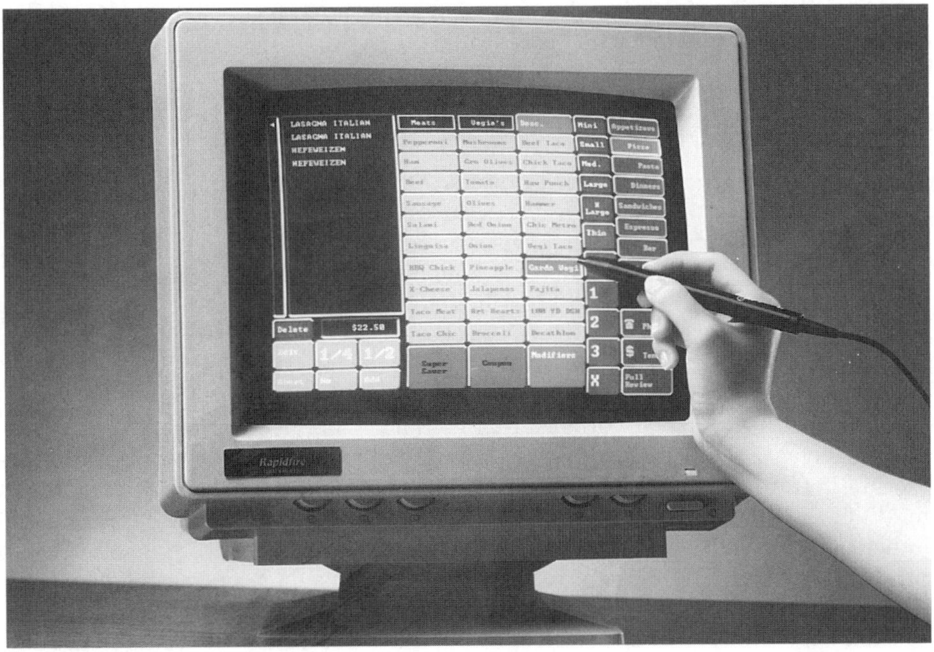

Source: RapidFire Solutions, Hillsboro, Oregon.

and void), legitimate price alteration (discount), and proper cash handling (no-sale).

Settlement keys are used to record the methods by which accounts are settled: cash, credit card, house account, charge transfer to the guest's folio (in a hotel), or other payment method.

The keys in the numeric keypad are used to ring up menu items by price, access price look-up data by menu item code number, access open guest check accounts by serial number, and perform other data entry operations. For example, if the register or terminal is used to record and store payroll data, the numeric keypad can be used to enter employee identification numbers as employees begin and end their work shifts. The numeric keypad may also be used to enter report codes that initiate the production of management reports.

Touch-Screen Terminals. Touch-screen terminals simplify data entry procedures and are increasingly used in place of traditional keyboards. A special microprocessor within the terminal is programmed to display data on areas of the screen that are sensitive to touch. Touching one of the sensitized areas produces an electronic charge, which is translated into signals processed by the terminal in much the same way that a terminal would process signals from a conventional keyboard (see Exhibit 8). This signal also instructs the microprocessor to display the next screen.[4]

Terminal designs vary. Flat touch-screen terminals are available that require significantly less space than the traditional POS terminals that they replace. Flat screens measure only three and one-half inches thick and can be mounted from walls, ceilings, counters, or shelving units. The design offers restaurants flexibility in determining where to locate the terminals.

Touch-Screens and POS Systems. Touch-sensitive screens simplify data entry and may be used in place of traditional cathode ray tube (CRT) screens and POS keyboards. Price look-up keys (PLUs) must often be used to enter orders because many systems maintain a limited number of preset keys. Using PLUs generally requires additional order-entry procedures related to product code numbers assigned to menu items. In some cases, servers memorize these codes, or management tapes a list of the code numbers at keyboard terminals. Most touch-screen terminals eliminate the need for PLUs altogether, decreasing the time necessary to enter orders into the system.

Touch-screen terminals are also interactive. The system provides on-screen prompts guiding servers through order-entry or settlement procedures. For example, after a server enters an order for a menu item that needs preparation instructions (such as a New York strip steak), the screen shifts to display the appropriate modifiers (rare, medium rare, medium, medium well done, well done). Forced modifiers will not allow the user to proceed with order entry until a response is indicated. This eliminates the possibility of servers sending incomplete orders to production areas. The interactive nature of these systems decreases the time it takes to train new employees. Touch-screen terminals may also be equipped with special magnetic strip reader devices that allow servers and managers to use bar-coded company identification cards to sign in and out of the system. One type of system ensures that immediately after employees sign into the system, a message screen is displayed. This message screen enables management to deliver different messages to different categories of employees, or to individual employees as well. For example, employees with job codes corresponding to food servers might receive messages about daily specials and prices. Or an individual employee might receive a message from a supervisor about work schedule changes. Since employees must touch the message screen to complete sign-in procedures, management is assured that employees have received their messages.

Bar Code Terminals. Bar code terminals also simplify data entry procedures and may be used in place of traditional keyboards or touch-screen terminals. With this system, servers use hand-held, penlike bar code readers to enter orders at service station terminals from a laminated bar-coded menu. Bar code terminals have not gained popularity and are in much less frequent use than their touch-screen terminal counterparts.

Hand-Held Server Computers. Hand-held server computers are remote order entry devices that may eventually replace traditional server order pads and precheck terminals.

Hand-held server computers, also referred to as portable server terminals, perform most of the functions of a precheck terminal and enable servers to enter orders at tableside. This technology can be a major advantage for large establishments with long distances between server stations and outdoor dining areas or with very busy lounges where it is difficult to reach a precheck terminal. In any

Hand held terminals can be used to ring cash bar transactions, to open and retrieve guest checks, and to print. The user interface on the touch screen of the hand held unit is almost identical to that of the fixed work station, simplifying training. (Courtesy of Comtrex Systems Corporation, Moorestown, New Jersey)

establishment, service is faster during peak business periods when servers do not have to walk to kitchen or bar areas to place orders, or wait in line to use a precheck terminal. In some cases, appetizers and drinks may be ready to serve just seconds after a server has finished entering the orders and has left the guest's table.

A two-way communications capability allows a server to deliver special instructions to production areas—"no salt" or "medium rare," for example—when keying in the order. Production employees can also communicate with the server. For example, they can immediately alert a server if an item is out of stock. Typically, when an order is ready for pickup, a production employee can alert the server by a signal sent to the server's hand-held computer.

Because all items must be entered through the server's hand-held unit, the common problem of coffee and/or desserts being inadvertently left off guest checks can be reduced. In addition, some units enable managers to monitor service through their own hand-held devices.

Magnetic Strip Readers. A **magnetic strip reader** is a device that connects to a cashier terminal. These devices do not replace keyboards, touch-screen terminals, or hand-held terminals. Instead, they extend the capabilities of these components. Magnetic strip readers are capable of collecting data stored on a magnetized film strip typically located on the back of a credit card or house account card. Credit card transactions can be handled directly with the ECR/POS system, thus eliminating the need for special processing.

Display Units

In addition to an order entry device, ECRs and POS terminals contain an operator display unit (a monitor) enabling the user to review and edit entries. An operator display unit helps the user check transactions in progress and respond to prompts necessary for carrying out various system procedures.

Some ECRs and POS terminals with cash drawers may also support a customer display unit. In food service operations where guests view settlement transactions, serious consideration should be given to the use of a customer display unit. Also, operators who elect not to use customer displays forgo an excellent method of tracking cashier and bartender recordings. A cashier may charge a guest for a $3.45 purchase and make change from a $10 bill. How does one prove that $3.45 was actually rung? Suppose the cashier only rung $.45 and later removed and pocketed $3.00 from the cash drawer? How can this act be detected and corrected? By after-the-fact audit trails, perhaps. However, a display of settlement amounts is a simple means of control at the point of order entry.

Video display units are used in many kitchens to enable order takers to more effectively communicate with preparation personnel. Most orders are entered by the server directly into the POS system for transfer to remote video display units in applicable production areas.

Printers

Output devices include guest check, workstation, and receipt printers. **Guest check printers** are standard ECR/POS output devices. Many guest check printers have **automatic form number reader** capability to facilitate order entry procedures. To access a guest check account, a server simply places the guest check into the terminal's automatic form number reader unit. A bar code printed on the check contains the check's serial number in a machine-readable format and provides rapid access to the correct guest check account.

Overprinting items and amounts on guest checks is a problem with some printers. Usually, servers must manually align the printer's ribbon with the next blank printing line on the guest check. If the alignment is not correct, the guest check appears disorganized and messy with items and amounts printed over one another or with large gaps between lines of print.

Printers with **automatic slip feed** capability prevent overprinting by retaining the number of the last line printed for each open guest check. The server simply aligns the top edge of the guest check with the top edge of the printer's slot and the terminal automatically moves the check to the next available printing line and prints the order entry data. Because guest checks are placed within the printer's slot the same way every time, servers may spend less time fussing with the guest check and more time meeting the needs of their guests.

Workstation printers are usually placed at kitchen preparation areas and service bars. As orders are entered at precheck or cashier terminals, they are also sent to a designated remote workstation printer to initiate production. This

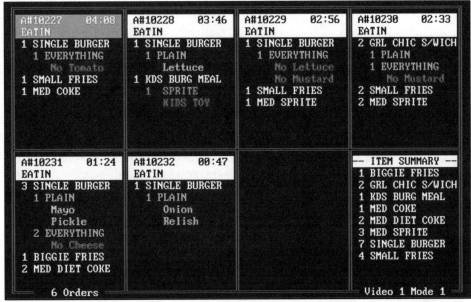

```
┌─────────────────┬─────────────────┬─────────────────┬─────────────────┐
│ A#10227   04:08 │ A#10228   03:46 │ A#10229   02:56 │ A#10230   02:33 │
│ EATIN           │ EATIN           │ EATIN           │ EATIN           │
│ 1 SINGLE BURGER │ 1 SINGLE BURGER │ 1 SINGLE BURGER │ 2 GRL CHIC S/WICH│
│   1 EVERYTHING  │   1 PLAIN       │   1 EVERYTHING  │   1 PLAIN       │
│     No Tomato   │     Lettuce     │     No Lettuce  │   1 EVERYTHING  │
│ 1 SMALL FRIES   │ 1 KDS BURG MEAL │     No Mustard  │     No Mustard  │
│ 1 MED COKE      │   1  SPRITE     │ 1 SMALL FRIES   │ 2 SMALL FRIES   │
│                 │     KIDS TOY    │ 1 MED SPRITE    │ 2 MED SPRITE    │
├─────────────────┼─────────────────┼─────────────────┼─────────────────┤
│ A#10231   01:24 │ A#10232   00:47 │                 │ -- ITEM SUMMARY --│
│ EATIN           │ EATIN           │                 │ 1 BIGGIE FRIES  │
│ 3 SINGLE BURGER │ 1 SINGLE BURGER │                 │ 2 GRL CHIC S/WICH│
│   1 PLAIN       │   1 PLAIN       │                 │ 1 KDS BURG MEAL │
│     Mayo        │     Onion       │                 │ 1 MED COKE      │
│     Pickle      │     Relish      │                 │ 2 MED DIET COKE │
│   2 EVERYTHING  │                 │                 │ 3 MED SPRITE    │
│     No Cheese   │                 │                 │ 7 SINGLE BURGER │
│ 1 BIGGIE FRIES  │                 │                 │ 4 SMALL FRIES   │
│ 2 MED DIET COKE │                 │                 │                 │
│      6 Orders   │                 │                 │  Video 1 Mode 1 │
└─────────────────┴─────────────────┴─────────────────┴─────────────────┘
```

Remote video systems expedite quick communication between order takers and preparation areas, improving customer service. This close-up of a video display unit shows six orders being sent to the kitchen without using any paper. (Courtesy of Comtrex Systems Corporation, Moorestown, New Jersey)

communication system enables servers to spend more time meeting the needs of guests while significantly reducing traffic in kitchen and bar areas.

If the need for hard copy output in production areas is not critical to an operation's internal control system, video display units (kitchen monitors) may be viable alternatives to workstation printers. Because these units are able to display several orders on a single screen, kitchen employees do not have to handle numerous pieces of paper. An accompanying cursor control keypad enables kitchen employees to easily review previously submitted orders.

Receipt printers produce hard copies on thin, narrow register tape. Although the usefulness of receipt printers is somewhat limited, these devices may help control the production of menu items that are not prepared in departments receiving orders through workstation printers.

For example, when servers prepare or pick up desserts for their guests and the pantry area is not equipped with a workstation printer, desserts could be served without ever having been entered into the POS system. When this happens, it is also possible that desserts could be served without ever being posted to guest checks. This situation can be avoided by using a receipt printer. Servers preparing desserts can be required to deliver a receipt tape to the dessert pantry area as proof that the desserts are properly posted to guest checks for eventual settlement. This procedure enhances management's internal control by ensuring that a record of every menu item served is stored somewhere in the computer system.

Automated Beverage Control Systems

Automated beverage control systems may enhance production and service capabilities while improving accounting and operational controls. A beverage control unit is the brain of an automated system. This control unit is generally located close to a beverage storage area and is primarily responsible for regulating all essential mechanisms within the system. The unit communicates requests from order entry terminals to the system's delivery network and directs the flow of beverages from a storage area to a dispensing unit.

Automated beverage control systems may use different kinds of sensing devices to increase operational controls within the system. Three common sensing devices are glass sensors, guest check sensors, and empty bottle sensors. A glass sensor is an electronic mechanism located in a bar dispensing unit that will not permit liquid to flow from the dispensing unit unless there is a glass positioned below the dispensing head to catch the liquid. Guest check sensors prevent the system from fulfilling beverage orders unless they are first recorded on a guest check or entered into the sales information system. When a server or bartender places a beverage order whose ingredients are out of stock, an empty bottle sensor relays a signal to the order entry device.

Sophisticated systems are able to record data input through order entry devices, transport beverage ingredients through a controlled delivery network, dispense ingredients for ordered items, and track important service and sales data that can be used to produce various reports for use by management. The following sections examine the basic components of an automated beverage control system: an order entry device, a delivery network, and dispensing units.

Order Entry Devices

In an automated beverage control system, the primary function of an order entry device is to initiate activities involved with recording, producing, and pricing beverage items requested by guests. There are two basic order entry devices: a group of preset buttons located on a dispensing unit, and keyboard units.

A group of preset buttons on a dispensing unit is the most popular order entry device. These devices may result in lower system costs because the dispensing unit serves as both an order taker and a delivery unit. However, since dispensing units will have a limited number of preset buttons, the number of beverage items under the control of the automated beverage system also is limited.

Keyboard units function like precheck terminals; beverage dispensing is performed by a separate piece of hardware. Because they support a full range of keys (including preset keys, price look-up keys, and modifier keys), keyboard units place a large number of beverage items under the control of the automated system. Keyboard units are most effective when equipped with a guest check printer that has an automatic form number reader and automatic slip feed capabilities.

Delivery Network

An automated beverage control system relies on a delivery network to transport beverage item ingredients from storage areas to dispensing units. Exhibit 9

Exhibit 9   Delivery Network of an Automated Beverage Control System

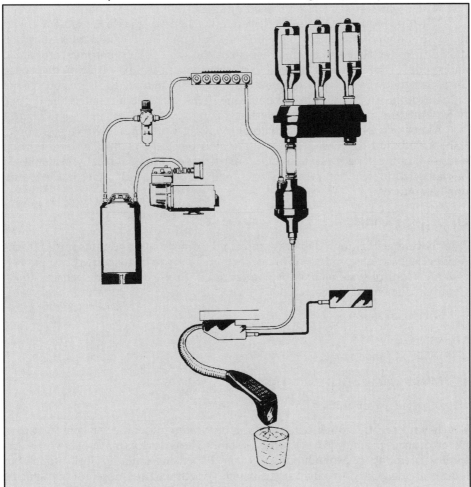

Source: Berg Company, a division of DEC International, Inc., Madison, Wisconsin.

provides an overview of one kind of delivery network. The delivery network must be a closed system capable of regulating temperature and pressure conditions at various locations and stages of delivery. To maintain proper temperature conditions, the delivery network typically uses a cooling subsystem that controls such mechanisms as cold plates, cold boxes, and/or cold storage rooms.

Most automated beverage control systems can deliver beverage ingredients by controlling pressure sources such as gravity, compressed air, carbon dioxide, and nitrous oxide. Gravity and compressed air are used for delivering liquor, nitrogen or nitrous oxide for wine, compressed air for beer, and a carbon dioxide regulator for post-mixes. A post-mix soft drink dispenser combines syrup and carbonated water together at the dispenser instead of storing, transporting, and distributing the soft drink as a finished product.

The type of pressure source selected to transport a specific ingredient affects the taste and wholesomeness of the finished beverage item. For example, if carbon dioxide were attached to a wine dispenser, the wine would become carbonated and spoiled; if compressed air were connected to a post-mix soft drink dispenser, the finished beverage item would not have any carbonation. Pressure sources not only affect the quality of finished beverage items, but may also affect the timing, flow of mixture, portion size, and desired foaming.

Almost any type of liquor and accompanying liquor ingredient can be stored, transported, and dispensed by an automated beverage control system. Portion sizes of liquor can be controlled with remarkable accuracy. Typically, systems can be calibrated to maintain portion sizes ranging from one-half ounce to three-and-one-half ounces.

Dispensing Units

After beverage item ingredients are removed from storage and transported by the delivery network to production areas, they are ready to be dispensed. Automated beverage control systems may be configured with a variety of dispensing units. Common dispensing units include:

- Touch-bar faucet
- Console faucet
- Hose-and-gun device
- Mini-tower pedestal
- Bundled tower unit

Touch-Bar Faucet. A **touch-bar faucet** can be located under the bar, behind the bar, on top of an ice machine, or on a pedestal stand. These devices may not have the versatility, flexibility, or expandability of other dispensing units. Typically, touch-bar faucets are dedicated to only a single beverage type and are preset for one specific portion size output per push on the bar lever.. To obtain a double shot of bourbon the bartender may have to push twice on the bar lever.

Console Faucet. Console faucet dispensing units are similar to touch-bar faucet devices in that they can be located in almost any part of the bar area. In addition, these units may be located up to 300 feet from beverage storage areas. Unlike touch-bar faucet devices, however, console faucet units are able to dispense various beverages in a number of portion sizes. Using buttons located above the faucet unit, a bartender can trigger up to four different portion sizes from the same faucet head. An optional feature of this kind of dispensing device is a double-hose faucet unit that can transport large quantities of liquids in short amounts of time.

Hose-and-Gun Device. The **hose-and-gun device** has traditionally been a popular dispensing unit. Control buttons on the handle of the gun can be connected by hoses to liquors, carbonated beverages, water, and/or wine tanks. These types of dispensers can be installed anywhere along the bar and are frequently included as standard dispensing equipment on portable bars and at service bar locations. Depressing a control button normally produces a premeasured flow of the desired beverage. The number of beverage items under the control of a hose-and-gun dispensing unit is limited to the number of control buttons the device supports. Some units offer the bartender up to 16 buttons for product dispensing.

Mini-Tower Pedestal. The **mini-tower pedestal** dispensing unit combines the portion-size capabilities of console faucet units with the button selection technique of hose-and-gun devices. In addition, the mini-tower concept offers increased control of bar operations. In order for a beverage to be dispensed, the mini-tower unit requires that a button be pressed and a glass-sensing device requires that a glass is placed directly under the dispensing head. This automated dispensing unit has been popular for dispensing beverage items that need no additional ingredients prior to service, such as wine and beer. A mini-tower unit can also be located on a wall, ice machine, or pedestal base in the bar area.

Bundled Tower Unit. The most sophisticated and flexible dispensing unit is the **bundled tower unit**, also referred to as a tube tower unit. The bundled tower unit is designed to dispense a variety of beverage items. Beverage orders must be entered on a separate piece of hardware, not on the tower unit. Bundled tower units may support more than 110 beverage products and contain a glass-sensing element. Each liquor has its own line to the tower unit and a variety of pressurized systems can be used to enhance delivery from storage areas. While other units sequentially dispense beverage item ingredients, the bundled tower unit simultaneously dispenses all ingredients required for a specific beverage item—bar servers merely garnish the finished product. This dispensing unit can be located up to 300 feet from beverage storage areas.

Management Considerations

There are several advantages to be gained from using automated equipment, from unit sales and revenue control to faster drink preparation. Sales control is possible because the number of ounces sold and potential revenue are known. In fact, the need for manual beverage control systems, especially for revenue, is reduced with automated beverage production service equipment.

Bartender errors—spillage, over- or underpouring, and pricing—are eliminated or reduced. Also, it is more difficult for bartenders to "beat the system." Bartender supervision and the bartender's work are made easier. Training time is reduced, and turnover can be easier to manage.

Other advantages include faster drink preparation; the opportunity to use large bottles, often at a lower per-ounce cost; less liquor stored behind the bar; and fewer employees if drinks are prepared more quickly.

There are also disadvantages associated with automated equipment. Equipment malfunctions create crises. Supplies must be brought to the bar, a non-operative cash drawer must be used, and untrained bartenders must hand-pour drinks.

Also, costs of maintenance, operation, and repair may add to the already high capital purchase costs of automated beverage equipment.

When patrons see the equipment in use they may feel they are receiving a smaller portion or lower-quality drink than they ordered. This may affect both revenue and customer perception of value. Another disadvantage is that it is difficult to evaluate objectively the payback period and therefore the cost-effectiveness of the equipment. Also, many types of equipment still require experienced and trained bartenders to prepare drinks that cannot be produced by the system.

Along with the advantages and disadvantages of automated beverage equipment, there are other considerations, including:

- Guest expectations of quality and value must be met. For example, if guests believe that the equipment is impersonal or, worse, that it reduces portion size or quality, this may be a good reason not to install the equipment. On the other hand, these problems can be reduced or eliminated if the equipment is used only in non-public service bars.

- When determining cost implications, use data applicable to the specific property rather than statistics for an "average" operation supplied by the equipment manufacturer or dealer.

- Employee resistance must be dealt with effectively.

- Before purchasing an automated beverage system, predict what changes in the existing control systems will be required. The manager will have to revise control systems in light of the automated beverage equipment.

- Plan for physical changes that may be required. These include such things as installation of dispensing equipment and bottle dispensing racks, and running beverage lines to equipment locations.

- Establish an effective working relationship with the supplier/dealer as equipment is installed and employees are trained. Automated equipment needs routine maintenance and repair and will probably break down at times. When this happens, an effective supplier relationship is helpful.

Automated beverage equipment undergoes constant change and improvement. Managers must attempt to keep up with the state of the art. They must be aware of technological changes while remaining sensitive to the needs of their properties. With this knowledge, effective decisions can be made. And if it is found that automated beverage equipment is desirable, then managers will be able to select that system which is most compatible with the property's existing control system and other requirements.

Endnotes

1. Readers interested in a detailed explanation of forecasting techniques used in the hospitality industry should read Chapter 9 of Raymond S. Schmidgall's *Hospitality Industry Managerial Accounting*, 3d ed. (Lansing, Mich.: Educational Institute of the American Hotel & Lodging Association, 1995).

2. Readers interested in a more detailed discussion of food and beverage service procedures should read Ronald F. Cichy and Paul E. Wise's *Managing Service in Food and Beverage Operations,* 2d ed. (Lansing, Mich.: Educational Institute of the American Hotel & Lodging Association, 1999).

3. Materials in this chapter relating to computerized precheck systems and automated beverage systems are adapted from Michael L. Kasavana and John J. Cahill's *Managing Computers in the Hospitality Industry,* 3d ed. (Lansing, Mich.: Educational Institute of the American Hotel & Lodging Association, 1997).

4. Adapted from Michael Kasavana and John Cahill. *Managing Computers in the Hospitality Industry,* 3d ed. (Lansing, Mich.: Educational Institute of the American Hotel & Lodging Association, 1997): 166.

Key Terms

automatic form number reader—A feature of a guest check printer that facilitates order entry procedures; instead of a server manually inputting a guest check's serial number to access the account, a bar code imprinted on the guest check presents the check's serial number in a machine readable format.

automatic slip feed—A feature of a guest check printer that prevents overprinting of items and amounts on guest checks.

bar code terminal—Servers use hand-held, penlike bar code readers to enter orders at service station terminals from a laminated bar-coded menu.

bundled tower unit—Part of one kind of automated beverage control system; a dispensing unit designed to dispense a variety of beverage items; also referred to as a tube tower unit.

console faucet dispensing unit—Part of one kind of automated beverage control system which may be located up to 300 feet from beverage storage areas; able to dispense various beverages in a number of portion sizes. Using buttons located above the faucet unit, a bartender can trigger up to four different portion sizes from the same faucet head.

electronic cash register (ECR)—Normally defined as an independent (stand-alone) computer system. The ECR frame houses all the necessary components of a computer system: an input/output device, a central processing unit, and storage (memory) capacity.

empower—To delegate to or authorize employees to use their own discretion in meeting the guests' wants and needs.

expediter—A staff member who helps communication between production and service personnel by controlling the process of turning in orders and picking up food items.

guest check printer—Sometimes referred to as a slip printer; guest check printers may be equipped with automatic form number readers and/or possess automatic slip feed capabilities.

hand-held server computers—Also referred to as portable server terminals, they perform most of the functions of a precheck terminal and enable servers to enter orders at tableside.

hose-and-gun device—A beverage-dispensing unit that has control buttons connected by hoses to liquors, carbonated beverages, water, and/or wine tanks.

magnetic strip reader—A device connected to a cashier terminal that collects data stored on a magnetized film strip typically located on the back of a credit card.

mini-tower pedestal—A beverage-dispensing unit that combines the portion-size capabilities of console faucet units with the button selection technique of hose-and-gun devices.

point-of-sale terminal—Contains its own input/output component and may even possess a small storage (memory) capacity, but usually does not contain its own central processing unit.

production planning—Designing or determining food and beverage preparation requirements in advance of actual production.

public bar—A bar where bartenders directly serve drinks to guests.

receipt printers—A device that prints hard copies on thin, narrow register tape. It helps control the production of menu items that are not prepared in departments receiving orders through workstation printers.

service bar—A bar where bartenders provide drinks to servers who deliver them to guests.

time series analysis—A forecasting method that assigns more importance (weight) to recent occurrences (trends).

touch-bar faucet—A beverage-dispensing unit that is dedicated to only a single beverage type and is preset for one specific portion size output per push on the bar lever.

touch-screen terminal—A unit containing a special microprocessor within the terminal programmed to display data on areas of the screen that are sensitive to touch.

workstation printer—A unit usually placed at kitchen preparation areas and service bars that relays orders submitted at precheck or cashier terminals to production personnel.

 Review Questions ─────────────────────────

1. Why is it difficult to control food production and service procedures?
2. Why is the menu an important element in controlling food and beverage production?
3. Why must quality requirements be considered as food and beverage products are produced?
4. Why are standard recipes important? How do automated recipe management systems work?

5. What are some ways to control beverage production?

6. What is an expediter? Why would a food and beverage operation use an expediter?

7. How do computerized precheck systems enhance management's control of production and service areas?

8. What are the different order entry devices used by computerized precheck systems?

9. What functions are performed by modifier and numeric keys?

10. What control factors should management consider when automating bar operations?

 **Internet Sites** —————————————————————————————

For more information, visit the following Internet sites. Remember that Internet addresses can change without notice. If the site is no longer there, you can use a search engine to look for additional sites.

Associations

American Culinary Federation (ACF)
http://www.acfchefs.org

American Hotel & Lodging Association (AH&LA)
http://www.ahlaonline.org

American School Food Service Association (ASFSA)
http://www.asfsa.org

Club Managers Association of America (CMAA)
http://www.cmaa.org

The Educational Foundation of NRA
http://www.edfound.org

The Educational Institute of AH&LA
http://www.ei-ahla.org

Hospitality Financial and Technology Professionals
http://www.hftp.org

Institute of Food Technologies
http://www.ift.org

International Hotel and Restaurant Association
http://www.ih-ra.com

National Association of College and University Food Services
http://www.nacufs.org

National Restaurant Association (NRA)
http://www.restaurant.org

Food and Beverage Resources

Barmedia
http://www.barmedia.com

Becoming a Chef
http://pages.prodigy.com/NY/chef/chef.html

Berg Company
http://www.berg-controls.com/

Chef Net
http://www.chefnet.com

Club Management Online
http://www.club-mgmt.com/dining/index.html

Food Service
http://www.nal.usda.gov:8001/Safety/safe.html

Microbrewery and brewpub guilde
http://www.realbeer.com

Prepared Foods. Product development, ingredients, suppliers
http://www.preparedfoods.com

Foodservice Software

Adaco Services, Inc.
http://www.adacoservices.com

Casio
http://www.casio.com

CMS Hospitality
http://www.cmshosp.com.au

Computrition, Inc.
http://www.computrition.com

Comtrex Systems Corporation
http://www.comtrex.com

Comus Restaurant Systems
http://www.comus.com

Cost Guard
http://www.costguard.com

Culinary Software Services
http://www.culinarysoftware.com

Eatec Corporation
http://www.eatec.com

Guestware
http://www.guestware.com

Hotel and Restaurant Systems
http://www.hrs.ru/products/restaurants/enterprise_solution_software.html

Infogenesis
http://www.infogenesis.com/

Integrated Restaurant Software
http://www.rmstouch.com

MAI Systems Corporation
http://www.maisystems.com

Micros Systems, Inc.
http://www.micros.com

MSI Solutions
http://www.msisolutions.com

National Cash Register Company
http://www.ncr.com/index2.htm

Posera
http://www.posera.com

Squirrel Systems
http://www.squirrelsystems.com/index.html

Sulcus Computer Corporation
http://www2.sulcus.nl

Management Companies

ARAMARK
http://www.aramark.com

Bon Appétit Management Company
http://www.bamco.com

Compass Group
http://www.compass-na.com

Sodexho Marriott
http://www.sodexhomarriott.com

The Wood Company
http://www.woodco.com

Publications—Online and Printed

Club Management Magazine
http://www.club-mgmt.com

Lodging Hospitality Online
http://www.lhonline.com

Electronic Gourmet Guide
http://www.foodwine.com

Lodging News, journal of the American
Hotel & Lodging Association
http://www.ei-ahla.org/webs/
lodging/index.html

Food and Hospitality Magazine
http://www.foodserviceworld.com

Nation's Restaurant News
http://www.nrn.com

Food Management
http://www.foodservicesearch.com

On the Rail—News for Food
Professionals
http://www.ontherail.com

Food Network: CyberKitchen
http://www.foodtv.com

Food Processing: The Magazine of
Strategy, Technology and Trends
http://www.foodprocessing.com

Restaurants and Institutions magazine
http://www.rimag.com

Internet Food Channel
http://www.foodchannel.com

Restaurant Business, Food Service, and
ID magazines
http://www.foodservicetoday.com

International Hotel and Restaurant
Association journal
www.hotelsmag.com

Restaurant Hospitality
www.foodservicesearch.com

International Journal of Hospitality
Management
http://www.mcb.co.uk/ijchm.htm

Restaurants and Institutions
http://www.rimag.com

Journal of Hospitality Financial
Management
http://hrta.fnr.umass.edu/sheel/
ahfme/jhfm/aboutjhfm.html

Restaurants USA, publication of
National Restaurant Association
http://www.restaurant.org/rusa

Wine Business Monthly
http://smartwine.com

Lodging Food and Beverage
http://www.lodgingnews.com/
lodgingfnb/

World Hospitality, management
magazine for hotel executives.
http://www.worldhospitality.com

 **Problems**

Problem 1

The following data recaps the number of portions of each menu item sold on Friday evening for the past five weeks:

	Week 1	Week 2	Week 3	Week 4	Week 5 Last Friday
Chicken	71	60	55	59	90
Pork Chops	60	43	57	61	81
Prime Rib	90	71	51	59	107
Lobster	82	63	75	80	91
Veal Cutlet	79	40	68	79	90
	382	277	306	338	459

a) What is the percentage of total items sold for each menu item averaged over the past five Fridays?

b) The manager notes that sales on the second Friday were lower than normal because of a weather problem. Sales on the last Friday were higher than normal because of an in-town sporting event. He believes the number of menu items to be sold this Friday will be about "average"; that is, they will exclude the one lower-than-normal Friday and one higher-than-normal Friday.

1. What is the total number of entrees expected to be served this Friday?

2. Assume also that the manager believes sales of each entrée this Friday will approximate those on the three "average" Fridays over the past three weeks; what is the expected sales of each entrée?

3. The manager is introducing entertainment during the dinner shift. This is expected to generate 20 additional sales of each menu item each Friday evening. Assuming that these additional guests select entrees in the same proportion as those over the last three "average" Fridays, what is the expected number of entrees to be sold?

Problem 2

What is the percentage of total sales represented by each of the following menu items during "average" Friday and Saturday evenings at the Green Pastures Restaurant?

Menu Item	Total Sales (Portions)	Percentage of Total Sales
Chicken	175	
Beef Stew	137	
Pork Chops	112	
Vegetarian Dinner	62	
Veal Cutlets	98	
Filet Mignon	128	

Problem 3

The manager of the Green Pastures Restaurant is expecting a busy weekend; the local college is celebrating homecoming with a football game against its big rival. The expected number of guests on Friday and Saturday night is, respectively, 950 and 1100 guests. Assuming the percentage of total sales remains tha same as in Problem 2, what is the total number of each menu item which is expected to be sold over the two-night period?

Problem 4

What is the total increase in expected meals to be served on Friday and Saturday nights at the Green Pastures Restaurant because of the college homecoming celebration?

Part IV

Using Information from the Control System

Chapter 9 Outline

Actual Food and Beverage Costs: Monthly
   Calculations
     Cost of Sales: The Basic Calculation
     Sources of Information for Basic Cost
       of Sales
     Calculating Value of Inventory
     Adjustments to Basic Cost of Sales
Actual Food Cost: Daily Calculations
     Components of Daily Food Cost
     Sources of Actual Daily Food Cost
       Information
     Calculating Actual Daily Food Cost
Computerized Pre/Postcosting Software
     Precost Analysis
     Postcost Analysis
Actual Beverage Cost: Daily Calculations
     Principles for Calculating Actual Daily
       Beverage Cost
     Procedures for Calculating Daily
       Beverage Cost
     Averaging Shift Costs
     Bartender Performance Review

Competencies

1. Calculate the basic monthly cost of
   sales for food and beverages.
   (pp. 289–294)

2. Use the FIFO method to calculate the
   value of products in inventory.
   (p. 295)

3. Use the LIFO method to calculate the
   value of products in inventory.
   (p. 296)

4. Use the weighted average method to
   calculate the value of products in
   inventory. (pp. 296–297)

5. Identify adjustments used to calculate
   a monthly net cost of sales for food
   and beverages. (pp. 298–301)

6. Identify factors that affect daily
   calculations of actual food and
   beverage costs. (pp. 301–306)

9

Calculating Actual Food and Beverage Costs

$\mathbf{A}$FTER A FOOD AND BEVERAGE operation has developed standards, constructed the operating budget, and designed effective control procedures, the next task in the control cycle is to assess the actual operating results. A necessary part of this process is calculating the actual food and beverage costs incurred to generate revenues during a specified period of time. This chapter discusses procedures for accomplishing these calculations.

To ensure that actual operating costs are comparable to standard or planned costs, several general rules must be followed. First, actual costs must be stated in the same manner as standard costs. This makes it easier to analyze the differences between them. For example, if standard food costs are stated as a specified percentage of revenues, then actual food costs must also be developed as a percentage of revenues. It is not possible—or at least it is very difficult—to compare a standard food cost expressed as a percentage with an actual food cost expressed in dollars.

A second rule for relating actual costs to standard costs is that both actual cost calculations and standard cost estimates must cover the same meal periods. The reason for this rule is the same as for the first—to make actual and standard costs truly comparable. For example, if standard costs are expressed as a specified percentage of revenue across all meal periods, actual costs should not be determined separately for breakfast, lunch, and dinner.

Third, all factors used to estimate standard costs must be included in the calculation of actual costs. For example, if food transfers, beverage transfers, employee meals, and complimentary meals are excluded from standard cost estimates, then they must also be excluded from the assessment of actual costs.

Finally, actual costs must be assessed on a timely basis. Decision makers must know as soon as possible if (and to what extent) actual costs differ from planned standard costs.

Clearly, calculations of actual costs must be accurate. Good decisions cannot be based on inaccurate cost information. Accuracy, however, is in part a function of the amount of time spent collecting the information. If the development of extremely accurate cost information requires an excessive amount of time, then the assessment procedures are not practical and, most likely, will not be done.

There is a cost-benefit consideration here. Managers must be able to justify the time they spend generating increasingly more accurate information. A decision needs to be made about how much time should be spent collecting accounting information used to develop financial statements. Information collected during this process generally becomes the basis for assessing actual costs.

Actual Food and Beverage Costs: Monthly Calculations

Calculations of **actual food and beverage costs** are based on the same set of information used to develop financial operating statements. Generally, financial statements for food and beverage operations are developed monthly. Occasionally, some properties may even out the days in the months by establishing 13 four-week accounting cycles containing 28 days each within the fiscal year. At any rate, all operations need financial information covering a period of several weeks, such as a month, for accounting purposes.

A strict accounting definition of the concept of "cost of sales" is beyond the scope of our discussion and can introduce many complications. For our purposes in this chapter, the following definition will be used: **cost of sales** is the food or beverage cost incurred to produce all food or beverage items sold during the accounting period.

Generally, the income statement will express cost of sales as total dollars and, frequently, as a percentage of revenue (sales income). The National Restaurant Association's *Uniform System of Accounts for Restaurants* includes a sample income statement (see Exhibit 1).[1] Note that total revenue (sales) is food revenue plus beverage revenue:

Food Revenue + Beverage Revenue = Total Food and Beverage Revenue

$1,030,000 + $257,500 = $1,287,500

To calculate the percentage of total revenue by revenue center, divide revenue for the revenue center by total food and beverage revenue and multiply by 100.

$$\frac{\text{Food Revenue}}{\text{Total Food and Beverage Revenue}} \times 100 = \text{Percentage of Revenue (Food)}$$

$$\frac{\$1,030,000}{\$1,287,500} \times 100 = 80\%$$

In this example, 80 percent of all revenue accrued from the food operations, while 20 percent (100 percent − 80 percent) was generated by the beverage operation.

To calculate the cost percentage for each food or beverage revenue source, divide the cost of sales by revenue and multiply by 100.

$$\frac{\text{Cost of Sales (Food)}}{\text{Food Revenue}} \times 100 = \text{Food Cost Percentage}$$

$$\frac{\$360,500}{\$1,030,000} \times 100 = 35.0\%$$

Exhibit 1   Sample Income Statement

Statement of Income for Full Service Restaurant Serving Food and Beverages

	Amount	Percentages*
SALES		
Food	$ 1,030,000	80%
Beverage	257,500	20
Total Sales	1,287,500	100
COST OF SALES		
Food	360,500	35
Beverage	68,240	27
Total Cost of Sales	428,740	33
GROSS PROFIT		
Food	669,500	65
Beverage	189,260	73
Total Gross Profit	858,760	67
OPERATING EXPENSES		
Salaries and Wages	386,250	30%
Employee Benefits	51,500	4
Direct Operating Expenses	77,250	6
Music and Entertainment	1,300	00.1
Marketing	25,750	2
Utility Services	38,600	3
Repairs and Maintenance	25,800	2
Occupancy	90,200	7
Depreciation	25,500	2
General and Administrative	39,000	3
Other Income	(6,440)	00.5
Total Operating Expenses	$ 754,710	59
OPERATING INCOME	104,050	10
INTEREST	6,500	00.5
INCOME BEFORE INCOME TAXES	$ 97,550	8%

All ratios are calculated as a percentage of total sales except food and beverage costs, which are based on their respective sales.

Source: *Uniform System of Accounts for Restaurants,* 7th rev. ed. (Washington, D.C.: National Restaurant Association, 1996).

$$\frac{\text{Cost of Sales (Beverage)}}{\text{Beverage Revenue}} \times 100 = \text{Beverage Cost Percentage}$$

$$\frac{\$68,240}{\$257,500} \times 100 = 27.0\% \text{ (rounded)}$$

Therefore, in this example, 35 percent of food revenue was used to purchase food products necessary to generate the food revenue, and 27 percent of beverage revenue was used to purchase beverage products necessary to generate the beverage revenue.

The *Uniform System of Accounts for the Lodging Industry* recommends a format (Exhibit 2) that a food department in a lodging property can use to gain relevant financial information.[2] Notice that:

- The form does not include beverage data. Another schedule is used to identify the financial status of the beverage operation.

- Adjustments to the cost of food are made (these are discussed later in this chapter), and allowable expenses must be allocated between the food department and other applicable departments.

These examples illustrate the kind of information food and beverage managers use to calculate actual food and beverage costs and to state them in ways comparable to standard cost assessments.

Cost of Sales: The Basic Calculation

The basic monthly cost of sales for food and beverages is calculated as follows:

Cost of Sales = Beginning Inventory + Purchases − Ending Inventory

For example, assume:

	Food	Beverage
Beginning Inventory	$ 124,500	$ 36,800
Purchases	+ 85,000	+ 29,500
Ending Inventory	− 112,250	− 27,500
Cost of Sales	$ 97,250	$ 38,800

The food or beverage cost percentage is calculated by dividing the cost of sales by the revenue amount and multiplying by 100:

$$\frac{\text{Cost of Sales}}{\text{Revenue}} \times 100 = \text{Cost Percentage}$$

For example, assume that food revenue is $284,500 and that beverage revenue is $154,500. The food cost percentage and the beverage cost percentage can be calculated as follows:

$$\frac{\text{Cost of Sales (Food)}}{\text{Food Revenue}} \times 100 = \text{Food Cost Percentage}$$

$$\frac{\$97,250}{\$284,500} \times 100 = 34.18\%$$

$$\frac{\text{Cost of Sales (Beverage)}}{\text{Beverage Revenue}} \times 100 = \text{Beverage Cost Percentage}$$

$$\frac{\$38,800}{\$154,500} \times 100 = 25.11\%$$

Exhibit 2   Sample Operating Statement Format

Food—Schedule 2

	Current Period
TOTAL REVENUE	$ _____
REVENUE	$
ALLOWANCES	_____
NET REVENUE	
COST OF SALES	
Cost of Food	
Less Cost of Employee Meals	
Less Food Transfers to Beverage	
Plus Beverage Transfers to Food	
Net Cost of Food	_____
Other Cost of Sales	_____
Total Cost of Sales	_____
GROSS PROFIT (LOSS) ON FOOD SALES	
OTHER INCOME	
Meeting Room Rentals	
Miscellaneous Banquet Income	
Service Charges	
Total Other Income	_____ _____
GROSS PROFIT (LOSS) ON OTHER INCOME	
EXPENSES	
Salaries and Wages	
Employee Benefits	_____
Total Payroll and Related Expenses	_____
Other Expenses	
China, Glassware, Silver, and Linen	
Contract Services	
Laundry and Dry Cleaning	
Licenses	
Miscellaneous Banquet Expense	
Music and Entertainment	
Operating Supplies	
Telecommunications	
Training	
Uniforms	
Other	_____
Total Other Expenses	_____
TOTAL EXPENSES	_____
DEPARTMENTAL INCOME (LOSS)	$ _____

Source: *Uniform System of Accounts for the Lodging Industry,* 9th rev. ed. (Lansing, Mich.: Educational Institute of the American Hotel & Lodging Association, 1996), p. 41.

Exhibit 3   Information for Basic Cost of Sales Calculation

Required Information	Cost of Sales: Food	Cost of Sales: Beverage
Beginning Inventory	Physical Inventory Forms (last month)	Physical Inventory Forms (last month)
+ Purchases	Daily Receiving Report* (columns 8 + 9)	Daily Receiving Report* (columns 10 to 13)
– Ending Inventory	Physical Inventory Forms (end of current month)	Physical Inventory Forms (end of current month)

*The source document for these purchases is the delivery invoice. Larger operations with formal accounting procedures may post information from the delivery invoices to a "purchase journal" after payment. This source, representing invoices for products received *and* paid for during the month plus delivery invoices representing products received but *not* paid during the month, may also be totaled to determine the value of purchases for the month.

Sources of Information for Basic Cost of Sales

Exhibit 3 illustrates the sources of information for calculating the basic cost of sales. As you review these sources, note that the value of product inventory is calculated only once monthly. The value of ending inventory on the last day of the fiscal period is the same as the value of beginning inventory on the first day of the next fiscal period.

The value of food and beverage purchases for the month can be obtained from the sum of the daily receiving reports for the period. Delivery invoices may be attached to these documents. If all the daily receiving reports are completed correctly, they will separate all food and beverage purchases. This reduces the time needed to make these calculations. If a daily receiving report is not used, the value of purchases will be represented by the sum of delivery invoices, adjusted as necessary by applicable request-for-credit memos. In this case, however, it will be necessary to separate invoice items into food and beverage categories before making purchase calculations.

Values of ending inventories for food and beverage items can be taken directly from a physical inventory form. Remember the importance of consistency in:

- The method used to calculate the cost of inventory items (some inventory valuation methods are discussed in the next section)

- Decisions such as how to treat the value of food supplies in workstations and the value of opened bottles behind the bar

- Whether items in broken cases, in miscellaneous storage areas, or in process are to be considered "in storage" and under inventory control

Calculating Value of Inventory

We have seen that the value of inventory is a critical element in calculating the cost of sales. We have also noted the importance of using a consistent method to calculate inventory. There are four generally accepted methods that can be used:

- **First-in, first-out (FIFO)**—The FIFO approach assigns the first, or earliest, product costs to *issues*—in other words, it values issues in the order in which the costs were incurred. As a consequence, the products in storage are valued *in the reverse order.* That is, since the earliest product costs were applied to the products that were issued, the most recent product costs are applied to the products left in inventory.

- **Last-in, first-out (LIFO)**—The LIFO approach assigns the last, or most recent, product costs to *issues.* As a consequence, the products in storage are valued in the reverse order—in other words, the order in which the costs were incurred. That is, since the most recent product costs were applied to the products that were issued, the earliest product costs are applied to the products left in inventory.

- **Actual cost**—The value of stored products is the total value represented by summing the individual unit costs.

- **Weighted average**—The quantity of products purchased at different unit costs is considered by "weighting" the prices to be averaged based on the quantity of products in storage at each price.

To explain further and clarify the differences among these methods of inventory valuation, let's assume that, at the end of the month, there are 28 cases of applesauce with a value of $22.00 per case among items in inventory. Therefore, at the beginning of the next month, there are also 28 cases of applesauce available as part of the "beginning inventory" for that month. Now, assume that delivery invoice records collected during this month show that 15 cases of applesauce with a value of $23.80 per case were purchased. Finally, suppose that at the end of this current month, the inventory count reveals there are now 20 cases available. From this, we know that 23 cases were issued (28 cases in beginning inventory + 15 cases purchased − 20 cases in ending inventory = 23 cases available). The problem is to determine the value of applesauce in inventory.

Let's see how the different inventory valuation methods are applied to this example.[3] Notice that the four methods yield significantly different values for the same amount of applesauce in inventory.

FIFO Method. Using the FIFO method, we value issues by assigning costs in the order in which they were incurred; consequently, we value inventory by assigning the most recent costs before earlier costs. As stated above, 23 cases were issued. Since 28 cases at the earlier cost of $22.00 were available, it is possible to assign this earlier cost to all 23 cases issued during the month. After we have done this, we have 5 remaining cases valued at the earlier cost and all 15 of the cases purchased at $23.80. The calculated value of the applesauce in inventory is:

Most Recent Costs:

$$\begin{array}{r} 15 \text{ Cases} \\ \times \quad \$23.80/\text{Case} \\ \hline \$357.00 \end{array}$$

Beginning Inventory Costs:

$$\begin{array}{r} 5 \text{ Cases} \\ \times \quad \$22.00/\text{Case} \\ \hline \$110.00 \end{array}$$

Value of Applesauce in Inventory:

$$\begin{array}{r} \$357.00 \\ + \quad 110.00 \\ \hline \$467.00 \end{array}$$

LIFO Method. Using the LIFO method, we value issues by assigning the most recent costs first. Since 23 cases were issued, we must assign the cost of all 15 of the more recently purchased cases *and* 8 of the earlier purchase. The 20 cases remaining in inventory are valued at the earlier cost. The calculated value of the applesauce in inventory is:

$$\text{Earliest Cost} \; = \; 20 \text{ Cases} \; \times \; \$22.00/\text{Case} \; = \; \$440.00$$

Suppose for the moment that only 10 cases had been issued during the month. In this situation, we would have 33 cases left in inventory $(28 + 15 - 10)$. Under the LIFO system, the 10 cases that had been issued would be costed at $23.80 each. Of the 33 remaining in inventory, 28 would be costed at $22.00 each and the other 5 at $23.80 each.

Actual Cost Method. If the actual cost method were used, each case of applesauce would be dated and marked with its actual purchase price when it was received and entered into storage. This marking system should be used regardless of the inventory valuation method in use for inventory control purposes. To calculate inventory costs, the number of cases of applesauce available at each purchase price would be counted. Let's assume that, according to an actual count made at the end of the month, there are 14 cases that were purchased at $23.80 per case and 6 cases that were purchased at $22.00 per case currently available in inventory. (In other words, for whatever reason, one of the new cases was issued before all of the older cases had been issued.) The actual cost method of calculating inventory value would determine the actual value of applesauce in inventory to be:

$$\begin{array}{rcl} 14 \text{ Cases} \; \times \; \$23.80/\text{Case} & = & \$333.20 \\ 6 \text{ Cases} \; \times \; \$22.00/\text{Case} & = & \$132.00 \\ \text{Value of Applesauce in Inventory} & = & \$465.20 \end{array}$$

Weighted Average Method. Finally, the weighted average method for inventory valuation also takes into account the actual number of cases acquired at each price. However, this method determines the value of inventory by multiplying the number of cases remaining in inventory at the end of the month by the average case price paid during the month. Thus, according to this method, the value of applesauce in inventory is calculated as follows:

$$
\begin{array}{rcl}
\text{Beginning Inventory} &=& 28 \text{ Cases} \ \times\ \$22.00/\text{Case} \ =\ \$616.00 \\
\text{Purchases During Month} &=& \underline{15 \text{ Cases}} \ \times\ \$23.80/\text{Case} \ =\ \underline{\$357.00} \\
&& 43 \text{ Cases} \qquad\qquad\qquad\quad =\ \$973.00
\end{array}
$$

$$
\text{Average Case Price} \ =\ \$973.00 \ \div\ 43 \text{ Cases} \ =\ \$22.63/\text{Case}
$$

$$
\begin{array}{ccc}
\begin{array}{c}\text{Number of Cases} \\ \text{in Inventory}\end{array} & \times\ \text{Average Case Price} \ = & \begin{array}{c}\text{Value of Applesauce} \\ \text{in Ending Inventory}\end{array} \\
20 \text{ Cases} & \times \qquad \$22.63/\text{Case} \qquad = & \$452.60
\end{array}
$$

Clearly, the method used to measure inventory can have a significant effect on the calculated value. In our example, the value of applesauce in inventory could be any of the following:

$467.00—FIFO method
$440.00—LIFO method
$465.20—Actual cost method
$452.60—Weighted average method

There is a range from $467.00 (FIFO method) to $440.00 (LIFO method). This difference of $27.00 represents only a small quantity of one product in inventory. When the values of large quantities of different products are assessed, the difference between the results obtained by the various methods can be several thousand dollars or more.

The food and beverage manager must determine the method of inventory valuation that will be used and ensure that whatever method is chosen is used consistently. There are tax implications and restrictions placed on changing inventory valuation methods.

Also, there is a need to develop consistent information for accounting purposes. The value of inventory will affect the operation's subsequent profit level. As the value of inventory increases, the value of actual product cost (cost of sales) will decrease. As this occurs, profit levels increase, and the income tax paid on profits will also increase. The reverse is also true. As the value of inventory decreases, actual product cost (cost of sales) will increase. As this occurs, profit levels will decrease because there is an increase in total costs. It is very important that the food and beverage manager obtain advice from an accountant knowledgeable about current tax laws when deciding which inventory valuation method would be appropriate for the specific food and beverage operation.

Inventory Counting Procedures. As a control measure, it is important that the task of assigning inventory values be given to someone not responsible for daily inventory/storage practices. Perhaps the food service manager or head cook can work with the accountant/controller/bookkeeper to determine the value of food products in inventory. Similarly, the manager or beverage manager might work with an accounting representative to determine inventory values in beverage storage areas. Of course, in small properties the manager/owner, perhaps working alone, will be responsible for determining the value of inventory.

Policies and procedures for counting inventory should be carefully developed and consistently followed. A policy should state whether products in specified storage areas should be consistently counted as "in inventory." For example, should

Exhibit 4 Adjustments to Basic Cost of Sales

Cost of Sales: Food	Charge to:	Cost of Sales: Beverage	Charge to:
Value of Beginning Inventory + Purchases − Value of Ending Inventory		Value of Beginning Inventory + Purchases − Value of Ending Inventory	
Unadjusted Cost of Sales: Food		Unadjusted Cost of Sales: Beverage	
+ Transfers to Kitchen	Food Cost	− Transfers to Kitchen	Food Cost
− Transfers from Kitchen	Bev. Cost	+ Transfers from Kitchen	Bev. Cost
− Employees' Meal Cost	Labor Cost		
− Value of Complimentary Meals	Promotion Expense	− Value of Complimentary Drinks	Promotion Expense
Net Cost of Sales: Food		Net Cost of Sales: Beverage	

items in "broken-case rooms," in workstation storage areas, and/or in process (or even leftovers) be included when inventory counts are taken? Also, to obtain ending inventory values (and beginning values for the next month), inventory counts should be taken at the close of the last day of the fiscal period.

Adjustments to Basic Cost of Sales

One reason to calculate the cost of sales is to determine, with reasonable accuracy, the product cost incurred in generating revenues. However, to make the information more meaningful and useful, some adjustments to the basic cost of sales may be helpful. This is because the unadjusted basic cost of sales will include costs not directly related to generating revenue. For example, in operations where meals are provided free of charge (or at a reduced charge) to employees, the dollars of food cost (and resulting food cost percentage) will be overstated if the cost of sales is not adjusted to compensate for employee meals. These food expenses were incurred to feed employees, not to generate revenue. The cost of meals to employees might more properly be considered as a labor cost or benefits cost rather than as a food cost.

Some food and beverage managers will use the unadjusted cost of sales as their monthly food and beverage costs because they believe that the increased degree of accuracy does not warrant the increased amount of time it takes to make adjustments. However, even food and beverage operations with relatively small annual revenue levels (less than $500,000) may note a significant difference in product costs when adjustments are made for a more accurate picture of the cost of generating revenues.

When adjustments are made to the basic cost of sales, the amount deducted must be charged to some other expense category. Managers who want a more accurate identification of the costs of food and beverage products that generated revenue may make any or all of the adjustments listed in Exhibit 4. These adjustments are examined in the following sections. Note, however, that any of these adjustments to the cost of sales must also be reflected in how standard food costs are calculated for comparisons to be meaningful. Also, the actual monthly cost of food or beverages, as

Exhibit 5   Sample Beverage and Food Transfer Memo

Date: _____			Memo Number: _____107801_____	
Issued to: ☑ Food ☐ Beverage			**Name of Employee** Issuing Food/Beverage: _____Joe_____ Receiving Food/Beverage: _____Sam_____	
Issued from: ☐ Food ☑ Beverage				

Item	Unit	No. of Units	Cost/Unit	Total Unit
House Burgundy	3L	2	8.15	16.30
Sauterne	L	1	3.90	3.90
			Total	$20.20

Source: Adapted from Jack D. Ninemeier, *Beverage Management: Business Systems for Restaurants, Hotels, and Clubs* (New York: Lebhar-Freidman, 1982).

described in detail in this chapter, should be compared with standard costs, budgeted performance expectations, and, if useful, past financial statements.

Food Transfers. Transfers from the kitchen to the bar decrease the cost of food sales. Examples of this are fruits used as drink garnishes or ice cream used for after-dinner drinks. Food served in bars during "cocktail hours" or at other times can be a large cost which, more appropriately, should not be charged to the food costs. Because these transfers were used to generate beverage revenue, they may be more appropriately charged to the beverage operation. This adjustment would decrease the food expense and increase the beverage expense.

Beverage Transfers. Transfers to the kitchen from the bar increase the cost of food sales. Examples of these are wine used for cooking or liqueurs used for tableside flaming of desserts. Although these expenses were initially charged to the beverage operation, they did not generate beverage revenue, but were used to increase food revenue. Therefore, these costs may be more appropriately charged to food. This adjustment would increase food costs and decrease beverage costs.

Transfer Memo. When adjustments are made for the cost of transfers, a beverage and food transfer memo (Exhibit 5) is used as the **source document**. A memo is completed each time products are transferred between the food and beverage departments. The forms can be hard copy or electronic. Once transferred, they can be held (hard copy) or electronically summed through the accounting period when the bookkeeper can total all transfers and make the adjustments in the cost of sales. Transfers to the beverage department will increase beverage costs and decrease food costs by the same amount. Transfers to the food department will increase food costs and decrease beverage costs by the same amount.

Large, multi-unit hotel food and beverage departments make still another use of transfer memos. Some of these properties set up support centers, such as bake shops, production kitchens, and even beverage storerooms. As revenue centers (restaurants or bars) requisition products, costs for those products are charged to the revenue centers. Charges may even include an allocated share of administrative and overhead costs that are incurred by the support center.

Employee Meals. Employee meal costs are usually calculated by multiplying a fixed amount, representing the property's food cost per meal, by the number of employee meals served. This food cost may be deducted from the cost of food sales and charged to the labor or employee benefits account. (Procedures for calculating employee meal costs are beyond the scope of this book. They can be complicated and have both legal—that is, wage and hour laws—and income tax implications. Interested readers can contact their state restaurant association, Department of Labor, or accountant for current information.)

Complimentary Food and Beverages. Complimentary meals and drinks—for example, those provided to prospective guests touring the operation or for other purposes—might reasonably be considered a marketing (promotion) cost. If so, the cost of food or beverage sales can be reduced by their value, and the costs can be transferred to the appropriate marketing account.

Actual Food Cost: Daily Calculations

Monthly calculations of actual food and beverage costs are sufficient to yield information required for monthly accounting statements. However, for control purposes, some food and beverage operators may want more timely information about actual costs against which to compare standard cost estimates. Suppose something goes wrong early in a month and continues to the end of the month. Another several days may elapse while actual operating data are developed into formal accounting reports. When these reports are then compared with standard costs, the problem is finally discovered. However, several weeks may now have passed since the problem first developed. Many dollars might have been saved if the problem had been detected earlier. Therefore, some properties use a practical daily food cost control system to help reduce this kind of problem.

Components of Daily Food Cost

The two components of daily food costs are directs and stores. Directs are typically inexpensive and perishable—fresh produce, bakery, and dairy products—purchased more or less on a daily basis for immediate use; they are not entered in inventory records. Directs are charged to food costs on the day they are received, even if they are not used on that day. Because directs are considered a food cost when received, they can be assessed daily. When received, directs are entered onto the Daily Receiving Report. They then may be sent to production immediately or to a storage area. For example, bread may be sent to the pantry as soon as it is received. By contrast, fresh produce may be placed in the refrigerator until the time of issuing one or two days later. However, because it is classified as a direct, it will not be entered into inventory records even though it is physically stored in an inventory area.

Stores are charged to food costs as they are issued. All foods are ultimately perishable, but these items can often be stored for a longer period of time than can directs. Since they are purchased on the basis of anticipated rather than immediate need, they are purchased, in effect, for inventory. When received, they are entered onto the daily receiving report. When needed for production, they are withdrawn from inventory through the issuing process. Food items removed from inventory are first listed on a food requisition form. Food items frequently classified as stores include frozen products, grocery (canned) items, and staples such as flour and sugar. Some fresh items, such as meats, poultry, and seafood, while extremely perishable, are also often considered stores since they are expensive and would otherwise significantly overstate food costs on daily records.

Sources of Actual Daily Food Cost Information

Two source documents provide reasonably accurate information for calculating actual daily food costs. Cost of daily directs comes from the daily receiving report. Cost of daily stores used in production comes from the sum of issue requisitions.

If an operation's standard food cost calculation includes adjustments for food transfers, beverage transfers, employee meals, and/or complimentary food and beverages (as discussed earlier in this chapter), these should also be made to daily food cost calculations.

Calculating Actual Daily Food Cost

If the daily receiving report and issue requisition forms are completed daily, it is easy to assess the actual daily food cost. While reviewing the actual daily food cost worksheet (Exhibit 6), note that information for each day is listed separately. The date is indicated in column 1. The unadjusted daily food cost (column 4) is calculated by adding the value of all storeroom issues for the day (the sum of costs of all issue requisition forms reported in column 2) to the value of all directs (calculated by adding the directs column on the daily receiving report and recorded in column 3).

Any factors that increase food cost, such as transfers to food from beverage, are listed in column 5. Similarly, factors that reduce food costs, such as transfers from food to beverage, cost of employee meals, and/or complimentary meals, are listed in column 6.

Exhibit 6   Sample Daily Food Cost Worksheet

	Cost of					Daily Food Cost		Food Revenue		Food Cost Percent	
Date	**Store-room Issues (Stores)**	**Directs**	**Total Food Cost**	**Add Adjust-ments**	**Less Adjust-ments**	**Today**	**To-Date**	**Today**	**To-Date**	**Today**	**To-Date**
Col. 1	**Col. 2**	**Col. 3**	**Col. 4**	**Col. 5**	**Col. 6**	**Col. 7**	**Col. 8**	**Col. 9**	**Col. 10**	**Col. 11**	**Col. 12**
8/1	$385.15	$176.85	$562.00	+42.50	−18.75	$585.75	$ 585.75	$1,425.00	$1,425.00	41.1%	41.1%
8/2	370.80	110.15	480.95	+31.80	−36.15	476.60	1,062.35	1,218.50	2,643.50	39.1%	40.2%

Month: August

Daily food cost (column 7) is calculated by adding total food cost (column 4) and increasing adjustments (column 5) minus decreasing adjustments (column 6). For example, for 8/1, the calculation is:

$$\text{Total Food Cost} + \text{Increasing Adjustments} - \text{Decreasing Adjustments} = \text{Total Daily Food Cost}$$

$$\$562.00 + \$42.50 - \$18.75 = \$585.75$$

In column 8, the food and beverage manager can keep a running total of daily food costs throughout the month. This is important because, for a single day, the total daily food cost is not likely to reflect actual costs. Suppose that a large shipment of fresh produce is received on 8/1. Even though some is used on 8/1 and the remainder is used on 8/2, the cost of all this produce is charged to food cost on 8/1 (column 3). This practice, while easy and fast, overstated the daily food cost (column 7) for 8/1. On the following day, the value of directs (column 3) is less, and total food cost (column 7) is reduced accordingly. A running total food cost, then, allows these factors to even out. As the number of days in the month increases, the food cost total in column 8 becomes more accurate. Column 8 is calculated by adding that day's food cost (column 7) to the previous day's to-date food cost (column 8). In the worksheet for 8/1, food cost (column 7) equals column 8 since it is the first day of the month. However, on 8/2 the to-date cost (column 8) is:

$$\$476.60 + \$585.75 = \$1,062.35$$

Column 9—food revenue today—is the revenue generated from the sale of the food in column 7. The source of this information depends on the revenue control system used. It may be the sum of food revenue from guest checks, electronic cash register (sales journal records), and/or from daily food revenue reports.

Column 10—food revenue to-date—is the food revenue generated by the total food cost to-date (column 8). It is the sum of today's revenue plus yesterday's to-date revenue. For example, on 8/2:

$$\$1,218.50 \ + \ \$1,425.00 \ = \ \$2,643.50$$

The day's food cost percentage is in column 11. It is calculated by dividing today's food cost (column 7) by today's food sales (column 9) and multiplying by 100. For example, on 8/2:

$$\frac{\$476.60}{\$1,218.50} \ = \ .391 \ \times \ 100 \ = \ 39.1\%$$

The food cost percentage to-date (column 12) is calculated by dividing the food cost to-date (column 8) by the food revenue to-date (column 10) and multiplying by 100. For example, on 8/2:

$$\frac{\$1,062.35}{\$2,643.50} \ = \ .402 \ \times \ 100 \ = \ 40.2\%$$

The food cost percentage is the actual food cost percentage to-date for the month. This actual food cost can be compared with standard costs and budgeted performance expectations and, if useful, with past financial statements. If, as the month continues, daily actual food cost percentages are higher (or lower) than standard food cost percentages, then some immediate corrective action may be needed.

Computerized Pre/Postcosting Software

The existence of an ingredient file, standard recipe file, and menu item file enables the development of effective precost (prior to service) and postcost (after service) calculations. The ingredient file contains a list of all purchased food items and their current purchase costs. The recipe file holds the formulations of ingredients needed to produce the operation's menu items. The menu item file consists of the list of recipes to be served and the number (projected or actual) of portions associated with each.

Precost Analysis

Precosting yields a standard cost that enables an operator to accurately evaluate a meal plan relative to budgetary plans before service. The precost analysis produces projected cost data based upon the application of ingredient costs across recipe offerings. For example, assume a four-entrée menu: tenderloin tips, steak, spaghetti, and lobster tail. Forecasted servings for each are 25, 57, 63, and 23, respectively. After determining each recipe's standard portion cost, the computer will report a food precost of $753.57 for this sales mix. This precost was the result of multiplying the number of projected servings for each entrée by its standard recipe cost and then summing the results for all entrées:

$$(25 \times \$2.50) + (57 \times \$5.00) + (63 \times \$3.89) + (23 \times \$7.00) = \$753.57$$

Computer speed and accuracy assure management of sufficient planning time. Manual equivalent procedures are tedious, cumbersome, and at best completed just prior to service.

Postcost Analysis

There are two types of postcost analyses—each performed with actual counts but with differing food (recipe) costs. Immediately after meal service, actual counts are multiplied by standard recipe costs (the same costs as in precost analysis) to produce an ideal food cost. Actual counts can be derived from an electronic cash register, a precheck system, or a manual count.

Once a physical inventory is taken and actual usage is known, actual counts are used again to generate actual costs. The computer employs previously constructed data files (ingredient, recipe, and menu) to produce analytical costing reports. This minimizes both data rehandling and elapsed time from input to output.

In addition to cost reports, pre/postcost systems can be used as a base to produce purchase orders, inventory replenishments, stockroom breakout quantities, labor scheduling forecasts, production area reports, and the like. Many operators also elect to use pre/postcosting for meal period simulations, ingredient substitution evaluation, and potential menu-item trending.

Actual Beverage Cost: Daily Calculations

The beverage manager, like the food manager, has access to monthly cost of sales information. However, the beverage manager may also want more timely information to make decisions as soon as possible after observing a problem. If a practical system to assess actual daily beverage costs can be designed to provide reasonably accurate information without requiring a significant amount of time, it will be a very useful control tool to beverage management. This section explains how to develop such a system. Once developed and implemented, it can collect daily beverage cost information as an integral part of the control process.

Principles for Calculating Actual Daily Beverage Cost

The cost of beverages issued to each bar at either the end or the beginning of the shift can be used to represent the actual beverage costs. If a bar par inventory is developed and issues are only made to restore the bar par on a bottle-for-bottle replacement basis, it is very simple to collect beverage cost information based upon the cost of issues. For each shift, the cost of issues reported on the beverage issue requisition form is the cost of beverages used for the shift. Beverage managers must decide whether to collect beverage cost information by shift or by day. When information is collected by shift, beverages are issued to the bar at the end or beginning of each shift.

Beverage Cost per Shift. Several factors influence the decision to collect beverage cost information by shift or by day. As more accuracy is desired, more specific data by shift is necessary. Also, as explained later in this chapter, collecting information by shift makes it very easy to assess beverage costs both by shift and by bartender—since only one more worksheet is necessary. In this way, detailed beverage control plans can specifically identify and help correct problems.

As the volume of revenue increases, it becomes even more important to collect beverage cost information by shift. Unless storage space for bar par inventories is very large, some issuing during the day may be necessary. Also, increased quantities of issued products and higher revenue levels may make it more difficult to identify causes of problems.

With more beverage outlets, the difficulty of identifying and correcting operational problems increases. If, for example, the beverage cost is too high, how does the beverage manager determine which bar and which bartender are responsible and when the problem(s) occurred?

As suggested, beverage costs can be represented by the costs of issues to the bar or bars at the end or the beginning of the shift or day. With this plan, no cost or inventory count is needed for central beverage storerooms, bar inventories, or changes in opened bottles behind the bar. Obviously, this is a simple procedure, but how much accuracy is sacrificed?

Behind-the-Bar Bottle Cost. On the average, each opened bottle behind the bar is half full. Some bottles are almost full or almost empty; others may be one-quarter or three-quarters full. But the average bottle (and the average becomes more accurate as both the number of bottles and the number of observations increase) is half full. Therefore, unless extreme accuracy is desired, there is little need to calculate quantities and cost of opened bottles behind the bar when taking inventory. (A computerized scale can be used if greater accuracy is desired.) A one-time cost of the opened-bottle inventory can be established based on the bar par and subject to increases over time as costs (inventory values) increase. This constant cost can be added to the value of beginning and ending inventories when calculating cost of revenue. Alternatively, no value may be assigned to opened-bottle inventory since, on the average, it is the same at the time of beginning and ending inventory counts.

When calculating daily beverage costs, changes in opened-bottle inventories become even less important. It is usually not practical to inventory opened bottles each shift or each day. Sometimes at the beginning of a shift, most of the bottles are almost full. Since few bottles may be emptied by the end of the shift, beverage cost, based upon issues to replace empty bottles, is low. However, at the beginning of the next shift, most of the bottles may be almost empty. With the same amount of drinks produced, more bottles will be emptied during this shift, and the resulting beverage costs will be high. Again, since the volume of opened-bottle inventory will even out over time, there is little need to account for these differences. Eliminating the cost of opened-bottle inventory allows reasonably accurate daily, or shift, beverage costs to be developed speedily and practically.

Procedures for Calculating Daily Beverage Cost

The following procedures can be used to calculate daily beverage costs:

1. At the beginning of a shift, the bartender reviews the inventory of opened and unopened bottles behind the bar to ensure that the bar par, for which the

bartender is held responsible during the shift, is complete. If the bar par is replenished at the beginning of a shift, the bar is now restocked.

2. During the shift, the bartender prepares drinks and collects revenue according to procedures established for the beverage operation.

3. At the end of the shift, bottles emptied during the shift are listed on the beverage requisition form. (The bar par can be replenished if restocking is done at the end of the shift.) If costs were marked on the bottles at the time of receiving, storing, or issuing, the bartender can easily record the unit costs while completing the form. (It is not necessary, at this time, to multiply the number of bottles to be issued by the unit cost to arrive at the total cost. The manager or bookkeeper can do this later when calculating the daily beverage cost.)

4. The operation's procedures for issuing the bottles from the beverage storeroom should be followed.

5. The actual beverage cost for the shift—represented by the cost of bottles issued at the end of the shift—is calculated by completing and summing the total cost column on the requisition form.

6. Working space for calculating the actual daily beverage cost percentage is provided at the bottom of the beverage issue requisition form. Revenue is obtained by reviewing electronic cash register revenue data, guest checks, precheck register equipment, or other method that generates information about beverage revenue. The beverage cost percentage is calculated by dividing the beverage cost for the shift by the beverage revenue during the shift and multiplying by 100.

$$\frac{\text{Beverage Cost/Shift}}{\text{Beverage Revenue/Shift}} \times 100 = \text{Beverage Cost Percentage/Shift}$$

Averaging Shift Costs

While this information may help in comparing the actual beverage cost with the standard and operating budget beverage costs, it is more accurate to average one shift's actual costs with those incurred during previous shifts. This can be done using a daily beverage cost percentage worksheet (Exhibit 7). When reviewing this form, note:

1. The form can accumulate information for up to four bars. In the sample form, only one bar is open during the lunch shift. In the evening that bar, the main and service bars, and a second public bar (called the French Bar) are open.

2. Each date of beverage operation is shown in column 1. The next eight columns list cost and revenue (in dollars) for each shift and each bar. This information is taken directly from beverage issue requisition forms used to replenish bar par levels in each bar.

3. To find today's total beverage cost (column 10), simply add up the beverage costs for all bars for the day. On 2/1, for example, the beverage costs are:

Exhibit 7   Sample Daily Beverage Cost Percentage Worksheet

	Bar: _Lunch_		Bar: _Main_		Bar: _Service_		Bar: _French_		Beverage Cost		Beverage Revenue		Beverage Cost Percent	
Date	Cost	Rev.	Cost	Rev.	Cost	Rev.	Cost	Rev.	Today	To-Date	Today	To-Date	Today	To-Date
1	2	3	4	5	6	7	8	9	10	11	12	13	14	15
2/1	$82.15	$410.75	$125.15	$585.75	$88.00	$465.00	$215.25	$1,052.35	$510.55	$510.55	$2,513.85	$2,513.85	20.3%	20.3%
2/2	$98.50	$415.80	$165.35	$625.00	$110.00	$565.35	$263.15	$1,182.30	$637.00	$1,147.55	$2,788.45	$5,302.30	22.8%	21.6%

$$\$82.15 \ + \ \$125.15 \ + \ \$88.00 \ + \ \$215.25 \ = \ \$510.55$$

4. The beverage cost to-date and beverage revenue to-date (columns 11 and 13 respectively) are calculated by adding the daily cost and revenue to yesterday's to-date cost and revenue. For example, on 2/2 the beverage cost to-date is calculated as follows:

$$\$637.00 \ + \ \$510.55 \ = \ \$1,147.55$$

5. Today's beverage percentage (column 14) is calculated by dividing the beverage cost today by beverage revenue today and multiplying by 100. For example, for 2/1:

$$\frac{\$510.55}{\$2,513.85} \ \times \ 100 \ = \ 20.3\%$$

6 Similarly, the to-date beverage percentage (column 15) is calculated by dividing the beverage cost to-date by the beverage revenue to-date and multiplying by 100. For 2/2, the to-date beverage percentage is calculated as follows:

$$\frac{\$1,147.55}{\$5,302.30} \ \times \ 100 \ = \ 21.6\%$$

The to-date beverage cost percentage (Exhibit 7, column 15) is the actual beverage cost percentage to-date for the month. If, as the month continues, the actual daily beverage costs are higher than the standard beverage costs, immediate corrective action may be in order.

Bartender Performance Review

With only one additional procedure, information from the daily beverage cost percentage worksheet (Exhibit 7) can be used to assess each bartender's performance separately. This is desirable because some bartenders may be contributing to a

Exhibit 8   Bartender Performance Review

Bartender Name											
Joe			Sam			Jack			Relief Only		Weekly Average
Date	Bar	%	Date	Bar	%	Date	Bar	%	Date	Bar	%	
2/1	Lunch	20.0	2/1	Main	21.4	2/1	Service	18.9	N	O N E		
2/2	Lunch	23.7	2/2	Service	19.5	2/2	French	22.3	N	O N E		
2/7	Lunch	22.8	2/8	Main	21.2	—	—	—	N	O N E		
		22.3			20.5			21.5			—	21.4%

higher-than-necessary beverage cost by not consistently using standard beverage control tools—standard recipes, standard portion tools, and standard ice size—and/or by failing to comply with the property's revenue control procedures. When reviewing the sample bartender performance review form (Exhibit 8), note:

1. Beverage percentage information, computed on the beverage issue requisition form, is transferred directly to the bartender performance review form. In the daily beverage cost percentage worksheet (Exhibit 7), cost and revenue data were listed for each bar and bartender, but the resulting individual beverage cost percentage by bar was not a component in calculating the actual beverage cost percentages.

2. Bartenders are listed across the top of the form. Each time the bartender works, the manager lists the name of the bar worked and the resulting beverage cost percentage on the form. This information comes directly from the beverage issue requisition form.

3. At the end of the week, the average beverage cost percentage for each bartender is calculated. Assume that one bartender (Joe) incurred the following beverage cost percentages during the six shifts worked during the week:

Date	Percentage
2/1	20.0
2/2	23.7
2/3	22.8
2/4	24.5
2/5	(off)
2/6	19.8
2/7	22.8

The average beverage cost percentage is determined by adding each percentage and dividing by the number of days worked:

$$\frac{133.6\%}{6} = 22.3\%$$

In addition to comparing the performance of each bartender against all other bartenders, the performance review form can be used to compare the performance of each bartender with the beverage cost percentage averaged across all bartenders and all shifts. This information is found in column 15 of the percentage recap form (Exhibit 7).

Comparisons may show a bartender's cost percentage is too high or too low. Perhaps the bartender is overpouring or stealing, or perhaps the bartender is underpouring or finding creative ways to bypass the property's revenue security system. In these cases, the bartender may require closer supervision, may have to be given additional training, or may otherwise be helped to better ensure that quality and control requirements are consistently met. Note that bartenders who always work on special shifts—for example, during low-price cocktail hours or high-price entertainment periods—will typically have, respectively, higher and lower beverage cost percentages, since revenue levels affect beverage cost percentages.

Endnotes

1. *Uniform System of Accounts for Restaurants*, 7th rev. ed. (Washington, D.C.: National Restaurant Association, 1996).

2. *Uniform System of Accounts for the Lodging Industry*, 9th ed. (Lansing, Mich.: Educational Institute of the American Hotel & Lodging Association, 1996).

3. The inventory valuation example in this chapter is adapted from Jack D. Ninemeier and Raymond S. Schmidgall, *Basic Accounting Standards* (Westport, Conn.: AVI, 1984), pp. 73–74.

Key Terms

actual cost—A method of valuing inventory that considers the actual cost paid for all products in inventory; the value of stored products is the total value represented by summing the individual unit costs.

actual food and beverage costs—The cost of items sold as determined by a factual weekly or monthly record.

cost of sales—The food or beverage cost incurred to produce all food and beverage items generating revenue during an accounting period.

first-in, first-out (FIFO)—A method of valuing inventory; the products in storage areas are valued at the level of the most recently purchased items to be placed in inventory.

last-in, first-out (LIFO)—A method of valuing inventory; the inventory value is assumed to be represented by the cost of items that were placed into inventory the earliest.

source document—The point of original entry of financial data into the accounting or control system.

weighted average—A method of valuing inventory; the quantity of products purchased at different unit costs is considered by "weighting" the prices based on the quantity of products in storage at each price.

 **Review Questions** ─────────────────────────

1. Why is it important to compare standard and actual food and beverage costs?

2. Why are revenues and product costs determined separately for food and beverage revenue centers?

3. How are food cost percentages and beverage cost percentages determined?

4. How is the cost of sales (for food and beverage) calculated?

5. What is the process for making adjustments to transfer food and beverage costs between revenue centers?

6. How would you decide upon the method of inventory valuation which should be used for a given property?

7. To what account should employee meals be allocated?

8. How are actual daily food costs and actual daily beverage costs calculated?

9. Why can it be important to separate beverage cost information by bartender?

10. What types of byproduct information are available through pre/postcosting software packages?

 **Internet Sites** ─────────────────────────────

For more information, visit the following Internet sites. Remember that Internet addresses can change without notice. If the site is no longer there, you can use a search engine to look for additional sites.

Associations

American Culinary Federation (ACF)
http://www.acfchefs.org

American Hotel & Lodging Association (AH&LA)
http://www.ahlaonline.org

American School Food Service Association (ASFSA)
http://www.asfsa.org

Club Managers Association of America (CMAA)
http://www.cmaa.org

The Educational Foundation of NRA
http://www.edfound.org

The Educational Institute of AH&LA
http://www.ei-ahla.org

Hospitality Financial and Technology Professionals
http://www.hftp.org

Institute of Food Technologies
http://www.ift.org

International Hotel and Restaurant Association
http://www.ih-ra.com

National Association of College and
University Food Services
http://www.nacufs.org

National Restaurant Association (NRA)
http://www.restaurant.org

Food and Beverage Resources

Club Management Online
http://www.club-mgmt.com/dining/
index.html

Controlling Beverage Costs
http://www.barmedia.com/
management.html

Controlling Food Costs
http://www.pdco.com

Costs of Goods Sold
http://taxguide.completetax.com/
text/Q12_2330.asp

Daily Beverage Costs
http://www.restaurantreport.com/
features/ft_bevcost.html

Inventory Valuation Methods
http://www.swcollege.com/
vircomm/gita/gita14-3.html

Prepared Foods. Product development,
ingredients, suppliers
http://www.preparedfoods.com

Management Companies

ARAMARK
http://www.aramark.com

Bon Appétit Management Company
http://www.bamco.com

Compass Group
http://www.compass-na.com

Sodexho Marriott
http://www.sodexhomarriott.com

The Wood Company
http://www.woodco.com

Publications—Online and Printed

Club Management Magazine
http://www.club-mgmt.com

Electronic Gourmet Guide
http://www.foodwine.com

Food and Hospitality Magazine
http://www.foodserviceworld.com

Food Management
http://www.foodservicesearch.com

Food Network: CyberKitchen
http://www.foodtv.com

Food Processing: The Magazine of
Strategy, Technology and Trends
http://www.foodprocessing.com

Internet Food Channel
http://www.foodchannel.com

International Hotel and Restaurant
Association journal
www.hotelsmag.com

International Journal of Hospitality
Management
http://www.mcb.co.uk/ijchm.htm

Journal of the American Dietetic
Association
http://www.eatright.org/
journaltoc.html

Journal of Nutrition, publication of American Society of Nutritional Sciences
http://nutrition.org

Lodging Food and Beverage
http://www.lodgingnews.com/lodgingfnb/

Lodging Hospitality Online
http://www.lhonline.com

Lodging News, journal of the American Hotel & Lodging Association
http://www.ei–ahla.org/webs/lodging/index.html

Nation's Restaurant News
http://www.nrn.com

On the Rail—News for Food Professionals
http://www.ontherail.com

Restaurants and Institutions magazine
http://www.rimag.com

Restaurant Business, Food Service, and ID magazines
http://www.foodservicetoday.com

Restaurant Hospitality
www.foodservicesearch.com

Restaurants and Institutions
http://www.rimag.com

Restaurants USA, publication of National Restaurant Association
http://www.restaurant.org/rusa

Wine Business Monthly
http://smartwine.com

World Hospitality, management magazine for hotel executives.
http://www.worldhospitality.com

 **Problems**

Problem 1

Use the following data to answer the question below about actual food and beverage costs for the Marina Bay Grill for July.

Ending Inventory (Food)	$68,000
Ending Inventory (Beverage)	$23,470
Food Purchases	$305,000
Beverage Purchases	$24,700
Beginning Inventory (Food)	$72,400
Beginning Inventory (Beverage)	$19,700
Transfers to Bar	$3,870
Theft/Pilferage	$510
Over-portioning Expense	$615
Transfers from Bar	$4,100
Complimentary Food	$2,160
Complimentary Beverages	$890
Employee Meal Cost	$11,225

Food Revenues	$878,000
Beverage Revenues	$116,500

What is the net cost of sales for food and beverage (indicate dollar and percentage costs)?

Problem 2

What are the unadjusted food and beverage costs for the Hillside Resort given the following information for April. Express your answer in dollars and percent.

	Food	Beverage
Beginning Inventory	$110,000	$38,500
Ending Inventory	$98,470	$41,000
Purchases	$488,000	$161,000
Revenues	$1,268,000	$742,000

The following additional information about April's food and beverage costs is also available. Use this data to calculate net costs of sales for food and beverage. Express your answer in dollars and percent.

Transfers to Bar	$5,170
Transfers from Bar	$6,850
Ending Inventory	$7,640
Purchases	$2,290
Revenues	$840

Problem 3

The Pleasant Meadows Restaurant uses frozen ground beef packed in 10 lb poly bags for many of its soup and casserole items. Use the following information to calculate the value of ground beef inventory at the end of January:

	January 1	January 31
Inventory Count	17 bags	28 bags
Ending Inventory	$28.00	$30.00

There were 37 bags purchased (delivered) during January.

    a. Calculate the value of ground beef inventory using the FIFO method.

    b. Calculate the value of ground beef inventory using the LIFO method.

    c. Calculate the value of ground beef inventory using the actual cost method. A proper inventory rotation system was in use.

    d. Calculate the value of ground beef using the weighted average method.

Problem 4

Complete the following Daily Food Cost Worksheet.

Date	Issues	Directs	Total Cost	Add Adjust	Less Adjust	Daily Food Cost Today	Daily Food Cost To-Date	Food Revenue Today	Food Revenue To-Date	Food Cost % Today	Food Cost % To-Date
7/1	$350.00	$210.00		$110.00	$120.00			$2400.00			
7/2	$870.00	$320.00		$85.00	$55.00			$2900.00			
7/3	$805.00	$290.00		$70.00	$50.00			$3100.00			

Problem 5

Using the worksheet below, calculate the Daily Food Cost for three days given the following data:

Date	Issues	Directs	Trans to Bar	Trans from Bar	Employee Meals	Revenue
8/1	$410.00	$205.00	$71.00	$60.00	$81.00	$1850.00
8/2	$370.00	$175.00	$45.10	$51.00	$65.75	$1790.00
8/3	$520.00	$199.00	$50.70	$40.60	$68.00	$2150.00

Worksheet

Date	Issues	Directs	Total Cost	Add Adjust	Less Adjust	Daily Food Cost Today	Daily Food Cost To-Date	Food Revenue Today	Food Revenue To-Date	Food Cost % Today	Food Cost % To-Date
8/1	$410.00	$205.00									
8/2	$370.00	$175.00									
8/3	$520.00	$199.00									

The desired food cost percentage is 27.8 percent. What should the manager do?

Problem 6

Complete the following Daily Beverage Cost Percentage Worksheet:

Date	Bar 1 Cost	Bar 1 Revenue	Bar 2 Cost	Bar 2 Revenue	Beverage Cost Today	Beverage Cost To-Date	Beverage Revenue Today	Beverage Revenue To-Date	Beverage Cost Percent Today	Beverage Cost Percent To-Date
(1)	(2)	(3)	(4)	(5)	(6)	(7)	(8)	(9)	(10)	(11)
7/1	$110.00	$470.00	$210.00	$840.00						
7/2	$180.00	$710.00	$295.00	$1280.00						
7/3	$161.00	$512.00	$300.00	$950.00						
7/4	$98.00	$480.00	$145.00	$615.00						

a. The beverage cost percent is budgeted at 23 percent What should the manager do?

b. The manager wonders whether one bar has a higher beverage cost than the other. What is the actual beverage cost of each bar?

c. Assume Bar 1 is only open at night and has a higher drink price than Bar 2. If the costs to purchase liquor (per bottle cost) are the same as for Bar 2 (and they are!), would you expect the Bar 1 beverage cost *percentage* to be higher or lower than Bar 2? Why?

Problem 7

What is the beverage cost percentage for Bartenders 1 and 2 given information in the following Bartender Performance Review Form. What is the weekly average beverage cost?

Bartender #1			Bartender #2		
Date	Bar	%	Date	Service	%
7/1	Main	24.1	7/1	Service	22.3
7/2	Main	23.8	7/2	Service	22.3
7/3	Main	23.4	7/3	Service	21.0
7/4	Main	24.0	7/4	Service	23.0
7/5	Main	24.6	7/5	Service	21.2

a. What is one example of an acceptable reason why Bartender 1 could have a higher beverage cost percentage than Bartender 2?

b. What is one example of an unacceptable reason for the higher beverage cost percentage by Bartender 1?

c. If prices are the same in both bars, what is an unacceptable reason for the lower beverage cost percentage by Bartender 2?

Chapter 10 Outline

Procedures for Comparison and Analysis
    The Comparison Process
    Questions to Consider during the
        Comparison Process
    Variance from Standards
    Analyzing Variances
    Potential Savings
Identifying the Problem
Taking Corrective Action
    Assigning Responsibility
Evaluating Corrective Action

Competencies

1. Identify the types of standards that food and beverage managers use to evaluate the results of operations. (pp. 317–320)

2. Explain how managers determine which variances from cost standards should be thoroughly analyzed. (p. 321)

3. Identify factors food and beverage managers consider when analyzing variances between standard costs and actual costs. (pp. 321–326)

4. Identify factors food and beverage managers consider when taking corrective action to control operations. (pp. 326–333)

10

Control Analysis, Corrective Action, and Evaluation

THE SEQUENCE OF the control process begins with setting standards—goals or expected results—for the food and beverage operation. The second step is measuring actual operating results. This chapter begins with a review of the third step in the control process: comparing standards with actual results. These comparisons may show that the fourth step of the control process is needed: taking corrective action. Once corrective action is taken, the control process concludes with evaluating the effectiveness of the action taken. Comparison, analysis, corrective action, and evaluation are the topics of this chapter.

Procedures for Comparison and Analysis

To compare expected results from the budget or other source of standard with actual results from operations, standards must be established and actual costs must be assessed. Using this information, standards can be compared with actual results to show how successful an operation has been in meeting its goals. Any differences (variances) between expected and actual results must be analyzed.

Exhibit 1 lists four sources of standard costs and briefly describes the information each source provides. A property's management team must carefully select the source of standard food and beverage cost information against which to compare actual operating results. As we will see later in this chapter, the method used for generating cost standards for a food and beverage operation affects the process used to compare standard and actual costs.

Sources of information for determining actual food and beverage costs are listed in Exhibit 2. Current income statements and selected management reports contain information about actual costs. The current income statement, prepared by the bookkeeper or accountant, shows the cost of sales—the food and beverage expense incurred in generating revenue for the current month. The other internal records report daily operating information. These are developed by management staff to reflect—daily and to-date—the actual costs of food and beverages.

The Comparison Process

There are a number of methods of evaluating the actual success of a food and beverage operation in meeting its goals. Each corresponds to a different way of establishing an expected goal—a standard cost—for the operation. The following sections examine standards based on:

Exhibit 1   Sources and Information Provided for Standard Food and Beverage Costs

Source	Information Provided
Averages	National or state restaurant or lodging association or other statistics on average food and beverage cost percents
Past financial statements	Previous income statements for the property that indicate food and beverage costs as a percentage of revenue for a specific period of time
Past or current operating budgets	Food and beverage costs in dollars and/or in percentage of estimated revenue for the property based upon past or current budget periods
In-house developed standard costs	Food and beverage costs developed specifically for the property after controlled study of results when all standard control tools are used

- Industry averages
- Past financial statements
- Operating budgets
- Specific property requirements

Industry Averages. The first source of information listed in Exhibit 1—industry averages—is the easiest to use but provides the least reliable basis for developing cost standards for a food and beverage operation. Using industry averages as standards against which to compare an operation's actual costs does little to address the specific concerns of a property whose needs likely differ from the "average" property.

While the success of an individual food and beverage operation may not be accurately measured by comparing it to industry-wide averages, many operations use such averages as standards. This approach is especially helpful when several units of a multi-operation chain are located near each other, in which case, food, labor, and related costs are likely to be similar, and external-property comparisons may be more relevant.

Consider the following example of an operation comparing its actual costs against industry averages. A property's food and beverage manager learns that 38 percent is the average food cost percentage for similar types of operations. The manager consults the current income statement and finds the property's actual food cost percentage is 42 percent. Since this percentage is higher than the standard of 38 percent, there may be a problem. If the property maintains internal daily records of actual food costs, such as the daily actual food cost worksheet, the manager could use these as a basis for reviewing actual costs to determine where reductions might be possible. However, note that the manager is assuming that the industry average supplied by an association or read in a trade journal applies to the property; this may not be true.

Exhibit 2   Sources and Information Provided for Establishing Actual Food and Beverage Costs

Source	Information Provided
Current income statement	Cost of food and beverage sales expressed as a percentage of revenue
Internal Records	
a) Daily food cost worksheet	To-date food cost percent calculated by: $$\frac{\text{Issues to-date} + \text{Directs to-date} + \text{ or } - \text{ Adjustments to-date}}{\text{Food revenue to-date}}$$
b) Daily beverage cost percentage recap	To-date beverage cost percent calculated by: $$\frac{\text{Issues to all bars to-date}}{\text{Revenue from all bars to-date}}$$
c) Bartender performance review form	Bartender's weekly beverage cost percent compared with the to-date beverage cost percent for all bartenders

Past Financial Statements. Financial statements that have been prepared for the property in the past can provide cost information that may be used to define standards for the property's current operations. A major disadvantage of using these records is that inefficiencies in past operations may continue unnoticed if management strives only to do as well as it did in a past financial period. For example, consider the situation in which a food and beverage manager bases the property's cost standards on a past income statement showing a relatively high food cost percentage. In this case, the food cost percentage noted on the past period's income statement would be compared with the actual food cost shown in the current income statement or in daily food cost records. If there is no variance, operational efficiency might be mistakenly assumed. However, if current costs are higher than the standard costs reported in the past financial statement, problems might exist.

Operating Budgets. Comparing actual costs to estimates in past or current operating budgets can also result in continuing of past inefficiencies. This may be largely avoided, however, if the property's operating budgets are developed according to procedures that incorporate specific profit requirements. If an operating budget for the current period has been developed, the food and beverage cost percentage calculated in that budget is compared with the actual cost percentages shown in the current income statement and/or in daily cost records.

Specific Property Requirements. The best and most accurate information about what costs should be is based on in-house cost standards developed specifically for the particular property. They incorporate the results to be expected when all aspects of the operation's control system are functioning properly. Standard costs are developed, then actual costs are compared with in-house standard costs. Actual costs can also be compared with anticipated costs based on the actual sales mix.

In each method of comparison described in this section, the food and beverage manager defines an operating goal—a standard cost—and compares it with the actual results of the operation as indicated by the income statement and/or internal daily records. The same process can be used to compare standard and actual costs for all other categories of expense.

Questions to Consider during the Comparison Process

Regardless of the source of standard costs or the method of assessing actual results, several basic questions should be asked when comparing standard and actual costs.

1. Is the standard cost correct? For example, if standards have been based on average costs applicable to a state or to a specific segment of the food and beverage industry, then some variance in actual costs may not be evidence of a problem. Even a standard developed specifically for the property may not be correct. Errors in calculating the standard cost may have been made, or the sales mix on which the standard was based may have changed. For example, a standard food cost developed during the summer, when many salads and light meals are eaten, may differ from one developed in the winter, when guests are more likely to choose heavier meals.

2. Is the actual cost correct? Calculations and other information in the property's accounting system should be checked for accuracy.

3. Have the components of food cost changed? Recall that actual costs and standard costs must be calculated on the same basis, including or excluding the same factors.

4. Are there similar variances between standard and actual costs when these are compared by different methods? If, for example, standard costs estimated from the operating budget are compared with actual costs from both the income statement and the daily food cost record, there should be some correlation in the variances exhibited.

5. Is the variance between standard and actual costs from this period significantly different from other periods? For example, if the variance between standard and actual costs has been about 1.5 percent for six months, a variance in the current month of four percent may indicate an increased need to look for problems.

6. Is the amount of variance great enough to warrant corrective action? As discussed later in this section, the cost area that represents the greatest amount of potential savings should normally receive priority for corrective action. This cost area may not necessarily be the one with the largest percentage of variance between expected and actual results; rather, the cost area with the largest dollar variance should be a priority for analysis.

Variance from Standards

Comparisons often reveal the actual cost to be greater than the standard cost. Does this mean that, in each instance, the manager must take corrective action? Standards, especially those developed in-house, indicate expected costs if nothing goes wrong. But even with the best management systems, things do go wrong. Therefore, managers commonly set a predetermined variance—a difference between standard and actual costs—that is regarded as permissible and not requiring corrective action.

For example, assume a standard beverage cost of 26 percent and an actual beverage cost of 27 percent. If a variance of no more than one percentage point is permitted, no further analysis or corrective action may be needed. On the other hand, if the actual beverage cost is 30 percent, the variance of four percentage points clearly requires investigation. Exhibit 3 shows the guidelines a restaurant executive might consider when analyzing alcoholic beverage costs.

How much of a variance is acceptable? In many operations, allowable variances are measured more often in dollars than percentages. For example, if beverage costs are $27,000 monthly, each one percent variance represents $270 (one percent of $27,000 = $270) of higher-than-expected costs and $270 of lost profits. In deciding when to take corrective action, management must take into account its profit requirements and the amount of freedom it has to reduce costs in other expense areas.

Management time and priorities must also be considered when setting variance levels. For example, if a four percent variance between standard and actual food costs represents $5,000, compared with the $270 in beverage costs, it would be better to concentrate on managing the $5,000 in excessive food costs.

Let's look at another example. Suppose there is a two percent variance between standard and actual food costs and a five percent variance between actual and standard beverage costs. Which profit center (food or beverage) should be studied first? If food revenues are $500,000 and beverage revenues are $50,000, the amount of lost profit is:

$$\text{Food Operation:} \quad \$500,000 \ \times \ .02 \ = \ \$10,000$$
$$\text{Beverage Operation:} \quad \$ 50,000 \ \times \ .05 \ = \ \$ 2,500$$

Clearly, there is a more significant problem with food costs. In this case, even though the variance percentage between standard and actual costs is lower, management should focus on controlling food expenses.

Finally, in deciding what level of variance between standard and actual costs to permit, remember that the savings realized by implementing controls must offset their cost. If it costs $500 monthly to save the $270 in excess beverage costs annually, the added control procedures are not justified. On the other hand, if it costs only $500 annually to save $270 monthly (or $3,240 annually), implementing additional control procedures may be justified.

Analyzing Variances

As already noted, a variance between standard and actual costs does not automatically mean that a problem exists that needs immediate corrective action. The

Exhibit 3   Analyzing Beverage Sales for Maximum Profit

Restaurant Report

Restaurant Report Email Newsletter
For hospitality professionals and food connoisseurs...

Subscribe
It's free!

Top 100 Food Sites

Articles

E-mail Newsletter

The Great Debates

Question & Answer

Buyer's Guide

Marketplace

Hospitality Jobs

James Beard Dateline

Print Subscriptions

Advertising Info

Contact Us

Home Page

For Profit's Sake - Inventory Your Beverage Cost

by Ron Gorodesky and Ed McCarron

The food and drink is great, the service fabulous and the restaurant is busier than ever, but are you wondering why the bottom line isn't all it should be?

Alcohol sales (beverage sales) are an easy way to increase profitability because the costs are lower and the gross margin is far greater for beverage than for food. However, beverage costs must be controlled if an operation is to reach maximum potential of gross profit from beverage sales. Every reduction in beverage cost percentage renders a higher gross profit. Beverage costs that are above industry averages can negatively impact your profitability. A profitable restaurant typically generates a 22% to 28% beverage cost. Because of the impact beverage costs can make on an operation, it is important to know where beverage cost falls in relation to total sales on a daily or weekly basis. Beyond the bottom line, beverage costs also reflect an operation's control systems, management skill level, and value provided to the customers...

ANALYZING YOUR BEVERAGE COST

What should your beverage cost percentage be? Successful restaurants generate beverage costs in the mid 20% range. However, different types of operations typically run higher or lower percentages; fine dining may run up to 35% (sales of bottles of wine are usually less profitable other alcoholic beverages) whereas brewpub restaurants may run about 15%. Comparing your cost percentage to restaurants with similar menus and service levels provides a more accurate perspective.

The 1997 RAS Report is a restaurant operations report for Pennsylvania restaurants which provides industry information and food and beverage cost averages based on menu-theme, sales volume, years in business and other categories. For example, the report lists an average beverage cost of 32.1% for American/Regional menu themed restaurants and 30.8% for a restaurant in a multi-unit organization.

How can you use your beverage cost percentage? The next step requires compiling the sales and costs consistently and regularly, as comparisons to previous performance can prove very helpful, identifying problems and trends, remembering that a *decrease* in beverage cost is as important to investigate as an increase. From here, your operation is positioned to tighten its beverage cost by looking closely at various methods used to control beverage cost, with the ultimate goal of positively impacting your bottom line.

Source: Restaurant Report On-Line, http://www.restaurantreport.com

difference may be explainable. For example, when the current sales mix has changed—more people buying higher- or lower-cost items than that mix observed in an earlier period—a variance should be expected. Studying sales history records may help clarify this situation.

Significant increases in food and beverage purchase prices may explain a variance, and may also indicate the need for improved precosting procedures and a change in menu selling prices. Revisions in recordkeeping procedures or changes in how financial reports are generated and revenue is collected might also explain differences between standard and actual costs.

If variances cannot be explained even after study, a serious problem may exist. If the actual costs are higher than planned and the manager cannot determine why, a close look at the food and beverage operation is in order. Variances can be caused by:

- Failure to follow required procedures designed to keep costs within acceptable limits.

- Theft of revenue or failure to collect all revenue. Both of these, of course, raise the food or beverage cost percentage. Often, the food cost percentage is excessive, not because food costs are too high, but because theft of cash is decreasing food revenues.

Potential Savings

Differences between standard and actual costs represent potential savings to the property. For example, if actual beverage costs are $270 greater than standard beverage costs, management could have increased profits by $270 during the financial period just by eliminating this variance. Each dollar of excess cost saved is a dollar of additional profit, provided that all other costs remain the same.

Converting percentage differences between standard and actual costs to dollar differences helps management understand when and if corrective action is in order. Exhibit 4, a potential savings worksheet, provides a format for making the necessary calculations. When reviewing the form, note:

- The source of standard percentage information used for the worksheet comparison is noted at the top of the form. As discussed previously, possibilities include averages, past financial statements, the past or current year's operating budget, or in-house developed standards (ideal costs).

- The formal worksheet comparison is made at least monthly (column 1). Quick, informal comparisons can be made daily by recalling the standard cost when reviewing forms such as the daily actual food cost worksheet and the daily beverage cost percentage recap.

- The best source of information about food costs for the month (column 2) is the cost of food sales reported in the monthly income statement. Monthly beverage costs (column 8) are reported on the income statement as the cost of beverage sales.

- Food revenue as reported on the monthly income statement is listed in column 3 and beverage revenue is noted in column 9.

Exhibit 4　Food and Beverage Potential Savings Worksheet

	Source of Standard Percent: Current Operating Budget											
	Food Cost						**Beverage Cost**					
	Actual			**Standard Percent**	**Difference**	**Potential Savings**	**Actual**			**Standard Percent**	**Difference**	**Potential Savings**
Month	**Cost**	**Revenue**	**Percent**				**Cost**	**Revenue**	**Percent**			
1	2	3	4	5	6	7	8	9	10	11	12	13
			2 ÷ 3		4 – 5	3 × 6			8 ÷ 9		10 – 11	9 × 12
Jan.	$118,545	$330,209	35.9%	33.5%	2.4%	$7,925	$13,875	$51,772	26.8%	21.0%	5.8%	$3,003
Feb.												
March												
April												
May												
June												
July												
Aug.												
Sept.												
Oct.												
Nov.												
Dec.												

- The actual food cost percentage for the month (column 4) is calculated by dividing the month's food cost (column 2) by the month's food revenue (column 3) and multiplying by 100. For example, in January:

$$\frac{\text{Month's Food Cost}}{\text{Month's Food Revenue}} \times 100 = \text{Actual Food Cost Percentage}$$

$$\frac{\$118,545}{\$330,209} \times 100 = 35.9\%$$

Similarly, the month's actual beverage cost percentage (column 10) is determined by dividing the month's beverage cost by the month's beverage revenue and multiplying by 100. In January, the calculation is:

$$\frac{\text{Month's Beverage Cost}}{\text{Month's Beverage Revenue}} \times 100 = \text{Actual Beverage Cost Percentage}$$

$$\frac{\$13,875}{\$51,772} \times 100 = 26.8\%$$

- The standard food cost percentage (column 5) is taken directly from the standard cost source, noted at the top of the form. The standard food cost percentage of 33.5 percent is the estimated food cost percentage for January, calculated when the operating budget was developed. The standard beverage cost percentage of 21 percent (column 11) is also taken from January's operating budget.

- The difference between the actual and standard food cost percentage (column 6) is:

$$\text{Column 4} - \text{Column 5} = \text{Column 6}$$

$$35.9\% - 33.5\% = 2.4\%$$

Similarly, the difference between the actual and standard beverage cost percentage (column 12) is:

$$\text{Column 10} - \text{Column 11} = \text{Column 12}$$

$$26.8\% - 21.0\% = 5.8\%$$

It is unlikely that the standard food and beverage cost percentages will be higher than the actual food and beverage cost percentages. Recall that the standards represent expected costs if nothing goes wrong. How often does that really occur? Reasons for standard costs being higher than actual costs include an incorrect standard, smaller portions, lower quality foods, poor recordkeeping, inadequate inventory, or some other improper practice. They all call for corrective action by management.

- The potential savings for the food operation (column 7) are determined by multiplying the difference between the actual and standard food cost percentages (as a decimal) by the food revenue. For example, consider January:

$$\begin{array}{ccc} \text{Food} & \times & \text{Percentage Difference} & = & \text{Potential Savings} \\ \text{Revenue} & & \text{(as a decimal)} & & \end{array}$$

$$\$330,209 \times .024 = \$7,925$$

In this example, the food operation spent approximately \$7,925 more on food than it should have during the month. Following more closely the procedures on which the food standards were based will decrease food costs and increase profit. The potential savings for the beverage operation are calculated in the same manner:

$$\begin{array}{ccc} \text{Beverage} & \times & \text{Percentage Difference} & = & \text{Potential Savings} \\ \text{Revenue} & & \text{(as a decimal)} & & \end{array}$$

$$\$51,772 \times .058 = \$3,003$$

Profit from the beverage operation could have been increased by up to \$3,003 by more closely following the procedures on which the beverage standards were based.

Identifying the Problem

Note the following principle: the more specific the standard cost, the easier it is to identify the problem; conversely, the more general the standard cost, the more difficult it is to identify the problem. For example, suppose separate food cost standards are established for lunch and dinner. If the actual food cost is higher than standard for lunch while the actual and standard costs for dinner are in line, the high food cost problem is clearly within the lunch operation. On the other hand, if the food cost standard is combined across both meal periods, it is more difficult to identify whether a problem is caused by lunch, dinner, or both.

Generally, all meals are combined in the standards developed for the food operation. Therefore, defining the problem contributing to high costs essentially involves questioning each operating procedure. Is it done the way it is supposed to be done? Can the procedure be improved? However, it is very difficult to know which procedures to review and to correct and whether changes in one will affect the others. The difficulty here is that all systems, and procedures within each system, are very closely related.

Identifying the problem requires asking such questions as: Are gross revenues decreasing? Why? Is the check average (revenue dollars divided by number of guests served) decreasing? Why? Is seat turnover (number of guests served divided by number of seats in the property) changing? Is there evidence of employee theft?

If revenues are decreasing while food costs remain the same, then variances from standards will increase. As noted previously, high food costs may result from lost revenue dollars as well as from increased operating costs.

It is important to know whether product costs are increasing. Trend analysis or indexing, which shows changes over time, may help put product costs in historical perspective.[1] When questioning product costs, it is also important to ask whether procedures used to control costs are reasonable at each control point, and whether they are followed consistently. Can practical changes be made in procedures to reduce costs without sacrificing product quality or the property's standards?

A checklist for profitable food operations (Exhibit 5) and a checklist for profitable beverage operations (Exhibit 6) list specific procedures to control food and beverage costs. The most important of these may become the basis for standard operating procedures utilized by a property. Management should study the lists routinely, update and revise them as necessary, and ensure that the procedures are being followed consistently. Tight systems become loose over time because employees find shortcuts and supervisors find other priorities. Without supervision, there is little assurance that procedures are being followed.

When variances between standard and actual costs are found, the checklists and standard operating procedures should be carefully reviewed. Are all the required procedures being followed? Are there any loopholes in the requirements that could cause costs to increase? Do staff, at any organizational level, have ideas about what is causing the trouble and how to correct it? Reviewing procedures may show managers which procedures are not being followed consistently or which ones need improvement. This practice may identify factors contributing to variances between standard and actual costs.

Taking Corrective Action

Once problems have been identified, management must determine the need for corrective action. Several factors become relevant when considering strategies to be implemented.

Exhibit 5   Checklist for Profitable Food Operations

Purchasing
- [ ] Food purchase specifications are used.
  When food is purchased:
  - [ ] Quality descriptions are given.
  - [ ] Items sold by several suppliers are purchased wherever possible.
  - [ ] Unit size is stated.
  - [ ] Best product for intended use is purchased.
  - [ ] Vendors know (have copies of) your quality standards (specifications).
- [ ] Seasonal and value buys are taken advantage of.
- [ ] Prices are obtained from several suppliers.
- [ ] Salespersons do not inventory and compute quantity needs of the operation.
- [ ] Lowest-priced supplier offering quality needed is given order.
- [ ] Beware of "deals."
- [ ] Don't buy for inventory (usually not more than for one month); weekly (or more frequently) may be much better.
- [ ] Bills are paid to take advantage of discounts.
- [ ] When possible, separate prices for food and its delivery are obtained.
- [ ] If it isn't needed, it isn't bought.
- [ ] A list with quantities needed is available when meeting with suppliers.
- [ ] The chef helps determine (is aware of) quantities of food purchased.
- [ ] Perishable items used in small quantities are purchased in small quantities.

Receiving
- [ ] Foods are checked to be sure:
  - [ ] Quality standards are met.
  - [ ] Amount received is amount ordered (items received are counted or weighed).
  - [ ] Amount received is amount charged for (per delivery invoice).
- [ ] Invoice extensions are verified.
- [ ] Foods are marked (date; cost).
- [ ] Proper receiving equipment is used; it is in good working condition.
- [ ] Deliveries are not accepted at peak business times.
- [ ] Someone is trained to receive food properly.
- [ ] Items are removed to storage promptly.
- [ ] Unacceptable items are refused.
- [ ] Spot-checking portion-controlled products is done to ensure that weight requirements are maintained.
- [ ] Meats, chicken, etc., are unboxed before weighing.
- [ ] Cartons of fruits and vegetables are checked throughout to ensure uniform quality.

Storage
- [ ] Oldest items are used first.
- [ ] Food is stored away from walls and off floor.
- [ ] Opened items are stored in containers with tight lids.
- [ ] Items giving off odors are stored away from items that absorb odors.
- [ ] Old items are used (and used first).
- [ ] Spoiled foods are removed promptly.
- [ ] Rodents and insects are professionally controlled.
- [ ] Proper storage temperatures are maintained.
- [ ] Foods in refrigerator are covered.
- [ ] Foods stored in freezer are in original container or in freezer bags or aluminum foil.
- [ ] Thawed foods are not refrozen.
- [ ] Storage areas are locked with limited access.
- [ ] Employee packages are checked.
- [ ] Special safeguards are set up for expensive items in storage.
- [ ] Inventory valuation and control recordkeeping procedures are followed.
- [ ] Items are shelved according to inventory records (or the reverse).

(continued)

Exhibit 5   *(continued)*

☐ Keys to storage areas are controlled.
☐ In-kitchen storage areas are locked when not in use.
☐ Monthly inventory valuation is done by someone other than the staff member responsible for storage.

Issuing
☐ Only items used for production are removed from storage.
☐ Oldest items are used first.
☐ Perishables are costed as a daily direct food cost.
☐ Generally, items are issued only at certain times of the day.
☐ Records are maintained for all items removed from storage.
☐ Issuing is done by the person responsible for storage.

Food Production
☐ Employees are trained to perform required tasks.
☐ Standard recipes are used and closely followed.
☐ Employees are properly supervised.
☐ Production equipment is adequate and maintained.
☐ Food production is scheduled according to need; leftovers are explained.
☐ There is agreement between the manager and the chef as to how much food must be produced.
☐ Leftovers are used in future production when possible.
☐ Employee meal and eating policies are enforced.
☐ Time between food production and service is minimized.
☐ High-cost convenience foods are offset with *reduced* labor cost.
☐ There is *not* an unnecessarily large variety of menu items.
☐ Proper food handling procedures result in minimum food spoilage.
☐ Amount of food left after service is reconciled with amount of food served.

Food Service
☐ Proper food ordering procedures are followed.
☐ Plate waste is analyzed.
☐ Portion size standards are maintained and followed.
☐ Food served meets the manager's quality standards.
☐ Food served is presented attractively.
☐ Proper serving equipment is available.
☐ Policies regarding returned food are followed.
☐ An effective food revenue control system is used.
   ☐ Revenue is received for all food served.
   ☐ Food and revenue control procedures minimize abuses by serving personnel.
☐ Dining room supervision prevents, or at least minimizes, guest walkouts.
☐ A system to account for food and beverage transfers has been set up and is used.
☐ Unprofitable, unpopular menu items are removed from the menu.
☐ The menu is designed to market high gross profit items.

- The probability of success—reduction of variances—must be weighed for all possible alternatives.

- All costs of implementing the corrective action must be known; there can be no surprises.

- Knowing what has or has not worked in similar situations in the past is an excellent clue to resolving current problems.

Exhibit 6 Checklist for Profitable Beverage Operations

Purchasing
- ☐ Purchasing is done in quantities necessary to build up a predetermined par stock level (the minimum/maximum system).
- ☐ Real costs of "deals" and special discounts are evaluated.
- ☐ Purchasing different house brands considers guest acceptance and value.
- ☐ Par stock levels are reviewed occasionally to determine if levels should be changed due to a changing sales mix.
- ☐ Inventory levels turn over at least twice monthly on the average. (No more than one-half the monthly beverage cost is in inventory at one time.)
- ☐ Beverages are purchased by brand names; unit size is stated.
- ☐ Salespersons do not inventory and compute quantities needed.
- ☐ Bills are paid to take advantage of discounts.
- ☐ A list with quantities needed is available when meeting with suppliers.
- ☐ The beverage manager (if separate from purchasing official) helps determine (is aware of) quantities of beverages purchased.
- ☐ Purchases are made in the largest practical bottle sizes.

Receiving
- ☐ Incoming beverages are checked against both the purchase order and delivery invoices for brand, quantity, and cost.
- ☐ Invoice extensions are verified.
- ☐ Deliveries are not accepted at peak business times.
- ☐ Incoming beverages are counted/weighed.
- ☐ Bottle prices are marked on bottles when received.
- ☐ Someone is trained to receive beverages properly.
- ☐ Items are removed to storage promptly.
- ☐ Unacceptable items are refused.
- ☐ Wet or punctured cases are inspected *very* closely before acceptance.
- ☐ Generally, the person purchasing beverages does not receive beverages.

Storage
- ☐ A perpetual inventory system is used; purchases are added to and issues are subtracted from amounts of stored items.
- ☐ Storage areas are locked with limited access.
- ☐ Employee packages are checked.
- ☐ Items are shelved according to inventory records (or the reverse).
- ☐ Keys to storage areas are controlled.
- ☐ Monthly physical inventories assess validity of the perpetual inventory system.
- ☐ Locks are changed at frequent intervals, especially when personnel with access to keys leave.
- ☐ Bottle stamps are used to identify the property's inventory.
- ☐ Someone other than bartenders keeps records.
- ☐ Par stock levels are established, used, and changed as necessary, both in central and bar storage areas.
- ☐ Proper storage temperatures, especially for beer and wine, are maintained.
- ☐ Spot-checks of inventory levels/records are made. Reasons for discrepancies are identified.
- ☐ Generally, more popular brands should be readily accessible; less popular brands can be stored in less accessible areas.

Issuing
- ☐ Issues are in amounts sufficient only to maintain the bar par(s).
- ☐ Full bottles are used only in return for empty bottles; empty bottles are broken (as laws permit).
- ☐ Requisition forms are completed.

(continued)

Exhibit 6 *(continued)*

☐ Generally, items are issued only at certain times of the day.
☐ Issuing is done by the person responsible for storage.

Service/Revenue Control
☐ Standard recipes, glassware, portion sizes, and bar par levels are used.
☐ Portion-control tools (jigger, shot glass, etc.) are *always* used.
☐ Employees are properly supervised.
☐ Beverages served meet the manager's quality standards.
☐ Beverages served are presented attractively.
☐ Policies regarding employees visiting/drinking at the bar during off hours are enforced.
☐ An effective beverage revenue control system is used.
  ☐ Revenue is received for all beverages served.
  ☐ Beverage and revenue control procedures minimize abuses by personnel preparing and serving beverages.
☐ A system to account for food and beverage transfers has been set up and is used.
☐ Only management determines drink prices.
☐ Shoppers are used as required.
☐ Only management personnel read cash registers.
☐ Policies regarding drinks on the house are strictly enforced.

- It must be possible to implement the chosen plan. Some food and beverage managers spend more time saying "things would be much easier if…" than they spend in evaluating the current problem and attempting to find the best solution within existing limitations.

- The best plan to resolve a problem is often a compromise or a mixture of several possible solutions.

- In some instances, alternatives can be tried on a limited basis rather than implemented throughout the operation. For example, if issuing practices are judged to be at fault, a new control procedure for issuing selected high-cost items—meats or liquor—might be tried before applying it to all items in inventory.

- Studying similar operations, reviewing books and articles from trade journals and the Internet, discussing problems with peers from other properties, and attending professional association meetings and educational seminars often generate useful ideas to help solve problems.

Assigning Responsibility

Another concern when considering strategies for corrective action is assigning responsibility for the action. There are several factors to consider in making this decision. First, how important is the problem? As the variance between standard and actual costs increases, more dollars become involved. As the importance of the problem increases, so does the need for higher levels of management to be involved in resolving it. Also, higher-level managers generally need to be involved if the proposed solution affects several departments.

Second, how specialized is the problem? If, for example, the corrective action involves changing procedures for determining the value of directs on the daily receiving report, it may be advisable to involve the receiving clerk and his or her supervisor. Who is responsible for the area of concern? Clearly, the management staff responsible and accountable for the area should be involved in some way in resolving the problem.

Should employees help determine necessary corrective action? Many human resource specialists stress participative management, which permits staff affected by management actions to help determine those actions. The employees who actually work with food and beverage products and procedures may have very good ideas about problems and how to correct them. By involving staff in making these decisions, the ideas for changing systems or procedures become the group's, as opposed to management's. This lessens the likelihood of staff resistance to revisions in operating plans.

Responsibility might be assigned to a person or persons in one or more of the following categories:

- Top management—those ultimately accountable to the owners; corporate-level officers; or the owners themselves

- Middle-level managers—those who have been delegated the authority and responsibility for operating specific segments of the property's activities

- Employees—those who most frequently perform and/or come in contact with control procedures

- External consultants—those who have special knowledge and experience

There are several concerns to keep in mind as corrective actions are implemented. Personnel affected by revised plans and procedures will often resist the changes; they may be more comfortable with the status quo. They may say, "We've always done things this way." This is especially true if staff members have not been involved in planning for change. Often, a situation like this is best resolved by involving affected personnel in analyzing and solving problems and by explaining, defending, and justifying the reasons for revised practices. Employees need to know how the changes will make things better from their perspective.[2] In Exhibit 7, a restaurant consultant shares some of his techniques for educating staff members and gaining their cooperation.

Employees should be trained to follow the new procedures.[3] Managers are often rushed and may give their staff members incomplete or incorrect instructions, perhaps because they aren't sure how the revised plan will work. Managers may believe they have effectively communicated when, in fact, staff members are not sure what has been said. Management must understand the new procedures to train staff and evaluate staff performance. Indeed, preparing for training sessions and effectively communicating instructions to employees encourages managers to fully think through new plans and procedures. For example, managers should ensure that all tools and equipment required by the revised procedures are available. In addition, it may be necessary to teach employees the proper ways to use new tools and equipment.

Exhibit 7   Restaurant Economics: A Team Approach

Restaurant *Report*

Articles

E-mail Newsletter

Hit enter to subscribe

Top 100 Sites

The Great Debates

Question & Answer

Buyer's Guide

Marketplace

Restaurants For Sale

Hospitality Jobs

James Beard Dateline

Print Subscriptions

Advertising Info

Contact Us

Articles By Department

Accountant's Corner
Beer
Chef's Report
Coffee
Core Biz Columns
Editorial Columns
Foodie Central
Internet Tips
Service Issues
Wine & Spirits

Newsletter Archives

Management Tip

DOLLARS AND SENSE
by Bill Marvin, "The Restaurant Doctor ®"

Recently I was consulting with a restaurant that had been losing 40 cents on the dollar for a number of years and the owners were tired of writing checks! The challenge was how to sensitize the staff to the situation without creating mass panic among the troops or revealing figures that were likely to find their way into a feature article in the local paper.

Before we started my first meeting with the staff, I asked them all to write down what percentage of the sales dollar they thought was profit. Then I gave them each $1.00 in change and we started to talk restaurant economics. The dollar represented a dollar in sales (they understood that) and they also understood that there were expenses against it. Reading from the NRA's Restaurant Industry Operations Report, we started "paying the bills" using median figures for full service restaurants -- 35 cents to food, 30 cents to labor, 5 cents to benefits and so on by dropping the coins into a cup. They were shocked to end up with 3 cents...and that was pre-tax profit!

Then I had them take the money out of the cup and talked about the results that their restaurant was achieving. We started with 50 cents for food and 50 cents for labor. Then I said, "OK, now we have to pay the rest of the bills -- utilities, telephone, rent, etc. -- so we need another 40 cents. Drop it in the cup. If you don't pay your bills, you can't stay in business." As their eyes got wide with panic, I gave the situation time to settle in before pointing out that when the income doesn't cover the expenses, you have to use your own money to stay in business...and that the owners were tired of it. They got the message loud and clear and started asking what they could do to help stop the bleeding.

I pass this along in case you want to conduct a little economics class of your own. In my experience, unless you educate them to the contrary, most restaurant workers think you make 25-50 cents on the dollar! By the way, the person who guessed closest to the right answer on profitability got the dollar's change from everyone at the meeting...and the restaurant's profitability picture has improved markedly in less than a month!

Source: Restaurant Report On-Line, a monthly business publication for owners, chefs, and key executives in the midscale/upscale restaurant market. http://www.restaurantreport.com

Evaluating Corrective Action

Evaluating the effectiveness of corrective actions is another step in the control system. The main concern here is assessing whether the variance between standard and actual costs has been reduced. If it has, the corrective action may have been helpful. On the other hand, if the variance has not been reduced, it is clear that the corrective action has not been successful. A revised plan or procedure must be implemented and evaluated.

There are several important considerations in the evaluation process. First, evaluation should not be done too early. Staff must have time to learn what they are supposed to do. Sufficient time must elapse between implementation of revised procedures and evaluation to allow for the elimination of start-up problems with the new system. During this transitional period, costs may continue to be higher than expected, so variance levels may continue to indicate a problem.

Choose an appropriate time frame for the evaluation. For example, to measure the success of corrective actions, the reduction of variance can be evaluated for the next fiscal period. Or, actual and standard costs could be compared one or two months after implementation to see whether the variance is reduced. Once the revised procedures succeed in making the operation more efficient, tightening up the standards themselves might be justified.

Evaluation of corrective actions may have spin-off effects on less obviously related parts of the food and beverage system. The evaluation itself may uncover other problems that must be resolved through further corrective action. For example, evaluation of changes in issuing procedures may uncover problems with the recordkeeping system used to assess issue values or with the stock rotation process.

Because all systems within an operation are very complex and interrelated, changes in one system may negatively affect another system. Suppose, for example, that to reduce food costs, new standard purchase specifications are written and new suppliers are chosen. If subsequent evaluation shows variances to be reduced, then the changes succeeded in reducing food costs. If evaluation stopped here, it would appear that the problem was resolved.

However, further evaluation might reveal that quality levels have been sacrificed. A change in purchase specifications might lead to inferior products. As a result, guests may become dissatisfied. At best, they may complain. At worst, they may stop visiting the property altogether and tell others about the problems they experienced. Sooner or later, unhappy guests result in decreased revenues. Therefore, evaluation must consider not only the specific target of corrective actions (controlling costs) but also the consequences of these actions for the entire food and beverage operation.

Endnotes

1. Trend analysis is beyond the scope of this text. Interested readers are referred to Raymond S. Schmidgall's *Hospitality Industry Managerial Accounting*, 4th ed. (Lansing, Mich.: Educational Institute of the American Hotel & Lodging Association, 1997).

2. For more information on how to manage change, interested readers are referred to Raphael R. Kavanaugh and Jack D. Ninemeier's *Supervision in the Hospitality Industry*, 3rd ed. (Lansing, Mich.: Educational Institute of the American Hotel & Lodging Association, 2001).

3. Readers interested in more information on training should read Lewis C. Forrest's *Training for the Hospitality Industry*, 3rd ed. (Lansing, Mich.: Educational Institute of the American Hotel & Lodging Association, 1989).

Review Questions

1. What are the most frequently used sources of information for defining standard food or beverage costs?

2. Is corrective action always necessary when actual costs are higher than standard costs? Why or why not?

3. What is meant by the concept of "potential savings"? Why must potential savings resulting from corrective actions be considered before implementing them?

4. What questions should be asked when comparing actual and standard costs?

5. Describe how unexplainable variances can occur.

6. Is corrective action necessary when variances between standard and actual costs cannot be explained? Why or why not?

7. Why should a standard cost which is higher than an actual cost be a concern to management?

8. What are some objectives of corrective action procedures?

9. Who should be involved in corrective action plans?

10. Why is it important to evaluate the effectiveness of corrective action plans?

 Internet Sites

For more information, visit the following Internet sites. Remember that Internet addresses can change without notice. If the site is no longer there, you can use a search engine to look for additional sites.

Associations

American Culinary Federation (ACF)
http://www.acfchefs.org

American Hotel & Lodging Association (AH&LA)
http://www.ahlaonline.org

American School Food Service Association (ASFSA)
http://www.asfsa.org

Club Managers Association of America (CMAA)
http://www.cmaa.org

The Educational Foundation of NRA
http://www.edfound.org

The Educational Institute of AH&LA
http://www.ei-ahla.org

Hospitality Financial and Technology
Professionals
http://www.hftp.org

Institute of Food Technologies
http://www.ift.org

International Hotel and Restaurant
Association
http://www.ih-ra.com

National Association of College and
University Food Services
http://www.nacufs.org

National Restaurant Association (NRA)
http://www.restaurant.org

Food and Beverage Resources

Club Management Online
http://www.club-mgmt.com/dining/
index.html

Decision-making
http://www.virtualsalt.com/
crebook5.htm

Prepared Foods. Product development,
ingredients, suppliers
http://www.preparedfoods.com

Restaurant Report On-Line
http://www.restaurantreport.com

Variance and Breakeven analysis
http://www.toolkit.cch.com/text/
P06_7500.asp

Management Companies

ARAMARK
http://www.aramark.com

Bon Appétit Management Company
http://www.bamco.com

Compass Group
http://www.compass-na.com

Sodexho Marriott
http://www.sodexhomarriott.com

The Wood Company
http://www.woodco.com

Publications—Online and Printed

Club Management Magazine
http://www.club-mgmt.com

Electronic Gourmet Guide
http://www.foodwine.com

Food and Hospitality Magazine
http://www.foodserviceworld.com

Food Management
http://www.foodservicesearch.com

Food Network: CyberKitchen
http://www.foodtv.com

Food Processing: The Magazine of
Strategy, Technology and Trends
http://www.foodprocessing.com

Internet Food Channel
http://www.foodchannel.com

International Hotel and Restaurant
Association journal
www.hotelsmag.com

International Journal of Hospitality
Management
http://www.mcb.co.uk/ijchm.htm

Journal of Hospitality Financial
Management
http://hrta.fnr.umass.edu/sheel/
ahfme/jhfm/aboutjhfm.html

Lodging Food and Beverage
http://www.lodgingnews.com/
lodgingfnb/

Lodging Hospitality Online
http://www.lhonline.com

Lodging News, journal of the American
Hotel & Lodging Association
http://www.ei-ahla.org/webs/
lodging/index.html

Nation's Restaurant News
http://www.nrn.com

On the Rail—News for Food
Professionals
http://www.ontherail.com

Restaurants and Institutions magazine
http://www.rimag.com

Restaurant Business, Food Service, and
ID magazines
http://www.foodservicetoday.com

Restaurant Hospitality
www.foodservicesearch.com

Restaurants and Institutions
http://www.rimag.com

Restaurants USA, publication of
National Restaurant Association
http://www.restaurant.org/rusa

Wine Business Monthly
http://smartwine.com

World Hospitality, management
magazine for hotel executives
http://www.worldhospitality.com

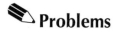 **Problems**

Problem 1

Financial information for a restaurant's beverage operation is as follows:

		Beverage Cost Percent	
Month	Beverage Revenue	Standard	Actual
January	$19,500	22%	26%
February	$21,005	22%	23.2%
March	$22,100	22%	24.7%

By what amount could profit levels have been increased if actual beverage cost percentages were on target with estimated standard costs?

Problem 2

Food revenues are $850,000; beverage revenues are $110,000. There is a one percent variance between standard and actual food costs and a four percent variance between standard and actual beverage costs. Which operation (food or beverage) likely has the most significant control problem? Why?

Problem 3

In regard to Problem 2 above:

a) How much higher would food profits have been if actual food costs were in line with standard food costs?

b) How much higher would beverage profits have been if actual beverage costs were in line with standard beverage costs?

Problem 4

a) Complete the Food and Beverage Potential Savings Worksheet below:

	Food and Beverage Potential Savings											
	Food Cost						**Beverage Cost**					
	Actual			**Standard**		**Potential**	**Actual**			**Standard**		**Potential**
Month	**Cost**	**Revenue**	**Percent**	**Percent**	**Difference**	**Savings**	**Cost**	**Revenue**	**Percent**	**Percent**	**Difference**	**Savings**
Jan.	$180,015	$485,510		38.7%			$80,100	$290,000		25.8%		
Feb.	$159,850	$397,480		38.7%			$61,700	$220,500		25.8%		
March	$152,700	$381,000		38.7%			$63,000	$200,400		25.8%		
April	$158,750	$382,750		38.7%			$62,775	$193,200		25.8%		
May	$161,420	$390,770		38.7%			$61,600	$195,400		25.8%		

b) What is the total amount of potential savings year-to-date in the food and beverage operations?

Problem 5

Control procedures during March have reduced the actual food cost percentage by .5 percent and the actual beverage cost percentage by 1.8 percent from the February levels calculated in Problem 4. If actual revenues in March were as follows, calculate the actual costs.

Data for March

Food Revenue	Actual Food Cost Percent	Actual Food Cost	Beverage Revenue	Actual Beverage Cost Percent	Actual Beverage Cost
$22,650			$17,000		

Problem 6

Following is selected information from three units of a fast-food restaurant chain from last month. All operate in the same metropolitan area. You are the district manager analyzing these results. What are the major problem areas, if any, with each unit?

	Net Revenue		Planned Revenue Growth		Marketing (Promotion) Costs	
	Actual	Budget	Actual	Budget	Actual	Budget
Unit 1	$110,000	$108,000	1%	0	3%	3%
Unit 2	$90,050	$107,000	3%	2%	4%	4%
Unit 3	$171,100	$160,000	(2%)	1%	2%	4%

		Food Cost		Labor Cost	
		Actual	Budget	Actual	Budget
Unit 1		29.3%	29.4%	23.8%	24.1%
Unit 2		30.5%	29.4%	23.1%	24.1%
Unit 3		28.8%	29.4%	22.9%	24.1%

Part V

Controlling Revenue

Chapter 11 Outline

Competencies

1. Describe revenue control procedures typical of food and beverage operations with manual guest check systems. (pp. 341–343)

2. Explain how point-of-sale technology simplifies guest check control systems. (pp. 344)

3. Distinguish server banking from cashier banking systems. (pp. 345–348)

4. Explain how managers use daily cashier reports as revenue control tools. (pp. 348–351)

5. Describe how managers use point-of-sale reports as revenue control tools. (p. 353)

6. Explain how managers in nonautomated operations control beverage revenue, and identify the advantages and disadvantages of automated beverage control systems. (pp. 353–361)

11

Revenue Control

THE LAST PHASE of the operational cycle is the collection of revenue for products and services offered to guests of the property. Planning for and controlling revenue is just as important as properly managing costs.

The first step in designing a control system for any resource, including revenue, is to set a standard. Revenue standards can then be compared against actual revenue. But how should a food and beverage operation define revenue standards? If a properly prepared operating budget (the operations profit plan) has been developed, it will indicate the liquor standard expected (revenue) for the fiscal period covered by the budget. As an integral part of the control process, the manager may compare the operating budget showing expected revenue with the income statement showing actual revenue. A manager may carry out corrective action plans, if needed. For example, new marketing strategies may be developed and implemented to increase revenue. It is also important for the manager to accurately estimate the amount of revenue which is generated for each "meal". How much revenue should be generated, for example, during a lunch or dinner shift? One method is based upon guest checks. The standard—the amount of revenue a property expects to collect from its operations—is represented by the totals from guest checks for a specific meal period or periods. A second method relies on unit sales information entered into electronic cash register equipment before menu items (food or beverages) are produced. The sum of this sales information defines revenue expectations.

This chapter begins by examining guest check control systems in relation to nonautomated and automated operations. Next, we discuss procedures that are designed to help ensure that the actual revenue collected corresponds with defined revenue standards. The final sections of the chapter examine the unique features of beverage operations that challenge revenue control systems for both nonautomated and automated operations.

Standard Revenue and Guest Check Control Systems

In some food and beverage operations, a guest check system is at the heart of revenue control. The standard (expected) amount of revenue is represented by the total of all amounts recorded on individual guest checks for a meal period (or periods) after all checks have been accounted for. The reliability of this standard depends upon servers following strict procedures when processing individual guest checks. These procedures will depend on the degree of automation within the operation.

The following sections examine guest check control systems for nonautomated and automated operations.

Manual Guest Check System

Manual guest check systems using hard-copy forms are increasingly being replaced in even relatively small operations by their automated counterparts. When used, a fundamental revenue control procedure requires that servers neatly write all food and beverage orders on guest checks. Servers generally use pens, not pencils, and mistakes must be crossed out rather than erased. In many operations, the server must have a supervisor initial a guest check that has items crossed out or voided. Before initialing, the supervisor makes sure that the deleted items were not prepared by kitchen or bar staff.

Before food or beverage items are produced, servers must provide appropriate production staff with **requisition slips**. Servers list items on a requisition slip and also record their name (or identification number) and the serial number of the corresponding guest check. Operations with manual guest check systems typically use a **duplicate guest check system** for food orders. With this system, each guest check has at least two parts. The server turns in the duplicate copy to the kitchen and keeps the original copy for presentation to the guest. When the guest is ready to pay, the guest check is tallied.

Requisition slips and duplicate checks are useful for routine **guest check audit** functions. At the end of a meal period, the manager matches requisition slips (or duplicate copies of guest checks) turned in to the kitchen with the corresponding guest checks for which revenue has been collected. This procedure identifies differences between what was produced and what was served. Routine audits of guest checks may also reveal mistakes made by servers in pricing items on guest checks or in calculating totals. By conducting routine audits of guest checks, management indicates to employees its concern about effectively controlling the property's revenue collection system.

Guest checks should be unique to the property. If they are purchased from a local restaurant supply company, anyone—including dishonest employees—can buy them. These checks can be used with no record of who has them or from whom revenue is due. It is best to order specially printed, hard-to-duplicate guest checks. Unused checks should be securely stored.

Guest checks should be sequentially numbered and a record kept of which checks are given to which employee. Beginning and ending numbers for all checks issued to servers should be listed on a guest check number log (Exhibit 1). Servers accepting the checks should sign the log to verify that they have received all checks for which they will be held accountable.

All checks issued to each server must be accounted for at the end of a shift. Checks will be either used and turned in with revenue, unused and turned in as part of the server-closing procedures, or kept in use and transferred to another server. Requisition slips or duplicate guest checks are helpful when a check is unaccounted for. If requisition slips (or the duplicate copy) corresponding to a missing guest check have been turned in to the kitchen, management knows that

Exhibit 1 Guest Check Number Log

Guest Check Log							
		Type Ticket			Guest Check No.		
Date	Shift	Food	Bev.	Server	Start	End	Signature
8/1/00	A.M.	✓		Phyllis	111789	111815	Phyllis
8/1/00	A.M.	✓		Joe	700100	700125	Joe
8/1/00	A.M.		✓	Janis	40010	40040	Janis
8/1/00	P.M.	✓		Joe	111850	111899	Joe
8/1/00	P.M.	✓		Andy	111900	111930	Andy

Source: Jack D. Ninemeier, *Food and Beverage Security: A Systems Manual for Restaurants, Hotels, and Clubs* (Boston, Mass.: CBI, 1982).

the missing guest check has been used, that items listed on it have been served, and that revenue is due from the server.

Automated Guest Check System

Some automated systems use preprinted, hard copy, serially numbered guest checks similar to those used by operations with manual guest check systems. Before entering an order, the server must "open" the guest check within the system. This is usually accomplished by inputting the server's identification number and the guest check's serial number. Once the system has recognized the server and "opened" the guest check, orders are entered and relayed to remote printers located at appropriate production areas. Precheck terminals are also equipped with guest check printers. As orders are relayed to production areas, the same items (with their selling prices) are printed on the server's guest check.

Once a guest check has been opened, it becomes part of the system's **open check file**. For each opened guest check, this file may contain the following data:

- Terminal number where the guest check was opened

- Guest check serial number

- Server identification number

- Time guest check was opened

- Menu items ordered

- Prices of menu items ordered

- Applicable tax

- Total amount due

A server adds orders to the guest check at the precheck terminal by first inputting the guest check's serial number and then entering the additional items.

There are many variations of this automated prechecking system. Some systems use guest checks with bar codes corresponding to the preprinted serial numbers. This eliminates the need for servers to input the guest check's serial number when opening a guest check or when adding items to guest checks already in use. When the guest check is placed in the guest check printer, the system reads the bar code and immediately accesses the appropriate file.

Modern systems eliminate the traditional guest check altogether. These increasingly popular systems maintain only an electronic file for each open guest check. A thin, narrow, receiptlike guest check can be printed at any time during service, but is usually not printed until after the meal, when the server presents it to the guest for settlement. Since no paper forms are used, the table number often becomes the tracking identifier for the order. With some systems, seat numbers are used for tracking multiple checks per table.

Electronic cash registers and point-of-sale technology simplify guest check control functions and eliminate the need for most of the time-consuming audit procedures required for manual systems. Automated prechecking functions eliminate mistakes made by servers in pricing items on guest checks or in calculating totals. When items must be voided after they have been entered into the system, a supervisor (with a special identification number) accesses the system and deletes the appropriate items. Generally, automated systems produce a report that lists all guest transactions with voided or returned items, the servers responsible for each guest transaction, and the supervisors who accessed the system and voided the items. It is important for automated systems to distinguish voided from returned items because returned items should be included in inventory usage reports, while voided items should not. If an item is voided after it has already been prepared, the item would be classified as "returned."

At any point in time, managers and/or supervisors can access the system and monitor the status of any open transaction. This check-tracking capability can be used to help identify potential walkouts, reduce server fraud, and significantly tighten guest check and revenue control. For example, the manager may walk by a guest table and notice two desserts have been served. The open check feature in the electronic cash register can be accessed to note if these desserts have been entered in the system.

The status of a guest transaction changes from open to closed when payment is received from the guest and it is recorded in the system. Most automated systems produce an **outstanding transaction report** that lists all open transactions (by server). These reports may list items such as the sequence number, server identification number, time at which the transaction began, number of guests, table number, and guest check total. This data makes it much easier for managers to determine responsibility for open transactions.

Collecting Revenue

To this point we have been discussing procedures to assess the amount of standard (expected) revenue to be generated from sales to guests. The next step in revenue control is to develop and implement revenue collection procedures to help ensure that actual revenue collected corresponds with defined revenue standards. The following sections examine procedures in relation to two types of revenue collection systems: the server banking system and the cashier banking system. In addition, revenue reports produced by computerized point-of-sale systems are examined.

Server Banking System

With the **server banking system**, servers (and bartenders) use their own banks of money to collect payments from guests and retain the collected revenue until they check out at the end of their shifts. In some operations, locking cash boxes are provided for each server to store collected revenue, credit card vouchers, and other sales materials.

At the end of a shift, the amount of revenue due the operation when a manual (hard copy check) system is used is determined by tallying the totals from all guest checks assigned to each server. The tally is made by the manager (or cashier) in the presence of the server. Totals from guest checks settled by credit card vouchers, personal checks, and house account charges are subtracted from the tally to arrive at the amount of cash to be collected from the server. The remaining cash represents the server's opening change bank and any cash tips earned. After the actual revenue collected by the manager (or cashier) balances with the tally of totals from all guest checks assigned to the server, charged tips (as recorded on credit card or house account vouchers) are paid out to the server.

In nonautomated properties, these closing procedures can be very time- consuming. Electronic cash registers and point-of-sale technology speed up the process by producing a report at the end of a shift that automatically tallies the total revenue due from each server. The report generally identifies transactions opened by the server and itemizes each of them in terms of:

- Table number
- Number of covers
- Elapsed time from opening to closing of the transaction
- Totals for food and beverage revenue
- Tax
- Tips due
- Settlement method

Exhibit 2 presents a sample report listing the daily transactions of one server. Using this report, closing procedures are greatly simplified for operations with server banking systems. Exhibit 3 summarizes unit sales, revenue totals, and related data for all servers for a shift or meal period.

Exhibit 2   Sample Daily Server Transactions (Sales) Report

	Net Sls	Comps	Promos	Taxes	Grs Sls (less Voids)	Check Avg.	Guest Avg.
				Kathryn		Page 1	
				Grs Sls 97.27		06/03/XX at 4:41 p.m.	
			Server Sales Report for 5/31/XX			3.659	
			Sales by Catagory				
Apps	5.50	0.00	0.00	0.33	5.83	0.97	0.45
Non-Alc	1.25	0.00	0.00	0.07	1.32	0.22	0.10
Salads	13.90	0.00	0.00	0.83	14.73	2.45	1.13
Soups	0.00	0.00	0.00	0.00	0.00	0.00	0.00
Chip & Frie	6.95	0.00	0.00	0.42	7.37	1.23	0.57
Dinners	0.00	0.00	0.00	0.00	0.00	0.00	0.00
Desserts	0.00	0.00	0.00	0.00	0.00	0.00	0.00
Burgers	15.75	0.00	0.00	0.94	16.69	2.78	1.28
Sandwiches	11.25	0.00	0.00	0.68	11.93	1.99	0.92
Pizza	0.00	0.00	0.00	0.00	0.00	0.00	0.00
Liquor	13.68	0.00	0.00	0.82	14.50	2.42	1.12
Kids	0.00	5.90	0.00	0.00	5.90	0.98	0.45
Beer	14.86	0.00	0.00	0.89	15.75	2.63	1.21
Wine	0.00	0.00	0.00	0.00	0.00	0.00	0.00
Theater	0.00	0.00	0.00	0.00	0.00	0.00	0.00
Open Pool	0.00	0.00	0.00	0.00	0.00	0.00	0.00
Happy Hour	0.00	0.00	0.00	0.00	0.00	0.00	0.00
Drink Mods	0.00	0.00	0.00	0.00	0.00	0.00	0.00
Food Mods	0.00	0.00	0.00	0.00	0.00	0.00	0.00
Billy's	0.00	0.00	0.00	0.00	0.00	0.00	0.00
Totals	83.14	5.90	0.00	4.98	94.02	15.67	7.23

Num Guests:

Lunch	13
Dinner	0
after hour	0
Total Guests	13

Num Checks:

Lunch	6
Dinner	0
after hour	0
Total Checks	6

Voids   3.25

Taxes by Tax ID

Non-Alc-x	0.07
Food	3.20
Liq	0.82
Beer	0.89
Wine	0.00
Modifier	0.00
Gift	0.00
Golf	0.00
Pool	0.00
Liq X	0.00
Beer X	0.00
Wine X	0.00
Game Room	0.00
Theater	0.00
non-alc	0.00
Total	4.98

Courtesy of Ibertech, Inc., Aloha Hospitality Software, Hurst, Texas

Exhibit 3   Summary of Unit Sales, Revenue Totals and Other Data for Meal Period

			PMIX Report—All Terminals						Page 6
			for 5/31/XX						06/04/xx at 8:36 a.m. 3.659

Rank	Category	Item Num	Item Name	Num Sold	Sales	Cost	Profit	Food Cost %	% Sales	% Cat Sales
	Grand Total:			4369	15147.70	0.00	15147.70	0.00	100.0	

Summary Section

Rank	Category	Item Num	Item Name	Num Sold	Sales	Cost	Profit	Food Cost %	% Sales	% Cat Sales
	Apps			116	617.45	0.00	617.45	0.00	4.08	
	Non-Alc			172	216.00	0.00	216.00	0.00	1.43	
	Salads			15	88.85	0.00	88.85	0.00	0.59	
	Soups			5	15.35	0.00	15.35	0.00	0.10	
	Chip & Frie			77	399.25	0.00	399.25	0.00	2.64	
	Dinners			40	360.50	0.00	360.50	0.00	2.38	
	Desserts			4	15.10	0.00	15.10	0.00	0.10	
	Burgers			62	320.30	0.00	320.30	0.00	2.11	
	Sandwiches			61	343.65	0.00	343.65	0.00	2.27	
	Pizza			28	279.60	0.00	279.60	0.00	1.85	
	Liquor			1016	3125.00	0.00	3125.00	0.00	20.63	
	Kids			11	35.05	0.00	35.05	0.00	0.23	
	Beer			2580	8331.35	0.00	8331.35	0.00	55.00	
	Wine			52	145.35	0.00	145.35	0.00	0.96	
	Theater			77	462.00	0.00	462.00	0.00	3.05	
	Open Pool			1	361.65	0.00	361.65	0.00	2.39	
	Drink Mods			22	11.00	0.00	11.00	0.00	0.07	
	Food Mods			30	20.25	0.00	20.25	0.00	0.13	
	Grand Total			4369	15147.70	0.00	15147.70	0.00	100.00	

Non-Sales Categories

Summary Section—Non-Sales Categories

************   **End of Report**   ************

Courtesy of Ibertech, Inc., Aloha Hospitality Software, Hurst, Texas

Cashier Banking System

With the **cashier banking system**, guests pay the cashier, the bartender, or the food or beverage server (who then pays the cashier or the bartender who has cashiering duties). Upon receiving a guest check for settlement, the cashier keys each item listed on the check into the register. The register tallies each item and imprints the total on the check for verification with the server's handwritten total. The cashier (or bartender) then retains the money and the accompanying guest checks.

With most electronic point-of-sale systems, the cashier does not have to key each item from every guest check into the register. The cashier's terminal simply accesses the transaction number opened by the server, and the cashier closes it by collecting and recording the revenue. At the end of the shift, the cashier's cash drawer and supporting documents are accounted for.

The following sections focus on revenue collection procedures used by food service operations with traditional cash register equipment.

At the end of the shift, cash register readings are taken and summarized. The cash, credit card vouchers, other types of payments, and any miscellaneous paid outs are then reconciled with the cash register readings using a **daily cashier's eport**. An operation with several stations and shifts may find it more convenient to use several daily cashier's reports, and summarize the data on a single report.

All daily cashier's reports are designed with common characteristics. These reports generally contain a heading showing the date and day of the week, and may contain information about the weather, number of guests, or other data helpful in analyzing and managing the operation. They usually consist of separate sections for register readings, accounting of cash register funds and transactions, and supporting documents.

For internal control reasons, register readings are taken by the manager or a designated individual other than the cashier. The differences between beginning and ending readings less any "voids" (voided register entries approved by supervisors) represent food revenue and sales taxes collected.

Exhibit 4 presents a sample daily cashier's report. Within this report, the accounting for the cash register funds and transactions is divided into two sections: the "To Be Accounted For" section and the "Accounted For" section.

The "To Be Accounted For" section represents net register readings, tips entered by guests on credit cards or charge accounts, collections from guests which are to be applied to prior balances of open accounts, and the initial change fund in the register. This section typically includes the following items:

- Food revenue
- Sales tax
- Tips charged
- Guest collections
- Change fund (start)

The result of this section provides a control total. The total of cash drawer funds and amounts represented on supporting documents should reconcile with this control total, except for minor cash shortages or overages. Minor shortages or overages are generally due to errors in processing the numerous cash transactions that an operation handles daily. Obviously, any large variances should be investigated for irregularities.

The "Accounted For" section represents the cash drawer funds, bankcard drafts (such as VISA and MasterCard), documents supporting items paid out of the cash drawer, and the return of the initial change fund (cash bank). This section typically includes the following items:

- Cash
- Purchases paid out
- Tips paid out
- Guest charges
- Change fund/cash bank (return)
- Cash shortages or overages

Exhibit 4   Daily Cashier's Report

Daily Cashier's Report

DATE 12/8/XX   Day: Sat.   Weather: Rainy + Cold

	Key A (Sales)	Key B (Sales Tax)
Previous shift's closing reading	62 113 14	9 002 03
This shift's closing reading	63 463 81	9 083 07
Difference	1 350 67	81 04
Voids	-0-	-0-
Net	1 350 67	81 04
TOTAL TO BE ACCOUNTED FOR:		
Food Revenue	1 350 67	
Sales Tax	81 04	
Tips Charged	50 00	
Guest Collections	185 00	
Change Fund (Start)	500 00	
CONTROL TOTAL	2 166 71	
TOTAL ACCOUNTED FOR:		
Cash for Deposit	1 407 06	
Purchases Paid Out	8 75	
Tips Paid Out	50 00	
Guest Charges	200 00	
Change Fund (Return)	500 00	
Total Receipts and Paid Outs	2 165 81	
Cash Short (+)	90	
Cash Over (−)		
TOTAL ACCOUNTED FOR	2 166 71	

EXPLANATION OF CUSTOMER COLLECTIONS & CHARGES:

CUSTOMER	TAB	COLLECTION	CHARGE
DEBCO, Inc.	1812		200 00
J.R. Rickles		185 00	
TOTAL		185 00	200 00

EXPLANATION OF PURCHASES PAID OUT:

PAID TO	PURPOSE	AMOUNT	
Ted's Market	Food items for kitchen	8 75	
TOTAL		8 75	

Source: Raymond Cote, *Understanding Hospitality Accounting I*, 4th ed. (Lansing, Mich.: Educational Institute of the American Hotel & Lodging Association, 1997), p. 220.

These total receipts and amounts paid out are reconciled with the control total, and any minor cash shortages or overages are computed. The final "Total Accounted For" must reconcile with the total of the items "To Be Accounted For" (the control total).

Processing the "To Be Accounted For" Section. The "To Be Accounted For" section is processed as follows:

1. Amounts for food revenue and sales tax are the result of totals of register readings, less any void rings.

2. Tips charged are tips that guests entered on credit card drafts or open account transactions.

3. Guest collections are payments received from guests to be applied toward their prior charges on open accounts. These collections are explained in a listing on a separate section of the report.

4. Change fund (start) represents the cashier's initial funds (cash bank) provided at the start of the day. This fund is a predetermined, fixed amount (also termed "imprest amount") established by management.

5. The total of the "To Be Accounted For" section serves as the control total. This control total will later be compared to the cash count and register documents to determine any cash shortages or overages.

Processing the "Accounted For" Section. The "Accounted For" section is processed as follows:

1. The change fund (cash bank) is restored to its original amount. The balance of the cash, personal checks, traveler's checks, and bank credit card drafts form the cash deposit. (To keep our example simple, the food and beverage operation using Exhibit 4 accepts only bankcards.)

2. Purchases paid out represent incidentals that were paid from the cash drawer during the shift. The cashier supports these amounts paid out by including documented vouchers in the cash drawer. These vouchers are explained in a listing on a separate section of the report. Paying for incidentals in this way eliminates the writing of checks for small items and averts the need for a separate cash fund.

3. Tips paid out represent payments to employees for the tips that were entered on credit card drafts or open accounts. The policy of many operations is to pay the server immediately upon receipt of the credit card draft or open account charge. In this case, the net result of tips charged and tips paid out will be zero.

4. Guest charges represent charges made by guests on their house accounts, and include the total of the guest checks. These charges are explained in a listing on a separate section of the report.

5. The total of the above items, referred to as "Total Receipts and Paid Outs," is compared with the control total (the total of the "To Be Accounted For" section). Any difference between these two totals is due to a cash shortage or overage.

6. The resulting "Accounted For" total must agree with the "To Be Accounted For" total (the control total).

Revenue Reports

Managers of automated food and beverage operations benefit from the speed and accuracy by which revenue reports are produced. Revenue reports enable managers to measure the sales performance of individual menu items by product category within certain time frames. These reports allow managers to track individual item sales, analyze product acceptance, and monitor advertising and sales promotional efforts. The time intervals are commonly referred to as day parts. Day parts often vary in relation to the type of food service operation. Fast-food restaurants may desire revenue analysis reports segmented by 15-minute intervals; table service restaurants, by the hour; and institutional food service operations, by meal period. The information reported is used for forecasting revenue and determining labor requirements.

A **revenue summary report** generally contains detailed revenue and tax information by such categories as food items, beer, wine, and liquor. Generally, totals for each category are printed for each meal period, and totals for each meal period are shown in different sections of the report. Exhibit 5 illustrates a sample revenue summary report of outlet sales for one day.

Productivity reports typically detail revenue activity for all assigned server revenue records. A **daily productivity report** may be generated for each server and cashier in terms of guest count, total revenue, and average revenue. In addition, a weekly productivity report may be generated, showing average revenue amount per guest for each server.

Assessing Standard Revenue: Beverage Operations —————

Just as in the control of food revenue, the expected revenue from beverage sales is based on the total number of items actually sold. However, procedures for controlling beverage revenue are different from procedures for controlling food revenue, and they are sometimes more complex to develop. One reason for this is the difficulty of basing the control of beverage revenue on a guest check system.

In properties with a nonautomated guest check system, procedures to control revenue include the following:

1. The bartender is assigned guest checks at the start of a shift and must adhere to all requirements regarding their use. For example, when a guest at the bar or lounge table orders a drink, the bartender writes the order on a guest check.

2. The bartender places the check face down on the bar or table in front of the guest and writes additional drink orders as necessary on the same check. If the

Exhibit 5   Sample Revenue Summary Report

	Revenue Summary Report for 5/31/XX		Page 2
	Net Sales by Period by Category		06/03/XX at 4:37 p.m.
			3.659
	Lunch	**Dinner**	**after hour**
Apps	29.30	493.45	94.70
Non-Alc	32.76	155.00	17.76
Salads	23.10	58.80	6.95
Soups	0.00	15.35	0.00
Chip & Frie	23.80	337.50	37.95
Dinners	9.25	341.30	9.95
Desserts	7.90	3.25	3.95
Burgers	87.65	222.75	9.90
Sandwiches	77.40	256.75	9.50
Pizza	12.75	257.90	8.95
Liquor	24.29	1014.62	1909.20
Kids	15.15	19.90	0.00
Beer	106.60	2512.97	5240.19
Wine	0.00	71.46	65.66
Theater	0.00	324.00	138.00
Open Pool	0.00	0.00	361.65
Happy Hour	0.00	0.00	0.00
Drink Mods	0.00	3.30	7.08
Food Mods	3.00	17.25	0.00
Billy's	0.00	0.00	0.00
Totals	452.95	6105.55	7921.39

Courtesy of Ibertech, Inc., Aloha Hospitality Software, Hurst, Texas

bar cash register has an accounts receivable function, the bartender can ring the check through the machine before serving the drink.

3. When the guest is ready to pay, the bartender rings the check into the register and deposits the funds.

4. The bartender puts used guest checks in a locked check box until the end of the shift when they are accounted for.

5. Totals from the guest checks are matched with register readings. Totals from all guest checks determine the standard expected revenue, which is compared to the actual revenue collected.

An obvious disadvantage of this method is the time required for the bartender to record guest check information. From a practical perspective, during busy rush periods, the procedure slows service. This is an excellent example of control procedures clashing with marketing and guest concerns. The issue must be resolved by management based on the unique costs and benefits of each procedure in each specific operation.

Increasingly, beverage operations utilize electronic cash register/point of sale (ECR/POS) systems. The basic procedures utilized to record data in these systems are the same for the food operations and for beverage service. For example, the bartender can take a drink order from the guest and enter it into the system using a keyboard or touch screen terminal. A drink can be prepared and served to the guests. Payment can be recorded and a receipt printer can produce hard copy on a narrow register tape for presentation to the guest.

One challenge in controlling beverage revenue is the impracticality of separating preparation, service, and collection activities. Bartenders frequently take an order, prepare and serve the drink, collect revenue, register the sale, and make change for guests. The possibilities for theft of revenue are numerous since there are fewer opportunities for managers to ensure that all required revenue control procedures are being followed.

With these problems in mind, how can the manager assess standard (expected) revenue for beverage sales? One possibility is to define the standard revenue level for beverage sales in terms of a percentage of total revenue that managers have come to expect on the basis of past revenue records.

Managers of nonautomated beverage operations can use a number of methods to control beverage revenue. Many of these methods match the number of ounces of liquor used with the amount of revenue generated. Some of these methods can be very time-consuming. The following sections examine the bottle revenue value method, which is practical and yields reasonably accurate information. In addition, automated beverage control systems are discussed in relation to beverage revenue control and the types of reports that can be produced for beverage managers.

Bottle Revenue Values: Manual System

The **bottle revenue value system** involves estimating the amount of revenue expected from a bottle of liquor. The beverage income standard is determined from the number of empty liquor bottles. This standard is then compared with the amount of actual revenue generated. Differences represent the variance between standard and actual revenue.

For example, suppose that, at the end of a shift, three bottles of bar Scotch are issued in exchange for three empty bottles. If each empty bottle had a revenue value of $40, then $120 in revenue should have been generated from the sale of Scotch during the shift. This system does not account for changes in opened-bottle inventory, but instead assumes that the value of liquor in opened bottles evens out over time.

This method is easy to use, but its usefulness depends on how accurately bottle revenue values are determined. The procedure for calculating bottle revenue values involves examining the historical sales mix to establish a weighted average revenue value per bottle. This procedure assumes that the historical sales mix is an accurate predictor of current usage rates. The following sections examine a step-by-step procedure for implementing a bottle revenue value system.

Classify All Liquor by Type. Two common classifications are house and call liquors. House liquor is served when no specific brand is ordered. Call liquor is that which is ordered by brand. (When even more specific standard revenue information for beverages is desired, it is possible to classify a third type of liquor—premium.)

Classify All Drinks by Kind. Two common classifications are mixed drinks and cocktails. Mixed drinks are liquor drinks to which a non-alcoholic mixer such as soda, tonic, or water is added. A cocktail is a drink made with two or more liquors or a drink containing a large amount of a single liquor. Typically, it is necessary for the beverage manager to specify classifications for other kinds of drinks to maintain consistency in the collection of revenue information during the study period.

Examine the Beverage Sales Mix. The beverage manager should establish a period of time to collect data about the beverage sales mix. Accuracy increases with the number of drinks reviewed. Review a proportionate number of drinks sold at all pricing periods. For example, if approximately 60 percent of all beverage revenue is generated from drinks sold at regular prices, then 60 percent of all drinks observed should be counted during regular price periods. Low- and high-price service times are other pricing periods that should be observed.

Count the Number of Each Type and Kind of Liquor Served. During the study period, a count is kept of the number of each type (house or call) and kind (mixed drink or cocktail) of liquor served. Guest checks, electronic cash register data, or physical counts can be used to determine the number of drinks served.

Determine the Revenue Value per Ounce. A revenue value per ounce calculation form (Exhibit 6) can be used to determine the revenue value per ounce of house and call liquors.

When reviewing Exhibit 6, note that a count from several low-pricing periods showed that 48 mixed drinks using house liquor were served. This is recorded in line A, column 1. Also note that, during the study period, 48 mixed drinks using house liquor were served at regular prices. This is recorded in line B, column 1. The total of all drinks served, line A plus line B, is shown in line C. In the example, 96 mixed drinks were served.

The number of ounces of liquor in each type of drink, line D, is multiplied by the number of drinks served, line C. In the example, the property has standardized its recipes to allow 1 ounce of liquor in each mixed drink.

The sales price for each drink type is noted in lines F and G. In the example, the low price of mixed drinks made with house liquor is $4.00; the regular price of house liquor cocktails is $4.50. In line H, the total revenue from low-priced drinks is reported. In the example, 48 mixed drinks at $4.00 each (line A times line F) amounts to $192. This is the revenue generated from the sale of house liquor mixed drinks during low-price periods. In line I, the same process is repeated for regular-priced drink sales. In the example, 48 regular-priced mixed drinks at $4.25 each equals $204. In line J, the total revenue is calculated. In the example, $192 from the sale of low-priced mixed drinks (line H) plus $204 from regular-priced mixed drinks (line I) yields $396 (line J).

In line K, the revenue value per ounce for house and call liquors is calculated. This per-ounce revenue value is determined by dividing the total number of ounces of each type of liquor into the total revenue generated by the liquor type. In the example, the total ounces of house liquor, 140 ounces (line E, column 3), is divided

Exhibit 6   Revenue Value per Ounce Calculation

	House			Call		
	Mixed Drink	Cocktail	Total	Mixed Drink	Cocktail	Total
Drinks	1	2	3	4	5	6
A) Low Price	48	20		28	4	
B) Regular Price	+ 48	+ 2		+ 40	+ 10	
C) Total (A + B)	96 +	22	= 118	68 +	14	= 82
Ounces						
D) Oz/Drink	× 1	× 2		× 1	× 2	
E) Total (C × D)	96 +	44	= 140	68 +	28	= 96
Revenue						
F) Low Price Charge	4.00	4.50		5.00	5.50	
G) Regular Price Charge	4.25	4.75		5.25	5.75	
H) Total (Low Price) (A × F)	192.00	90.00		140.00	22.00	
I) Total (Reg. Price) (B × G)	+ 204.00	+ 9.50		+ 210.00	+ 57.50	
J) Total (H + I)	396.00 +	99.50	= 495.50	350.00 +	79.50	= 429.50
Revenue Value per Ounce						
K) Value = (J ÷ E)			3.54			4.47

To calculate bottle revenue value:
revenue value per ounce (line K) × number of ounces per bottle

Ounces per Bottle

Bottle Size	Number Ounces (approx.)
750 ml	25.4
Liter	33.8
1.5 Liter	50.7

Source: Adapted from Jack D. Ninemeier, *Beverage Management: Business Systems for Restaurants, Hotels, and Clubs* (New York: Lebhar-Freidman, 1982).

into the total revenue for house liquor, $396 (line J, column 3). Therefore, the weighted average revenue value per ounce of house liquor (line K, column 3) is $3.54 ($495.50 divided by 140 equals $3.54, rounded). The same process used for house liquor is repeated for call liquor. In the example, the revenue value per ounce of call liquor (line K, column 6) is $4.47 ($429.50 divided by 96 equals $4.47, rounded).

To calculate the bottle revenue value, the number of ounces of liquor in each bottle is multiplied by the revenue value per ounce. In the example, since there are 33.8 ounces of house liquor in a liter bottle, each liter bottle of house liquor has a potential revenue value of $119.65 ($3.54 times 33.8 ounces equals $119.65, rounded).

The potential revenue values for each bottle of house liquor and each bottle of call liquor become the basis for defining standard beverage revenue levels when the number of empty bottles is counted at the end of each shift. All liter bottles of house liquor, whatever type, have the same revenue value. The same is true for all liter bottles of call liquor. In the preceding example, a liter bottle of house liquor—whether Scotch, gin, or bourbon—will be expected to generate $119.65 in revenue. A liter bottle of call liquor has a sales value of $151.09 ($4.47 per ounce times 33.8 ounces per bottle).

This may seem strange since each type of liquor costs a different amount. However, most operations do not charge a different amount for each house liquor. The selling price of a mixed drink made with house liquor is generally the same regardless of whether it is made of Scotch, gin, or bourbon. The relationship between the cost of liquor and its selling price is less direct than the relationship between the cost of a food menu item and its selling price.

Furthermore, it would be impractical to manually keep track of all types of liquor and their different revenue values. In the procedure outlined above, information has to be assembled only for two types of liquor—house and call. To establish a bottle revenue value for each individual type of liquor would mean assessing sales information for the 70 to 100 different types and brands that might be carried by the beverage operation.

After the revenue value per bottle for house and call liquors is established, standard beverage revenue for liquor can be assessed. As full bottles are issued to replace empty bottles, the revenue value of each bottle is noted. A beverage issue and revenue value sheet (Exhibit 7) is simply a modified version of the basic beverage requisition form. Using this form makes it easier to tally bottle revenue value information. The sum of revenue values for all bottles issued, as listed on the form, is the standard (expected) revenue generated during the shift.

The standard revenue can be compared with actual revenue generated as taken from cash register tapes or other source documents. A form to compare standard with actual revenue (Exhibit 8) can be used for this purpose. When reviewing this form, note the following:

1. For each date, daily standard revenue is shown (column 2) as assessed on the beverage issue and revenue value sheet (Exhibit 7). The actual revenue (column 3) is determined from sources such as cash register and/or precheck terminal printouts.

2. To-date standard and actual revenue are reported in columns 4 and 5, respectively. This information should show that the effects of changes in opened-bottle inventory average out over time. Column 4 is the total of daily entries in column 2. Column 5 is the total of daily entries recorded in column 3.

3. Column 6 indicates the percentage of standard revenue actually received. It is calculated by dividing actual revenue to-date by standard revenue to-date and multiplying by 100. For 10/2, the calculation is as follows:

$$\frac{\$1,061.78}{\$1,092.45} \times 100 = 97.2\%$$

This means that as of 10/2, the beverage operation had actually received 97.2 percent of the revenue expected from liquor sales.

Exhibit 7   Beverage Issues and Sales Value Sheet

Beverage Issue/Sales Value						

Shift: _P.M._   Date: _10/1/XX_
Bar: _Main_   Bartender: _BT_

Liquor	Number of Bottles		Unit Cost	Total Cost	Sales Value	
	Number	Size			Unit	Total
B. Scotch	3	750 ml	$12.75	$38.25	$119.65	$358.95
B. Vodka	3	750 ml	11.50	34.50	119.65	358.95
B. Gin	2	liter	12.00	24.00	119.65	239.30
B. Rum	1	liter	12.50	12.50	119.65	119.65
S. Seven	1	750 ml	15.85	15.85	151.09	151.09
Tia Maria	1	750 ml	19.80	19.80	151.09	151.09
Drambuie	1	750 ml	19.75	19.75	151.09	151.09
				$164.65		$1530.1

2
Total Bottles: _12_   (Cost)   (Value)
OK to issue: _JN_
Issued by: _KT_
Received by: _BT_   Check one
☐ low price

$164.74 ÷ 1530.12 × 100 = 10.8%   ☑ reg. price
(Cost)   Revenue   (Beverage Cost Percent)   ☐ high price

Source: Adapted from Jack D. Ninemeier, *Beverage Management: Business Systems for Restaurants, Hotels, and Clubs* (New York: Lebhar-Freidman, 1982).

Exhibit 8   Sample Form for Comparing Standard and Actual Revenue

Standard and Actual Revenue Comparison					

Month: _October_   Bar: _Main_

Date	Daily Revenue		To-Date Revenue		Percent Difference To-Date
	Standard	Actual	Standard	Actual	
1	2	3	4	5	6
10/1	$690.45	$666.28	$ 690.45	$ 666.28	96.5%
10/2	402.00	395.50	1,092.45	1,061.78	97.2

Source: Adapted from Jack D. Ninemeier, *Beverage Management: Business Systems for Restaurants, Hotels, and Clubs* (New York: Lebhar-Freidman, 1982).

The above process is repeated to calculate standard and actual revenue for the day or any future date. As the days in the month progress, the variance between actual revenue and standard revenue should decrease. Acceptable variances should be established, and when this variance is exceeded, corrective action for tighter control may be necessary. For example, the beverage manager may decide that a variance greater than two percent by the tenth of the month requires investigation.

Automated Beverage Systems

Automated beverage systems significantly reduce many of the time-consuming management tasks for controlling beverage operations. While automated beverage systems vary, most systems can:

- Dispense drinks according to the operation's standard recipes

- Count the number of drinks poured

- Assess the standard (expected) revenue for beverage sales

- Provide timely management reports

Automated beverage systems can be programmed to dispense different portion sizes. They can also generate standard revenue information based on different pricing periods as defined by management. With most systems, the station at which drinks are prepared may be connected to a guest check printer that records every sale as drinks are dispensed. Some systems require that a guest check be inserted into the printer before the drink will be dispensed. Most equipment can, and should, be connected to the bar cash register to automatically record all revenue generated through the automated equipment.

With one type of automated beverage system, liquor is stored at the bar. Price-coded pourers (special nozzles) are inserted into each bottle. These pourers cannot dispense liquor unless they are used with a special activator ring. The bartender slips the neck of a liquor bottle (with the price-coded pourer already inserted) into the ring and prepares the drink with a conventional hand-pouring motion. A cord connects the activator ring to a master control panel that records the number of drinks poured at each price level. The master control panel may be connected to a point-of-sale system that records the sale. Some master control panels are equipped with printers and can produce revenue reports for each station. Reports indicate the number of drinks poured at different price levels and the total standard (expected) revenue for each station.

With another type of automated beverage system, liquor is stored in bottle racks in a locked storage room. The bartender prepares a drink by pushing the appropriate key on a keyboard. The liquor and necessary mixes travel to a dispensing device at the bar through separate plastic tubing. The system dispenses the drink when the bartender holds the glass (with ice) under the serving device. The drink is then garnished and served to the guest. Extensive revenue and inventory reports can be produced with this type of system. Also, transactions can be tied to an automated transaction control system. For each shift and each station during a shift, separate reports can indicate:

- Revenues by major beverage category

- Revenues by time of day

Exhibit 9   Sales by Food and Beverage Categories

			Sales By Revenue Center for 5/31/XX		Page 1 06/03/XX at 4:47 p.m.
			Net Sales by Catagory		3.659
	Bar	**Restaurant**	**Game Room**	**Theater**	**Banquet**
Apps	67.95	505.95	4.95	0.00	38.60
Non-Alc	32.48	165.65	0.00	3.86	3.54
Salads	0.00	53.15	0.00	0.00	35.70
Soups	5.90	6.20	0.00	0.00	3.25
Chip & Frie	45.60	330.55	0.00	0.00	23.10
Dinners	0.00	351.25	9.25	0.00	0.00
Desserts	0.00	15.10	0.00	0.00	0.00
Burgers	46.35	269.00	0.00	0.00	4.95
Sandwiches	6.25	328.70	0.00	0.00	8.70
Pizza	33.80	245.80	0.00	0.00	0.00
Liquor	1322.41	1374.06	18.16	165.80	67.69
Kids	0.00	35.05	0.00	0.00	0.00
Beer	2904.01	2629.25	2100.33	133.02	93.16
Wine	58.96	64.15	0.00	10.94	3.07
Theater	0.00	0.00	0.00	462.00	0.00
Open Pool	0.00	0.00	361.65	0.00	0.00
Happy Hour	0.00	0.00	0.00	0.00	0.00
Drink Mods	0.00	8.49	0.00	0.00	1.89
Food Mods	2.75	16.75	0.00	0.00	0.75
Billy's	0.00	0.00	0.00	0.00	0.00
Totals	4526.46	6399.10	2494.34	775.62	284.40

Courtesy of Ibertech, Inc., Aloha Hospitality Software, Hurst, Texas

- Revenues by server
- Settlement methods
- Outstanding guest checks
- Sales mix by beverage product

Exhibit 9 indicates the standard beverage revenue by major beverage category for five separate stations, as well as total revenue figures including food sales for the five outlets. Exhibit 10 indicates revenues by beverage server. When bartenders close their stations, the system generates a settlement methods report (Exhibit 11) which indicates the amounts due in the form of credit card vouchers, house account charges, and cash. Note: the total of the settlement report (the amount of revenue that the bartenders will be held accountable for) does not include revenues due from outstanding guest checks.

Unquestionably, automated beverage systems can greatly enhance management's control of beverage operations. At the least, the system can provide accurate information about the number of drinks and/or ounces sold. At best, such a system will not allow a drink to be served without its being entered as a sale within the system.

However, automated equipment cannot totally solve the problem of assessing expected revenue from beverage sales because:

Exhibit 10   Revenue by Beverage Server

Ring Off #22		—2:52 a.m.	1/06							
Accumulators Cleared		—8:00 a.m.	1/05							

Server	Reported Tips	Total Sales	Cash	Visa	Dine	Amex	Prom	Comp	Disc	Dire
						(All Sales Include Tax and Tips)				
1	6.10	1252.05	1160.45	.00	.00	91.60	.00	.00	.00	.00
4	.00	197.45	197.45	.00	.00	.00	.00	.00	.00	.00
5	.00	223.40	223.40	.00	.00	.00	.00	.00	.00	.00
6	.00	493.50	493.50	.00	.00	.00	.00	.00	.00	.00
12	1.50	785.65	553.70	.00	179.70	52.25	.00	.00	.00	.00
15	.00	644.75	644.75	.00	.00	.00	.00	.00	.00	.00
16	.00	5.00	5.00	.00	.00	.00	.00	.00	.00	.00
17	.00	288.90	288.90	.00	.00	.00	.00	.00	.00	.00
27	.00	111.75	111.75	.00	.00	.00	.00	.00	.00	.00
35	.00	21.00	21.00	.00	.00	.00	.00	.00	.00	.00
37	.00	28.25	28.25	.00	.00	.00	.00	.00	.00	.00
39	.00	36.50	36.50	.00	.00	.00	.00	.00	.00	.00
40	.00	276.20	276.20	.00	.00	.00	.00	.00	.00	.00
41	.00	18.00	18.00	.00	.00	.00	.00	.00	.00	.00
43	.00	244.25	233.50	10.75	.00	.00	.00	.00	.00	.00
44	.00	5.95	5.95	.00	.00	.00	.00	.00	.00	.00
45	.00	85.95	85.95	.00	.00	.00	.00	.00	.00	.00
47	5.00	30.50	25.50	.00	.00	5.00	.00	.00	.00	.00
56	.00	166.25	166.25	.00	.00	.00	.00	.00	.00	.00
58	.00	84.25	84.25	.00	.00	.00	.00	.00	.00	.00
60	.00	7.75	7.75	.00	.00	.00	.00	.00	.00	.00
65	.00	13.00	13.00	.00	.00	.00	.00	.00	.00	.00
66	.00	235.50	235.50	.00	.00	.00	.00	.00	.00	.00
67	.00	2.50	2.50	.00	.00	.00	.00	.00	.00	.00
68	.00	21.00	21.00	.00	.00	.00	.00	.00	.00	.00
71	.00	24.25	.00	.00	.00	24.25	.00	.00	.00	.00
78	.00	208.25	208.25	.00	.00	.00	.00	.00	.00	.00
80	.00	10.50	10.50	.00	.00	.00	.00	.00	.00	.00
93	.00	1.75	1.75	.00	.00	.00	.00	.00	.00	.00
Totals	12.60	5524.05	5140.50	10.75	179.70	173.10	.00	.00	.00	.00

Courtesy of American Business Computers, Akron, Ohio

- Some beverage products will not be on the system. For example, bottled beer and some mixed cocktails such as frozen daiquiris are not generally metered by automated equipment.

- Dishonest personnel can almost always find a way to beat the system.

- When the equipment breaks down, manual revenue control systems are still necessary.

Perhaps the best approach for controlling revenue with an automated beverage system is to make sure that it complements the revenue collection system used in the food and beverage operation.

Exhibit 11   Settlement Methods Report

Ring Off #22	—2:52 a.m.	1/06			
Accumulators Cleared	—8:00 a.m.	1/05			

Settlement Methods	STATION 1 SALES	STATION 2 SALES	STATION 3 SALES	STATION 4 SALES	TOTAL SALES
Cash	1548.65	1560.20	1368.00	683.65	5160.50
Visa/MC	.00	10.75	.00	.00	10.75
Diners	179.70	.00	.00	.00	179.70
Amex	52.25	.00	96.60	24.25	173.10
Promo	.00	.00	.00	.00	.00
Company	.00	.00	.00	.00	.00
Discovery	.00	.00	.00	.00	.00
Direct Bill	.00	.00	.00	.00	.00
Total Settlements	1780.60	1570.95	1464.60	707.90	5524.05

Courtesy of American Business Computers, Akron, Ohio

Key Terms

bottle revenue value system—In relation to nonautomated beverage operations, a procedure for estimating the amount of revenue expected from a bottle of liquor.

cashier banking system—In relation to food and beverage operations, a revenue collection system by which guests pay the cashier, the bartender, or the food or beverage server (who then pays the cashier or the bartender who has cashiering duties).

daily cashier's report—A revenue collection control document used to record cash register readings, cash count, bank deposits, and other transactions handled by a cashier.

daily productivity report—In relation to food and beverage operations, a report produced by automated point-of-sale equipment; the report details revenue activity for all assigned server records; may be generated for each server and cashier in terms of guest count, total revenues, and average revenues.

duplicate guest check system—A manual revenue control system in which the server turns in the duplicate copy to the kitchen and keeps the original copy for presentation to the guest.

guest check audit—In relation to food and beverage operations, a manual control function that identifies differences between what was produced and what was served. At the end of a meal period, the manager matches requisition slips (or duplicate copies of guest checks) turned in to the kitchen with the corresponding guest checks for which revenue has been collected.

open check file—In relation to food and beverage operations, an electronic file maintained by automated point-of-sale equipment that records information for each guest check used; information may include: terminal number where the guest check was opened, guest check serial number, server identification number, time guest check was opened, menu items ordered, prices of menu items ordered, applicable tax, and total amount due.

outstanding transaction report—In relation to food and beverage operations, a report produced by automated point-of-sale equipment; the report lists all open transactions (by server); information may include the sequence number, server identification number, time at which the transaction began, number of guests, table number, and guest check total.

requisition slips—In relation to food and beverage service, slips provided by servers to production staff before items are produced in a manual revenue control system; the slips indicate items for preparation, the server's name or identification number, and the serial number of the corresponding guest check.

revenue summary report—In relation to food and beverage operations, a report produced by automated point-of-sale equipment; the report contains detailed revenue and tax information by such categories as food items, beer, wine, and liquor. Generally, totals for each category are printed for each meal period, and totals for each meal period are shown in different sections of the report.

server banking system—In relation to food and beverage operations, a revenue collection system by which servers and bartenders use their own banks of change to collect payments from guests and retain the collected revenue until they check out at the end of their shifts.

 Review Questions ⎯⎯⎯⎯⎯⎯⎯⎯⎯⎯⎯⎯⎯⎯⎯⎯⎯⎯⎯⎯

1. How are requisition slips or duplicate checks useful in determining standard revenue for nonautomated food operations?

2. How do electronic cash registers and point-of-sale systems simplify guest check control functions? How do they help simplify the collection of accurate unit sales and revenue data?

3. What is a server banking system?

4. What is a cashier banking system?

5. How is a daily cashier's report used to compare standard revenue and actual revenue collected?

6. How are revenue and productivity reports useful to managers of automated food and beverage operations?

7. What are the advantages and disadvantages of using a guest check system to control revenue in nonautomated beverage operations?

8. How can a bottle revenue value system help managers determine standard revenue for nonautomated beverage operations?

9. How can automated beverage systems reduce many of the time-consuming tasks in controlling beverage operations?

10. What are some problems that may arise in assessing standard revenue from beverage sales in operations with automated beverage systems?

Internet Sites

For more information, visit the following Internet sites. Remember that Internet addresses can change without notice. If the site is no longer there, you can use a search engine to look for additional sites.

Associations

American Culinary Federation (ACF)
http://www.acfchefs.org

American Hotel & Lodging Association (AH&LA)
http://www.ahlaonline.org

American School Food Service Association (ASFSA)
http://www.asfsa.org

Club Managers Association of America (CMAA)
http://www.cmaa.org

The Educational Foundation of NRA
http://www.edfound.org

The Educational Institute of AH&LA
http://www.ei-ahla.org

Hospitality Financial and Technology Professionals
http://www.hftp.org

Institute of Food Technologies
http://www.ift.org

International Hotel and Restaurant Association
http://www.ih-ra.com

National Association of College and University Food Services
http://www.nacufs.org

National Restaurant Association (NRA)
http://www.restaurant.org

Food and Beverage Resources

Club Management Online
http://www.club-mgmt.com/dining/index.html

Prepared Foods. Product development, ingredients, suppliers
http://www.preparedfoods.com

Management Companies

ARAMARK
http://www.aramark.com

Bon Appétit Management Company
http://www.bamco.com

Compass Group
http://www.compass-na.com

Sodexho Marriott
http://www.sodexhomarriott.com

The Wood Company
http://www.woodco.com

Publications—Online and Printed

Club Management Magazine
http://www.club-mgmt.com

Electronic Gourmet Guide
http://www.foodwine.com

Food and Hospitality Magazine
http://www.foodserviceworld.com

Food Management
http://www.foodservicesearch.com

Food Network: CyberKitchen
http://www.foodtv.com

Food Processing: The Magazine of
Strategy, Technology and Trends
http://www.foodprocessing.com

Internet Food Channel
http://www.foodchannel.com

International Hotel and Restaurant
Association journal
www.hotelsmag.com

International Journal of Hospitality
Management
http://www.mcb.co.uk/ijchm.htm

Journal of Hospitality Financial
Management
http://hrta.fnr.umass.edu/sheel/
ahfme/jhfm/aboutjhfm.html

Lodging Food and Beverage
http://www.lodgingnews.com/
lodgingfnb/

Lodging Hospitality Online
http://www.lhonline.com

Lodging News, journal of the American
Hotel & Lodging Association
http://www.ei–ahla.org/webs/
lodging/index.html

Nation's Restaurant News
http://www.nrn.com

On the Rail—News for Food
Professionals
http://www.ontherail.com

Restaurants and Institutions magazine
http://www.rimag.com

Restaurant Business, Food Service, and
ID magazines
http://www.foodservicetoday.com

Restaurant Hospitality
www.foodservicesearch.com

Restaurants and Institutions
http://www.rimag.com

Restaurants USA, publication of
National Restaurant Association
http://www.restaurant.org/rusa

World Hospitality, management
magazine for hotel executives.
http://www.worldhospitality.com

 **Problems** ————————————————————————

Problem 1

What is the potential revenue given the following sales information which applies to last
Saturday at the Marina Boulevard Café?

Item	Number Sold	Selling Price	Potential Revenue
Chicken	94	$ 8.95	
Veal	73	12.50	
Pork Chops	68	11.95	
Vegetarian Entrée	55	9.50	
Lobster Newburg	38	14.75	
Beef Casserole	81	12.95	

a) Assume that the total food cost to prepare all the above items is $1,470.50; what is the standard food cost percentage?
b) What is the guest check average for the Saturday under study?

Problem 2

What is the total revenue expected from the sales information presented below?

Item	No. Produced	No. Leftover	No. Sold	Sales Price	Total Revenue
A	28	2		$8.95	
B	45	0		$10.50	
C	64	8		$7.95	
D	55	5		$8.50	
E	49	4		$7.95	

Problem 3

Use the following information to calculate the total cost of issues and the revenue value of the bar in the Pleasant Hollow Restaurant.

Liquor	No. Bottles Issued	Unit Cost	Total Cost	Revenue Value Unit	Total
Bar Gin	2	$9.70		$ 69.50	
Bar Vodka	2	$8.65		69.50	
Bar Rum	1	$8.75		69.50	
Bar Scotch	3	$10.70		69.50	
Dewar's Scotch	1	$16.50		115.40	
Kaluha	1	$17.25		98.70	

a) What is the standard beverage cost percentage?
b) If the cost of all bottles of house (bar) liquor increased by $1.50 each, what would be the new cost of issues and beverage cost percentage?

Problem 4

Complete the Standard and Actual Revenue Comparison Sheet below:

Standard and Actual Revenue Comparison					
Month: _July_			Bar: _Main_		
	Daily Revenue		To-Date Revenue		Percent Difference To-Date
Date	Standard	Actual	Standard	Actual	
7/1	$650.10	$644.50			
7/2	712.40	703.90			
7/3	595.50	605.50			
7/4	625.10	610.10			
7/5	710.00	701.50			

If on 7/5, the actual amount of revenue received to-date had been $3,140.50 instead of $3,265.50, what would be the percent difference between standard and actual revenue?

Problem 5

What is the revenue value per ounce for house and call liquors given the following information?

Drinks	House			Call		
	Mixed Drink	**Cocktail**	**Total**	**Mixed Drink**	**Cocktail**	**Total**
Low Price	155	95		110	75	
Regular Price	225	125		190	85	
Total						
Ounces						
Oz/Drink	1.0	1.75		1.0	1.25	
Total	___ +	___	= ___	___ +	___	= ___
Revenue						
Low Charge	$2.75	$3.50		$3.75	$4.25	
Regular Charge	$3.50	$4.00		$4.25	$4.75	
Total (Low)	___	___		___	___	
Total (Reg.)						
Total	___ +		= ___	___ +		= ___
Revenue Value per Ounce			___			___

What is the revenue value for house and call liquors given the information above? (Assume 750 ml [25.4 oz] bottles are used.)

Problem 6

Complete the Food Service Revenue Recap Sheet for Joe's Café—a very small operation using a manual revenue control system.

Food Service Revenue Recap Sheet			
	Revenue		
Server	**Standard**	**Actual**	**Difference**
Jack	$110.50	$105.50	
Ray	$98.70	$98.70	
Mike	$125.40	$130.50	
Ron	$180.10	$177.50	

You are Joe, the owner of the Café. What should you do about Jack's and Ron's shortages? What should you do about Mike's overage?

Chapter 12 Outline

Theft by Bartenders
    Theft by Misuse of the Bar Cash
      Register
    Theft by Misuse of Beverage Products
    Theft Prevention through Shopper
      Services
Theft by Cashiers
Theft by Food and Beverage Servers and
    Other Staff
Theft by Guests
Employee Theft from Guests
Control of Cash after Collection
    Preventing Theft of Bank Deposit
      Funds
    Preventing Theft when Bills Are Paid
    Preventing Bookkeeper Theft

Competencies

1. Describe some of the ways bartenders
    can steal, and identify precautions
    managers can take to reduce this kind
    of theft. (pp. 369–376)

2. Explain how shopper services work
    and why food and beverage
    operations use them. (pp. 376–377)

3. Describe some of the ways food and
    beverage servers can steal, and
    identify precautions managers can
    take to reduce this kind of theft.
    (pp. 377–380)

4. Describe some of the ways guests can
    steal, and identify precautions food
    and beverage managers can take to
    reduce this kind of theft. (pp. 380–382)

5. Describe cash control procedures
    appropriate for food and beverage
    operations. (pp. 387–391)

12

Preventing Theft of Revenue

$\mathbf{F}$OOD AND BEVERAGE CONTROL PROCEDURES require constant review of standard and actual cost percentages. When actual cost percentages exceed standards established for a food and beverage operation, most managers try to reduce costs. Yet, often the problem is not that costs are too high but that revenue is too low. Even though expenses may, in fact, be reasonable, theft reduces revenue levels and increases food and/or beverage cost percentages. Therefore, managers must consider both expenses and revenue levels when assessing the effectiveness of control systems.

A large percentage of the revenue for many food and beverage operations is in the form of cash, in contrast to credit cards, company charge plans, or personal checks. Without effective control systems, this cash resource is extremely vulnerable to theft. Consider the following:

- Personnel who handle cash, including bartenders, cashiers, and service staff, often hold low-paid, entry-level positions. Many of these employees frequently move from job to job and have little identification with or loyalty to a property.

- The busy environment of a food and beverage operation and the complexity of production and service tasks provide the opportunity for personnel who handle money to take advantage of loopholes in revenue collection systems.

- To some extent, many managers are unconcerned about employee theft. Some feel that theft is inevitable and simply increase prices to cover it.

Guests' demands for value are increasingly important factors in establishing food and beverage selling prices. If the costs of theft are built into selling prices, the operation may lose its competitive edge in pricing. A more reasonable way to minimize the consequences of employee theft is to design and implement a system incorporating the basic principles of revenue control. Even after a revenue control plan is in effect, it is still important to supervise operations to ensure that the system works and that staff members have not found creative ways to steal.

While not being unduly alarmed, food and beverage managers must realize that some employees steal, others will if they have the opportunity, and all staff are likely, at times, to make mistakes. The net result of all theft and employee error is reduced profit. This cannot be tolerated when it can be controlled.

It is difficult, perhaps impossible, to design a revenue control system that will prevent clever, dishonest employees from stealing. This is especially true when we consider the possibilities for **collusion**—cooperation between two or more dishonest staff members. However, well-designed and supervised revenue control systems make it difficult for one staff member, working alone, to steal.

Theft by Bartenders

Because the bartender prepares and serves products, and also, at least in public bars, collects and records revenue, it is perhaps easier for the bartender to steal revenue than for any other employee. Basically, bartender theft centers upon misuse of the bar cash register machine and/or misuse of beverage products. The following sections discuss each of these problems separately.

Theft by Misuse of the Bar Cash Register

Today's electronic cash register is much more than just a storage drawer for money collected. Used properly, it is critical to the property's revenue control and record-keeping systems. Management staff should develop specific procedures to be followed not only by bartenders, but also by food service cashiers. A sample of policies and procedures for operating the cash register is shown in Exhibit 1. The bartender (or food service cashier) will have less opportunity to steal revenue when control policies and procedures are strictly enforced.

There are many ways in which the bar register can be misused. Just as managers need to know about the complex, interrelated procedures incorporated into an effective revenue control system, so too must they be aware of the inappropriate procedures that allow employees to misuse the bar register. The following sections describe misuses of cash registers that can result in errors or permit employee theft of revenue.

"No-Ring" Sales. In no-ring sales, the bartender collects revenue from guests, opens the cash drawer by pressing a "no sale" or similar type of key and makes change for currency collected. In this way, the sale has not been entered into the register's revenue data or on the register's tape. Although the collected revenue has been placed in the cash drawer, this is only a temporary arrangement. The register operator does not want to remove stolen funds several times during a shift since this increases the likelihood of being observed. So the dishonest bartender generally keeps a record of the unrecorded revenue and removes it from the register only one time near the end of the shift.

While practices differ, bartenders keep track of unrecorded revenue by numerous creative schemes. For example, a bartender may place coins under the cash drawer—ten pennies can mean ten dollars in unrecorded drink revenue. Separating or bending swizzle sticks or matches is another technique. Managers should go behind the bar frequently and carefully look for things out of the ordinary. Why are some bottle caps lying in the corner of the bar? Why is a napkin with several tears lying on the back bar? Why is one glass with several lemon twists or toothpicks in an unusual place? Using a shopper service, a control method discussed later in this chapter, can also help reduce the opportunity for no-ring sales.

Underringing. Bartenders who use guest checks in a manual system can collect the proper amount of revenue from guests but record a lower sales value on the check.

Exhibit 1   Cash Register Operating Procedures

Cash Bank:

At the beginning of each shift, personnel who will operate a cash register are given a cash bank. The amount of money in the bank will be set by management and will not vary from shift to shift. A minimum amount of currency to ensure that change can be made throughout the shift should be determined. For example, in a lounge with drink prices set on a 25-cent graduated basis ($3.25, $3.50, $3.75, etc.) the following amounts for a $400 cash bank may be very effective.

NUMBER	UNIT	TOTAL DOLLARS
50	$1.00	$50.00
10	10.00	100.00
12	5.00	60.00
8	20.00	160.00
2 ROLLS	.25	20.00
1 ROLL	.10	5.00
2 ROLLS	.01	1.00
2 ROLLS	.05	4.00

The balance ($25.00) will be composed of dollar bills and "broken roll" change.

At a minimum, currency in the amounts shown will be needed to make up the cash bank. Responsibility for securing change should be assumed by management, who will be able to obtain change from the bank when deposits are made. Cashiers and bartenders should not be permitted to bring in their own change. The bank should remain intact. No IOUs, petty cash receipts, personal loans, or other deductions from the cash balance will be carried in the bank.

Personnel receiving a cash bank should sign a document showing that they have done so. From that point, personnel will be responsible for their own cash bank until the end of their shift. The employee should be permitted to count the beginning bank in the presence of management to make sure that the correct amount of cash is in the beginning bank.

At the end of the shift, the value of the beginning bank should be counted out first. The remaining funds in the cash drawer should, of course, equal the value of revenue collected to satisfy register tape and/or guest check and precheck register totals. Register operators will be liable for any shortages in cash banks or revenue.*

Specific Register Operating Procedures:

The cash drawer is to be closed when not in use.

Each guest check must be rung up separately. At no time should two or more guest checks be totaled in the bartender's head and rung as a total. Each ticket will be closely checked to ensure that the printed ring-up agrees with the total charge due from the guest.

At no time is the bartender's tip jar to be near the cash register. The tip jar should be located away from the cash register to eliminate the possibility of the bartender making change from it or removing money from the register to the tip jar.

Bills over $20.00 should be placed under the currency tray. Bills collected from the customer should remain on the register shelf until the transaction is acceptable to the guest. When making change, count from the amount of the sale to the amount of money given by the customer. Call the manager on duty if there are any questions regarding cash collection or change making.

Only the bartender or cashier should have access to the register. No employee other than the one with responsibility should use, enter, or otherwise have any contact with the cash register for any reason whatsoever. Management may, of course, conduct spot audits of tapes and currency as believed necessary.

---

* Restaurant managers should check with their attorney or other officials to determine the legality of requiring employees to make up cash register shortages.

(continued)

Exhibit 1 *(continued)*

The appropriate department key must be depressed to record the type of transaction represented by the guest check being rung up. All procedures in register ring-up should be designed to provide revenue information on a department basis for greater accuracy in financial accounting.

Separate cash drawers (or separate cash registers) should be used by each person having access to the cash register.

The register user should not be able to read or total the machine. Information regarding total revenue should not be made known to the cashier/bartender.

Cashiers/bartenders should begin each shift with a new bank.

Each register user should have a separate key to the register. A separate identification number should be used to identify transactions on cash register tapes.

Each sale must be rung up in proper sequence, in the proper amount, and without "bunching" or totaling tickets. Each ticket or transaction must be rung separately.

Each register user should have a written copy of procedures for use of the cash register.

Register users, when practical, should call out the price of items being rung on the register.

The cash drawer should only be opened by depressing the sales price or "no sale" key. It should not be possible to enter the machine by use of a lever or other mechanical device, except in case of power outage.

Detail tapes should be replaced before they run out (there is generally a colored strip or other marking which becomes noticeable as the tape supply diminishes).

Registers should be empty, unlocked, and left open when not in use (or drawers should be removed) to prevent damage to machine during possible theft attempts.

Voids, overrings, or other problems should be reported to management as soon as possible after they occur.

Cash register audits, including the counting of money in the drawer(s), should be made on a random basis.

Management should watch the cash register and its operation closely as part of its ongoing supervisory responsibilities.

Detail tapes should be studied on a random basis to uncover possible fraud.

Cashiers are not allowed to accept postdated checks or IOUs in payment or as collateral for loans.

Only a minimum number of supervisory personnel should have access to cash register keys.

Register banks should be counted and exchanged at each change in cashiers; cash register tapes are read or totaled and cleared at this time.

All checks accepted from employees are immediately marked "FOR DEPOSIT ONLY." Forms should be available to record, by shift, revenue from each register (point-of-sale) for food and beverage service for the entire day (or other period).

Register balances should be reconciled with cash receipts at least once each shift.

Revenue from miscellaneous cash sales (vending proceeds, grease, returnable bottles, etc.) must be properly recorded in business accounts if it is first deposited in a cash register.

Cash register bell, alarm, or buzzer systems should not be bypassed; a noise should be heard each time the cash drawer is opened.

The cash register should be located in a position visible to guests, employees, and management.

If a register is used by a food cashier who collects revenue directly from guests, the machine should be located close to the exit.

Cash registers should be kept locked during service periods when the register operator is not at the machine.

Exhibit 1   *(continued)*

Audits of detail tapes should ensure continuity in transaction numbers. The first transaction number for a new shift should be in sequence with the last transaction number from the previous shift's detail tape.

Constant cash overages should be investigated. (The register user may be underringing and removing only part of the money to avoid a shortage which might alert management.)

Random and unexpected audits should be made of the cash register. The machine should be read to determine the amount of revenue during the shift. This revenue plus the amount of the beginning cash bank should be in the register. If there is more money in the machine, it may be because the operator has "not rung" or has underrung revenue and has not had time to remove the cash.

Cash register readings should not be made by the cashier/bartender.

No money should be paid out of cash register funds without the approval of management, and then only with writing up of a paid-out slip; if applicable, an invoice or sales slip should be attached.

The cash register should not be used as an imprest petty cash fund.

All employees who handle cash should be bonded.

The bartender rings the lower value into the machine and steals the difference between this amount and what was actually collected from the guest. This practice is called underringing. To reduce the opportunity for underringing, managers need to randomly check the amount rung into the machine or printed on the check. Automated equipment using preset keys and video touch-screen monitors for data entry make underringing more difficult in the traditional sense. They can, however, use proper procedures to ring an inexpensive drink and then prepare, serve and collect revenue for a more expensive drink.

Bunched Sales. Bunched sales occur when employees add guest check totals or drink charges in their heads and enter only the totals into the machine. Theft occurs when an employee purposely lowers the total of a guest check, collects the full amount from the guest, and pockets the difference. This type of theft can be prevented by requiring handwritten totals on all guest checks, and by enforcing policies that hold employees accountable for failing to follow proper procedures. Display terminals require that each order be placed separately; this reduces the possibility of this problem occurring with automated equipment.

Substituting Bottle Sales for Drink Sales. Operations that sell liquor by the bottle as well as by the drink offer another opportunity for theft. If, for example, $1\,1/4$ ounce portions are served and a liter bottle is used, a bartender can serve approximately 25 drinks and deposit the revenue from each without ringing the sale. Later, the bartender can record a bottle sale at a much lower revenue value and steal the difference between what the property should collect—revenue from the sale of 25 drinks—and what is actually collected—the value of a bottle sale. This maneuver helps explain an increased beverage cost percentage because drinks are prepared without a sale being recorded.

Misuse of Guest Checks. When bartenders are required to use guest checks, one guest's check can be reused when another guest places the same order. The revenue from this second guest is not recorded in the machine and the bartender can steal it. A locked box for all used tickets—those run through the register after payment—can deter this technique, especially when supplemented with other control procedures such as routine security shopping, discussed later.

Register operators can steal guest checks or purchase similar checks and use them to undermine the property's revenue control system. Increased use of automated systems which eliminate the use of hard copy guest checks are very helpful in reducing the opportunities for employee theft of revenue.

Substituting Stolen Bank Checks or Credit Card Vouchers for Cash. Register users can steal personal bank checks from anyone or emboss additional credit card vouchers from guests and replace cash in the register with the stolen check or charge voucher. Credit card and check acceptance procedures, discussed later in this chapter, can help prevent this type of theft.

Mixing Revenue with Tips. Bartenders might also use the tip jar to steal revenue from the property. Basically, the bartender collects revenue from guests and deposits it directly in—or makes change from—the tip jar. Suppose, for example, when paying for two drinks at $2.25 each (a $4.50 charge), the guest says, "Here's a five; keep the change." The bartender can then put the entire $5 in the tip jar. The guest who does not wait for change will hardly notice what is happening. A locked tip box placed away from the register, along with regular supervision and use of a shopping service, will help prevent this method of employee theft.

"Borrowing" from the Register. The best intentions to pay back borrowed funds too often don't materialize. When the beginning cash bank is counted and removed at the end of each shift—along with the actual revenue collected—borrowing is no longer possible.

In many loosely controlled operations, bartenders simply remove cash from the income drawer. It is impossible to overemphasize the need to double-check the amount of revenue expected to be in the cash drawer.

Stealing from Other Bartenders. Bartenders can also ring sales on another bartender's key and pocket the revenue, thereby making the other bartender short. The dishonest bartender can remove the "excess" cash from the register without detection, and the honest bartender will be suspect. Funds owed to the property as reported on the victimized bartender's sales tape will be overstated and monies in the register will be short. The best precaution here is a separate register—or, at the very least, a different cash drawer—for each bartender. Modern systems utilizing an employee identification number, key, key card or other security device have made this theft method increasingly difficult to implement.

Many beverage managers believe that an effective way to reduce the potential for bartender misuse of the cash register involves removal of the cash drawer during the bartender's shift. The manager using this technique will go to the bartender's register at a random time during the shift to "x" the register print transactions and remove the cash drawer. A new cash drawer with a precounted cash bank is inserted into the machine so the bartender can continue working. After reading the register and removing the drawer, the manager can count the amount of money in the drawer and compare it to the amount of revenue rung on the register. The amount that should be available is the amount of the beginning cash bank plus the amount of revenue from sales registered up to the time the drawer was removed. This procedure is an effective control technique. If the register count indicates a shortage of funds in the cash drawer, there is clearly a problem with employee theft or errors. Beverage managers must also be concerned when the comparison shows there is too much money in the cash drawer. As noted earlier, bartenders using a no-ring theft method will typically leave unrecorded revenue in the cash drawer until the end of the shift. If the count of money in the drawer indicates that the amount of cash is greater than that which can be accounted for, it is possible that the bartender is not ringing all unit sales and has yet to remove unrecorded revenue from the drawer.

Theft by Misuse of Beverage Products

Bartenders can find many ways to steal revenue by misusing beverage products when they prepare drinks for guests. These theft methods often result in higher beverage cost percentages since beverages are used but no revenue—or an incorrect amount of revenue—is collected.

Underpouring Drinks. Bartenders can underpour drinks by using an improper shot glass or jigger. Freepouring—not using a measured pour at all—can also result in underpoured drinks. For example, if 1-ounce drinks are underpoured by $1/4$ ounce, the bartender can steal the revenue from every fifth drink without affecting the beverage cost percentage. Managers can protect the property against this type of theft by requiring that portion control tools—a proper jigger or shot glass—be used every time liquor is poured, or by using a metered or computerized beverage-dispensing system.

Diluting Liquor Bottles. Diluting liquor is another technique that might be used to get more drinks out of a bottle without affecting the beverage cost percentage. The bartender steals the revenue from the "extra" drinks. To detect this problem, managers should check bottles since liquors often become lighter in color or cloudy when water or soda is added. Frequent complaints from guests regarding beverage quality are also clues to this method of bartender theft.

Substituting Lower-Quality Liquor for Call Brands. With this method of theft, bartenders charge the higher price, and pocket the difference. This practice can be prevented by requiring that orders be written on the guest checks and that the check be rung through the register. This problem may be uncovered by random examinations of guest checks and by observing the way that orders are written and rung up. Automated systems requiring separate order entry for each drink are also helpful deterrents.

Pouring Drinks from Private Bottles. Bartenders can bring in their own bottles and pour from them. This kind of theft will not result in higher beverage cost percentages for the property because the bartender incurs all costs and collects all revenue. Essentially, the operation has a "partner" in the business—one who does not share in the payment of overhead expenses. Bottle marking can help prevent bartenders from substituting their own liquor for the property's. This is especially effective when access to the marking stamp or other marking device is controlled. As always, careful supervision, including frequent behind-the-bar checks, is an important control tool.

Misrepresenting Sales as Spilled, Complimentary, or Returned Drinks. Bartenders can sell drinks for cash, keep the revenue, and report the drinks as spilled, complimentary, or returned. Management should view all returned drinks before disposal. Policies regarding complimentary drinks should be developed and consistently followed. Bartenders reporting excessive spillage and returns should be retrained, closely supervised, or terminated.

Collusion with Beverage Servers. Bartenders can work in collusion with beverage servers. Drinks can be prepared for the server, and revenue split between the two employees. Supervision is needed to ensure that the procedures of the property's revenue collection system are followed. Shift rotations and close comparisons of standard and actual beverage costs may help detect and prevent this problem.

Collusion with Food Production Employees. Bartenders can trade liquor for food products from the kitchen. Managers should ensure that all eating and drinking policies are consistently followed. Signs of policy violations—glasses in the kitchen or plates at the bar, restroom, or locker areas—should be followed up with corrective action.

Pouring Free Drinks. Bartenders can rob the property of revenue by giving away drinks to friends or employees. They also may try to promote bigger tips by providing free beverages to guests. The need for policies regarding complimentary drinks has already been stressed. An effective way to prevent and discover these problems is by regular use of shopper services.

Theft Prevention through Shopper Services

The value of using shopper services to detect bartender theft has been mentioned several times. With this technique, the manager hires someone to pose as a guest, sit at the bar, and watch the bartender work. Many operations bring in shoppers every month or even more frequently. Bartenders or other employees should not know the shoppers. Shoppers could be friends of the management staff or employees of a professional shopping service.

Informing the staff that a shopper service is used routinely to assess the effectiveness of the operation's revenue control system may itself help deter theft. Remember that the purpose of the control system is to prevent and reduce the opportunities for employee theft.

Shopper Training. Before the on-site visit, it is important that management meet with the person who will be "shopping" the property. The usefulness of shopper services to management's control system depends on shoppers knowing what to look for.

A shopper is not simply an undercover security person looking for overt cases of employee theft. It is much more likely that a shopper will note an improper procedure than an actual theft taking place. Therefore, the exact procedures that should be followed by the food and beverage staff must be fully explained to the shopper before the visit. Shoppers should be familiar with all cash register, drink preparation, and revenue collection procedures established by management. This includes such things as how, if permitted, guest charges should be transferred between the lounge and restaurant, how appetizers should be accounted for in the lounge, and how guest bar tabs should be run.

During the visit, all bartenders should be randomly observed by the shopper. However, a manager can ask the shopper to more carefully observe specific staff members, such as a bartender suspected of theft, or a new bartender who may still be trying to learn the property's procedures.

With this information, the shopper can closely monitor the actual procedures during the visit. For example, the shopper may order a drink and carefully observe all procedures for taking the order, preparing and serving the drink, collecting cash, and ringing the sale on the register. The shopper generally remains at the bar and casually observes the various transactions and procedures. At the conclusion of the visit, the shopper should report all findings to the manager, perhaps using a form such as that in Exhibit 2.

Shoppers as Marketing Consultants. Shoppers can and should be concerned with more than just a study of the bartender's handling procedures for beverages and revenue. Shoppers may also be used to view the operation from the guest's perspective. For example, they can note whether service was efficient and hospitable and whether products meet quality expectations. They can also determine whether sanitation procedures are being followed and whether facility cleanliness meets their expectations. In effect, then, the shopper can serve as a consultant to the food and beverage manager, looking at both procedures and facilities from the point of view of guest satisfaction.

Theft by Cashiers

Cashiers have the same opportunities for electronic cash register misuse as we indicated in the examples of bartender theft. Therefore, the operating procedures shown in Exhibit 1 apply equally to cashiers. However, creative cashiers can use still other methods to steal revenue. Exhibit 3 notes some of the more common cashier theft methods and also indicates preventive measures. In several theft methods, the dishonest act affects employees other than the cashier. Management must actively try to prevent theft to protect honest employees.

Theft by Food and Beverage Servers and Other Staff

Food and beverage servers can use a variety of common methods to steal from the operation. With some manual check and cash collection systems, servers may be able to receive cash from a guest without using a guest check and simply steal the

Exhibit 2   Sample Shopper Report

Shopper Report

OPERATIONAL AND SERVICE REPORT

Name of Property: _____   **Date:** _____

☐ AM

Address: _____   **Time:** _____   ☐ PM

_____

Employee Reviewed: Badge/ID ____

  Sex _____   Other

  Age _____   Descriptive

  Build _____   Features:

  Hair Color _____

  Glasses _____

Items Purchased

Quantity	Item	Charge

Tax _____

Amt. Paid _____

Part I — Service Details

	Yes	No
A. Was service cordial?	☐	☐
B. Were you greeted?	☐	☐
C. Were soiled items present when you were seated?	☐	☐
D. Was service prompt?	☐	☐
E. Was server neat/clean?	☐	☐
F. Was server aware of prices/brands?	☐	☐
G. Was serviceware clean?	☐	☐

Part III — Other Information

A. Cash Register Operation

B. Production/Service Concerns

C. Interaction with Other Employees

Parv IV — Miscellaneous

Part II — Revenue Collection

When check was issued:

	Yes	No
A. Was check presented immediately upon service?	☐	☐
B. Were check charges/ arithmetic correct?	☐	☐
C. Was new check presented?	☐	☐
D. Check Number		_____
E. Served At: ☐ Counter ☐ Table		

When money was collected:

	Yes	No
A. Was payment requested upon service?	☐	☐
B. Was amount of purchase quoted?	☐	☐
C. Were charges correct?	☐	☐
D. Was charge called back?	☐	☐
E. Was revenue rung up immediately/correctly?	☐	☐
F. Were you thanked after payment?	☐	☐

(Use continuation sheet as necessary)

Exhibit 3　Common Methods of Theft by Cashier

Theft Method	Affects	Prevention Method
1. Collect cash and void sales checks	Cashier	Sales checks must be matched with duplicates; management must okay all voids
2. Collect cash and record sales as a charge	Cashier	See procedures for processing credit card charges
3. Collect cash, claim guest walked out ("dine and dash" claim)	Cashier Server	Walkouts should be tallied by employee; more than very occasional walkouts call for retraining or more supervision
4. Remove cash, claiming shortage	Cashier	Actual revenue known via double-check or automated register system
5. Make payments from register for personal expenses	Cashier	Imprest petty cash system
6. Underadd cashier's reports	Cashier	A non-cashier employee should process or at least review all revenue reports detailing cashier transactions
7. Fail to record miscellaneous revenue (vending machine proceeds, grease sales, etc.)	Cashier	Miscellaneous revenue should be paid to management, not to the cashier
8. Incorrectly use register/other equipment	Cashier	All register-operating procedures reviewed in Exhibit 1 should be consistently followed
9. Ring up on another cashier's key	All Cashiers	When possible each cashier should have a separate register, drawer, or access key
10. Collect revenue, claiming guest refusal to pay	Cashier	These situations should be referred to management
11. Receive cash, destroy ticket claiming ticket was not received	Cashier Server	If problem occurs more than very occasionally, a sign off system should require the cashier to accept responsibility for tickets received from servers
12. Collect cash and change ticket to show reduced amount owed	Cashier Server	All procedures for guest check control should be in use; match up original and duplicate checks

revenue. This practice becomes difficult with an effective guest-check or automated control system.

When guest checks are used, servers may receive or take products without entering the required information on the guest check. With few exceptions, the control system should prohibit production staff (cooks and bartenders) from giving products to service personnel until they present appropriate requisition slips or duplicate guest checks or until orders are entered into an automated system. Servers may use guest checks purchased at a local restaurant supply store to bypass the existing guest check system. This cannot happen if unique, hard-to duplicate checks are issued, used, and stored securely. The following sections describe how servers may steal by abusing the guest check control system. Many of these techniques won't work if automated systems are used and required procedures are followed.

Servers may reuse a check to obtain an identical order for another guest. This can be prevented by requiring that servers present appropriate requisition slips or duplicate checks to kitchen staff before receiving food. In the bar area, a stamp, marking, or register imprint can certify which drinks on a guest check have already been served.

Servers may underadd a check, delete items to help a friend, or overadd to influence the tip. Guest checks should be regularly audited. If requisition slips or duplicate checks are used, copies should be matched with the original guest check on either a routine or a random basis.

Servers may collect cash and destroy a check, claiming that it was lost or that the guests left without paying. Because checks will be accounted for, the missing check will be noticed. When a server loses checks or has guests "walk," the server, at the least, needs close supervision or additional training.

A dishonest food server may collect revenue for a beverage charge transferred from the lounge, destroy the guest check, steal the money, and claim that the transfer was never received. This may be prevented by requiring that the supervisor, host, or cashier verify transactions by recording the appropriate guest check numbers alongside items that have been transferred.

A server may claim that a dissatisfied guest returned an item listed on the guest check, pocket the money, and turn in only the revenue for the other items. The manager should approve all returned menu items and approve any changes to totals recorded on guest checks.

Servers may pocket the revenue from items that they can pick up without presenting requisition slips or duplicate checks. Management should design procedures that minimize the number of menu items to which servers can help themselves.

In addition to bartenders, cashiers, and food and beverage servers, other employees who do not normally come in direct contact with revenue may still present problems. Exhibit 4 lists common methods of theft used by non-cash-handling personnel, as well as corresponding methods of prevention. (Special concerns regarding embezzlement by secretarial or accounting staff are discussed later in this chapter.)

Theft by Guests

Unfortunately, some guests will also steal from the food and beverage operation if given the opportunity. Knowing the possible ways dishonest guests can steal from the property enables managers to incorporate practical preventive procedures into the control system. The following sections describe some methods guests may use to steal.

Guests may take advantage of staff errors. Guests can take advantage of server errors in calculating charges. This problem is reduced if servers use a calculator with

Exhibit 4   Theft by Non-Cash-Handling Personnel

Theft Method	Prevention Method
1. Housekeeping personnel steal cash left unattended in electronic cash registers or in the office when cleaning.	Lock or empty electronic cash registers when unattended. Keep cash in office areas under lock.
2. Revenue awaiting deposit in bank is stolen.	Keep revenue locked in bank bags in the safe or other secure area(s).
3. Employees pass bad checks or request loans that are difficult to collect.	Do not accept employee checks. Keep loans small, and do not give others if any loan remains unpaid; loan total should not exceed the amount of salary or wage due.
4. Employees misuse petty cash funds.	Follow imprest petty cash fund procedures.
5. Buspersons or other staff steal tips or revenue from service staff.	Have service personnel keep close track of their guests. Have the server keep money collected in a server banking system on his or her person or in a locked box.
6. Employees intercept mail, remove checks.	Deny employee access to all incoming and outgoing mail.

a printing tape in a manual check system. Then, work carefully, double-check the numbers, and attach the calculator tape to the guest check before presenting it. A similar problem occurs when guests do not point out omissions on the guest check. Again, recording everything on checks and adding carefully can help reduce this type of problem. Use of automated equipment reduces the possibility of simple authentic errors on guest transactions.

Guests may walk out before paying the bill. Service staff should present bills promptly and pay attention to guests who appear to be finishing and getting ready to leave. Service staff can also be trained to notice guests being served in other workstations who appear to be ready to leave. They can then notify the guests' server. Also, positioning the cashier or hostess station at the entrance to the dining area helps reduce the possibility of walkouts.

Guests may disclaim transfer charges. Some guests may disclaim beverage charges incurred in the lounge that are transferred to the restaurant. Staff should have guests sign transferred guest checks or slips and process them in a manner that ensures payment for all transferred checks.

Guests may steal property. Guests can also steal flatware, glassware, room furnishings, and other easily transportable items. While this is not theft of cash, there are clear cost implications. Service staff should be trained to remove all soiled items from tables promptly to reduce opportunities for this kind of theft. They should also be alert to items missing from the table or surrounding areas as guests leave and should promptly notify management if they are suspicious. Some properties make embossed and/or unique items available for sale to guests. In this way, the property can generate additional revenue at the same time that it reduces the potential for theft-incurred costs.

Guests may pass worthless checks. Managers or designated staff members should approve all payments by guests using personal checks or traveler's checks. The information presented in Exhibit 5 can help those approving such payments to spot forged checks. As part of the control system, managers should maintain a list of all personal and business checks that are not to be accepted. National check approval services, which provide full payment for checks they approve that are later dishonored by the bank, should be considered. Guests wishing to pay by check should be asked to present two forms of identification, one of which should be a major credit card accepted by the property. Personal checks without the depositor's name printed on them should not be accepted. Exhibit 6 suggests steps to follow when accepting checks. Additional procedures may include the following:

- Accept checks only for the amount of the bill.

- Postdated or two-party checks are not acceptable.

- All checks should be legible and made out to the correct name of the food and beverage operation. Those showing any sign of tampering are not acceptable.

- Checks marked "For Deposit Only" are not acceptable.

- The guests must sign the check in the presence of the manager or designated staff member.

- Checks should be marked or stamped "For Deposit Only" as soon as they are accepted.

Guests may use fraudulent credit cards. Managers should ensure that before accepting payment, bartenders, servers, and cashiers follow all rules required by credit card companies regarding authorization. Today, most operations process the guest's credit card through an automated authorization device. Additional procedures for approval of credit card payments may include the following:

- Have the guest sign the credit card voucher as well as applicable guest checks or slips.

- "Loans" should not be made on credit cards. Food and beverage operations pay a discount fee for the value of credit card charges.

Guests may pass counterfeit currency. Food and beverage operations often serve as convenient places for dishonest guests to pass counterfeit currency. Exhibit 7 suggests how to detect counterfeit currency, what to do if counterfeit currency is detected, and pertinent facts about paper currency in the United States. Note that in many cases the passer may not have made the bills, but may be able to help police trace their origin.

Guests may shortchange cash-handling employees. The fast pace of busy meal periods presents another convenient opportunity for dishonest guests to shortchange employees handling cash payments. Exhibit 8 describes the tricks of a shortchange artist and suggests how to avoid being victimized.

Exhibit 5 How to Spot Forged Checks

How to Spot Forged Checks

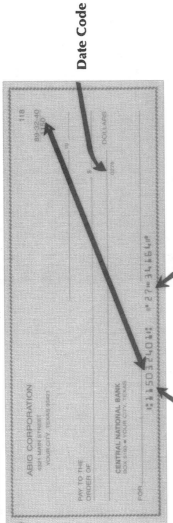

Date Code

Federal Reserve Districts

Check for Perforations

You'll be able to feel perforations on at least one edge of all legitimate checks except for government checks printed on computer card stock. Perforation equipment is expensive and bulky, so most forgers use a regular paper cutter — leaving all four sides smooth.

Watch for Clues Revealing Color Copied Checks

Magnetic routing numbers at the bottom of a check will be raised off the surface — almost like braille — because of the dull ink's effect on the reflective light duplicating process. The numbers on the copy will be shiny instead of dull. Also, because the color is created by a chemical process rather than by ink, the moisture from your fingers will often cause them to smear an opposite color.

Check Magnetic Numbers for Dull Finish

The special magnetic ink required for automated check sorting is extremely flat and dull. If you spot shine, or reflected light, off these numbers when you tilt the check under normal lighting, it is probably a forgery. This ink is expensive, and restricted, so the forger will usually not go to the trouble to obtain it. Being aware of the short cuts taken by forgers due to expense and unavailability of certain papers and inks, will help you to quickly and easily spot forged checks.

Verify Federal Reserve District Numbers

The nine place number between the brackets is the routing code for the bank the check is drawn on. The first two indicate which of the 12 Federal Reserve Districts the bank is located in. Refer to the codes below. It is important that you compare this to the location of the bank since a forger will sometimes change these in order to buy more float time while the check is routed to a distant, incorrect Reserve Bank. It should also agree with the routing fraction printed in the upper right hand corner.

Federal Reserve Bank Codes

01—Massachusetts, Maine, New Hampshire, Connecticut, Vermont, Rhode Island
02—New York, New Jersey, Connecticut
03—Pennsylvania, Delaware, New Jersey
04—Ohio, Pennsylvania, Kentucky, West Virginia
05—Virginia, Maryland, North Carolina, Washington, D.C., South Carolina, West

Virginia
06—Georgia, Alabama, Florida, Tennessee, Louisiana, Mississippi
07—Illinois, Michigan, Indiana, Iowa, Wisconsin
08—Missouri, Arkansas, Kentucky, Tennessee, Indiana, Illinois, Mississippi
09—Minnesota, Montana, North Dakota,

South Dakota, Wisconsin, Michigan
10—Missouri, Colorado, Oklahoma, Nebraska, Iowa, Wyoming, Kansas, New Mexico
11—Texas, Arizona, New Mexico, Louisiana
12—California, Oregon, Washington, Utah, Hawaii, Alaska, Idaho, Nevada, Arizona

©1990 by Frank Abagnale & Associates
Not to be reproduced under penalty of federal law.

Source: Frank W. Abagnale & Associates, Tulsa, Oklahoma.

Exhibit 6   Steps to Follow when Accepting Checks

Steps to Follow when Accepting Checks

1   **Be cautious of new checking accounts**

Of all the insufficient, "hot" checks, 90% are drawn on accounts less than a year old. The consecutive numbers in the upper right hand corner begin with 101 and you should be especially careful when taking low numbered checks. Because knowing the age of the account is so important, some banks now print a code of when the account was opened (for example, 0278 means February, 1978) on all checks.

2   **Place all information on front of check**

As described in Regulation CC, either write the information consecutively across the top of the front or use the cross method.

Driver's license number	Credit card number
Clerk's initials	Other ID or manager's approval

3   **Examine driver's license carefully**

After you have the license out of the customer's wallet and in your hand, quickly ask yourself the following questions: Is the person in the photo and in front of you the same person? Are the addresses on the check and license the same? When does the license expire? More than 60% of the forged checks last year were cashed with an expired driver's license. Also, the courts have ruled that licenses are legally worthless for identification as soon as they expire. Be sure you examine the driver's license carefully.

4   **Other Negotiable Instrument Codes**

On drafts issued by savings and loan institutions and mutual savings banks, magnetic bank routing numbers may start with the digit 2 or 3. Credit union drafts are honored by the bank on which they are drawn. International traveler's checks have routing numbers starting with 8000. U.S. Government checks contain the routing number 000000518.

5   **Traveler's check identification**

VISA—When held above eye level, a globe of the world will appear on the front left and a dove in the upper right.
MASTERCARD and THOMAS COOK—When held above eye level, on the right side of the check in a circle, a woman with short black hair will appear.
CITICORP—When held above eye level, a Greek god will appear on the right.
BANK OF AMERICA—No distinguishing watermarks.
AMERICAN EXPRESS—Turn check over. Moisten your finger tip and run it over the left denomination. If it smears it is good. Right side will not smear.

6   **Be impressed with the check—not the person**

Don't let a customer's appearance lull you into ignoring any of these steps. Frank Abagnale, the retired master forger, once cashed a $50 check written on a cocktail napkin, before a hidden camera for television, because the bank teller was more impressed by his appearance than by the item he presented. When you're in a hurry, or want to make an exception, think how you will defend your decision if the check is returned. Then, only the check will matter —not the circumstances in which you took it.

Developed by Frank W. Abagnale

 & Associates/PO Box 701290, Tulsa, Oklahoma 74170/Telephone 918-492-6590

Source: Frank W. Abagnale & Associates, Tulsa, Oklahoma.

Exhibit 7   Counterfeit Paper Currency Test

WOODROW
FEDERAL RESERVE BANK OF MINNEAPOLIS

Counterfeit Protection

Whether altering the design of ancient coins or making photocopies of bills with high-tech machines, counterfeiters have made illegal money throughout history. The Secret Service, an agency of the U.S. Treasury, has investigated suspected counterfeit operations since 1865. Over the past decade, the Secret Service has seized approximately 90 percent of all known counterfeit currency printed before it reached circulation.

In the printing process, the Bureau of Engraving and Printing uses complicated techniques to stifle counterfeiters. Beginning with the $100 bill in 1996, currency will be redesigned to include more security features. The following pictures explain how the Bureau protects your money.

Portrait
The portrait on the bill is a lifelike picture, distinctly different from the screen-like background. Each portrait is only on one denomination. For example, George Washington appears only on the $1 bill, **not** on the $100 bill. Portraits on counterfeit bills appear unclear or unnaturally white.

Feel of Paper
Money is printed on high-quality paper made of cotton and linen. It has a strong "feel" to it, different from regular paper.

Border
The artwork along the side of the bill has intricate, crisscrossing lines which are clear and unbroken. Lines in counterfeit bills are often smudged or broken.

Threads
Bills have tiny red and blue fibers that are embedded inside the bill.

Ink
The special "never-dry" ink that is used can be rubbed off. However, this isn't a fool-proof test since ink on some counterfeit bills also rubs off.

Recent Measures

Security Thread
Beginning with series 1990, a polyester thread, which can't be reproduced by photocopiers, is woven inside $10, $20, $50 and $100 bills. USA TEN, USA TWENTY, etc. is printed on it to match the denomination.

Microprinting
"The United States of America" is printed in miniature letters around the border of the portrait. To the naked eye the words appear as a black line, which is also how photocopiers print them.

What to do if you have counterfeit currency
Since the consequences for passing counterfeit currency include fines up to $5,000 or imprisonment up to 15 years, you need to be careful. If you have a suspicious bill:

- Write your initials on the back so you can identify it later.
- On a separate sheet of paper write in detail how you got it:
    1. **Who** gave it to you.
    2. **Where** you got it.
    3. **When** you got it.
- Handle it as little as possible to preserve any fingerprints.
- Contact the nearest Secret Service office or local police.

You are not reimbursed for turning in counterfeit bills; however, you protect yourself from trouble by following proper procedures.

Source: Federal Reserve Bank of Minneapolis. http://www.woodrow.mpls.frb.fed.us

Exhibit 8   Tricks of a Short-Change Artist

Tricks of a Short-Change Artist

The short-change artist is a master of the art of deception and persuasion. Each has a particular individual style and technique. The short-change artist may be a man, woman, teenager, even a child, but regardless of sex or age, he/she usually operates within these four basic rules:

(1) Establishes credibility and trust. (2) Gains the confidence of the prospective victim. (3) Confuses the prospective victim without making him suspicious. (4) Short changes the victim without the victim even knowing what has happened.

FOLLOW THE PHOTO SEQUENCE CAREFULLY, AND YOU WILL SEE THAT I STARTED WITH $20.00 AND ENDED WITH $29.02. THAT IS A $9.02 SHORTCHANGE PLUS A FREE 98¢ PACKAGE OF RAZOR BLADES . . . OR A TOTAL OF $10.00 IN MERCHANDISE AND CASH.

4

5

Frank: (gives Clerk a five and four ones) "please count it."

1

Frank: "Here's a $20 bill for these razor blades."

2

Clerk: (puts bill on register) "And here is your change. Thank you, sir."

6

Clerk: "Sir, you're short a dollar."
Frank: "I'm sorry. Let me have the twenty back and we'll start over."

3   ALERT   *Mistake!*

Frank: (takes change) "May I have a $10 bill for a five and five ones?"

7   *Mistake!*

(Clerk hands the twenty back)
Frank: "Now, how much do you have?" **Clerk:** "Nine dollars."

8

Frank: "OK, here's a one and another ten; that makes twenty. Now we have it. Thank you!"

A $10 LOSS!

The Answer: 1. Be Alert! 2. Have the customer's money in your hands before making change!
3. Never mix transaction A with B

Developed by Frank W. Abagnale

Frank W Abagnale ——— & Associates/Box 701290, Tulsa, Oklahoma 74170   918-492-6590

Source: Frank W. Abagnale & Associates, Tulsa, Oklahoma.

Employee Theft from Guests

While employee theft from guests may not immediately affect the property's revenue, it may significantly affect the property's reputation and, therefore, its long-term profitability. Guests who discover that they have been cheated will often blame the property, not the dishonest employee. This is reasonable since the employer selects and trains employees and has an obligation to design and enforce procedures and policies to protect guests.

Staff members with the greatest opportunity to steal from guests are bartenders, cashiers, and servers. Several of the methods used to steal money from guests are:

- Attempting to increase tips by padding bills—putting items not ordered on guest checks.

- Charging higher prices for items than those established by management and pocketing the difference.

- Altering credit card charges after the guest leaves, or imprinting additional vouchers with the guest's credit card before returning it. The dishonest employee can then use these vouchers fraudulently.

- Altering personal checks that guests use for payment.

- Making change incorrectly by shortchanging or fast-counting.

Guests are also cheated when they are served items of lower quality than they order and pay for. With the appropriate control systems, properties can prevent or reduce employee theft from guests. The most effective control methods include:

- Proper operation of the electronic cash register.

- Guest check control (if manual hard copies are used).

- Audits.

- Close supervision.

- Use of shoppers.

- Compliance with the check and credit card procedures reviewed earlier.

Control of Cash after Collection

Even if all actual revenue due the property is collected, theft may occur when bank deposits are made, when bills are paid, or when bookkeeping/accounting tasks are performed.

Preventing Theft of Bank Deposit Funds

All revenue must be deposited in the food and beverage operation's bank account. Revenue should be deposited at least on a daily basis. Moreover, all revenue should be deposited intact. This means that bills should not be paid with cash from the daily revenue. Instead, bills should be paid by check. This policy makes it easier to trace the flow of revenue into the property, on to the bank, into the proper account, and back out again through proper disbursement procedures when paying bills.

The separation of duties is a basic element in effective control. When possible, different employees should collect revenue, audit and account for guest checks (if used), and prepare the tallies of daily revenue. These employees should not normally be involved in preparing bank deposits or paying bills. In small properties, the manager or owner will perform many or all of these tasks. For example, the manager should be able to double-check revenue levels from source documents such as guest checks and electronic cash register data, verify the amount of revenue collected as reported on recorded tallies, make adjustments, and note the amount of revenue reported on a bank deposit slip.

In addition to the basic control policies noted, specific practices that can help control revenue at the time of deposit include the following:

- Compare the amount of each bank deposit with records of daily revenue collected.

- Cash received from miscellaneous sources, such as grease sales or bottle returns, should be in the form of a check and deposited in the bank as "other revenue" along with deposits from daily operations.

- Deposits for nonrecurring transactions, such as the sale of equipment or insurance proceeds, should be made separately from revenue.

- Personnel who open mail should not make bank deposits. This reduces the possibility of employees diverting revenue from checks received that should be deposited.

- All persons involved with money, deposit assessment, and cash disbursements should be bonded.

- The person preparing the deposit should not make the deposit—unless the owner/manager takes responsibility for these tasks.

- All involved personnel should be aware of and consistently follow deposit procedures. Close supervision of this task is extremely important.

- All checks should be marked "For Deposit Only," preferably at the time of receipt. Instruct local banks not to issue cash for any checks made payable to the food and beverage operation.

- Checks returned as "NSF"—Not Sufficient Funds—should be turned over to the bank to be held for collection. This way funds deposited in the account will first be used to meet NSF obligations. If the check is redeposited, cash can be stolen in an amount equal to the value of each returned check.

- Checks returned as "Account Closed" should be turned over to a collection agency.

Two final rules are important for handling revenue receipts. First, change safe combinations periodically. As few staff members as possible should know how to open the safe. Second, require all employees who handle cash to take uninterrupted annual or more frequent vacations. This way another employee can assume the cash-handling duties and may uncover improper practices.

Preventing Theft when Bills Are Paid

To reduce the opportunities for theft, bills should be properly processed and paid. Basic procedures for paying bills should be incorporated into the cash disbursement system. The following procedures should be implemented to safeguard against theft when bills are paid:

- Pay bills by check. Do not use cash, except for minor expenses to be paid with petty cash funds.

- When processing bills for payment, compare the in-house copy of the purchase order or purchase record, the suppliers' delivery invoices, and the in-house receiving report.

- Develop and use control procedures for issuing checks. If practical, use check protectors that imprint the check amount. Print all checks with the name of the property and mark them "void after 60 days." Never sign blank checks. Inform banks of all management staff authorized to sign checks. Checks in excess of a specified dollar value may require more than one manager's signature. Keep unused checks locked in a secure area.

- The person who signs the checks should mail them. They should not be returned to the employee who processed the bills.

- Personnel who sign checks should not normally have access to petty cash funds and should not be permitted to approve cash disbursements or to record cash receipts—unless it is the manager or owner who performs all these tasks.

- Make out all checks to a specific company or person. Never make out checks to "cash" or "bearer."

- Clearly mark invoices and statements "PAID" after processing. The date, check number, invoice, and check amount should all be clearly noted on the forms. File these documents, with supporting information, by supplier.

- Investigate outstanding checks that are not promptly returned or cashed.

- Place all returned checks in sequential order and properly reconcile bank statements.

Although bills should be paid by check whenever possible, writing checks for minor expenses can be a nuisance. For this reason, many food and beverage operations set up a petty cash fund. Proper procedures for handling petty cash are an important aspect of the cash control system. The basic plan for using a petty cash system should include these steps:

1. Set the total of the petty cash fund at the amount normally needed for very small purchases over several weeks. To establish the fund, write a check charged to

Exhibit 9 Sample Petty Cash Voucher

```
┌─────────────────────────────────────────────────────────────┐
│              Petty Cash Voucher                              │
│                                                              │
│                            Voucher Number: _____   │
│  Date: _____                         │
│  Purpose: _____  │
│           _____  │
│                                                              │
│  Account: _____    Account To Be Charged: _____ │
│  Authorized By: _____  │
│                                                              │
│              (Attach Receipt to This Voucher)                │
└─────────────────────────────────────────────────────────────┘
```

"petty cash." This amount—in dollars or in supporting receipts—should always remain in the fund. When replenishing the petty cash fund, write a second check for the total amount of receipts in the fund to bring it back up to its proper level. Make out the checks to "petty cash," not to "cash" or to the name of the person managing the fund.

2. Assign responsibility for the fund to one staff member and keep the fund in a secure place. It should not be mixed with funds in cash registers.

3. Do not authorize the person responsible for managing the fund to write or sign a check to replenish it—unless the owner/manager is responsible for the fund.

4. Develop definite policies regarding what can and cannot be purchased with funds from petty cash. These policies should also specify how often purchases can be made and a dollar limit above which checks must be written for purchases.

5. Support all purchases with a receipt for the amount of the purchased items.

6. Use a petty cash voucher (see Exhibit 9) to summarize petty cash transactions.

7. Cash advances or loans for employees should not come from the petty cash fund.

8. Spot-check petty cash funds to ensure that the fund is at the proper level and that all purchases are for authorized purposes and supported by receipts.

Preventing Bookkeeper Theft

Many types of theft are related to the misuse of bookkeeping and accounting procedures. Managers need to remain constantly alert to this wide range of opportunities for theft. Examples include:

- Changing revenue records to show lower daily revenue and stealing the difference between revenue reported and actual revenue collected.
- Removing cash from the petty cash fund and either allowing the fund to remain short or submitting false expense receipts to cover the shortage.
- Billing charge customers at the full amount but recording a lower amount and pocketing the difference.
- Showing higher than actual discounts when reimbursement checks from credit card companies are deposited.
- Claiming a guest's check was marked "NSF" (Not Sufficient Funds) or "account closed" and then converting the check to personal use.
- Preparing checks payable to oneself and forging signatures or using signed blank checks, then destroying paid checks when returned from the bank.
- Manipulating bank statement reconciliations—overstating deposits not yet recorded, understating outstanding checks, and/or purposely miscalculating on reconciliation worksheets—to cover cash shortages.
- Overstating expenses but paying only the supplier's correct charge.
- Overpaying a supplier's invoice and converting the supplier's refund check for personal use.
- Resubmitting invoices previously paid for a second payment and splitting payment with the suppliers in collusion with a company thief.
- Setting up a "dummy" company to submit invoices for payment.
- Padding the payroll by preparing checks for employees who have been terminated or adding fictitious employees to the payroll.
- Adding overtime or additional hours to payroll records in order to increase wages.
- Converting unclaimed payroll checks and cashing them with forged signatures.

Key Terms

collusion—A relationship between two or more employees that allows them to work together to steal revenue and/or products from the operation.

Review Questions

1. Why is it important to develop and implement specific procedures for using the electronic cash register?

2. What are some of the ways that a bartender can steal from a property? What procedures can be implemented to reduce the opportunities for bartender theft? How can use of an electronic cash register/point of sale system (ECR/POS) reduce opportunities for bartender theft when a manual hard copy guest check system is used?

3. What is a shopper service? Why and when should this service be used?

4. What are some of the ways that food service staff can steal from a property? What procedures can be implemented to reduce these possibilities? How can use of an ECR/POS system reduce opportunities for server theft when a hard copy guest check system is used?

5. What are some of the ways cashiers can steal from a property? What procedures can be implemented to reduce these possibilities? How can ECR/POS systems help reduct cashier theft?

6. What are some of the ways guests can steal from a property? What procedures can be implemented to reduce these possibilities?

7. What are some of the ways employees can steal from guests? What procedures can be implemented to reduce these possibilities? How do ECR/POS systems reduce employee theft from guests?

8. When should revenue be deposited in the bank? Why?

9. What are some good procedures for handling petty cash?

10. How can bookkeepers steal from a property? What procedures can be implemented to reduce these possibilities?

Internet Sites

For more information, visit the following Internet sites. Remember that Internet addresses can change without notice. If the site is no longer there, you can use a search engine to look for additional sites.

Associations

American Culinary Federation (ACF)
http://www.acfchefs.org

American Hotel & Lodging Association (AH&LA)
http://www.ahlaonline.org

American School Food Service Association (ASFSA)
http://www.asfsa.org

Club Managers Association of America (CMAA)
http://www.cmaa.org

The Educational Foundation of NRA
http://www.edfound.org

The Educational Institute of AH&LA
http://www.ei–ahla.org

Hospitality Financial and Technology Professionals
http://www.hftp.org

Institute of Food Technologies
http://www.ift.org

International Hotel and Restaurant Association
http://www.ih–ra.com

National Association of College and University Food Services
http://www.nacufs.org

National Restaurant Association (NRA)
http://www.restaurant.org

Food and Beverage Resources

Club Management Online
http://www.club-mgmt.com/dining/
index.html

Prepared Foods. Product development,
ingredients, suppliers
http://www.preparedfoods.com

Management Companies

ARAMARK
http://www.aramark.com

Bon Appétit Management Company
http://www.bamco.com

Compass Group
http://www.compass-na.com

Sodexho Marriott
http://www.sodexhomarriott.com

The Wood Company
http://www.woodco.com

Publications—Online and Printed

Club Management Magazine
http://www.club-mgmt.com

Electronic Gourmet Guide
http://www.foodwine.com

Food and Hospitality Magazine
http://www.foodserviceworld.com

Food Management
http://www.foodservicesearch.com

Food Network: CyberKitchen
http://www.foodtv.com

Food Processing: The Magazine of
Strategy, Technology and Trends
http://www.foodprocessing.com

Internet Food Channel
http://www.foodchannel.com

International Hotel and Restaurant
Association journal
www.hotelsmag.com

International Journal of Hospitality
Management
http://www.mcb.co.uk/ijchm.htm

Journal of Hospitality Financial
Management
http://hrta.fnr.umass.edu/sheel/
ahfme/jhfm/aboutjhfm.html

Lodging Food and Beverage
http://www.lodgingnews.com/
lodgingfnb/

Lodging Hospitality Online
http://www.lhonline.com

Lodging News, journal of the American
Hotel & Lodging Association
http://www.ei-ahla.org/webs/
lodging/index.html

Nation's Restaurant News
http://www.nrn.com

On the Rail—News for Food
Professionals
http://www.ontherail.com

Restaurant Business, Food Service, and
ID magazines
http://www.foodservicetoday.com

Restaurant Hospitality
www.foodservicesearch.com

Restaurants and Institutions
http://www.rimag.com

Restaurants USA, publication of
National Restaurant Association
http://www.restaurant.org/rusa

World Hospitality, management
magazine for hotel executives.
http://www.worldhospitality.com

Theft Prevention

Employee Theft
http://www.metrokc.gov/proatty/
fraud/theft.htm

Theft Prevention in Hotels
http://cepcoproducts.com

Theft
http://www.crimedoctor.com/
identity.com

Part VI

Controlling Labor Costs

Chapter 13 Outline

Managing Human Resources
    Basic Staffing Tools
    Recruitment and Selection Procedures
    Employee Orientation Procedures
    The Training Process
    Employee Supervision
    Employee Performance Evaluation
        Process
Factors Affecting Work Performance and
    Productivity
Work Simplification and Labor Cost Control
    Increasing Productivity
Labor Control and Employees
    Get to Know Your Employees
    Employee Motivation
    Increasing Interest in Work

Competencies

1. Describe how food and beverage managers use staffing tools such as job descriptions, job specifications, and organization charts in planning for labor cost control. (pp. 397–401)

2. Describe how food and beverage managers use recruitment and selection tools to ensure that the most qualified applicants are hired for open positions. (pp. 401–404)

3. Explain how orientation programs, training programs, and employee performance evaluations help control labor costs. (pp. 405–414)

4. Explain how food and beverage managers can increase staff productivity by simplifying work processes and revising performance standards. (pp. 415–417)

5. Explain how food and beverage managers use techniques such as job rotation, job enlargement, and job enrichment to increase productivity and employees' interest in work. (pp. 420–421)

13

Labor Cost Control

FOOD AND BEVERAGE managers are well aware of the need to control labor costs. To put the issue in perspective, consider the following:

- The food service industry is labor-intensive. Technology has not found a way to replace people with equipment. Even an increased emphasis on convenience food usage in many properties has not eliminated the need for a large staff. Employees are needed to produce, serve, and clean up in food and beverage operations. And many employees occupy entry-level hourly positions, where problems of turnover, accidents, absenteeism, tardiness, and low morale are often prevalent.

- Direct labor costs are increasing. Minimum wage scales increase periodically. Many employees in the hospitality industry are paid at rates significantly higher than minimum wage in efforts to attract and retain them. Competition for qualified people from other food and beverage operations and especially from other service industries raises labor rates. And, in many areas, there is a need for larger incentives to attract people to work in entry-level positions.

- Increases in labor costs are usually not balanced by increases in productivity. Labor needed just to maintain operations becomes increasingly expensive.

- Fringe benefits packages are often very creative—and expensive. Not long ago, a benefits package generally included employer contributions for social security, meals, uniforms, and unemployment taxes. Today, however, employees often receive such additional benefits as dental and health insurance, vacation time, education and training assistance, contributions toward retirement plans, and many others.

- It is difficult to manage people in any industry, but in the hospitality industry it is especially true that people with differing attitudes, beliefs, problems, goals, and personalities are commonly found among staff.

- In addition to economic and supervisory concerns, managers often recognize the need to help employees find meaning and satisfaction in their jobs. Labor costs, then, are difficult to control because people cannot—and should not—be managed in the same way that food and beverage products are managed.

Managing Human Resources

From management's point of view, the major human resources objective is to control labor costs while attaining the operation's goals. If inexperienced, uninterested, or untrainable employees are hired, these major objectives will never be realized. In an all-too-familiar situation in some food and beverage operations, managers are forced to hire whoever walks in the door. This might be due to some "emergency," a failure to plan for staffing needs, a lack of knowledge about principles of human resources administration, or few qualified applicants. At any rate, considerable time and money are spent in training and closely supervising the new employee. During this orientation period, when the new staff member is learning about the job and its responsibilities, productivity is low. In addition, other problems may be encountered such as less-than-ideal product quality, increased accidents and errors, misuse of equipment, and breakage. After a short time of unsatisfactory job performance, the employee quits. This situation is repeated too often in many food and beverage operations. Managers come to believe that this is to be expected: they think that high turnover goes with the job and the industry.

This example emphasizes that labor cost control must begin with the procedures used to recruit, select, orient, and train employees. Managers must be concerned with each employee's reactions to human resources administration and control procedures. In addition to orienting and training new employees, the control system for labor must include procedures for the supervision and appraisal of all employees.

Basic Staffing Tools

The first step in the human resources administration process—employee recruitment—begins with writing **job descriptions** that summarize each job, list its major tasks, and tell who supervises the employee and whom the employee supervises. Personal qualities necessary for someone to do the job well are often worked into the job description. Exhibits 1 and 2 present sample job descriptions for a dining room server and a bartender.

Some properties also use a second document—a **job specification**—to list personal qualities judged necessary for successful performance on the job.

When writing job descriptions, remember that they are developed for a position, not for a particular person. A job description is task-oriented. Don't think, "I have a cook named John. What does he, or should he, do?" Instead, focus on work that any cook in that position might reasonably be expected to do.

Do not overstate personal attributes needed to perform the job. As qualifications for the job increase, it becomes more difficult to find employees. As experience and other requirements increase, so will labor costs since operations must pay more for highly qualified employees. Finally, if overqualified applicants are hired, they may become bored since they are underemployed. Stated simply, then, food and beverage managers should hire people who are properly qualified to perform required tasks.

Job descriptions are useful in several ways. They help managers recruit and select job applicants. Because managers know the work to be done and the type of person generally qualified to do it, they can evaluate applicants against these standards. Job descriptions assist in the design of training programs. Staff members must be trained to perform each task required by the job description. Job descriptions also help with daily supervision, answering questions such as who should

Exhibit 1   Job Description for Dining Room Server

POSITION DESCRIPTION

POSITION: *Server*	JOB NO.: _____
REPORTS TO: *Dining Room Manager*	DATE: _____
DEPARTMENT: *F & B*	PREPARED BY: _____
WAGE & HOUR CLASS: *Hourly*	APPROVED BY: _____
	(Supervisor)
COMPANY: _____	CLASSIFICATION CODE: _____

POSITION PURPOSE:

To be responsible for the proper service of meals to guests in an assigned area of the dining room.

DIMENSIONS:

NATURE AND SCOPE:

This position reports to the Manager of the dining room.

Before the restaurant opens, the incumbent sets the tables in his/her assigned area and makes sure everything is in order.

The incumbent may assist the Hostess in seating the guests in her area. She takes orders from the guests in an efficient manner and after checking to see if everything ordered is on the ticket, she turns the orders in to the kitchen to be filled. Before the food is delivered to the tables, the incumbent checks the orders to see if they have been correctly filled. He/she serves the meals by courses, making sure that the proper orders are placed in front of the guests. If the busperson has not placed ice water, bread and butter on the tables, the incumbent sees that this is done and makes sure they are replenished as needed. She also replenishes coffee or tea, and remains alert to the needs of the guests at all times.

The incumbent presents the checks to the guests with a pleasant "Thank You."

After the guests have left the tables, the incumbent clears the tables and resets them if the busperson is busy.

The incumbent assists in training new waitresses and buspersons and performs other related duties as required.

It is imperative that the incumbent perform her duties efficiently and pleasantly in order to ensure continued patronage by the guest and the high standard of quality and service of the restaurant.

PRINCIPAL ACTIVITIES:

1. Sets tables in assigned area prior to serving time.

2. Takes orders and serves meals in an efficient manner to the complete satisfaction of the guests.

3. Presents tickets which have been correctly tabulated to the guests with a pleasant "Thank You."

4. Clears tables and resets them if the busperson is busy.

THE USE OF PERSONAL PRONOUNS SHOULD NOT BE CONSIDERED SEX-BIASED.

Courtesy of Opryland Hotel, Nashville, Tennessee

Exhibit 2   Job Description for Bartender

POSITION DESCRIPTION

POSITION: *Bartender*

REPORTS TO: *Beverage Manager*

DEPARTMENT: *Beverage*

WAGE & HOUR CLASS: *Hourly*

COMPANY: _____

JOB NO.: _____

DATE: _____

PREPARED BY: _____

APPROVED BY: _____
(Supervisor)

CLASSIFICATION CODE: _____

POSITION PURPOSE:

To be responsible for the preparation of alcoholic drinks according to set standards as they relate to size, recipe, and quality; to operate cash register; to be responsible for seeing that the bar is kept clean and properly stocked; to assist in inventories, and in the training of new bartenders and barbacks; and to perform other duties as required.

DIMENSIONS:

NATURE AND SCOPE:

This position reports to the Beverage Manager.

The incumbent ensures that prior to serving time, the bar is ready for service and that all supplies, utensils, and glassware are on hand to serve the guests. (Day shift bartenders must make sure that the bar is fully stocked and cleaned for the night bartenders.)

The incumbent is responsible for checking of bar par and making sure it is on par and checking liquor requisitions.

The bartender mixes drinks, cocktails, and bar beverages ordered. He is also responsible for preparing fruits and garnishing drinks. The orders should be filled as they are turned in by the cocktail waitresses and the amount rung up on the guest checks. After the waitresses collect the money from the guests, they turn it in to the incumbent, who rings it up on the cash register and ensures transmittal to the accounting office.

The incumbent is responsible for seeing that the bar is clean at all times and assists the barback in washing glassware and utensils.

The bartender assists in taking inventory after bar closing and assists in training new bartenders and barbacks.

The customer must be given the receipt portion of the guest check on all transactions.

The incumbent performs other related duties as may be generally assigned.

PRINCIPAL ACTIVITIES:

1. Ensures that, prior to serving time, the bar is ready for service and all supplies are on hand to serve the guests.
2. Mixes drinks, cocktails, and bar beverages as ordered by the cocktail waitress and rings up the amount of the order on the check.
3. Receives payments and checks from cocktail waitresses, rings them up on the cash register, and ensures transmittal to the accounting department.
4. Is responsible for seeing that glasses and bar utensils are washed and the bar is kept clean at all times and is properly stocked.
5. Assists in inventories and in the training of new bartenders and barbacks.
6. Performs other related duties as required.

THE USE OF PERSONAL PRONOUNS SHOULD NOT BE CONSIDERED SEX-BIASED.

Courtesy of Opryland Hotel, Nashville, Tennessee

Exhibit 3 Sample Organization Chart for the Dining Room of a Large Hotel

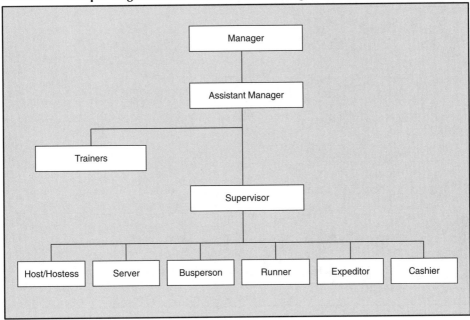

Courtesy of Opryland Hotel, Nashville, Tennessee

prepare salad greens: the assistant cook or food service worker? Finally, job descriptions also help with employee evaluation. Each staff member should be able to adequately perform the tasks included in his or her job description.

After job descriptions are developed, an **organization chart** should be used to show the relationships among all positions in the food and beverage operation. Exhibit 3 presents an organization chart for the food service positions in a dining room of a large hotel, while Exhibit 4 presents a bar and beverage organization chart. Notice that the charts do not indicate the number of individuals employed in each position; rather, they indicate only how each position relates to all others. The charts, developed to fit the needs of individual properties, let each staff member know where he or she fits into the organization. The charts show channels of communication and coordination by illustrating the chain of command. With an organization chart as a guide, specific decisions and problems can be referred to the right position and to the responsible person.

Recruitment and Selection Procedures

After the tools of labor control planning (job descriptions, job specifications, and the organization chart) are developed, specific procedures can be designed to obtain the best possible employees for all positions in the food and beverage operation. Recruitment begins with attracting qualified applicants for vacant positions

Exhibit 4   Sample Organization Chart for a Bar/Beverage Operation

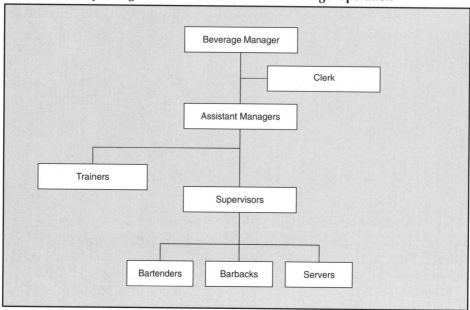

Courtesy of Opryland Hotel, Nashville, Tennessee

and continues with screening procedures so that employees can be selected from a pool of the best-qualified people.

Sources of Job Applicants. The list for potential job applicants includes friends and relatives of current staff. There are both advantages and disadvantages of this source of job applicants. One advantage is that current employees know what it is like to work at the property. If they have a favorable impression, they might be good salespersons for attracting others. A possible disadvantage is that, if one member of the group is disciplined, terminated, or otherwise affected by human resources administration, there may be a spin-off effect on the others. In addition, collusion may occur between friends or relatives.

Promoting current employees is another way to fill vacant positions. A career ladder that indicates advancement opportunities within the food and beverage operation is often a good idea. Promotion from within may build morale, encourage existing staff to perform better, and reduce turnover.

Applicants for vacant positions may learn of openings through newspaper or trade magazine advertisements, state or private employment agencies, word of mouth, schools with education and training programs in food and beverage operations, and other sources of information about employment opportunities. Exhibit 5 lists possible strategies to use in recruiting applicants. Lists of applicants may also be available from state employment services, single parent organizations, and veterans' groups, among others.

Exhibit 5 Recruitment Strategies

RECRUITMENT STRATEGIES

1. **Youth**
   Schools, Vo-Techs, Colleges
   — Meet with counselors
   — Speak to classes
   — Sponsor work study programs
   — Participate in career days
   — Invite classes to tour hotel

2. **Minorities**
   — Meet with representatives from minority community agencies and invite for lunch and tour of hotel
   — Advertise in minority newspapers
   — Visit schools in minority neighborhoods
   — Notices at churches in minority communities
   — Visit youth centers and place notices there

3. **Disabled Persons**
   — State Rehabilitation Agencies
   — National Alliance of Business
   — Private Industry Councils
   — National Association of Retarded Citizens
   — Goodwill Industries
   — Other local agencies

4. **Women**
   — Local organizations which assist women in transition
   — Community colleges, universities
   — Bulletin board notices in supermarkets, libraries, YWCAs, exercise centers
   — Flyers in parking lots
   — Displaced Homemakers organizations
   — Craft centers
   — Child care centers

5. **Older Workers**
   — AARP Senior Employment Services
   — Senior Citizen Centers
   — Synagogues and churches
   — Retirement communities and apartment complexes
   — Newspaper ads worded to attract
   — Retired military

6. **Individuals in Career Transition**
   — Newspaper ads
   — University evening programs
   — Referrals
   — Teachers
   — Unemployed actors
   — Laid off workers from other industries
   — Speak at community functions, i.e., Rotary, Toastmasters

7. **Lawfully Authorized Immigrants**
   — Ads in foreign language newspapers
   — Churches
   — English as a Second Language classes
   — Citizenship classes
   — Refugee resettlement centers
   — Employee referrals

Courtesy of Radisson Hotel Corporation, Minneapolis, Minnesota

Application Form. Once prospective employees are identified, they must be evaluated. The use of an employment application form helps determine whether the applicant meets minimum job qualifications. The form should be simple and require only information relevant to judging the applicant's suitability for the job, since federal, state, and perhaps local laws prohibit discrimination based on factors such as age or race. Employment applications, properly developed, help screen out unsuitable applicants. Information on the application can become the basis for conducting interviews.

Employee Interviews. The next stage of the selection process is to conduct interviews with job candidates chosen from among the employment applications. Through the initial employee interview, managers gain additional information about applicants and can tell them about the company and the position. This is also a time to answer applicants' questions. In large operations, the human resources department conducts the opening interview. Applicants judged eligible are then interviewed in the department in which the position is located. In smaller operations, the owner/manager or department head may handle interviews personally.

Reference Checks. After the initial pool of applicants has been narrowed by the interview process, a reference check can be performed for the remaining applicants. Such a check may help verify information provided on the application form. Telephone conversations with past employers named on the application form can be a helpful start. Additionally, if the employer knows staff members in any of the properties where the applicant has worked, a second reference may be available. (Note: increasingly, past employers provide little information other than to verify employment dates because of concern over lawsuits by applicants who are rejected by firms to which they have applied.)

Selection Tests. After examining the application form, conducting interviews, and making reference checks, employers may give each eligible applicant a **selection test**. Selection tests require applicants to demonstrate skills required by the job description for the desired position. A simple arithmetic test for certain positions may give the employer an initial idea about how much training will be necessary. For example, an applicant for a cashier's position should know how to make change, and a cook may need to know how to extend recipes.

Supervisor Interview. The staff member who will supervise the new employee should have the opportunity to interview applicants, since the supervisor will be directly affected by the selection. This can be a second interview in which the supervisor asks very specific questions, and, with the applicant, considers how their personalities and attitudes will mesh on the job.

All concerned parties—the human resources manager or owner/manager, department head, and position supervisor—should be involved in the hiring decision. The final decision should be based on a careful review of the information gained from the sources described previously. This requires that ample time be given to the recruitment and selection process. It also implies that as many applicants as possible should be recruited and evaluated, in contrast to the common alternative of recruiting one person at a time and using selection procedures to ensure that he or she can do the work.

Employee Orientation Procedures

An orientation program must be set up for the new employee. Although often overlooked, orientation is very important because it sets the tone for the relationship between the new employee and the organization.

The new staff member's first experiences on the job affect later performance. Experienced food and beverage managers agree that employees are more likely to leave relatively soon after hiring than after many years on the job. When this happens, it indicates that perhaps the employee was not a good choice. Or, it may suggest something happened soon after hiring that made the employee unsuitable or want to leave the position. Either way, the human resources administration process appears to be at fault.

Usually, new employees are eager employees or, at least, can be motivated. Management should build upon this attitude so that new employees will want to perform effectively. An inadequate orientation program tells new employees that the supervisor doesn't care about them and that the property may not really be a good place to work.

An employee orientation program should be built on the following basic principles:

1. The new staff member should receive an updated employee handbook covering the basic facts about the company and the job—background on the property, organization chart, job description/specification, rules and policies, and job benefits.

2. All forms to be completed—tax withholding, insurance, and similar documents—should be assembled so the employee can complete them during the first day on the job.

3. The employee should be given a job orientation that includes a tour of the property's facilities and introductions to all staff members with whom he or she will work. The work group should be informed in advance about the new employee's arrival.

4. The employee's workstation should be viewed, and a locker, uniform, small tools, or similar items, as applicable, should be available.

5. The employee(s) responsible for on-the-job training, if this technique is used, should be selected and specific plans for training developed (see the following discussion).

6. The trainer or contact person should work very closely with the new staff member over the first several days. The new employee should not be neglected. Perhaps answering the question, "How would I like to be treated if I were a new employee?" can be the guide to carrying out the orientation.

7. The supervisor should check with the new staff member frequently during the first several days, then adjust the degree of supervision according to the nature of the work the employee does and the amount of person-to-person help that the specific employee needs.

An orientation checklist (Exhibit 6) can identify topics of importance during the process of orienting new staff members.

The Training Process

Training is important for both new and current employees to learn or improve necessary job knowledge, skills, and attitudes. Properly trained employees are absolutely critical to the success of the labor cost control program as well as to attaining all the property's goals. The company, after all, is only as good as its employees.

In planning a training program, managers should consider exactly what trainees need to learn, how to evaluate if trainees have, in fact, learned the material (at least to a minimum performance level), and the amount of training time needed. Exhibit 7 presents a general property, department, and position orientation and training schedule for servers. Note that the general property orientation lasts almost two days. The department and position orientation and training continues for eight more work days.

How is a training program developed and implemented? Details are beyond the scope of this chapter.[1] However, a basic outline of the process is illustrated in Exhibit 8. Note that the first step is to observe the needs for training.

Employee Supervision

The most important responsibility of most food and beverage managers is supervising other staff members.[2] Unless employees receive direction as they undertake their work, labor cost control goals cannot be met. Therefore, supervision is essential to the overall labor control system. The supervisor must accept the responsibility for directing the work of employees in addition to performing other job requirements. This means that supervisors must spend the amount of time necessary to properly direct employees while they work.

Supervisors are responsible to several groups. First, they are responsible to themselves because they want to be competent and feel satisfied that they are doing well. Responsibilities to peers and colleagues include cooperating in a team effort to meet goals. Supervisors must also help solve problems within budget and cost restrictions, provide timely and accurate information, and, in general, help higher-level managers with ongoing work.

Supervisors also have some very direct responsibilities to employees. For example, they must:

- Try to understand the employee as an individual in a human relations approach to supervision.

- Place people in positions according to job descriptions. To fit jobs to employees may not benefit the property or the employee.

- Support employees when they perform as required, and criticize constructively when individual staff members need to improve work performance.

- Provide adequate training and appraisal.

- Be fair and reasonable in all relationships with employees.

Exhibit 6   New Employee Orientation Checklist

New Employee Orientation Checklist

Name of New Employee: _____   Position: _____

Department: _____   Supervisor: _____

Date Hired: _____

Instructions—Initial and date when each of the following is completed.

Part I—Introduction

☐ _____ Welcome to new position (give your name, find out what name the employee prefers to be called, etc.)
☐ _____ Tour of property
☐ _____ Tour of department work area
☐ _____ Introduction to fellow employees
☐ _____ Introduction to trainer
☐ _____ Explanation of training program
☐ _____ Review of job description
☐ _____ Explanation of department

Part II—Discussion of Daily Procedures

☐ _____ Beginning/ending time of workshift
☐ _____ Break and meal periods
☐ _____ Uniforms (responsibilities for, cleanliness of, etc.)
☐ _____ Assignment of locker
☐ _____ Employee meals (if any)
☐ _____ Parking requirements
☐ _____ First aid and accident reporting procedures
☐ _____ Time clock or "sign-in log" requirements
☐ _____ Other (specify)
☐ _____

Part III—Information About Salary/Wages

☐ _____ Rate of pay
☐ _____ Deductions
☐ _____ Pay periods
☐ _____ Overtime policies
☐ _____ Complete all payroll withholding, insurance, and related forms
☐ _____ Other (specify)

Part IV—Review of Policies and Rules

☐ _____ Safety, fires, accidents
☐ _____ Maintenance and use of equipment
☐ _____ Punctuality
☐ _____ Absenteeism
☐ _____ Illness
☐ _____ Emergencies
☐ _____ Use of telephone
☐ _____ Leaving work station
☐ _____ Smoking/eating/drinking
☐ _____ Packages
☐ _____ Vacations
☐ _____ Other (specify)

(continued)

Exhibit 6   *(continued)*

Part V—Employee Handbook/Related Information

☐ _____ Received and reviewed
☐ _____ Review of employee appraisal process
☐ _____ Review of organization chart
☐ _____ Review of job description
☐ _____ Review of department's responsibilities
☐ _____ Review of all benefit plans
☐ _____ Discuss performance standards/expectations
☐ _____ Discuss career path possibilities

Part VI—Miscellaneous Orientation Procedures (Review all other areas covered with the new employee)

_____

_____

_____

I certify that all the above activities were completed on the date indicated.

Employee _____   Date _____

Supervisor _____   Date _____

Source: Raphael R. Kavanaugh and Jack D. Ninemeier, *Supervision in the Hospitality Industry,* 3rd ed. (Lansing, Mich.: Educational Institute of the American Hotel & Lodging Association, 2001), pp. 118–119.

- Be concerned about employee safety and well-being.

- Provide an example of acceptable behavior while on the job—often referred to as being a role model for staff.

Supervisors who meet such responsibilities help control labor costs within the food and beverage operation.

Good supervisors want to work with employees in an effort to do the best job. They do not write off employees as unmanageable. If they were to do so, turnover, absenteeism, and low productivity would typically result. They develop ways to involve employees in the work as much as possible and to satisfy desires and needs of individual employees on the job.

Employees, in turn, must be able to accept the authority for and responsibility to complete assigned work. They must have both the physical ability and mental desire to perform this work. Supervisors should be willing to involve staff members in designing their work to the extent they wish to be involved.

Supervisors must be able to relate to and understand employees, recognize them as individuals, and treat them accordingly in work relationships. Employees are individuals on and off the job, and their personal problems can affect their work. Generally, it is best for supervisors to have only professional, rather than personal, relationships with staff.

Management personnel should display a positive attitude and a commitment to the food and beverage operation in general. They should be consistently honest and fair in all relationships with employees, peers, and superiors. Finally,

Exhibit 7   Server Training Schedule

FOOD AND BEVERAGE TRAINING PROFILE				
Department: Beverage			Position: Server	

Week 1

Mon	Tue	Wed	Thu	Fri
8:00 A.M.–4:00 P.M. Hotel Orientation	8:00 A.M.–4:00 P.M. Hotel Orientation 3:30 P.M. Training Manual Program Handout	9:00 A.M.–4:00 P.M. 9:00 A.M. Department Introduction 1:00 P.M. Introduction to IBM	8:45 A.M.–3:30 P.M. 8:45 A.M. "Drink Presentation" 1:00 P.M. IBM Role Play	10:00 A.M.–5:00 P.M. 10:00 A.M. "Service Fundamentals Beverage Style" 12:00 P.M. Floor Observation, All Outlets
4:00 P.M. Home	4:00 P.M. Home	4:00 P.M. Home	3:30 P.M. Home	5:00 P.M. Home

Off Saturday & Sunday

Week 2

Mon	Tue	Wed	Thu	Fri
5:00 P.M.–Closing Follow Seasoned Trainer Paperwork	5:00 P.M.–Closing Follow Seasoned Trainer Paperwork	2:00 P.M.–8:00 P.M. Follow Trainer No Paperwork	10:30 A.M.–6:00 P.M. Training Station Paperwork	10:30 A.M.–6:00 P.M. Training Station Paperwork

Courtesy of Opryland Hotel, Nashville, Tennessee

supervisors should use their knowledge, experience, and common sense in dealing with people and in solving job-related problems.

The quality of employee supervision affects how closely the actual operating results approximate established labor performance standards and whether plans to control labor costs are successful. Although supervision is an essential aspect of the entire labor control system, the process of supervising and directing staff is too vast to discuss here.

Employee Performance Evaluation Process

Each staff member's work must be evaluated regularly. This happens informally as supervisors interact with employees and make decisions about work quantity and quality. However, more formal evaluations are also needed to better explain to each employee how supervisors view the adequacy of their work. Employees cannot improve their performance unless they understand what their supervisors expect and where, if at all, supervisors believe problems exist. An effective

Exhibit 8   Flow Chart of Training Program Development and Implementation

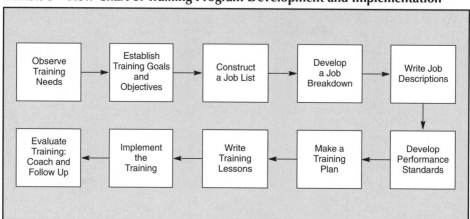

evaluation process also permits employees to offer ideas for improving the operation. As training needs are identified, as bases for discipline are established, and, in general, as the labor cost control program is improved, good work can be recognized through wage increases and/or promotions.

Procedures for evaluating employees include the following:

1. Decide what factors are to be considered and ensure that employees accept them as a way to judge the quality of performance. To the maximum extent possible, factors should be measurable and objective.

2. Inform employees about purposes, frequency, factors judged, and quality standards expected in the evaluation.

3. Review work daily, or at some other regular time interval, to collect information about employee performance. Note critical incidents illustrating very good or very bad performance.

4. In private meetings with each employee, discuss the employee's general job performance. Critical incident information can be used to illustrate or defend the points made. Formal employee appraisals should normally take place at least every six months.

5. The employee should be permitted to express views about the job, the supervisor's comments, or how job performance and relationships with others might be improved.

6. In concluding the evaluation session, the supervisor should emphasize the employee's strong points and indicate a desire to work with the employee to improve performance in weak areas. Finally, the supervisor should suggest that the employee can talk with him or her about problems encountered at any time.

See Exhibit 9 for a set of guidelines useful in conducting performance evaluations.

Employees can be evaluated with a form indicating qualities considered important in performing the job. Exhibit 10 is an example of a sophisticated

Exhibit 9   Conducting Performance Evaluations: Guidelines

1. Interview in a setting that is informal, private, and free of distraction.
2. Provide a courteous, supportive atmosphere.
3. Encourage the employee to participate actively.
4. Clearly explain the purpose of the interview.
5. Explain problem areas thoroughly but tactfully.
6. Listen when the employee talks; don't interrupt.
7. Criticize job performance, not the employee.
8. Criticize while you're calm, not angry.
9. Avoid confrontation and argument.
10. Emphasize the employee's strengths, then discuss areas which need improvement.
11. To set goals for improvement, focus on future performance, not past.
12. Assume nothing; instead, ask for clarification.
13. Ask questions to gather information, not to "test" the employee.
14. Expect the employee to disagree.
15. Try to resolve differences; don't expect total agreement.
16. Avoid exaggerations (such as "always" or "never").
17. Help the employee maintain self-esteem; don't threaten or belittle.
18. Keep your own biases in check.
19. Allow the employee to help you set goals for improvement.
20. Assure the employee that you will help him/her reach the goals.
21. Maintain appropriate eye contact.
22. End on a positive note.

Source: Raphael R. Kavanaugh and Jack D. Ninemeier, *Supervision in the Hospitality Industry,* 3rd ed. (Lansing, Mich.: Educational Institute of the American Hotel & Lodging Association, 2001), p. 174.

performance evaluation form covering an extensive period of time. It can be modified to suit individual properties and specific positions.

Benefits of properly conducted performance evaluation programs include the following:

1. The employees learn about ways to improve performance.
2. The supervisor learns about employees' job-related problems.
3. Both the supervisor and employees become aware of the importance of achieving output of an acceptable quantity and quality.
4. The process by which employees are identified for promotion and salary increases is formalized.
5. Employee suggestions for improving the job are obtained.

Exhibit 10   Sample Performance Evaluation: Food Server

FOOD SERVER PERFORMANCE REVIEW

FOOD SERVER NAME _____

DIRECTIONS: Rate the performance level of the employee.

4 — Excellent — Usually meets established standards
3 — Good — Acceptable but could improve
2 — Fair — Definite need for improvement
1 — Unacceptable — Definite need for counseling

Performance Area	Date	Before Training	After Training	25-Day Eval.	90-Day Eval.	180-Day Eval.	270-Day Eval.	360-Day Eval.	Comments — Indicate Date by Each Comment
		/ /	/ /	/ /	/ /	/ /	/ /	/ /	
Policies and Procedures (Knowledge)									
Use of exits and entrances									
Uniform exchange/cleaning procedures									
Sign-in and sign-out sheets									
Cafeteria hours									
Restaurant hours of operation									
Employee schedules									
Fire procedures									
Accident reports									
Absenteeism, sick calls, tardiness									
Table numbers and stations									
Pre-meal meetings									
Bulletin board information									
Performance reviews and evaluations									
Rules of conduct									
Locker issue and use									
Personal phone call rules									
Transfers and promotions									
Exit interview policy									
Paycheck procedures									
Service Concept (Knowledge)									
Upper Level service standards									
Personal appearance specifications									
Restaurant safety									
Menu knowledge									
Wine knowledge									
Beverage knowledge									
Service scenario									
Opening Sidework (Knowledge/Skills)									
Preparing flowers									
Preparing butter									
Preparing sugar bowls									
Preparing salts and peppers									

(continued)

Exhibit 10 (continued)

Performance Area	Before Training	After Training	25-Day Eval.	90-Day Eval.	180-Day Eval.	270-Day Eval.	360-Day Eval.	Comments
Date	/ /	/ /	/ /	/ /	/ /	/ /	/ /	Indicate Date by Each Comment
Preparing gueridons								
Folding napkins								
Preparing silverware (regular/special)								
Setting up service trays								
Stocking chilled forks/plates								
Checking Benny Wafers								
Stocking ashtrays and matches								
Setting tables								
Checking overall station appearance								
Service Procedures (Knowledge/Skills)								
Greeting guests								
Taking cocktail order								
Picking up drinks								
Serving cocktails								
Presenting menus								
Taking the food order								
Presenting the seafood tray								
Suggestive selling								
Taking the wine order								
Assisting with wine selection								
Performing pre-check operation								
Ordering food								
Serving wine/champagne								
Picking up food orders								
Serving food orders								
Serving food courses								
Clearing between courses								
Preparing table for each course								
Checking tables for needs								
Changing ashtrays								
Removing soiled dishes to dishroom								
Clearing after entree course								
Crumbing the table								
Taking dessert and coffee order								
Serving dessert and coffee								
Serving hot tea and Sanka								
Selling and serving cordials								
Preparing the guest check								
Presenting the guest check								

Exhibit 10 *(continued)*

Performance Area	Date	Before Training	After Training	25-Day Eval.	90-Day Eval.	180-Day Eval.	270-Day Eval.	360-Day Eval.	Comments
		/ /	/ /	/ /	/ /	/ /	/ /	/ /	Indicate Date by Each Comment
Processing payment									
Assisting guests upon departure									
Delivery of the service scenario (Server)									
Resetting tables									
Closing Sidework (Knowledge/Skills)									
Storing flowers									
Cleaning gueridons									
Taking linens to laundry									
Storing condiments									
Breaking down breads and butters									
Breaking down coffee station									
Breaking down wine buckets									
Breaking down water pitchers									
Straightening and cleaning side stands									
Setting station for next meal (w/o silver)									
Securing all silverware									
Bussing all soiled items to dishwasher									
Vacuuming carpet									
Personal Attributes									
Attitude toward work									
Appearance and uniform									
Cooperation with fellow workers									
Acceptance of directions									
Attendance									
Desire to learn in job									

RATED BY (INITIALS)

Describe specific training needs (areas with scores of 2 or below):

Source: Lewis C. Forrest, Jr., *Training for the Hospitality Industry*, 2d ed. (Lansing, Mich.: Educational Institute of the American Hotel & Lodging Association, 1990), pp. 356–357.

Factors Affecting Work Performance and Productivity

To control labor costs, it is first necessary to identify those factors that influence the required number of labor hours—and therefore labor costs. While varying among properties, possible influences on productivity include several factors, such as the following:

Menu Items. Items involving difficult production techniques require more production hours. For example, a menu with 15 difficult entrées—such as beef Wellington and chicken Kiev—requires more labor time than a menu with several hamburger variations.

Convenience Foods. Menu items made on-site require more preparation time than similar menu items made with convenience foods. Convenience food products are purchased with "built-in" labor.

Service. A restaurant featuring elegant tableside cooking and service requires more labor than a walk-up or drive-up fast-food operation.

Quantity of Meals. The number of labor hours needed for most positions will vary according to the volume of meals produced and served.

Number of Meal Periods. Using different menus for different meal periods requires setup and tear-down labor time and also means a larger variety of menu items.

Facility Layout and Design. Efficient layout of space and equipment positively affects worker productivity.

Production Equipment. Using equipment to do work otherwise done manually reduces labor time.

Labor Market. If properly skilled or experienced employees are not available, other employees will need training. During training, they will be less productive than when fully trained.

Allocation of Labor Hours. Work performance relates to productivity levels that compare labor hours to meals or revenue produced. If, for example, labor costs are allocated between food and beverage departments, or indirect labor not previously charged to a revenue center is charged to a department, it affects labor costs relative to output.

Human Resources Administration Policies. When effective policies and procedures of human resources administration are used, work performance generally improves.

Supervision. Effective supervision implies that employee output will be high. The quality of supervision influences labor costs and, in general, the quantity and quality of output.

Employee. The individual worker's experience, abilities, knowledge, and attitudes affect performance. This supports the need to recruit and keep the most qualified employees.

Work Methods. Work simplification principles help worker performance, as discussed later in this chapter.

Work Environment. The places in which employees work influence productivity. Temperature and humidity, ventilation, lighting, colors, and noise levels should add to employee comfort, not hurt performance.

Number of Hours Worked. Long hours and hard work are common in many food service jobs. Legal restrictions and common sense are now reducing the number of hours worked, at least for nonmanagement staff. These changes help minimize negative influences on worker performance.

Other Worker-Related Factors. Adequacy of training, staff morale, relationships among staff members, type of leadership exerted by supervisors, time pressures, the worker's health and physical condition, and similar considerations all affect work performance.

All these and other possible factors affecting worker performance must be understood when developing labor standards.

Work Simplification and Labor Cost Control

When more work is done in less time, labor costs are reduced. (However, quality standards should not be reduced in the process of reducing costs.) Certain basic procedures can simplify work. The operation benefits since labor costs are better controlled, and the employee benefits since the job is made more efficient. There are several indicators of inefficient work procedures:[3]

- Service delays requiring guests to wait beyond reservation times or for food or beverages to be served
- Labor hours in excess of labor performance standards
- Guest and employee complaints
- Peaks and valleys in workloads
- Excessive breakage or theft
- Poor use of employee skills and knowledge
- Frequent accidents or errors
- Low employee morale and motivation
- Ineffective use of space
- Too much paperwork
- Inadequate forecasting of production and service needs
- Difficulty in meeting production and service schedules
- Poor working conditions

When supervisors observe these or similar problems, they should consider implementing work simplification procedures. Priority should go to studying those jobs that can benefit most from work simplification, such as those that:

- Involve large amounts of labor time and therefore labor costs.

- Directly involve food production and service, in contrast to recordkeeping or exterior maintenance tasks.

- Will continue indefinitely.

- Create bottlenecks or excessive overtime hours.

- Involve many employees performing the same tasks, such as cleaning vegetables or washing dishes.

- Consistently do not meet quality or quantity standards.

Increasing Productivity

One of the most difficult and challenging tasks for supervisors is to create new ways of getting work done in the department. Too often supervisors get caught up in routine, day-to-day functions and fail to question the way things are done. One of the best ways to increase productivity is to continually review and revise performance standards. The following sections present a five-step process for increasing productivity by revising performance standards.

Step 1—Collect and Analyze Information about Current Performance Standards. Often this can be done by simple observation. If you know what must be done to meet current performance standards, observe what is actually being done and note any differences. When analyzing tasks listed in performance standards for positions within the department, supervisors should ask the following questions:

- Can a particular task be eliminated? Before revising how a task is performed, the supervisor must ask whether the task needs to be carried out in the first place.

- Can a particular task be assigned to a different position? For example, perhaps some food preparation duties can be assigned to dishwashers during low-volume times; a part-time food preparation position might be eliminated.

- Are the performance standards of another department decreasing the productivity of employees in your department? For example, the hotel's on-premises laundry may not be supplying the amount of table linen needed by the food and beverage department. Productivity suffers when dining room staff must make frequent trips to the laundry area to pick up clean linen as it becomes available.

Step 2—Generate Ideas for New Ways to Get the Job Done. Generally, when work problems arise, there is more than one way to resolve them. Performance standards for many hospitality positions are complex, and it is often difficult to pinpoint the exact reasons for current problems or new ideas about how to get the job done more efficiently.

Employees, other supervisors, and guests are important sources of information that can help a supervisor pinpoint tasks for revision. Employees who actually perform the job are often the best source for suggested improvements. Other supervisors may be able to pass on techniques which they used successfully to increase productivity in their areas. Also, networking with colleagues often results in creative ideas that you can apply to your own area of responsibility. Completed guest comment cards and/or personal interviews with selected guests may reveal aspects of the operation that supervisors may consistently overlook.

Step 3—Evaluate Each Idea and Select the Best Approach. The actual idea you select may be a blend of the best elements of several different suggestions. When selecting the best way to revise current performance standards, be sure that the task can be done in the time allowed. It is one thing for a "superstar" employee to clean the dining room or cook a meal within a specified time; it may not, however, be reasonable to expect that an average employee—even after training and with close supervision—can be as productive. Performance standards must be attainable to be useful.

Step 4—Test the Revised Performance Standard. Have only a few employees use the revised performance standard for a specified time so you can closely monitor whether the new procedures do indeed increase productivity. Remember, old habits are hard to break. Before conducting a formal evaluation of the revised performance standard, employees will need time to become familiar with the new tasks and build speed.

Step 5—Implement the Revised Performance Standard. After the trial study has demonstrated that the new performance standard increases productivity, employees must be trained in the new procedures. Continual supervision, reinforcement, and coaching during the transitional period will also be necessary. Most important, if the increased productivity is significant, make the necessary changes to the department's staffing guide and base scheduling practices on the new productivity standard. This will ensure that increased productivity translates to increased profits through lower labor costs.

Labor Control and Employees

The labor control system must effectively manage employees, work, and associated costs. Viewing the job from the perspective of the employee may help supervisors discover what the employees want and provide it to the maximum extent possible. This will reduce labor problems and associated costs.

Get to Know Your Employees

Supervisors develop a motivated staff by creating a climate in which employees want to work *toward*—rather than *against*—the goals of the department and those of the organization. To help employees become motivated, supervisors must understand their needs, interests, and goals. What motivates one employee may have little effect on another because needs, interests, and goals vary from employee to employee. These motivational factors are a function of each individual's background, personality, intellect, attitudes, and other characteristics. The challenge is for supervisors to get to know employees they supervise.

To be a successful motivator, supervisors need to know what it takes for employees to become motivated. This is not an easy task because some employees may not know, or at least cannot verbalize, their needs or goals. Much motivation is subconscious. For example, some "high energy" employees may be

Exhibit 11 What Do Employees Want from Their Jobs?

Factors	Rank Given By	
	Employees	Supervisors
Full appreciation of work done	1	8
Feeling of being in on things	2	10
Help with personal problems	3	9
Job security	4	2
Higher wages	5	1
Interesting work	6	5
Promotion in the company	7	3
Personal loyalty of supervisor	8	6
Good working conditions	9	4
Tactful discipline	10	7

Source: Adapted with permission from John W. Newstrom and Edward E. Scannell, *Games Trainers Play: Experiential Learning Exercises* (New York: McGraw-Hill, 1980), p. 121.

top performers because they fear rejection from co-workers if they do not produce above-average results. These employees may not even be aware that they are seeking approval from their peers.

Exhibit 11 shows that significant differences can exist between what supervisors *believe* employees want and what employees *actually* want from their jobs. Workers were asked to rate the factors that most affected their morale and motivation level. Likewise, supervisors were asked to indicate what factors they believed were most important to their employees. Note that the top three items ranked by employees (full appreciation of work done, feeling of being in on things, and help with personal problems) are the last three items ranked by supervisors.

The first two items judged most important by employees are fully within the control of a supervisor. In fact, there are a number of things one can do to improve the motivational climate at little or no cost to the organization. By acknowledging the good performance of employees and by providing appropriate recognition, a supervisor can convey an appreciation to their employees. Also, a supervisor helps employees feel that they are "in on things" by effectively communicating the objectives of the department and significant events affecting the organization.

The third item judged most important by employees may not be fully within the control of a supervisor. Personal problems are generally better addressed by trained professionals. However, a supervisor can communicate understanding and concern for employees experiencing personal problems beyond the workplace. They may also be able to refer troubled employees to the appropriate professional. This kind of attention may be all that many employees expect and may be greatly appreciated.

Employee Motivation

The fact that individuals have unmet needs that stimulate them to do something provides the basis for understanding approaches to motivation. One basic approach was advanced by Herzberg and his associates many years ago.[4] They identified factors that must be present to some extent within the work environment before an employee can be motivated. In other words, if these factors are not present, employees will become dissatisfied. One strategy involves providing these factors on the job with the hope that employees will make some commitment to their job.

The following maintenance factors, in amounts employees individually judge necessary, become part of what employees want from their jobs:

- Acceptable company policies
- Acceptable administration/management
- Adequate relations with supervisors, subordinates, and peers
- Adequate salary and working conditions
- Appropriate job security assurances
- Proper status

Herzberg and his associates also suggested another set of factors which, when provided in the quantity employees judge important, may increase worker satisfaction and job performance:

- Challenging work
- A sense of personal accomplishment
- A feeling of being appreciated for performing acceptable work
- Increased responsibility and the opportunity to advance in the job
- Feelings of importance and contributing to the organization
- Participation in job-related matters that affect the worker

Each of these, then, is an ingredient in a complete answer to the question, "What does an employee want from the job?" Supervisors who feel they have something in common with their employees may use a golden-rule approach: "What I want from my job is what my employees may want from their jobs. The way I want to be treated in my job is the way that my employees want to be treated in their jobs."

Increasing Interest in Work

To the greatest extent possible, improvements in work should benefit both the organization and the employee. This assumes that people have been matched with jobs to some degree. Hiring people qualified to perform tasks outlined in the job description should help to eliminate:

- Underemployment and employees who become bored because their work provides no challenge
- Overemployment and employees who are frustrated because they are not qualified to perform the work

Assuming employees are performing adequately, several techniques may help generate increased interest in the work.

Job Rotation. Job rotation is a system of moving employees among jobs they are able to perform. The employee advantages include reduced boredom from constantly repeating the same tasks. It may also enable the employee to discover other positions of interest and so develop more appropriate career tracks. Job rotation has other advantages to the organization. When not bored, employees may be more efficient and produce higher quality work. Employees who can do several jobs can fill in as required. Also, training time for jobs reached through promotion may be lessened.

Job Enlargement. Job enlargement increases the number of tasks included in a job. The additional tasks may or may not increase the variety of the work, nor will additional tasks always be of interest to the employee.

When enlarging jobs, managers should consult with affected employees to determine jointly how job tasks might be recombined.

Job Enrichment. In **job enrichment**, job tasks are changed to generate interest, involvement, and challenge. Increasing employee responsibility and making employees more accountable for their own work are examples of job enrichment. Job enrichment techniques introduce more and/or different types of motivation factors into the job. The approach generally involves getting workers interested in doing things they want to do within the job.

Endnotes

1. For more information on training, see Lewis C. Forrest, Jr., *Training for the Hospitality Industry,* 2d ed. (Lansing, Mich.: Educational Institute of the American Hotel & Lodging Association, 1990).

2. For more information on this subject, see Raphael R. Kavanaugh and Jack D. Ninemeier, *Supervision in the Hospitality Industry,* 3rd ed. (Lansing, Mich.: Educational Institute of the American Hotel & Lodging Association, 2001), pp. 17–18.

3. First reported in E. Kazarian, *Work Analysis and Design for Hotels, Restaurants, and Institutions* (Westport, Conn.: AVI, 1969), pp. 4–5.

4. F. Herzberg et al., *The Motivation to Work,* 2d ed. (New York: Wiley, 1959). The discussion here simplifies the material.

Key Terms

job description—A written, detailed summary of duties, requirements, and supervisory relationships for each employee position within the hospitality operation.

job enlargement—Increasing the number of tasks included in a job.

job enrichment—Changing a job by adding motivational factors—such as responsibility, decision making, variety, and challenge—to the job itself.

job rotation—A system of moving employees among jobs they are able to perform.

job specification—A selection tool that lists the personal qualities judged necessary for an employee's successful performance on the job.

organization chart—A visual picture of the hierarchical structure of positions within a hospitality organization.

selection test—An examination requiring job applicants to demonstrate skills included in the job descriptions for the desired positions.

Review Questions

1. When should labor control begin? Why?

2. Is it always necessary to have job descriptions and job specifications? Why or why not?

3. What are the steps in the process of selecting a new employee? Why are these steps important?

4. Why is it important to properly orient and train new employees as soon as they are hired?

5. What are the steps in conducting an employee performance evaluation? Why are they important?

6. What are some factors that influence employee work performance and productivity?

7. What are some questions to ask when analyzing work procedures?

8. What can be done to increase an employee's interest in work?

9. What can supervisors do to increase employee productivity?

10. Why is it important that supervisors get to know their employees?

11. What are examples of ways that Herzberg's motivation theory can be used in interactions with food and beverage employees?

Internet Sites

For more information, visit the following Internet sites. Remember that Internet addresses can change without notice. If the site is no longer there, you can use a search engine to look for additional sites.

Associations

American Culinary Federation (ACF)
http://www.acfchefs.org

American Hotel & Lodging Association (AH&LA)
http://www.ahlaonline.org

American School Food Service Association (ASFSA)
http://www.asfsa.org

Club Managers Association of America (CMAA)
http://www.cmaa.org

The Educational Foundation of NRA
http://www.edfound.org

The Educational Institute of AH&LA
http://www.ei-ahla.org

Hospitality Financial and Technology Professionals
http://www.hftp.org

Institute of Food Technologies
http://www.ift.org

International Hotel and Restaurant Association
http://www.ih-ra.com

National Association of College and University Food Services
http://www.nacufs.org

National Restaurant Association (NRA)
http://www.restaurant.org

Food and Beverage Resources

Club Management Online
http://www.club-mgmt.com/dining/index.html

Hospitality Human Resources
http://www.msue.msu.edu/msue/imp/modtd/33129714.html

Prepared Foods. Product development, ingredients, suppliers
http://www.preparedfoods.com

Management Companies

ARAMARK
http://www.aramark.com

Bon Appétit Management Company
http://www.bamco.com

Compass Group
http://www.compass-na.com

Sodexho Marriott
http://www.sodexhomarriott.com

The Wood Company
http://www.woodco.com

Publication—Online and Printed

Club Management Magazine
http://www.club-mgmt.com

Electronic Gourmet Guide
http://www.foodwine.com

Food and Hospitality Magazine
http://www.foodserviceworld.com

Food Management
http://www.foodservicesearch.com

Food Network: CyberKitchen
http://www.foodtv.com

Food Processing: The Magazine of Strategy, Technology and Trends
http://www.foodprocessing.com

Internet Food Channel
http://www.foodchannel.com

International Hotel and Restaurant Association journal
www.hotelsmag.com

International Journal of Hospitality Management
http://www.mcb.co.uk/ijchm.htm

Journal of Hospitality Financial Management
http://hrta.fnr.umass.edu/sheel/ahfme/jhfm/aboutjhfm.html

Lodging Food and Beverage
http://www.lodgingnews.com/
lodgingfnb/

Lodging Hospitality Online
http://www.lhonline.com

Lodging News, journal of the American
Hotel & Lodging Association
http://www.ei-ahla.org/webs/
lodging/index.html

Nation's Restaurant News
http://www.nrn.com

On the Rail—News for Food
Professionals
http://www.ontherail.com

Restaurants and Institutions magazine
http://www.rimag.com

Restaurant Business, Food Service, and
ID magazines
http://www.foodservicetoday.com

Restaurant and Hospitality
www.foodservicesearch.com

Restaurants and Institutions
http://www.rimag.com

Restaurants USA, publication of
National Restaurant Association
http://www.restaurant.org/rusa

World Hospitality, management
magazine for hotel executives
http://www.worldhospitality.com

Chapter 14 Outline

Competencies

1. Explain how food and beverage managers determine labor standards. (pp. 427–429)

2. Identify factors food and beverage managers consider when constructing a staffing guide. (pp. 431–432)

3. Distinguish between fixed and variable labor in relation to food and beverage operations. (pp. 432–436)

4. Explain how food and beverage managers use staffing guides as labor scheduling tools. (pp. 436–440)

5. Explain how food and beverage managers use staffing guides as labor cost control tools. (pp. 440–444)

14

Implementing Labor Cost Controls

Labor standards form the basis for effective labor control systems. However, before labor standards can be developed and implemented, managers must consider quality requirements. For example, labor standards for service staff depend on the level of service defined by management. The level of service may depend on the relationship between the number of labor hours scheduled and the number of guests served. As more labor hours are scheduled for a constant number of guests, employees can give each guest more attention. Conversely, fewer scheduled labor hours for the same number of guests could mean lower or, at least, different quality service because less attention can be paid to each guest.

Labor standards for kitchen staff must take into account the amount of time necessary to produce food of the required quality. The amount of time required is based on procedures dictated by standard recipes. Elaborate buffet presentations, ice carvings, fancy cake decorating, and similar labor-intensive tasks require extra time, but quality should not be sacrificed.

These quality requirements form the foundation of labor standards. Training programs should be designed to provide employees with the knowledge and skills necessary to meet quality requirements.

This chapter begins with a discussion of how managers can measure labor activity in such a way that meaningful comparisons can be made between labor standards and actual labor costs. Next, labor standards are defined in relation to productivity rates that managers can establish by conducting position performance analyses. Once labor standards are determined, they can be used to construct a staffing guide. Much of this chapter focuses on how managers can use a staffing guide to implement labor cost controls consistent with budgeted goals.

The final sections of the chapter address special labor scheduling techniques used by fast-food operations and how labor cost control can be enhanced by automated labor and payroll information systems.

Establishing a Unit of Measurement for Labor Standards

When developing labor standards, managers must decide how labor activity will be measured and specify the level of detail needed to adequately control labor costs. Recall that standard cost information for food and beverage products is

427

generally expressed in dollars and percentages. Actual food and beverage costs are measured in the same way so that comparisons can be made with standard cost information. But what unit of measurement applies to labor?

Several factors must be considered in choosing a labor measure to define standard and actual labor costs. First, the unit of measurement must be used consistently. If one unit of measurement is used in developing labor standards and another unit is used to report actual labor costs, managers will be left comparing "apples to oranges," and the labor control system will yield meaningless results. Second, the unit of measurement must be simple enough so that managers can explain it to staff members. Using a ratio of labor costs to total costs may be useful for management tasks, but is it easily understood by supervisors and other staff members who may work with it on a daily basis? Third, the unit of measurement also must be compatible with the operation's accounting system. The method for measuring labor standards and actual labor activity should incorporate information from the property's payroll and accounting systems. It is a waste of time to keep two sets of books—one for internal labor control and a second for payroll and accounting.

Labor activity may be expressed in terms of labor dollars and/or labor hours. When dollars are used as the unit of measurement, managers may work with a designated number of labor dollars per day or with predetermined labor cost percentages. Advantages of measuring labor standards in dollars include the following:

- Budgets are generally expressed in dollars rather than labor hours.

- Financial operating statements are expressed in dollars—not labor hours.

- Labor costs can be separated by shift for each position within each department.

Labor activity may also be measured in labor hours. For example, a unit of measurement might be based on the number of labor hours required to produce a given number of meals or generate a certain level of revenue. Reasons for measuring labor standards in hours, rather than dollars, are as follows:

- When productivity is emphasized instead of labor cost reduction, it is easier to incorporate quality requirements into work tasks (or, at least, to remember the need for them).

- Labor hours must be calculated for many staff members' wages even if labor cost measurements are used, since the number of hours determines wages.

- Systems to control labor dollars are often time-consuming and difficult to use. Different wages and salaries for personnel within each position make calculating labor standards in dollars a challenge.

- Fixed labor costs (labor costs that do not vary with the volume of meals served or the amount of revenue produced) may distort labor costs as meal counts decrease or as revenue increases.

- On some occasions, concentrating on labor dollars may obscure variations in productivity and, hence, costs.

- Calculating labor hours, rather than dollars, keeps the measure from being affected during times of economic inflation.

Deciding whether to base labor measurement systems on labor dollars or labor hours is difficult. In many large food and beverage operations, a combined approach is practical and yields accurate and useful information. The approach used in the remainder of this chapter focuses on the control of labor hours. However, procedures to convert hours into dollars are included to facilitate the combined approach.

Determining Productivity Rates

Productivity can be measured by comparing the number of labor hours expended to the number of meals served and/or to the amount of revenue generated. Managers must decide whether to determine productivity rates by department, by shift, by position, or by position and shift.

A detailed standard makes it easier to take corrective action when variances between standards and actual results occur. This is because a more detailed standard affords greater accuracy in analyzing the causes of variances and, as a result, makes it easier to develop corrective action procedures. The greater usefulness of more specific information in the corrective action phase of the control system must be taken into consideration when assessing the trade-off between accuracy and the time required to collect information.

Determining productivity rates by position and shift yields the most accurate, detailed information. Suppose a food and beverage manager, after carefully studying the operation, determines that a productivity rate of 15 meals per labor hour is a desired efficiency level; that is, for every hour of labor (input), there should be 15 guests served (output). Let's assume that productivity rates for cooks, dishwashers, and service personnel were not considered separately. After a given meal period, the manager discovers that the actual productivity rate was only 13 meals per labor hour. Since the productivity rate was established without considering positions separately, the manager cannot pinpoint the cause of the lower overall productivity. If, however, the manager had known that the labor performance standard for cooks was 15 meals per labor hour, while the actual productivity rate was only 12, then at least part of the problem could have been immediately traced to the kitchen.

Establishing productivity rates by position makes it easier to examine the efficiency of each staff member. Experienced food service managers realize that productivity rates for different positions—cooks versus dishwashers, for example—vary. These different rates must be determined and incorporated into labor standards.

After determining minimum quality requirements, the unit of measure for labor activity, and how productivity rates are to be measured, managers can develop labor standards by considering the number of labor hours required to perform assigned tasks. In one traditional approach, an observer using a stopwatch and clipboard develops labor standards based on observing employees perform tasks. There are also very sophisticated procedures adapted from industrial

Exhibit 1   Position Performance Analysis Form

Position Performance Analysis

Position: _____Service_____   Name of Employee: _____Joyce_____

Shift: _____A.M.—Lunch_____

	4/14	4/15	4/16	4/17	4/18
No. of Guests Served	38	60	25	45	50
No. of Hours Worked	4	4	4	4	3.5
No. of Guests/Labor Hour	9.5	15	6.3	11.3	14.3
Review Comments	Even workflow; no problems	Was really rushed; could not provide adequate service	Too much "standing around"; very inefficient	No problems; handled everything well	Worked fast whole shift; better with fewer guests

General Comments

   Joyce is a better than average server; with all the tasks that service personnel must do in our restaurant, approximately 10 guests per labor hour can be served by one server. When the number of guests goes up, service quality decreases. When Joyce really had to rush, some guests waited longer than they should have had to. When the number of guests per labor hour dropped and Joyce was not busy, there was a lot of unproductive time.

Suggested Guests/Labor Hour
(for this position): _____10_____   Performance Review by: _____W. Brown_____
                                                                            Restaurant Manager

engineering techniques. However, time, cost, and expertise probably prohibit using sophisticated approaches in all but the largest food and beverage operations or in fast-food operations where some tasks are very repetitive. While not strictly scientific, the following technique—position performance analysis—yields reasonably accurate results.

   Position performance analysis determines labor standards for each position and shift. An observation period is set during which employees are instructed to carefully follow all established policies and procedures. They are closely supervised to ensure compliance. For example, a cook would be told to follow all standard recipes, and all staff would be instructed to observe rest breaks and to perform tasks at the required quality levels. No changes in employee scheduling are made. During the study period the manager closely observes and analyzes job performance.

   Exhibit 1 presents a worksheet that a manager can use to determine a labor standard for food servers. The worksheet provides columns for recording data and observations on the work of a single server over five lunch shifts. For each lunch shift, the manager records the following data:

• Number of guests served

• Number of hours the server worked

- Number of guests the server served per hour worked

- Comments concerning how well the server performed

The exhibit shows that on April 14, Joyce served 38 guests during a four-hour shift. This resulted in 9.5 guests served per hour worked (38 guests divided by four hours of work). Over a five-day period, the manager observed her work and then recorded comments relating to her efficiency.

Before calculating a labor standard for this position, the manager would have completed worksheets for several trained servers who worked similar lunch shifts. In our example, the manager determined a labor standard of 10 guests per labor hour. That is, in the manager's view, trained servers should be able to serve 10 guests for each hour worked without sacrificing quality requirements.

With slight alterations, Exhibit 1 can be used to determine labor standards for other positions in the operation. For example, a worksheet for a lunch cook would have space to record the number of meals prepared, the number of hours the cook worked, and the number of meals prepared per hour worked. A position performance analysis should be completed for each position and shift. This is because productivity rates for positions are different for each meal period due to the different tasks required by the various menus and service styles.

Constructing a Staffing Guide

A staffing guide answers the question, "How many labor hours are needed for each position and shift to produce and serve a given number of meals while meeting minimum quality requirements?" The **staffing guide** incorporates labor standards and tells managers the number of labor hours needed for each position according to the volume of business forecasted for any given meal period. By converting the labor hour information into labor dollars, the manager can also establish standard labor costs. Procedures for converting labor hours into labor dollars are discussed later in this chapter.

The staffing guide serves as a tool for both planning work schedules and controlling labor costs. When the number of actual labor hours exceeds the standard labor hours identified by the staffing guide, managers should take corrective action.

A staffing guide can be developed either for each department within the food and beverage operation or for each position within each department. If the staffing guide is developed for a department, first analyze and summarize each position within the department (such as cook, assistant cook, and kitchen helper in the food production department). Then, average the required labor hours. For example, suppose that the standard labor hours for each position in the food production department (as determined by position performance analyses) are as follows:

Cook	30 meals / labor hour
Assistant cook	20 meals / labor hour
Kitchen helper	10 meals / labor hour
Total	60

$$\frac{\text{Total Meals per Labor Hour}}{\text{Number of Positions}} = \text{Average Meals per Labor Hour}$$

$$\frac{60}{3} = 20 \text{ Meals per Labor Hour (Average)}$$

In this example, when scheduling staff for the food production department, the manager should schedule one labor hour for every 20 meals forecasted. However, this standard does not indicate the number of labor hours needed for each position within the department. Lacking this detail, if standard labor hours are exceeded, how can the manager identify which positions (cooks, assistant cooks, or kitchen helpers) are using the extra time?

A second method for developing a staffing guide separates hours worked by position. With this approach, the schedule maker can plan the number of labor hours needed for each position. If actual labor hours exceed standard labor hours, it becomes obvious which position incurred the additional hours. This procedure yields more accurate and useful labor control information.

When constructing staffing guides, managers should keep in mind the following points:

- Each property must set specific labor standards. Standards developed by another operation are generally meaningless because different properties have different menus, equipment, quality standards, etc.

- Use the productivity rates of good employees to set labor standards for average employees.

- As employees become more efficient through practice, work simplification ideas, and other efficiency measures, change the staffing guide to reflect the higher productivity rates.

- The standard labor dollars resulting from following the staffing guide must be consistent with the standard labor dollars permitted by the operating budget. This point is discussed later in the chapter.

Fixed Versus Variable Labor

Before deciding on procedures for developing staffing guides, managers must understand the difference between fixed and variable labor. **Fixed labor** refers to the minimum labor required to operate the food and beverage operation regardless of the volume of business. For example, when a restaurant is open for guest service at least one cook, server, and bartender may be needed, up to a certain volume of guests, before additional cooks, servers, and bartenders are required. This minimum amount of labor must be considered and incorporated into the staffing guide. Up to a certain volume of business (a point determined by management), no additional staff are necessary. Above this defined level, however, additional labor is needed. This additional labor is referred to as **variable labor**, which varies according to the volume of business activity. Therefore, as more guests are served or as more meals are produced, additional service and/or kitchen labor is needed.

Exhibit 2   Standard Labor Hour Staffing Guide: Dinner

Standard Labor Hour Staffing Guide: Dinner

Number of Meals

Position	50	75	100	125	150
Food Server	8.5 5:00–9:30 7:00–11:00	9.5 5:00–9:30 6:30–11:30	16.0 5:00–9:30 6:30–10:00 7:00–10:00 7:30–12:30	16.0 5:00–9:30 6:30–10:00 7:00–10:00 7:30–12:30	19.0 5:00–10:00 6:00–11:00 6:00–11:00 7:30–11:30
Bartender	9.0 4:00–1:00	9.0 4:00–1:00	9.0 4:00–1:00	9.0 4:00–1:00	9.0 4:00–1:00
Cocktail Server	6.5 4:30–11:00	6.5 4:30–11:00	6.5 4:30–11:00	6.5 4:30–11:00	6.5 4:30–11:00
Cook	7 4:00–11:00	14 3:00–10:00 5:00–12:00	14 3:00–10:00 5:00–12:00	14 3:00–10:00 5:00–12:00	16 3:00–11:00 4:00–12:00
Steward	6.5 5:00–11:30	6.5 5:00–11:30	9.0 3:00–12:00	9.5 3:00–12:30	9.5 3:00–12:30
Busperson	—	2 7:30–9:30	4 7:30–9:30 7:30–9:30	5 7:00–9:30 7:30–10:00	7 7:00–9:30 7:30–10:00 7:30–9:30
Host (Manager serves as host on slow evenings)	—	3 6:00–9:00	3.5 6:00–9:30	4.0 6:00–10:00	4.0 6:00–10:00

NOTE: Labor hour standards are used for illustrative purposes only. Information must be developed for a specific property based upon factors that influence worker efficiency within that food and beverage operation.

Exhibit 2 provides a sample staffing guide format for variable labor positions. The hours noted in the staffing guide include the fixed hours required regardless of business volume. To understand the staffing guide, look at the position of food server. When 50 dinners are forecasted, 8.5 food server labor hours should be scheduled. The 8.5 labor hours represent the standard of meals per labor hour based upon a position performance analysis. That is, the labor standard (8.5 labor hours) equals the total hours which should normally be scheduled to serve 50 meals. The manager must decide how many and which food servers to schedule. The times listed (5:00 to 9:30 and 7:00 to 11:00) represent a staff schedule that incorporates typical peaks and valleys in business volume each shift.

Determining Fixed Labor Requirements. Remember that each food and beverage operation has fixed labor needs (the minimum amount of labor necessary regardless of business volume) that dictate, in effect, a minimum staffing level. The amount of fixed labor should be established department by department. Several times during the course of the year, for example, when seasonal business fluctuations occur, managers should evaluate the amount of fixed labor recommended by department heads. Many factors affect the amount of fixed labor required (such as changes in quality requirements, operating procedures, the menu, and guest expectations).

The work performed by fixed labor staff must be carefully analyzed to ensure that these employees are as productive as possible. During this analysis, managers may consider temporary actions to reduce labor expense during slow business periods. For example, it might be possible to curtail or eliminate the hours of dining room service or valet parking service. Also, the tasks performed by hourly fixed staff could be adjusted. For example, given the proper cross-training, a cook may be able to perform certain baking duties.

Controlling Salaried Labor Costs. Salaried labor costs do not increase or decrease according to the number of guests served. One manager, paid at a predetermined salary rate, creates a fixed labor cost. Normally, salaried personnel should be scheduled to perform only the work their job descriptions require. Management tasks such as recordkeeping, purchasing, and work scheduling should be scheduled during nonpeak production periods. During busy times, managers must be available to perform supervisory and operational duties.

During slow business periods, salaried staff could be assigned duties normally performed by hourly employees. For example, an assistant restaurant manager might be stationed at the host stand, seating guests and taking reservations. However, salaried staff should not be used indiscriminately to reduce hourly labor costs. Although management staff must know how to perform all the tasks in the operation, salaried staff members should not be the first chosen to replace hourly employees who fail to report to work. Efficiency, attitude, and ability decrease as the length of the workweek increases. Management turnover can often be traced to overwork and/or to poorly assigned work.

When developing the staffing guide, the tasks of salaried staff, as indicated on current job descriptions, should be analyzed thoroughly. Schedules should allow enough time for them to do their required work. Also, the personal preferences of salaried staff should be considered when developing schedules. It is often wise to develop responsibilities, tasks, and the volume of work for salaried staff first; then schedule variable labor staff to perform the remaining tasks.

Aligning the Staffing Guide with Budgeted Labor Costs

When budgeted labor costs are based on the same productivity rates as the staffing guide, it is relatively easy for managers to keep labor costs in line with budgeted goals. When this is not the case, managers must ensure that standard labor hours permitted by the staffing guide remain within budgeted labor costs. To evaluate the staffing guide in terms of budgeted goals, managers must compare the labor costs projected by the staffing guide to the allowable labor costs defined by the operating budget. In some cases, the staffing guide may need to be revised to remain within labor costs allowed by the operating budget.

Let's assume that the manager of an operation constructed the staffing guide shown in Exhibit 2. Before scheduling employees according to the staffing guide, the manager wants to ensure that the resulting labor costs will be within the limits established by the operating budget. Assume that the current operating budget limits labor costs for variable labor to 18.9 percent of total food and beverage revenue. The manager must calculate a comparable labor cost percentage based on the labor hours expressed by the staffing guide. Therefore, for each level of business volume within the staffing guide, the manager must:

1. Convert labor hours into labor dollars.

2. Determine the total labor cost.

3. Estimate the total food and beverage revenue.

4. Determine a labor cost percentage.

Converting Labor Hours into Labor Dollars. Labor hours expressed by the staffing guide are converted into labor dollars by multiplying the number of hours allowed for each position by the average hourly rate for the position. For example, Exhibit 3 notes that 16 standard labor hours are necessary for the cook when 150 meals are served. The standard labor cost for the cook's position is calculated as follows: 16 standard labor hours × $11.00 average hourly rate = $176 standard labor cost. (Note that if labor cost calculations for the operating budget include employee benefits, the cost of employee benefits must also be added when converting labor hours into labor dollars; normally these are calculated separately on budgets and income statements.)

Determining a Total Labor Cost. Total labor costs are determined by adding the labor dollars for each position for each level of business volume. For example, Exhibit 3 shows that when 150 meals are served, the total variable labor cost is expected to be $475.75.

Estimating Total Food and Beverage Revenue. Estimates for total food and beverage sales for each level of business volume can be made by multiplying the number of meals (identified in the staffing guide) by the guest check average. Let's assume that a review of current revenue information shows that the guest check average is $32.08 (Total revenue ÷ number of quarts = $32.08). When 150 meals are served, the total food and beverage revenue would be estimated at $4,812 (150 meals × $32.08).

Determining a Labor Cost Percentage. For each level of business volume identified in the staffing guide, a labor cost percentage can be determined by dividing the total labor cost by the estimated total of food and beverage revenue. Therefore, when 150 meals are served, the labor cost is 9.8 percent ($475.75 total labor cost divided by $4,812 total revenue multiplied by 100).

Exhibit 3 shows the results of these calculations. Note that the labor cost percentage for each level of business volume remains within the limits established by the operating budget (18.9 percent). Note that as the number of meals served *increases*, the labor cost percent *decreases*. This is generally the case because

Exhibit 3 Converting Standard Labor Hours into Standard Labor Dollars

| Position | Number of Meals | | | | | | | | | |
| | 50 | | 75 | | 100 | | 125 | | 150 | |
	Stand. Avg. Labor Hourly Hours Rate	Stand. Labor Costs	Stand. Avg. Labor Hourly Hours Rate	Stand. Labor Costs	Stand. Avg. Labor Hourly Hours Rate	Stand. Labor Costs	Stand. Avg. Labor Hourly Hours Rate	Stand. Labor Costs	Stand. Avg. Labor Hourly Hours Rate	Stand. Labor Costs
Food Server	8.5/5.00	42.50	9.5/5.00	47.50	16.0/5.00	80.00	16.0/5.00	80.00	19.0/5.00	95.00
Bartender	9.0/8.00	72.00	9.00/8.00	72.00	9.0/8.00	72.00	9.0/8.00	72.00	9.0/8.00	72.00
Cocktail Server	6.5/5.00	32.50	6.5/5.00	32.50	6.5/5.00	32.50	6.5/5.00	32.50	6.5/5.00	32.50
Cook	7.0/11.00	77.00	14.0/11.00	154.00	14.0/11.00	154.00	14.0/11.00	154.00	16.0/11.00	176.00
Steward	6.5/6.50	42.25	6.5/6.50	42.25	9.0/6.50	58.50	9.5/6.50	61.75	9.5/6.50	61.75
Busperson	—	—	2.0/5.50	11.00	4.0/5.50	22.00	5.0/5.50	27.50	7.0/5.50	38.50
Host	—	—	—	—	—	—	—	—	—	—
Total Standard Labor Cost	$266.25		$359.25		$419.00		$427.75		$475.75	
Revenue (Meals × Avg. Checks)	$1,604.00		$2,406.00		$3,208.00		$4,010.00		$4,812.00	
Standard Labor Cost Percentage*	16.6%		14.9%		13%		10.7%		9.8%	

NOTE: Hourly rate and number of hours worked for varying numbers of meals are for illustrative purposes only. Food and beverage operations must develop this information based on factors that influence worker efficiency in their own specific properties.

*In no instance does the labor cost percentage exceed the allowable variable labor cost percentage (18.9 percent) as calculated for the operating budget.

production and service efficiencies can be built into the standards. (For example, it takes the same amount of time to clean a steam kettle if 100 or 150 portions were prepared. This means that the manager can use the staffing guide to schedule employees and remain safely within budgeted labor cost standards.

However, what would happen if the staffing guide yielded higher labor costs than those permitted by the operating budget? One course of action would be to revise the budget accordingly. If costs could not be reduced in other expense areas or if revenue could not be increased, profit expectations would have to be lowered. Another course of action would be to revise the quality requirements and productivity rates on which the staffing guide is based. In this case, productivity might be increased and labor costs could be reduced through further position performance analyses to increase worker efficiency.

The Staffing Guide as a Scheduling Tool

The staffing guide and business volume forecasts are tools managers and supervisors can use to schedule employees. Once the staffing guide has been developed to

Exhibit 4 Schedule Worksheet

Position/Employee	Planned Total Hours
Joe	7.0
Sally	6.5
Phyllis	4.5
	18.0

Day: _Monday_   Estimated Guests: A.M. | P.M. _250_   Department: _Food Service_
Date: _8/1/XX_   Position: _Assistant Cook_
Shift: _P.M._

Time columns: 6:00 a, 7:00 a, 8:00 a, 9:00 a, 10:00 a, 11:00 a, 12:00 p, 1:00 p, 2:00 p, 3:00 p, 4:00 p, 5:00 p, 6:00 p, 7:00 p, 8:00 p, 9:00 p, 10:00 p, 11:00 p, 12:00 a, 1:00 a, 2:00 a, 3:00 a, 4:00 a, 5:00 a

Position: _Assistant Cook_
Standard Labor Hours: _18_
Planned Labor Hours: _18_
Difference: _0_

indicate labor hours and labor dollars, work schedules can be constructed on the basis of labor hours or labor dollars. In practice, it is much easier and more efficient to schedule employees on the basis of labor hours. It is difficult and even unreasonable to expect managers or supervisors to consider specific hourly rates when developing work schedules.

Some managers and supervisors find it convenient to schedule required labor hours during the midweek for the next workweek (Monday through Sunday). Others may develop work schedules for longer or shorter time periods. In any case, the important point is to establish a routine scheduling procedure.

Some supervisors use a schedule worksheet to determine when employees are needed to work. Let's review how the supervisor might have completed the schedule worksheet shown in Exhibit 4. After receiving the forecast of 250 estimated guests for Monday evening, the supervisor checked the staffing guide for the dinner meal period and found that 18 labor hours should be scheduled for the position of assistant cook. Knowing that the peak hours during the dinner period are between 7:30 P.M. and 9:30 P.M., the supervisor staggered the work schedules of three assistant cooks to cover these peak hours. Joe was scheduled to work earlier to perform duties at the beginning of the shift, and Phyllis was scheduled to work later to perform closing duties at the end of the shift. All three assistant cooks would be available for regular duties during the peak business hours.

There are times when managers or supervisors need to schedule more labor hours than those indicated by the staffing guide. For example, additional labor hours may need to be scheduled while training new staff members or when introducing a new menu.

Before considering specific methods of employee scheduling, however, let's examine some principles relevant to all employee scheduling methods.

Staggered Work Schedules. In most food and beverage operations, the work flow is rarely constant throughout a shift. There is usually a mixture of rush, normal, and slow periods. Therefore, it is generally not a good idea to have all staff begin and end workshifts at the same time. By staggering and overlapping workshifts, managers can ensure that the greatest number of employees are working during peak business hours.

For example, one server might begin work an hour before the dining room opens. The server can use this time to check or set up tables and perform other miscellaneous **mise-en-place** tasks. A second server could be scheduled to arrive one-half hour before opening to perform other preopening duties. Both employees can begin serving when needed. Staggered ending times are also encouraged to ensure maximum worker efficiency. The first employee to check in might be the first to leave. Of course, it is necessary to comply with property policies and applicable laws as scheduling decisions are made.

Full-Time versus Part-Time Staff. Part-time staff can be hired to work short shifts of, for example, three to five hours. If some of these staff members want more hours, a split shift—two short shifts in one day separated by time off—may be possible. Since staggered scheduling often reduces labor hours, there may be less need for full-time personnel. However, full-time personnel will likely be needed to fill key administrative positions.

If there are not enough administrative tasks to justify certain full-time positions, some full-time jobs can be composed of management and nonmanagement tasks. For example, a full-time head bartender or head dishwasher position could be developed. The head dishwasher could handle management duties such as supervising personnel and developing cleaning schedules. However, the position might also include the nonmanagement task of dishwashing. With these types of arrangements, salaries or wages are set on the basis of reasonable pay for all work performed so that both the food and beverage operation and employees benefit.

Temporary Employees. Temporary employees can also be used. Many properties keep a file of names of people who do not want steady work but like to work occasionally. A large banquet, employee illness, seasonal business fluctuations, or similar circumstances may create a need for temporary assistance.

While these scheduling principles are helpful, two of the most useful scheduling tools are the manager's past experience in developing work schedules and the manager's knowledge of the staff's capabilities. In many food and beverage operations, the pattern of business volume stabilizes, creating a recognizable pattern of labor requirements. The more experience the manager acquires in relation to a specific operation, the easier it becomes to stagger work schedules, balance full-time and part-time employees, and effectively use temporary workers. Similarly, the

Exhibit 5   Sample Employee Schedule

	Week of: 7/14/XX						
Shift: P.M.				Supervisor: Julie			
Position: Cook							

Employee	7/14 Monday	7/15 Tuesday	7/16 Wednesday	7/17 Thursday	7/18 Friday	7/19 Saturday	7/20 Sunday
Syrus	12:00-7:00	—	12:00-7:00	1:00-7:30	—	12:00-7:00	—
Ann	—	12:00-7:00	1:00-7:30	12:00-7:00	—	—	12:00-7:00
Jean	3:00-8:00	1:00-5:00	3:00-8:00	—	—	1:00-7:30	1:00-7:30
Sue	—	3:00-8:30	12:30-8:30	12:30-7:30	12:00-7:00	—	—
Gabridle	12:30-6:30	12:30-6:00	—	—	3:00-7:00	3:00-8:00	3:00-8:00
Stacey	3:00-7:00	3:00-7:00	3:00-7:30	3:00-7:30	—	—	12:30-8:30
Phyllis	1:00-5:00	1:00-5:00	—	—	3:00-8:00	12:30-8:30	3:00-7:00
Andres	1:00-7:00	—	—	1:00-7:00	1:00-8:30	3:00-7:00	—
Sally	—	—	3:00-8:00	1:00-7:00	3:00-7:30	—	1:00-6:00
Karen	1:00-7:00	1:00-7:00	—	—	1:00-5:00	1:00-6:00	2:00-7:00
Bettina	—	—	3:00-7:00	3:00-8:00	3:00-7:00	2:00-7:00	—

better the manager understands the capabilities of the operation's staff, the easier it becomes to schedule the right employees for particular times and shifts. For example, some servers may work best when they are scheduled for the late dinner shift, or some cooks may not be able to perform well when experiencing the stress of a dinner rush. These factors can be taken into account when planning work schedules.

Whenever possible, managers or supervisors with scheduling responsibilities should consider employees' preferences. Employees can be given schedule request forms to indicate which days or shifts they want off. These requests should be submitted by employees several weeks in advance and honored by management to the maximum extent possible.

Once the working hours for each employee are established, they should be combined in a schedule and posted for employee review and use. Note that the sample employee schedule, shown in Exhibit 5, indicates for each cook the days and hours of each shift for an entire week. The posted schedule attempts to provide employees with the best possible advance notice of their work hours.

Of course, schedule plans do not always work. Employees might call in sick or fail to show up without warning. Also, the number of actual guests and the volume of meals might be lower or higher than expected. Therefore, it is often necessary to revise posted work schedules.

Management must continually encourage employees to follow posted work schedules. Policies providing for on-call staff members may help protect the operation when the attendance problems of staff members result in a reduced number of employees. Managers, of course, must comply with all union, legal, and other restrictions regarding policies requiring employees to call in or be available for work on days when they are not scheduled.

The Staffing Guide as a Control Tool

Using the department's staffing guide and a reliable business volume forecast to develop employee work schedules does not guarantee that the hours employees actually work will equal the number of hours for which they were scheduled to work. Managers must monitor and evaluate the scheduling process by comparing, on a weekly basis, the actual hours each employee works with the number of hours for which the employee was scheduled to work. Information about actual hours worked is usually obtained from the accounting department or from a staff member assigned to maintain payroll records.

Exhibit 6 presents a sample weekly department labor hour report. Actual hours worked by each employee are recorded for each day of the week in columns 2 through 8. Actual total hours worked for each employee and for the position categories are totaled in column 9. These actual hours worked can be compared with the scheduled labor hours shown in column 10. Significant variances should be analyzed and corrective action taken when necessary.

Variance Analysis

The sample report (Exhibit 6) shows that during the week of July 14, 216.5 labor hours were scheduled for dining room employees, but the actual hours worked totaled 224.5. This indicates a variance of 8 hours. Is 8 hours a significant variance? Should the manager or supervisor investigate it? To answer these questions, let's do some quick calculations. Assuming that the average hourly wage for the staff is $8, the variance of 8 hours costs the operation a total of $64 for the week of July 14. If actual hours worked differed from scheduled labor hours at this rate for the entire year, it would cost the operation a total of $3,328 ($64 weekly, for 52 weeks, equals $3,328) in lost profits. Since no manager wants to lose any amount of potential profit, the variance is significant.

The remarks at the bottom of the report address the variances in relation to each employee. If similar variances and remarks occur over a period of several weeks, corrective action may be necessary. For example, the manager or supervisor may need to do a better job at planning and scheduling necessary cleaning for the dining room and storage areas.

A weekly department labor hour report will almost always reveal differences between the hours scheduled and the actual hours worked. Generally, a small deviation is permitted. For example, if the labor performance standard for a position is 210 hours for the week, a variance of 2 percent, approximately 4.2 hours, might be tolerated. So, if actual labor hours do not exceed 214.2 (210.00 + 4.2 = 214.2), no investigation is necessary. If actual labor hours increase beyond 214.2, analysis and corrective action may be required.

There may be legitimate reasons for a difference between standard and actual results. While management must decide what acceptable reasons are, examples may include:

Exhibit 6 Weekly Department Labor Hour Report

Weekly Department Labor Hour Report

Week of: 7/14/XX Department: Food Service Supervisor: Sandra
Shift: P.M.

Actual Labor Hours Worked

Position/Employee	7/14 Mon	7/15 Tues	7/16 Wed	7/17 Thurs	7/18 Fri	7/19 Sat	7/20 Sun	Total Labor Hours Actual	Std.
DINING ROOM 1	2	3	4	5	6	7	8	9	10
Jennifer	7	—	7	6.5	7	6	—	33.5	31.0
Brenda	—	7	6.5	7	6.5	6.5	5	38.5	38.5
Sally	—	5	8	7	8	10	—	38.0	36.0
Patty	8	6	6	4.5	—	—	6	30.5	31.0
Anna	4	4	6.5	—	4.5	—	5	24.0	22.0
Thelma	6	5	5	5	5	—	—	26.0	24.0
Elsie	6	—	—	6	6	8	8	34.0	34.0
								224.5	216.5
COOK									
Peggy	4	4	4	4	4	—	—	20.0	20.0
Kathy	4	4	4	—	—	4	4	20.0	20.0
Tilly	4	—	—	4	4	4	4	20.0	18.0
Carlos	—	4	4	4	4	4	—	20.0	20.0
Sam	4	4	—	—	—	—	4	12.0	12.0
								92.0	90.0
DISHWASHING									
Terry	—	—	6	6	6	—	—	18.0	18.0
Andrew	6	6	—	—	8	5	5	30.0	30.0
Robert	8	8	8	8	—	—	6	38.0	38.0
Carl	5	—	5	5	5	6	—	26.0	26.0
								112.0	112.0
Total (all personnel)								428.5	418.5
Difference								+ 10.00	

Remarks: 7/18 — Jennifer, Sally and Elsie given extra hours to learn tableside flaming
7/19 — Sally stayed 2 hours—special cleaning
7/20 — Tilly stayed 2 hours—cleaned storeroom shelves

- Hours worked by new employees and included in the weekly department labor hour report that represent training time rather than time spent on productive work.

- Out-of-order equipment results in additional manual labor.

- New menu items or new work procedures create a training or transitional period, thereby increasing labor hours.

- A rush of late shift business that requires staff to remain on duty longer than scheduled.

If such circumstances explain reasons for variances, corrective action is not needed. The food and beverage manager is aware of the problem, as well as its cause, expected duration, and estimated economic cost. These reasons for variances are understood by management and are within its control.

Occasionally, problems may exist for which immediate causes or solutions are not apparent. In these situations, the manager or department supervisor could ask employees for ideas about the problem. Also, the manager or supervisor could work in the affected position for a shift or two. Unknown reasons for variances, while rare, deserve high priority to ensure that the operation is in control of labor costs at all times.

The procedures discussed so far use one week as the time period for comparing labor standards and actual labor hours. If comparisons are made too infrequently, time is wasted and labor dollars are lost before managers notice that a problem may exist. On the other hand, if comparisons are made too frequently, excessive time and money is spent in assembling data, performing calculations, and making comparisons. Some time is necessary for labor hours and costs to average out. Obviously, labor hours can be higher than established labor standards on some days and lower on other days.

When a comparison of labor standards with actual labor results indicates unacceptable variances, answering several questions may help uncover potential causes:

- Are the labor standards established by position performance analyses correct? If they are incorrect, the staffing guide itself will be incorrect. A recurring problem may call for reviewing position performance analyses and evaluating the accuracy of the labor standards used to construct the staffing guide.

- How accurate are the forecasts used for scheduling staff? Additional labor hours may have been necessary if more meals were produced and served than forecasted. If this happens frequently, the forecasting techniques should be evaluated.

- Are employees performing tasks that are not listed in their job descriptions? These tasks may not have been considered in the initial position performance analyses which established labor standards.

- Are there new employees who do not perform as efficiently as employees did during the initial position performance analyses?

- Have factors affecting labor efficiency changed (such as menu revisions or new equipment purchases)? If so, updated position performance analyses (leading to revised labor standards) may be necessary.

- Are personal or professional problems among the staff affecting efficiency?

Comparing Actual Labor Costs to Budgeted Labor Costs

It is important that the information recorded in a weekly labor hour report is consistent with information developed for other aspects of the labor control system. For example, Exhibit 7, a department weekly labor hour and cost report, provides the same information as Exhibit 6, but also lists hourly rates for each employee and

Exhibit 7   Department Weekly Labor Hour and Cost Report

Week of: _____7/14/XX_____

Department: _____Food Service_____   Supervisor: _____Sandra_____

Shift: _____P.M._____

Actual Labor Hours Worked

Position/ Employee	Mon 7/14	Tues 7/15	Wed 7/16	Thurs 7/17	Fri 7/18	Sat 7/19	Sun 7/20	Total Labor Hours Actual	Standard	Hourly Rate	Total Labor Costs Actual	Standard
1	2	3	4	5	6	7	8	9	10	11	12	13
DINING ROOM												
Jennifer	7	—	7	6.5	7	6	—	33.5	31.0	$5.00	$167.50	$155.00
Brenda	—	7	6.5	7	6.5	6.5	5	38.5	38.5	5.15	198.28	198.28
Sally	—	5	8	7	8	10	—	38.0	36.0	5.25	199.50	189.00
Patty	8	6	6	4.5	—	—	6	30.5	31.0	5.10	155.55	158.10
Anna	4	4	6.5	—	4.5	—	5	24.0	22.0	5.10	122.40	112.20
Thelma	6	5	5	5	5	—	—	26.0	24.0	5.40	140.40	129.60
Elsie	6	—	—	6	6	8	8	34.0	34.0	5.05	171.70	171.70
								224.5	216.5		$1,155.33	$1,113.88
COOK												
Peggy	4	4	4	4	4	—	—	20.0	20.0	11.00	220.00	220.00
Kathy	4	4	4	—	—	4	4	20.0	20.0	11.15	223.00	223.00
Tilly	4	—	—	4	4	4	4	20.0	18.0	11.50	230.00	207.00
Carlos	—	4	4	4	4	4	—	20.0	20.0	11.00	220.00	220.00
Sam	4	4	—	—	—	—	4	12.0	12.0	11.10	133.20	133.20
								92.0	90.0		$1,026.20	$1,003.20
DISHWASHING												
Terry	—	—	6	6	6	—	—	18.0	18.0	6.50	117.00	117.00
Andrew	6	6	—	—	8	5	5	30.0	30.0	6.25	187.50	187.50
Robert	8	8	8	8	—	—	6	38.0	38.0	6.55	248.90	248.90
Carl	5	—	5	5	5	6	—	26.0	26.0	6.50	169.00	169.00
								112.0	112.0		$722.40	$722.40
											$2,903.93	$2,839.48

converts actual and standard labor hours into labor dollars. The labor dollars sections enable managers to compare actual labor costs with budgeted labor costs. For example, during the course of each month, the manager can total the actual labor costs to date by adding actual costs from all previous weekly department labor hour and cost reports. The to-date figure can be subtracted from the total labor costs allowed by the operating budget for that month. The result indicates the amount of labor dollars left in the current month's budget. This helps managers plan future expenses and remain within the budgeted allowance for labor costs.

Alternatively, the manager could divide the actual labor costs to date by the amount of food and beverage revenue to date. This yields a to-date actual labor cost percentage, which can be compared with the budgeted labor cost percentage for the period.

The weekly labor hour and cost report can also be used to monitor **overtime** labor costs. Some companies use the term overtime to refer to a situation in which an employee has worked more than the time the staffing guide lists for his or her position. Federal guidelines specify that non-exempt employees who work in excess of the standard 40-hour work week are generally entitled to receive overtime pay of one and one-half times the hourly rate. Any number of situations may arise that force a supervisor to schedule overtime for some employees. However, most operations require management approval for any scheduled overtime. Unscheduled and excessive overtime costs are generally signs of poor forecasting and/or scheduling problems.

The weekly labor hour and cost report alerts the manager to all situations in which an employee's actual labor hours exceed the number of hours for which that employee was scheduled. If previous approval of a variance was not granted, the discrepancy may signal an attempt by one or more dishonest employees to steal through payroll fraud.

Planning Corrective Action

A corrective action program should follow a sequence that ensures that important elements of the control system are not overlooked:

1. Identify variations between labor standards and actual labor results. The department supervisor should briefly explain these on the weekly department labor hour report (Exhibit 6).

2. A senior manager analyzes the form.

3. The supervisor and senior manager meet to discuss the problem and agree on corrective actions and a time by which labor hours and costs should return to normal.

4. Implement corrective action procedures. Both managers should closely monitor the effectiveness of the corrective action.

5. After the time limit has elapsed, managers should again meet to review the effectiveness of the corrective action(s) which occurred. Any findings applicable to other positions or departments can be noted. The need for an updated position performance analysis can also be reviewed at this point.

Developing the best corrective action plan is important. Managers must know exactly what the problems are, consider effective management strategies, supervise workers, and evaluate them to ensure that corrective action is successful. Exhibit 8, a checklist for labor control, can help managers spot potential problems and take corrective action.

Employee Scheduling and Fast-Food Operations ———

When developing labor standards, some fast-food companies conduct relatively sophisticated time studies of trained employees in several operations. In a fast-food operation, where there is typically a limited variety of food products and a consistent repetition of procedures required to produce these products, this system creates exciting possibilities.

The time study analysis used to develop labor standards is similar to procedures used in manufacturing industries where conveyer assembly lines or

Exhibit 8   Checklist for Labor Control

Personnel Administration

☐ Job descriptions for all tasks performed by all positions in all sections of the food and beverage operation are available, accurately reflect the positions, and are revised as necessary.

☐ Personnel are aware of tasks in job descriptions; job descriptions effectively set boundaries of responsibility for each position.

☐ Job specifications are available and are used in employee selection to ensure that properly qualified personnel are hired.

☐ An organization chart, revised as necessary, shows relationships between and among departments and positions within the property.

☐ New employees are given copies of job descriptions, specifications, and an organization chart, along with other materials in an employee handbook, at hiring. Orientation is completed.

☐ Supervisors, by interviewing applicants and participating in decisions, are involved in hiring for vacant positions in their sections.

☐ When possible, eligible current employees are promoted to fill vacant positions; there is a "career ladder" for employees. For example, a food service worker can be promoted to assistant cook and the assistant cook to head cook.

☐ Supervisors are aware of and work with informal employee groups.

☐ Only qualified applicants are considered for vacant positions.

☐ An employee application form is the initial step in selecting employees.

☐ References on employee application forms are contacted for additional information.

☐ Food and beverage managers interview applicants.

☐ The supervisor/section head interviews the applicants.

☐ Top managers and the section supervisor discuss and make a joint decision regarding the applicant.

☐ Simple tests, such as extending a recipe or working the dishwashing machine, are used to ensure that experienced personnel have basic knowledge upon which the facility can build through training.

☐ Several applicants are considered for each position; the best is selected.

☐ The selection process allows the applicant to learn about the facility, in addition to food service personnel learning about the applicant.

☐ New employees are not thrown into the job. They are given a tour of the property and introduced to other employees before being taken to the work station.

☐ The formal work group is notified in advance of new employees' arrivals and their job qualifications are explained.

☐ Supervisors spend time with new employees on their first day, making them feel comfortable and answering basic questions.

☐ An experienced employee is assigned to the new employee to help with other questions and to begin on-the-job training.

☐ A planned training program ensures that the new employee can do required tasks according to required procedures.

☐ The trainer and supervisor formally discuss any need for additional training and evaluate the new employee's progress.

☐ Training is used to bring long-time employees up to minimum quality standards if they are not working according to required procedures.

☐ A formal employee evaluation program allows the supervisor to inform employees about their strengths and weaknesses and permits employees to talk with supervisors about ways to improve their jobs.

☐ Employees know, in advance, the job standards on which they will be evaluated and are trained to achieve these standards.

Labor Control System

☐ A standard labor hour staffing guide is available to help supervisors schedule variable labor employees.

☐ Salaried labor is scheduled according to need; salaried labor is not generally used to replace hourly employees; tasks performed by salaried personnel are in line with salaries.

☐ The supervisor and top management staff know, for each position in the department, the number of labor hours needed to produce minimum quality levels for varied revenue volumes.

☐ The department supervisor and other managers regularly observe personnel in all positions to ensure that the staffing guide accurately reflects the number of labor hours needed.

(continued)

Exhibit 8   *(continued)*

☐ There are separate staffing guides for each shift if the type of menu, variety of items, etc., are judged to affect worker productivity.

☐ Supervisors use the standard labor hour staffing guide when scheduling employees, scheduling only the maximum number of labor hours judged necessary for each shift.

☐ Supervisors use split shifts, part-time personnel, and staggered scheduling to ensure that personnel are available only when needed.

☐ Employees are informed about their work schedules through a formal schedule posted in an employee area; schedules for at least one week are prepared one week in advance.

☐ Supervisors confirm the number of labor hours worked by hourly employees. A report, signed by each supervisor, indicating the number of labor hours worked by each employee is an integral part of the property's payroll system.

☐ Supervisors must explain the reasons when the actual number of labor hours worked by employees within a position exceeds the standard number.

☐ Top management officials carefully review all weekly reports to note trends and to take corrective action(s) when actual labor hours within a department consistently exceed standard labor hours.

☐ The reasons for excessive labor hours are known and necessary corrective action is taken.

☐ Managers and supervisors work together to plan and monitor results of corrective action.

☐ A standard labor hour cost control system, at the least, is used to monitor and control labor costs; systems involving labor cost dollars and budget development and use are considered according to their applicability to the individual property.

Personnel Supervision

☐ All supervisors recognize that employee motivation and training are part of their jobs.

☐ All supervisors recognize that employee problems are manageable; problems frequently result from improper supervisory techniques.

☐ Supervisors know how to give instructions properly; they seek cooperation and, when necessary, take time to explain, defend, and justify reasons for actions.

☐ Supervisors have been taught procedures for motivating and directing employees.

☐ Supervisors are aware of and attempt to provide those things that employees want from their jobs.

☐ Supervisors know what affects employee morale and constantly work to improve morale.

☐ Supervisors can make decisions and solve problems to do their jobs as effectively as possible.

☐ Supervisors solicit ideas from all affected parties when making decisions.

☐ Supervisors and top managers are aware that, in some instances, the supervisor is part of the problem. The supervisor as well as employees must sometimes change.

☐ Supervisors are fair and reasonable in disciplining employees; discipline is designed to create adherence to fair and reasonable procedures, rather than to punish.

☐ Supervisors help make decisions regarding promotion.

☐ Supervisors are involved in decisions regarding termination.

Work Simplification

☐ Supervisors know how to analyze jobs to improve the work performed.

☐ The philosophy of work simplification is an integral part of the supervisor's job.

☐ Supervisors are constantly reviewing work with the intent to eliminate, simplify, or combine tasks.

☐ Supervisors are alert to signs that examination of work tasks is in order.

☐ Supervisors know how to analyze a job for work simplification improvements.

☐ Supervisors can recognize problems and know how to correct them when jobs are examined.

☐ Supervisors encourage employees to help with work simplification.

Source: Adapted from Herman Zaccarelli and Jack D. Ninemeier, *Cost Effective Contract Food Service: An Institutional Guide* (Rockville, Md.: Aspen Systems Corporation, 1982).

similar processes are studied. For example, employees may be videotaped while performing selected tasks. Careful analysis of the videotaped activity often suggests ways to simplify and speed work procedures. Such study also generates

Exhibit 9   Sample Staffing Grid

Position	$0–$150	$151–$250	$251–$450	$451–$600	$601–$750	$751–$900	$901–$1,050
	Hourly Revenue						
Manager	1	1	1	1	1	1	1
Delivery Person	2	3	3	4	4	5	6
Phone Operator	0	0	1	2	2	2	2
Cook	0	0	1	1	2	2	2
Total	3	4	6	8	9	10	11

ideas for improved placement of equipment and for combining tasks within each job position. When the videotaped employees consistently use the standard operating procedures prescribed by the company, it becomes possible to determine the minimum amount of time needed for employees in each position to complete their work.

Fast-food operations may base the allowable number of labor hours (or labor dollars) for each position on estimated revenue for the scheduling period. With many of these operations, it is even possible to use hourly revenue estimates as the basis for labor control and employee scheduling. Exhibit 9 illustrates a staffing plan for a pizza operation using this labor control system. Notice that when less than $150 will be generated during a specific hour of operation, one manager and two delivery persons should be scheduled. If, during a busy hour of operation, revenue levels are estimated at between $451 and $600, there is still a need for only one manager. However, four delivery persons, two phone operators, and one cook would be required.

According to this staffing grid, the lower the revenue levels, the more responsibilities must overlap from one position to the next. For example, the manager answers the phone and also cooks during slow periods. By contrast, a cook who only does activities associated with this position is not required until revenue increases beyond $250 per hour. Also, as more pizzas are ordered, there is a greater likelihood that several orders will be delivered to the same area, and fewer delivery persons may be required on a per-unit (pizza) basis.

To use the staffing grid, the schedule planner can estimate hourly revenue for the scheduling period by averaging hourly revenue recorded for four or five previous weeks. For example, to estimate revenue to be generated on Monday from 11:00 A.M. to noon, a manager could review the revenue generated from 11:00 A.M. to noon on the previous five Mondays and divide that total by five. (Note: automated systems allow this data to be easily generated.)

Once the hourly revenue estimates are made, the manager can schedule employees according to the procedures already described. This approach to scheduling tries to match input (number of employee hours) with output (amount of revenue generated). As pressures for reduced labor costs increase, this approach, which has relevance to other segments of the food and beverage industry, may become more useful.

Exhibit 10   Hourly Revenue Report 5/31

Through Time	Revenue	Guests	Checks	Labor Hrs	Labor $$	Lbr/Rev
8:00 AM	0.00	0	0	0.00	0.00	0.00%
9:00 AM	0.00	0	0	0.13	0.70	0.00%
10:00 AM	0.00	0	0	5.52	27.46	0.00%
11:00 AM	0.00	1	1	10.28	47.68	0.00%
12:00 PM	100.45	12	5	16.30	65.98	65.68%
1:00 PM	93.40	7	8	17.78	67.81	72.60%
2:00 PM	139.05	14	13	18.00	67.81	48.77%
3:00 PM	76.80	6	10	18.00	67.81	88.29%
4:00 PM	615.89	86	56	17.67	64.42	10.46%
5:00 PM	240.55	7	12	25.17	85.85	35.69%
6:00 PM	609.85	48	28	39.73	137.82	22.60%
7:00 PM	1,319.29	141	89	45.42	160.94	12.20%
8:00 PM	1,573.40	167	131	52.70	190.49	12.11%
9:00 PM	1,815.77	92	169	56.95	213.66	11.77%
10:00 PM	1,376.40	67	213	57.50	229.18	16.65%
11:00 PM	1,317.80	159	237	51.53	203.61	15.45%
12.00 AM	1,281.95	34	237	47.18	181.08	14.13%
1:00 AM	1,220.30	22	231	38.62	152.32	12.48%
2:00 AM	791.30	122	161	32.97	128.98	16.30%
3:00 AM	2,575.50	3	3	20.90	78.13	3.03%
4:00 AM	0.00	0	0	6.73	11.67	0.00%
5:00 AM	0.00	0	0	0.00	0.00	0.00%
6:00 AM	0.00	0	0	0.00	0.00	0.00%
7:00 AM	0.00	0	0	0.00	0.00	0.00%
Total	15,147.70	988	1604	579.08	2,183.40	14.41%

Courtesy of Ibatech, Inc., Aloha Hospitality Software, Hurst, Texas

Hourly revenue forecasting and labor scheduling are easily accomplished by many automated fast-food operations. Exhibit 10 illustrates an **hourly revenue eport** that reveals revenue and labor figures for each hour of a workday. These daily reports can be processed to project revenue for every hour of each day of the coming week. Exhibit 11 illustrates a **labor requirements report** that shows the amount of projected revenue and the number of employees required for every hour of each day of the coming week. The projections are calculated by averaging the revenue for each hour of the past four weeks. The labor standards specified by management are then used to arrive at the number of employees needed to service each hour of projected revenue.

Automated Labor and Payroll Information Systems

Calculating each employee's pay, developing the accounting records, and preparing the necessary reports required by federal, state, and local governments are recurrent tasks carried out by every food service operation. Payroll activities can be time-consuming tasks in nonautomated properties. Not only do pay rates vary with job classifications but also, in many food service operations, a single

Exhibit 11 Sample Labor Requirements Report

		MONDAY		TUESDAY		WEDNESDAY		THURSDAY		FRIDAY		SATURDAY		SUNDAY	
FROM	TO	SALES	PEOPLE	SALES	PEOPLE	SALES	PEOPLE	SALES	PEOPLE	SALES	PEOPLE	SALES	PEOPLE	SALES	PEOPLE
0 -	1 A.M.														
1 -	2														
2 -	3														
3 -	4														
4 -	5														
5 -	6														
6 -	7														
7 -	8														
8 -	9	37	5	37	5	39	5	42	7	55	8	55	8	55	8
9 -	10	61	8	61	8	61	8	61	8	79	9	79	9	79	9
10 -	11	85	9	85	9	85	9	85	9	111	9	111	9	111	9
11 -	NOON	97	9	99	9	99	9	100	9	127	10	127	10	130	10
12 -	1 P.M.	115	9	169	13	114	9	114	9	169	13	171	15	171	15
1 -	2	132	10	132	10	132	10	132	10	154	12	189	15	163	13
2 -	3	130	10	133	10	172	15	121	10	168	13	172	15	175	15
3 -	4	157	12	157	12	157	12	234	15	213	15	220	15	213	15
4 -	5	210	15	205	15	195	15	171	15	208	15	217	15	213	15
5 -	6	126	10	127	10	129	10	171	15	201	15	203	15	207	15
6 -	7	115	9	112	9	116	9	103	9	174	15	172	15	171	15
7 -	8	82	9	67	8	70	8	100	9	115	9	150	11	120	9
8 -	9	36	5	73	9	58	8	51	8	138	10	138	10	136	10
9 -	10														
10 -	11														
11 -	MID														

```
01  - CHICKEN DELICIOUS INC.              LABOR REQUIREMENTS           LS2043  PAGE    1
001 - CHICKEN DELICIOUS #1               FOR WEEK BEGINNING 10/01/8-    17.44.00    10/01/8-
```

	MONDAY	TUESDAY	WEDNESDAY	THURSDAY	FRIDAY	SATURDAY	SUNDAY
TOTAL SALES	$1383.00	$1457.00	$1427.00	$1485.00	$1912.00	$2004.00	$1944.00
TOTAL HOURS	120.0	127.0	127.0	133.0	153.0	162.0	158.0
AVG. SALE PER HOUR	$ 11.53	$ 11.47	$ 11.23	$ 11.17	$ 12.50	$ 12.37	$ 12.30

TOTAL PROJECTED WEEKLY SALES $11,613.00
TOTAL LABOR HOURS 980.0
AVERAGE SALE PER HOUR . . . . $ 11.85

Source: Tridata, Inc., Atlanta, Georgia.

employee may work at different tasks over a number of workshifts, each of which may call for a separate pay rate. In addition, unlike many other accounting functions, payroll system requirements arise from sources other than property management officials. Government agencies, unions, pension trust funds, credit unions, banks, and employees themselves often have input into how payroll information is stored and reported.

In an increasing number of properties, a **computerized time-clock system** records time in and time out for employees as they enter and leave the work area. Exhibit 12 illustrates a time card produced by a computerized time-clock system. When a time-clock system is interfaced with a computer system, relevant data may

Exhibit 12   Sample Time Card from a Computerized Time-Clock System

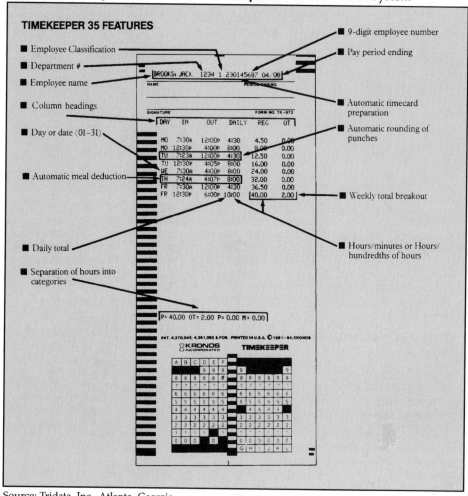

Source: Tridata, Inc., Atlanta, Georgia.

be transferred each day to the automated payroll system and the previous day's pay calculated for each employee.

Sophisticated point-of-sale (POS) systems may maintain (or, alternatively, can be interfaced to an electronic file that contains) a labor master file containing the following data for each employee:

- Name
- Employee number
- Social Security number
- Authorized job codes and corresponding hourly wage rates

Exhibit 13   Sample Daily Labor Report

```
            SMITH'S RESTAURANT  1050              ◄──── User-specified name

   12/12/XX                              14:25    ◄──── Date and time

               DAILY LABOR REPORT                 ◄──── Report title

   JOB CODE: 10                                   ◄──── User-specified job code

   EMP   IN    OUT   HOURS  WAGES  D WAGE          ─── Employee line for this job code
   210  09:34 15:05   5:31  31.86   26.76    ◄──── (D WAGE means declared wages)
    •
    •
   224  13:05 18:08   6:03  36.18   30.39
             SUBTOTAL 11:34
                              68.04          ◄──── Totals for this job code
                                     57.15


   JOB CODE: 16

   EMP   IN    OUT   HOURS  WAGES  D WAGE
   321  06:00 14:18   8:18  42.95    0.00
    •
    •
   387  08:26 14:07   5:41  40.76    0.00
             SUBTOTAL 13:59
                              83.71
                                      0.00

          TOTAL      25:33                  ◄──── Totals for all job codes
                             151.75
                                     57.15
```

This file may also contain data required to produce labor reports for management. Each record in the labor master file may accumulate data on:

- Actual hours worked
- Total hourly wages
- Tips
- Credits for employee meals
- Number of guests served
- Gross sales

Data accumulated by the labor master file can be accessed to produce a number of reports. A labor master report contains general data maintained by the labor master file. This report is commonly used to verify an employee's hourly rate(s), job code(s), Social Security number, and other information. Exhibit 13 illustrates a sample daily labor report that lists the employee number, hours worked, wages earned, and wages declared for each employee on a given workday.

Automated payroll systems must be flexible enough to meet all the demands placed on the system with a minimum of actual programming changes. In many cases, a utility program enables a property to define its own particular pay period (daily, weekly, biweekly, or monthly). Automated payroll systems are generally able to perform the following functions:

- Maintain an employee master file
- Calculate gross and net pay for salaried and hourly employees
- Print paychecks
- Produce payroll tax registers and reports
- Prepare labor cost reports for use by management
- Provide overtime warnings (which alert employers to employees who are nearing the hour limit after which overtime pay will be required)
- Reduce lost time (by not allowing an employee to check in a maximum number of minutes before the scheduled time or to check out after a specified time beyond schedule)

Employee Master File

An employee master file maintains payroll and personnel data on each employee. Data contained in this file may include:

- Company employee number
- Name of employee
- Address of employee
- Social Security number
- Job classification code(s)
- Wage rate code(s)
- Withholdings
- Deductions

This file can be extensive. Appropriate deductions and withholding amounts are subtracted from each employee's gross pay to arrive at net pay. **Withholdings** are for income and social security taxes. Since federal tax regulations frequently change, and since state withholdings vary across the country, many payroll modules are designed so that the user is able to make the necessary programming adjustments. **Deductions** are usually voluntary and depend on the types of benefits available from the employer. Exhibit 14 lists some of the kinds of deductions made from the gross pay of employees.

Payroll Register File

To calculate gross and net pay for hourly employees, the payroll module relies upon a payroll register file to access the number of hours each employee worked during the pay period and other data that may require special tax calculations, such as:

Exhibit 14   Sample Payroll Withholdings and Deductions

TAXES

- Federal, state, and city withholding amounts for income taxes
- Federal Insurance Contribution Act tax (Social Security tax)
- State unemployment compensation (selected states)

OTHER

- Savings bonds
- Medical insurance
- Life insurance
- Retirement contribution
- Charitable contribution
- Capital stock purchase plan
- Savings plan, credit union
- Charge for meals
- Payroll advance
- Garnishment of wages
- Union dues

- Sick leave pay

- Bonus pay

- Tips

- Expense reimbursements

As noted earlier, the automated payroll system must be flexible enough to automatically handle several pay categories per employee and several nontax deductions (which may be required on either a fixed or a variable basis). Payroll-systems typically provide override options which management may exercise in connection with pay rate calculations and adjustments.

Automated payroll systems may also print paychecks, paycheck registers, payroll detail registers, and deduction registers. These systems generally maintain a government reporting file for quarter-to-date and year-to-date federal and state tax histories. Deduction reports can be produced with year-to-date computations. Exhibit 15 illustrates a sample detailed check history produced by a food and beverage back office accounting system. The check register summarizes important payroll information for each employee.

Automated payroll systems can accommodate manually written payroll checks and voided payroll checks. Systems typically reconcile outstanding paychecks (checks which have been issued) with paychecks that have cleared the bank and appear on bank statements. Generally, at the end of a check reconciliation routine, the system prints an updated list of outstanding checks.

In addition to printing paychecks, payroll modules are generally able to calculate sick leave and vacation hours accrued (earned) by employees. This may be done in any one of several ways: accrual each pay period, accrual periodically (for

Exhibit 15   Sample Payroll Check Register

UNIVERSITY CLUB OF MSU
EMPLOYEE SS# XXX-XX-XXXX
NAME: MARY ADAMS

PAYROLL
DETAILED CHECK HISTORY

CHECK # DATE	REG GRAT	OVT OTHER	HOL HOLWK	VAC XTIP	SICK	TIP WAGES TOTAL GROSS	FIT SIT	CITY #1 W/H CITY #2 W/H	OTHER W/H S.D.I.	FICA TOTAL DED
	(1)	(2)	(3)	(4)	(5)	(6)	(7)	(8)	(9)	(10)
046713 10/19/XX	244.05	.00	.00	.00	.00	.00	51.22	4.43	.00	33.93
	199.44	.00	.00	.00	.00	443.49	18.63	.00	.00	.00
						TOTAL HOURS-			NET PAY-	335.28
	244.05	.00	.00	.00	.00	.00	51.22	4.43	.00	33.93
	199.44	.00	.00	.00	.00	443.49	18.63	.00	.00	.00
EMPLOYEE TOTAL						TOTAL HOURS-			NET PAY-	335.28
	244.05	.00	.00	.00	.00	.00	51.22	4.43	.00	33.93
	199.44	.00	.00	.00	.00	443.49	18.63	.00	.00	.00
FINAL TOTALS						TOTAL HOURS-			NET PAY-	335.28

EXPLANATION OF COLUMN HEADERS

(1) Regular Wage
Gratutities

(2) Overtime
Other (such as bonus)

(3) Holiday Pay
Holiday work
(Holiday Pay &
Hourly Compensation)

(4) Vacation
Extra Tip

(5) Sick Pay

(6) Tip Wages
Total Gross Wages

(7) Federal Income Tax
State Income Tax

(8) City #1 withholding tax
City #2 withholding tax

(9) Other withholding tax
State disability insurance

(10) Federal Insurance Corporation of America
(Social Security; includes Medicare)
Total Deductions
(Employee share of insurance, 401(k) plans, etc.)

Courtesy of The University Club, Michigan State University, East Lansing, Michigan

example, on the first pay period of the month), or accrual yearly on the basis of the employee's anniversary date.

Based on each employee's hourly rate (which has been previously stored in the system) and calculations of pay for salaried employees, payroll modules are capable of determining departmental labor costs. A payroll cost report, by department and/or job classification, may also be prepared for use by management.

Key Terms

computerized time-clock system—Records time in and time out for employees as they enter and leave the work area; when interfaced with an automated payroll system, relevant data may be transferred each day and the previous day's pay calculated for each employee.

deductions—Subtractions from gross pay that are usually voluntary and depend on the types of benefits available from the employer.

fixed labor—The minimum amount and type of labor required to operate the food and beverage operation regardless of the volume of business.

hourly revenue report—Shows revenue and labor figures for each hour of a day; used by some fast-food operations as the basis for scheduling employees.

labor requirements report—Shows the amount of projected revenue and the number of employees required for every hour of each day of the coming week; the projections are calculated by averaging the sales for each hour of the past four weeks.

mise en place—A French phrase meaning "everything in its place"; it is necessary to stock work stations and do necessary preparation tasks before guests arrive.

overtime—Some companies use the term overtime to refer to a situation in which an employee has worked more than the time the staffing guide lists for his or her position. Federal guidelines specify that non-exempt employees who work in excess of the standard 40-hour work week are generally entitled to receive overtime pay of one and one-half times the hourly rate.

position performance analysis—A technique for determining labor standards for each position and shift.

staffing guide—A labor scheduling and control tool that incorporates labor standards and tells managers the number of labor hours needed for each position according to the volume of business forecasted for any given meal period.

variable labor—Labor requirements that vary according to the volume of business activity; for example, as more guests are served or as more meals are produced, additional service and/or kitchen labor is needed.

withholdings—Subtractions from gross pay for income and social security taxes.

Review Questions

1. Why must managers consider quality requirements before developing labor standards?

2. What are the advantages of expressing labor standards in terms of labor dollars? in terms of labor hours?

3. How can managers use a position performance analysis to determine labor standards for each position and shift?

4. What are some factors managers must consider when constructing a staffing guide?

5. How is fixed labor different from variable labor?

6. How can managers evaluate a staffing guide in relation to budgeted goals?

7. How can managers use a staffing guide as a scheduling tool? as a control tool?

8. How do managers of fast-food operations schedule employees on the basis of estimated sales?

9. Why can payroll activities become time-consuming activities for managers of nonautomated operations?

10. What functions can be performed by an automated payroll system?

Internet Sites

For more information, visit the following Internet sites. Remember that Internet addresses can change without notice. If the site is no longer there, you can use a search engine to look for additional sites.

Associations

American Culinary Federation (ACF)
http://www.acfchefs.org

American Hotel & Lodging Association (AH&LA)
http://www.ahlaonline.org

American School Food Service Association (ASFSA)
http://www.asfsa.org

Club Managers Association of America (CMAA)
http://www.cmaa.org

The Educational Foundation of NRA
http://www.edfound.org

The Educational Institute of AH&LA
http://www.ei-ahla.org

Hospitality Financial and Technology Professionals
http://www.hftp.org

Institute of Food Technologies
http://www.ift.org

International Hotel and Restaurant Association
http://www.ih-ra.com

National Association of College and University Food Services
http://www.nacufs.org

National Restaurant Association (NRA)
http://www.restaurant.org

Food and Beverage Resources

Club Management Online
http://www.club-mgmt.com/dining/index.html

Prepared Foods. Product development, ingredients, suppliers
http://www.preparedfoods.com

Food Service Software

Adaco Services, Inc.
http://www.adacoservices.com

CMS Hospitality
http://www.cmshosp.com.au

Computrition, Inc.
http://www.computrition.com

Comtrex Systems Corporation
http://www.comtrex.com

Comus Restaurant Systems
http://www.comus.com

Cost Guard
http://www.costguard.com

Culinary Software
http://www.culinarysoftware.com

Eatec Corporation
http://www.eatec.com

Instill Corporation
http://www.instill.com

Integrated Restaurant Software
http://www.rmstouch.com

MAI Systems Corporation
http://www.maisystems.com

Micros Systems, Inc.
http://www.micros.com

MSI Solutions
http://www.msisolutions.com

Sulcus Computer Corporation
http://www2.sulcus.nl

Management Companies

ARAMARK
http://www.aramark.com

Bon Appétit Management Company
http://www.bamco.com

Compass Group
http://www.compass-na.com

Sodexho Marriott
http://www.sodexhomarriott.com

The Wood Company
http://www.woodco.com

Publications—Online and Printed

Club Management Magazine
http://www.club-mgmt.com

Electronic Gourmet Guide
http://www.foodwine.com

Food and Hospitality Magazine
http://www.foodserviceworld.com

Food Management
http://www.foodservicesearch.com

Food Network: CyberKitchen
http://www.foodtv.com

Food Processing: The Magazine of
Strategy, Technology and Trends
http://www.foodprocessing.com

Internet Food Channel
http://www.foodchannel.com

International Hotel and Restaurant
Association journal
www.hotelsmag.com

International Journal of Hospitality
Management
http://www.mcb.co.uk/ijchm.htm

Journal of Hospitality Financial Management
http://hrta.fnr.umass.edu/sheel/ahfme/jhfm/aboutjhfm.html

Lodging Food and Beverage
http://www.lodgingnews.com/lodgingfnb/

Lodging Hospitality Online
http://www.lhonline.com

Lodging News, journal of the American Hotel & Lodging Association
http://www.ei–ahla.org/webs/lodging/index.html

Nation's Restaurant News
http://www.nrn.com

On the Rail—News for Food Professionals
http://www.ontherail.com

Restaurants and Institutions magazine
http://www.rimag.com

Restaurant Business, Food Service, and ID magazines
http://www.foodservicetoday.com

Restaurant Hospitality
www.foodservicesearch.com

Restaurants and Institutions
http://www.rimag.com

Restaurants USA, publication of National Restaurant Association
http://www.restaurant.org/rusa

World Hospitality, management magazine for hotel executives.
http://www.worldhospitality.com

 **Problems**

Problem 1

What is the standard labor cost percentage to serve 50, 75, and 100 lunches given the following number of standard labor hours (assume a guest check average for lunch of $14.75)?

	Number of Lunches					
	50		**75**		**100**	
Position	Stand. Avg. Labor Hourly Hours Rate	Stand. Labor Costs	Stand. Avg. Labor Hourly Hours Rate	Stand. Labor Costs	Stand. Avg. Labor Hourly Hours Rate	Stand. Labor Costs
Server	9.5/5.25		11.0/5.25		15.75/5.25	
Bartender	4.75/7.75		4.75/7.55		4.75/7.75	
Cook	12.0/11.50		16.0/11.50		19.0/11.50	
Steward	9.5/6.75		9.5/6.75		11.0/6.25	
Busperson	8.5/4.25		8.5/4.25		8.5/4.25	
Host	4.0/7.00		4.0/7.00		6.0/7.00	
Total Standard Labor Cost	══		══		══	

Problem 2

Following is the hourly payscale for the Southern Center Restaurant:

Cook	= $7.95
Food Server	= $4.10
Bartender	= $5.75
Dishwasher	= $5.20

The schedule for the upcoming week requires the following number of hours for each position:

Cook	190 hrs
Food Server	285 hrs
Bartender	75 hrs
Dishwasher	90 hrs

a) If all persons work the number of hours on the schedule, what will be the expected wage for each position and for all positions for the work week?

b) What is the average hourly labor cost for the Southern Center Restaurant given the financial data above?

c) The manager of the Southern Center Restaurant is interested in the average hourly labor cost for "Back of House" ("Heart of House") positions; what is that average hourly rate?

d) What is the average hourly rate for "Front of House" positions in the Southern Center Restaurant?

Problem 3

Complete the weekly Department Labor Hour Report shown below for the cook's position.

				Actual Hours				Total	
Employee	7/16	7/17	7/18	7/19	7/20	7/21	7/22	Actual	Standard
Bill	—	—	5	8	8	8	7		34
Phil	5	—	—	5	8	8	8		30
Latoya	8	4	—	—	8	7	8		32
Enid	8	8	8	—	—	8	8		40
Pasco	7	8	8	8	7	—	—		36
									172

What are your comments as you compare the actual to the standard (expected) number of hours worked?

Problem 4

Complete the Weekly Department Labor Hour and Cost Report for the cook's position.

Employee	7/14	7/15	7/16	7/17	7/18	7/19	7/20	Actual	Standard	Rate	Actual	Standard
Phyllis	8	—	8	7	8	—	8		40	$11.00		
Ahmed	7	8	7	8	—	8	—		35	$10.90		
Tom	8	8	7	8	—	—	8		35	$10.55		
Orlando	8	8	—	—	8	8	7		40	$11.25		
Moses	—	—	8	7	8	8	8		38	$9.95		
									188			

What comments would you make to the schedule planner?

Index